CHEEKY SLAPPERS

Published by 2023

Paperback ISBN: 978-1-7395086-0-9
ePub ISBN: 978-1-7395086-1-6
Hardback ISBN: 978-1-7395086-2-3

CHEEKY SLAPPERS

Mark Delstanche

‘Cheeky Slappers’

The name I gave to waves that crept up out of a completely different direction to the others, slapping the side of the boat and drenching me, generally just after I’d just dried out and was preparing to go on a break, eliciting a cry of ‘Oooh, you cheeky slapper!’ on good days. Bad days, by contrast, would give rise to a somewhat less repeatable response.

This book is dedicated to two of the most amazing parents anyone could wish for, who gave me the tenacity and belief to conquer all, and to my wonderful wife and kids who gave me the strength to carry on throughout the darkest of times.

Contents

Introduction

Thank you for picking up this book. I hope that you have as much fun reading it as I have had in writing it!

Though it is a book inspired by my attempt to become the first person to row solo and unsupported from New York to London, I'm afraid you're going to have to endure a fair bit before we get to the point where I'm standing on the dock in New York getting ready to set out on what would prove to be the biggest challenge of my life.

As with all adventurers, I didn't drop out of the womb carrying an ice axe or holding a pair of oars (thankfully). Thus this story is as much about how I came to find myself in a seven-metre rowing boat, crossing the world's most dangerous ocean, as it is about the adventure itself.

For the wannabe ocean rower, I've included a few hints and tips as well as some technical stuff, based on my experience, which may be of some use to you. For the less technically minded, I'll give plenty of warning so you can skip these bits rather than running the risk of dozing off and spilling your cocoa. Some lessons were learned the hard way, such as, 'If you're going to sit cross-legged and naked whilst making porridge, be sure not to fumble the stove', so hopefully you can benefit from my mistakes. This particular example can be used either literally or, if you prefer, as a metaphor for life.

Part I

From Humble Beginnings

As already stated, I wasn't born an adventurer. I don't come from a privileged upbringing nor – to answer a question I often get asked – do I have a military background.

Though a very proud Brit, I'm no 'thoroughbred', as you may have guessed from my surname. Going back three generations, I'm a blend of Belgian, Maltese, Irish and Jewish descent which, if you were to take the stereotypical views of each of those races, would probably not produce an adventurer. I'm not sure quite what it would produce; I'll leave that to your imagination. I do rather enjoy honeycomb-centred chocolate balls, *moules et frites*, a pint of Guinness and the occasional smoked salmon bagel, though.

My biggest advantage in life was being born to two extraordinary parents who, despite very humble and difficult beginnings, showed me that I could achieve anything I set my mind on through sheer hard work and determination. They gave me the courage to overcome in the face of adversity and to believe that the impossible is only a state of mind. It is therefore only fair that I start with a little bit about them.

1

Mum and Dad

If I have seen further, it is by standing on the shoulders of giants.
Isaac Newton

Well, alright, anyone who knows my parents knows that they are not actually giants, with Mum standing a shade over five foot tall and Dad around five foot nine inches, but as human beings they tower above most. Both proud Londoners, they had a pretty rough start to life, which makes the love, compassion and support that they showed to my sister and me throughout our lives all the more remarkable. In retrospect, I suppose their hard upbringing gave them a very clear idea of how they would not raise us!

Mum was born in Whitechapel hospital in 1949 and brought up in the remains of Stepney in East London. The area still bore the scars of extensive bombing during the Second World War, being very close to the strategic London Docks which was a big target for the Luftwaffe. Her mother being somewhat errant, Mum was primarily brought up by her grandmother, a tough Irish Immigrant who, having come to Liverpool in the 1930s as a Catholic single mother (something that was practically unheard of in those days), did whatever she had to do in order to make ends meet. I remember her as a heavily lined old lady with a gravelly voice, sitting in a chair smoking one cigarette after another, a drink never far from hand. Visiting her at her dark flat in Stepney Green was always a chore; following a trek across London, we would have to negotiate a filthy hallway and elevator smelling of pee, only to be greeted with a thick wall of smoke the moment we stepped through the door. Everything in the flat seemed to be stained with nicotine or covered in a film of that all-pervading smoke. By the time we left, we'd probably inhaled a good portion of the eighty cigarettes a day that my great grandmother smoked until the day she died.

Mum was brought up in what would now be perceived as slum dwellings, which were later condemned, demolished and replaced by new tower blocks which stand to this day (though no longer quite as shiny and new). Fortunately for the local authorities, Mum's elder brother helped them with this process when he went into the coal hole one day and, torches being unavailable, used a lit taper instead. Mum was subsequently greeted on her way back from school by one of the local kids who informed her in typically diplomatic East End fashion, 'Eeer, your aaas 'as burned daaan' (try saying it out loud in a cockney accent, it'll make more sense). The house was completely gutted by the fire, but a few days later the council came round and put plywood up to replace floors, ceilings and walls as a temporary solution. It only took three years until they found somewhere else to live.

Mum's nan and her then husband (whom I only ever knew as 'Nannu') took a lease out on a house in Greenwich. The idea was that they would live in the front room leaving my mum, her mum and her two brothers the rest of the three-bedroom house. Unfortunately, however, this was never going to work as my grandmother and her mum never got on. Eventually my great grandmother and her husband moved back to Stepney where they were rehoused in the flat in Stepney Green. This meant that Mum and her two brothers were forced to move back in with her mother in Greenwich when she was seven years old.

Suffice to say Mum's upbringing was fairly loveless with none of the caring and nurturing that a child should have. She also suffered abuse at the hands of the Catholic Church. Her mother and father were separated when she was two and, if her mother was on the scene, it wasn't for long and as the moment a new boyfriend arrived the kids were forgotten.

Mum's school days, though not exactly a bundle of fun, did at least offer her a sanctuary from her home life. Though the nuns were incredibly strict (this was back in the day when being left-handed was considered a sign of the devil and literally beaten out of her younger brother), Mum received a good education. She did well in her exams and would have loved to have gone to university, but it was never an option, as there was no money and wages were needed. Upon leaving school, she therefore took a job as a telephonist in an office next door to the Royal Mint opposite the Tower of London. It was an exciting environment, and Mum enjoyed the work.

Mum was paid on Fridays and the wages came in cash in a little brown envelope, which she said was always quite exciting. When she went home her wages were taken by her mother and she was given half a crown, the equivalent of two pounds fifty today, and her bus fare for the week. Her elder brother, Frank, had left home as soon as he'd got a job and gone to his nan's. Mum tried to follow him, but there was no room at the inn.

Eventually, the lease on the house in Greenwich expired so the family – which now consisted of Mum, her mother and her younger brother Steve – were rehoused in one of the new satellite suburbs in Harold Hill in Essex. In Mum's words: 'It was a horrible place and I hated it. I had to give up my job because it was too far away so had to take a job in a garage over the summer as a petrol pump attendant but that had a silver lining. One day your Dad walked in, we got talking and when he invited me to watch the Chelsea versus Fulham match the following Saturday, I told him how much I enjoyed footie!!!! I quickly asked my brother Frank, a West Ham supporter, to give me the rudiments of the beautiful game. The rest, as they say, is history. Also one of our regular customers took a shine to me and asked if I would be interested in a telephonist/receptionist job for a fashion retailer in the West End. I went for the interview and got the job, so began my life working in London.'

Mum and Dad were married in 1970 and two years later she fell pregnant with my sister Penny so gave up travelling to London. They'd bought a house in Surbiton which is where I was born and raised.

Dad was also what would now be termed 'disadvantaged', but in those days that was the norm for working class kids. He was brought up in Fulham in South West London where nowadays you'd struggle to find a two-bedroomed flat for much less than a million pounds, but back in the late 1940s it was quite a different place. It too still bore the scars of the Second World War, as it lay close to the River Thames and strategic targets such as Lots Road Power Station which supplied electricity to the London Underground. After the war, his family benefitted from one of the government's temporary solutions to the housing crisis caused by the bombing, being moved into a 'prefab', a pre-fabricated house plonked right on the site where brick-built houses had once stood.

Back then, building technology was still in its infancy. If you were to get a bunch of kids to build a single-storey dwelling out of cardboard and other bits around the house and upscale it, you wouldn't be far from the family's new house. It did however boast many modern conveniences such as an indoor loo and hot and cold running water, including on the inside of the windows due to the poor insulation. These 'temporary' solutions would still be in use well into the 1960s.

Though Dad was not subjected to the abuse that my Mum had to deal with, both he and his mother suffered beatings from my granddad who sadly had his own daemons from his upbringing to exercise. Dad lived in what now would be considered poverty, with cardboard patching the holes in his shoes and suppers often consisting of little more than a boiled egg, but, as I've said, this was commonplace at the time.

Dad thoroughly enjoyed his schooldays at one of the newly formed comprehensive schools – Holland Park in West London – mainly because he was hardly ever there, spending most of the time 'bunking off', smoking cigarettes and getting up to mischief with his mates. He left school with very few qualifications apart from RSAs in technical drawing and maths, but he was street smart and able to get himself in and out of trouble with equal measure. One thing that he did gain from his time at school, which was to have a great impact on his life, was his participation in the Duke of Edinburgh's Award, which not only taught him camping and map-reading skills but, as is its aim, greater confidence and self-esteem. Both he and his brother took part in the scheme, becoming the first brothers in history to attain the Gold Award.

Upon leaving school, receiving no guidance from his parents, he looked through the classified ads in the *Evening Standard* newspaper to see what was on offer. Dad was keen to learn a skill and tried a few options. First he applied to the Merchant Navy, wanting to become a cook or an engineer. He passed the entrance exam but was told that he could only become an able seaman to start with, an offer he decided not to take up after being advised by a mate of his who had joined that this was boring. Next he went to the youth employment office where he was offered a job in a sheet-metal works in North Kensington that urgently needed someone to make washing machine parts. When being shown around the works, he recognised a guy who had left his school the previous year and asked how he was doing.

Apparently the guy had done very well for himself and after just three months of operating a piece of machinery, stamping out metal parts, had been moved on to another piece of machinery stamping out different metal parts. With the pay two pounds ten shillings a week (£50 in today's money), out of which he would have to buy his own apron, Dad politely declined the position.

Going back to the *Evening Standard*, Dad found a firm that needed a motorbike messenger. The wage was seven pounds ten shillings a week with a motorbike supplied; all they required was somebody with a clean licence. Dad's was very clean, so clean in fact that it didn't exist, a fact he managed to conceal from the firm who hired him.

Dad has always loved motorbikes and this was his first, a 'crappy' 125cc BSA, held together with tape and with Brillo pads stuffed up the exhaust to act as silencers. He managed to keep that on the road and was subsequently rewarded with a bigger bike with a sidecar which, fortunately for him, he could remove and use the bike at weekends to go racing along the newly built A3. Dad would pick up a 'bird' and drop her off at the Ace of Spades café where she could watch from the flyover as he and the lads roared past on their bikes. He was envious of the other 'rockers' with their bigger bikes and would always be bringing up the rear, leader of the 'also rans' by virtue of the fact that his bike was newer than theirs.

At the same time, due to his completion of the Gold Duke of Edinburgh's Award, he was asked to go with a group of other boys to introduce the scheme to King Hussein of Jordan. The company that he was working for, upon hearing of the royal connection, gave him four weeks off to do so and he had a great time, teaching the Jordanian Army how to make maps, visiting Petra and meeting the King who, he always said, was a charming man.

He returned home after the trip to find that his dad had buggered off to the United States. This was far from being any great loss and he actually benefitted from it when his mum bought him a Hillman Minx for twenty-five pounds from his uncle. The only thing she missed when her husband left was someone to drive her places and she wasn't too keen on being ferried around on the back of a motorbike in her twin set.

The firm that Dad was working for was called Sperry and Hutchinson. It was American with a rather laidback attitude which suited Dad just fine. After a few months, they asked him if he wouldn't mind delivering cars for them and he started doing so throughout the length and breadth of the country which he loved, having a fairly heavy right foot in the days before speed cameras.

On one occasion, he was asked to take three company executives to Birmingham, stay there overnight and return the next day. They were all having a great time and after a few beers they asked him when he'd passed his driving test. He revealed very quietly that he actually hadn't, whereupon they asked him if he would please do so. Soon after, he drove to the test centre and, though having had no lessons, aced it. Although by the sounds of it, keeping under the speed limit must have been a heck of a strain.

He had risen again in the company, to the role of merchandiser, when he met Mum at the petrol station. They immediately hit it off and, as mentioned, married in 1970 on a shoestring budget that amounted to the cost of a new suit for him and forty pounds for my Uncle Bert to do the catering. The reception was at Mum and Dad's house, while Mum received her dress as a present from the fashion company where she was working.

In 1973 my sister was born, followed by me fifteen months later. The following year Dad applied for and got a job as a fireman in the London Fire Brigade which he loved, eventually rising to the rank of Station Officer until a motorbike accident on the way to work put an end to his career in 1993.

2

The Early Years

As a kid, you always think of the friends who get the latest toys or the trendiest clothes as being the lucky ones. For me, it was always Lee Porter or Stephen Bryant who got the Sergio Tacchini tracksuit or Tin Can Alley for Christmas. It is only later in life that you realise that the greatest gifts your parents can give you is time, love and guidance. These my sister and I received in bucketloads.

Growing up in Surbiton, a suburb on the outskirts of Southwest London, there wasn't a huge amount of scope for adventure and weekends were often spent going to the park for a kick around or riding my bike with mates. TV was strictly limited to an hour or so on Saturday and Sunday mornings. Otherwise we occupied ourselves with 'family time', which we spent both in and out of doors, playing games with Mum and Dad. Sadly, my sister and I fought like cats and dogs, so I'm sure that part of the reason for keeping us occupied was to stop us from squabbling (which I now know as a parent is utterly infuriating).

Summer holidays were often spent camping either in Wales, where my Dad had done his Duke of Edinburgh's Award expeditions, or in Italy, close to where Mum and Dad got engaged.

My fondest memories are probably of those outings in Wales where we'd pitch the tent in a field with no amenities other than a standpipe for fresh water and make our own amusements. I'm not sure that my mum or sister would agree, but the days spent playing in the freezing River Towy or hiking up the local mountains, more often than not in wind and rain, left their mark. I always enjoyed the exhilaration of the physical effort and the sense of achievement gained in those early years.

Then there were the half-term holidays in the spring and autumn when Dad and I would go off on our own to do 'boys' stuff' whilst Mum and Penny did their thing. Dad's experiences with the outward-bound courses and the Duke of Edinburgh had obviously paid dividends as he was great at teaching me the basics of fieldcraft, map-reading and orienteering. Armed with not much more than a plastic sheet and some rope to make a bivouac, we'd camp out in places we probably shouldn't have been in while spending our days hiking up hill and down dale in truly spectacular countryside.

On one memorable trip in Dorset, we approached the tank ranges at Lulworth to find that the ten-foot-high gates topped with razor wire were closed and red flags were flying to indicate that firing was in progress. This would force us to add an awkward eight-mile detour to our original route of a little more than two miles to get to our planned destination.

In his typical never-say-die way, Dad noted that there were lots of cows grazing in the alleged firing area and deduced accordingly that there could not possibly be firing in progress. He also pointed out small gaps in the razor wire on top of the gateposts which suggested that the Ministry of Defence wasn't serious about keeping us out – clearly, he said, the flags had been left up by mistake.

A few minutes later, we were over the fence, albeit with a few nicks and cuts from the razor wire (which, true to its name, really is very sharp), and on our merry way. We'd marched perhaps a mile when we were approached by a flustered-looking man on a bicycle, who asked us what the bloody hell we were doing there and how the hell did we get in. I can't remember what Dad's exact answer was, but the general gist was that it would be just as dangerous to go back as it was to carry on and, anyway, the cows seemed to be doing alright for themselves. Confounded by this logic, the range master, as he turned out to be, reluctantly let us carry on.

Around this time, I was fortunate enough to pass my 11-plus exam and gained entry to the local grammar school, Tiffin Grammar School for Boys. I clearly remember getting the letter informing me of the pass and the overwhelming sense of joy and pride I felt as one of only two boys in my school to do so.

Dad always cut my hair for me and Tiffin Grammar had a strict hair and uniform code so, as the end of the summer holidays approached, he asked me if I wanted a haircut. The crew cut that he usually gave me was not allowed at the school, and as 'flat tops' were 'in' at the time, he waited till Mum was out of the house before saying he'd give it a go even though he'd never tried one before. (He's seventy-six now and I don't think he's ever passed up an opportunity to give anything a go.)

As the work progressed, it became fairly obvious that he may have bitten off more than he could chew. He continued regardless but after about half an hour he was forced to confess, 'Sorry, son, I might have made a bit of a cock-up there,' which turned out to be something of an understatement.

Fortunately, he found an old cap and we had a barber shop at the end of the street. We went there together and upon arrival he whipped off the cap and asked the barber with his usual laugh, 'S'cuse me, mate, do you do crash damage?'

The barber took one look at my head and asked, 'What exactly do you want me to do with that?'

To this Dad replied, 'Well, can you just even it up, mate?'

And so it came to pass that I turned up to my first day at Tiffins with a shaved head. This and the fact that I was the only kid in the year with a cockney accent saw me immediately labelled a thug.

Tiffins was (and still is) an exceptional school, frequently in the top ten schools in the country academically with an exceptional record in sports too. Sadly, I didn't really fit in and, having been a big fish in a small pond at my previous school, I was disappointed to find myself no longer top of the class and began to slip behind in my studies. I also showed no aptitude for team sports or anything to do with a ball (a shortcoming which persists to this day, a ball being far more likely to hit me square between the eyes before I've any chance catching it) so I often found myself left out of selections. More often than not, I found it easier to play the class clown, particularly in the subjects I saw absolutely no point in doing, Music, French, Religious Education and Latin being top of that list. Though I enjoyed the Sciences, Geography and Maths, I realise in hindsight that I lacked the confidence necessary to knuckle down and make the most of the education that was on offer.

Being situated close to the River Thames, the school had its own rowing club. So when at the age of thirteen I was given the option to ditch ball sports and get in a boat, I grasped it with both hands (and didn't subsequently drop it!). Dad had done a bit of rowing with the London Fire Brigade so I guess he steered me in that direction, his opinion no doubt formed while standing on the sidelines during rugby matches observing how bloody useless I was. (He recently came to one of my son's school matches and, with a mile-wide smile on his face, remarked, 'He's definitely yours!')

Upon starting rowing at Tiffins, you had to first pass a sculling test in a boat they called the 'gig'. This was akin to something you might see on any lake, a big, wide, heavy craft with a two-person bench seat at the back where your basic abilities to control a boat were assessed. The assessor was a lovely old guy called Keith Southern, a volunteer at the club who soon became the butt of our jokes on account of a story he often repeated, the key line of which was, 'Back in my day, you didn't have wheels on the seats, you had to wear leather trousers and oil them up so that you could slide up and down!'

Though perfectly innocent, I'm sure that these days a comment like that would have landed him on some kind of register. Back then, life was more innocent somehow and fortunately nobody took him up on the offer to squeeze into a well-oiled pair of *Lederhosen*. Keith was indeed quite old, but even so I'm pretty certain that the wheel had been invented before he started rowing. Still, as with many things that perplexed me at school, I guess I'll never know the truth behind the story.

Most of the prestige in rowing centres around the eights, in which the eight men in the boat each has an oar. As at Oxford and Cambridge, a lot of effort was put into producing a crew to compete in the national school championships. Unfortunately, the main focus at Tiffins was on rugby and cricket, which meant there wasn't a huge pool of potential oarsmen to choose from. This and the additional challenge of convincing everybody to turn up to training at weekends generally saw us splitting up into 'small boats', which was anything other than eights.

Furthermore, I always felt, perhaps unfairly, that there were people in the boat not working as hard as me. I found this really frustrating. In hindsight, I realise that, though I gave 100 per cent at every training session and in every race, I would have probably done everyone a favour if I'd dialled it back and tried to row as one with the team rather than trying to prove that I was the fittest, strongest bloke in the boat.

We trained hard with sessions on the water before school in the summer. We'd be out on the water by six in the morning; sometimes we'd run up to five miles during lunch breaks and there'd be occasional outings after school. We also trained on Saturdays, often a double session, out on the water by around eight o'clock before a short break, then going out again at around eleven for another couple of hours.

The boat club was situated on a perfect stretch of the non-tidal Thames, one of the longest sections between locks stretching from Hampton Court Palace, the former residence of King Henry VIII, down to Teddington Lock, the barrier that marks the tidal limit of the river. It was just under five miles in length, about the same as the Oxford-Cambridge Boat Race and also roughly that of the annual Head of the River Race, a hugely contested national time trial over the same course. This made it a terrific place to train.

With all our training, we managed to form a pretty decent four and had some success in local events, once making the semi-finals at the National Schools Championships. Yet we were generally outgunned by private schools with better equipment, superior coaching and a bigger pool of students to draw from.

Post-training on a Saturday, I'd cycle the three miles or so home, stopping at Kingston Market on the way to pick up the fruit and veg for the week for the family which would often weigh twenty or thirty pounds. To this day, I am thankful for the extra training and determination this gave me, the latter especially necessary on the big hill that stood in the way!

Although I enjoyed my time in the fours and later in a pretty successful double with my rowing partner, Alex Barker, my true passion was the single sculls where the only person responsible for my success or failure was me. It is this that I have my fondest memories of as I was able to train as hard as I liked and whenever I wanted and didn't have to rely on anybody else. Some of my best memories are of cool spring mornings with a mist hanging over the river, rowing the last half mile on water as smooth as glass up to Hampton Court Bridge with just the sound of my oars in the water and the reflection of the banks to keep me company. There have been few moments in my life when I have felt absolute contentment, tranquility and a true sense of everything being right with the world, but this was certainly one of them.

My first win in single sculls came at the Kingston Regatta, a five hundred meter sprint on home turf which ended at the boat house that I was based at. After progressing through the first three knockout rounds, I found myself in the final where any home advantage was nullified by being up against another guy who rowed out of the same boat house as me.

As we set off, I quickly gained a small advantage and was cheered on by Dad who was following the race on a bicycle path adjacent to the river. Rowing not being a sport particularly popular amongst your average cockney, the umpire following in a launch was rather taken aback upon hearing the shouts of 'GO ON SON, YOU'RE DOIN 'IM!' and other such encouragements not often heard from the banks of the Thames during a regatta.

Obviously ruffled by this display of most un-gentlemanly behaviour, the umpire started to chastise Dad with calls from his loud hailer 'NO COACHING FROM THE BANK PLEASE!' but, undaunted and seemingly carried away by the moment, Dad's calls continued, much to the protestation from the umpire and it wasn't until I managed to shout out 'SHUT UP DAD, YOU'RE GOING TO GET ME DISQUALIFIED' in between gasping lung fulls of air that he eventually started to pipe down. Not entirely of course, just enough to allow me to take the win.

This was the late 1980s and on TV there was a soap opera called *Howards' Way*, based on yachting around the South Coast of England. We rarely watched it, but there was a competition at the end of the series to win a Westerly 34 sailing boat. Having never sailed before but fancying 'giving it a bash anyway', Dad decided to enter the competition. Unsurprisingly, we didn't win but it did pique Dad's interest. He was still serving in the London Fire Brigade at the time and they had a sailing association so he contacted them to see if he could try his hand. Fortunately, he was given the opportunity to do so and, after a couple of trips, he asked if I fancied giving it a go.

As previously mentioned, I loved going away on adventures with Dad and having one-on-one time away with him. This was especially so as he was often working in between shifts in the Fire Brigade to put a bit more bread on the table, which made such opportunities precious. I therefore leapt at the chance that presented itself.

A few years previously, in our only ever dabble in the stock market, TSB Bank had decided to float. Shares were sold at a pound each and we had been allocated 175. I was too young to own shares so I gave Dad £86.50 out of my savings from birthdays and Christmases as well as money I'd earned from my paper round to buy half of them. I gave these back to him to pay for the trip and, a few months later, we took the train out to Sheerness to meet the boat.

For most of my life I'd been used to being around firefighters. so it was a bit of a shock when we turned up to meet the rest of the crew which consisted of a lady in her thirties called Jackie, a bespectacled chap called Chris who looked more like a librarian than a firefighter, an ex-headmistress called Margaret whom we initially thought was a bit snooty but who turned out to be lovely, and a short, rotund fella whose name eludes me but whom we ended up christening 'Gizmo' on account of the fact that he had a lot of gadgets and was equally useless with all of them.

Dad and I have always had a very strong bond and, imbued with the Fire Brigade sense of humour I'd grown up with, I guess we made a formidable pair, always quick to take the piss out of most other people's foibles. We couldn't quite work out the relationship between Chris and Jackie, as she was quite sparky and good fun and he had the personality of a limp lettuce leaf. We thought he was trying to woo her, after first assuming he was trying to get his leg over before coming to the conclusion that he wouldn't know what to do if the opportunity did arise.

Anyhow, we headed out of Sheerness and across the Channel. Conditions were good and we were heeled over a good way in fairly smooth seas. Dad and I were seated on the leeward bench with Chris and Jackie on the windward side (we were at the bottom and they were at the top) with the boat over at about 30 degrees where both my Dad and I had a glorious view of one of Chris's testicles which had popped out of the side of his shorts to say hello. Dad and I burst out in fits of laughter whilst he was trying to make small talk with Jackie, until eventually he could no longer hold his curiosity as to the source of our mirth. Dad duly informed him that one of his balls was hanging out, much to our increased hilarity and to his absolute horror. He didn't say much to us after that but it was a memorable start to the trip.

By the time we reached France, the weather was closing in on us. This made things awkward as we had to turn around and get the boat back to Brighton. The forecast was for winds up to force 7 to 8, which is essentially a gale, and rough seas, but we had to go anyway. This was fortunate, as it was an incredibly exhilarating journey with all the crew barring the skipper, Dad and I suffering from seasickness, leaving us to sail the boat back pretty much by ourselves in torrid conditions.

We didn't have much money for decent kit and I remember Dad and I sharing a fleece, depending on who was on the helm at the time, accompanied by a modified bin bag to keep the rain off (a tactic repeated in Greece a few years later when we managed to hit a once-in-fifty-year storm which washed away half the roads on some of the islands). The thrill of climbing up the face of the waves on the 42-foot boat before surfing down into the troughs only to face the next wall of water is something that I will never forget. Maybe through complete ignorance or sheer bravado, we had the time of our lives, although I'm not sure the rest of the crew would share the same memories.

Fourteen hours later, we eased into Brighton Marina, cold, wet, salt-encrusted and wind-battered, and couldn't have been happier!

Through such experiences, the seed was sown from an early age to take perverse pleasure in overcoming adversity through sheer grit and determination. This somewhat masochistic attitude in the pursuit of happiness would certainly stand me in good stead for later experiences, although it baffles both my wife and my mum to this day.

Having by now been severely bitten by the sailing bug, Dad enrolled in a night school to do his Yachtmaster theory exam with a view to one day selling up and buggering off into the blue yonder with Mum. One of the advantages of this was that Dad would come home from his classes to go over what he had learnt with me which, as I had a bit of a penchant for Maths and Geometry, was right up my street.

Dad later passed his practical exam and thereafter, when time and money allowed, we would charter small boats for family holidays, starting in the UK and heading over to France or the Channel Islands or exploring the lovely little spots along the South Coast. I always look back fondly on those trips which were a great way to learn the ropes and grow to respect Mother Nature and her ever-changing moods. In particular, due to a combination of our enthusiasm and lack of experience, I learnt a huge amount in regard to crisis management and problem-solving which would come in handy in my future career and lifestyle choices.

Looking back, I would have loved to have seen us through the eyes of other, more experienced yachties as we pulled in and out of harbours, much as I like to do now, having gained a wee bit of experience in how to handle a boat. To this day, I've yet to see somebody chugging out of a port with one of the crew hanging onto the end of the boom, perpendicular to the boat, in order to get the boat to tip over enough to clear the muddy bottom on a dropping tide, but I reckon that's their loss.

I should add at this point that though the big plan was for Mum and Dad to 'sell up and sail', Mum was somewhat of an unwilling participant, being a poor swimmer and having very little love for the sea. The sea itself seemed to recognize this and took every opportunity to chastise her for her gall in gracing it with her presence. To compound matters, she suffers from seasickness, although I think that this was probably driven in no small part by the anxiety she felt about being on a boat with us pair of idiots. My sister, though never suffering from seasickness, was a very hormonal teenager at this stage and took little joy in being stuck in a confined space with any of us and, probably rather sensibly, spent a lot of the time below decks.

As mentioned, Mum enjoyed being at sea about as much as it seemed the sea enjoyed having her there. On one trip, to Alderney in the Channel Islands, Mum had the boom dropped on her head twice in the space of three days, nearly passing out on the second occasion. Upon reaching our destination, we took a stroll ashore to stretch our legs and sat on the wall of a flower bed for a family photo. Under normal circumstances, this would have been fairly innocuous, but Poseidon hadn't finished with Mum and, assisted by a small nudge from my sister, she toppled over backwards to hit the exact same spot on her head on an ornamental anchor.

On another occasion, during a bit of a wobbly crossing, Mum really needed a wee. For those of you who have spent any time on smaller sailing boats, you will appreciate that this requires good timing, excellent balance, a fair amount of luck and preferably a spare pair of arms to hold yourself steady whilst trying to get your clothing off and position yourself on a small loo whilst being tossed about like a pea in a drum.

At the time, knowing very little about sailing, Dad and I thought that the more sail you had up and the harder you fought the helm, the better you must be doing as you were getting everything you could out of the boat. It was only later in life, upon meeting my now wife (who is a far better technical sailor than me but much less experienced in getting out of shit, mainly because she hasn't had to) that I realised that, though very exhilarating, this might not be the fastest or best way to sail a boat.

One of the problems seemed to be that the rudder never seemed to be quite big enough for the boats that we sailed, particularly in heavy weather when it wasn't powerful enough to make the boat go in a straight line. (For the land-lubbers amongst you, there was nothing wrong with the rudder, we just had way too much sail up!) This invariably led to involuntary tacking or, even worse, gybing where the boat would spin around violently and go onto the opposite tack meaning that what had moments before been up suddenly became down, and vice versa.

Unfortunately for Mum, it was during one of these occasions that she decided to empty her bladder. Worse, she had failed to secure herself properly when the boat lurched over. With her ankles firmly shackled together by her trousers, she flew through the toilet door, landing upside down in the wet locker opposite, bum pointing skyward, and wondering what the hell she'd signed up for. Fortunately, in the next moment, Dad wrestled the boat back onto the right tack, pitching us back and rolling Mum out of the locker and into the loo, the door slamming firmly behind her.

This event wasn't exactly atypical during our sailing 'holidays', so you mightn't be surprised to learn that Mum and Dad never did set off into the blue yonder, which is probably just as well. Then again, if they had, they probably wouldn't have been held by the Taliban whilst driving across Pakistan or nearly eaten alive whilst unwittingly parking off the beaten track in a game reserve in India, but these are other stories entirely.

In the meantime, I had joined the Air Training Corps, a voluntary military youth organisation sponsored by the Ministry of Defence and the Royal Air Force, as I harboured a desire to be a fighter pilot. It was basically an Air Force-orientated scouts group in which you got to go flying once in a while and do all kinds of other field activities.

I had applied for a cadetship to join the Royal Air Force which would pay for me to do a university degree before training to become an officer. However, upon going to the Officer and Aircrew Selection Centre at Biggin Hill, I soon discovered that I might not have the requisite skills to fly an aircraft; in fact, I probably didn't have the requisite skills to sit in one without falling off my seat or breaking something.

I remember one of the tests where you had a joystick to control movement up and down and pair of foot pedals to control movement left and right. It was a pretty good test for an organisation looking to recruit somebody to fly a multi-million-pound aircraft, I suppose. The aim of the game was to keep a little white cross in the centre of a computer screen whilst the program would try and send it elsewhere. If it were an exercise in escape and evasion, I would have won it hands down as shortly after the start of the test the cross shot off to some unknown part of the screen only to reappear fleetingly as it darted to another corner whilst I frantically wrestled with the controls.

To my dismay, those around me seemed to have much easier controls than I did as their white cross stayed very central with, it seemed, little effort on their part! At the end of the first day, we were split into two groups and it was suggested that maybe I should not be aiming to be a pilot but rather think about becoming a navigator which I took as, ‘Good luck, there’s the door, find your own way home.’

Part II

School's Out

Though my prowess in a rowing boat undoubtedly gave me a huge boost of confidence at my school due to me finally being better than others at something, I was far from the top of the class in most subjects. The focus among students was on getting the right A-Levels to go to university. However, having come from a working-class background (and as a two-fingered salute to the somewhat middle-class-orientated school and bourgeois elite), I vowed not to even entertain the thought.

Instead, I decided to make my dad proud and applied to join the London Fire Brigade in the Autumn of 1992. It was only in later years that I came to realise that nothing would have made my parents prouder at the time than if I had made the most of my education and gone to university, becoming the first person from our side of the family to do so. That year, Tiffins had their best ever results, 99 per cent of the boys in my year attaining three or more A-Level grades A–C and going on to further education. There were around a hundred boys in my year, so I'll let you do the maths!

3

Out of the Frying Pan...

The year I applied to join the London Fire Brigade, only 140 places were available for forty thousand applicants so the process was rather drawn out.

In the meantime, I did various jobs, everything from working in a clothing store to gardening, painting and decorating, to cleaning kitchens and pulling beers in a pub. The goal was to earn a few quid to go off travelling with a buddy of mine in the US.

Jim and I had got to know each other through the Air Training Corps. We had a few adventures together, most notably kayaking the 'length of the Thames', starting at the first bit you can actually kayak (though there was a fair bit if dragging involved to begin with), near Cricklade in Wiltshire, and paddling back to our home town of Kingston. We had a couple of old slalom kayaks which are pretty useless for long-distance kayaking as they are built to go around corners rather than in straight lines. However, they did have a spray deck which kept the water out and ample storage for our camping supplies. They also leaked like sieves so everything was wrapped up in bin bags, allowing us to keep kit relatively dry, but it meant that we had to unload the boats at every lock and empty varying amounts of the Thames that we had collected on the way.

The main point of ingress was along the seam that joined the top to the bottom of the fiberglass kayak. This would have been fine had we not weighed ourselves down with kit which meant that the kayaks spent a lot of the time submerged (which of course let in more of the river and submerged us further). It certainly gave us a greater sense of urgency on the longer stretches.

Late on the second day of paddling, the heavens opened. We tried to find a secluded spot to stop and camp for the night but failed. Finally, with it raining cats and dogs, we hauled the kayaks ashore at the bottom end of a pub garden and tried to shelter underneath a bench. After about ten minutes of this, now totally drenched and covered in mud, we looked for another option.

Close by, there was a beautiful Henley river cruiser, a classic boat with a roomy interior protected by a canopy and flappy canvas sides. This we managed to bundle ourselves under for the duration of the storm which lasted throughout the night. Come first light, the rain had stopped and we snuck out of our shelter leaving as little trace of ourselves as possible. Unfortunately, this amounted to quite a lot of mud on an otherwise pristine white interior.

Efforts to sluice down the interior using what little we had only made matter worse. Thus an executive decision was made to get out of there and as far away as we could as quickly as possible. Jim even somehow managed to lose a pair of his underpants which we assumed were still onboard and could be used as DNA evidence in the case that this should ever come to prosecution. I'm glad to say that Jim wasn't put off kayaking by our early trips and has since completed the Devizes to Westminster International Canoe Race, an event still on my bucket list.

Having left school I decided to join the local rowing club, but found the members to be so far up their own arses that I'd rather have plucked my own scrotum than compete for them. Instead I started rowing out of a club called Tideway Scullers, based on the Thames at Chiswick. My aim was to get some coaching to further improve myself in the hope that I would make the Great Britain Under-21s rowing squad. A number of the other rowers at the club represented the country and I was planning to hang on to their coat-tails.

It was quite a shock when I turned up for my first training session. At school warm-ups had consisted of a couple of laps of the local playing field followed by some stretching and then out onto the water. So when my new mentors said that we were off for a warm-up run I was expecting similar. Seven miles later, we hit the gym for an intense ninety-minute circuit session after which we went out on the water for an hour and a half. Following this, I cycled the thirteen miles home.

The next morning, I woke up and couldn't move a single muscle. It was another four days before I could do anything without wincing.

Amazingly, as the months passed, the training became more bearable and I found myself doing five hours a day 7 days a week and starting to keep up with the big boys, or so I thought. I remember being out on the river one day and seeing Sir Steve Redgrave just downstream of us. (For those of you who don't know him, Steve is a mountain of a man who has won five gold rowing medals in five consecutive Olympics between the years 1984 and 2000.) *Ah yes*, thought I, *but he's a sweep oarsman, not a sculler, I reckon I might do OK here!* Off we went, side by side, gradually piling on the pressure with the stroke rate climbing.

I was still with him past Mortlake Bridge and under Hammersmith

Bridge. By the Harrods Depository we remained neck and neck, both of us going full tilt, and I was thinking to myself, '*You've got him now!*' which was when I found out why he had won five gold medals and I didn't have any.

Basically, he pulled away and I didn't see him again. I think that by the time I reached Putney Bridge he'd got his boat out of the water, given it a wash, gone for a shower and headed home, eaten half a cow and a dozen raw eggs and nodded off in front of the telly (hopefully remembering how he'd almost had to break into a sweat to keep up with me).

Come the late summer of '92, Jim and I had saved enough money to go to the States. We headed off to California for eight weeks, initially staying with the parents of friends that Mum and Dad had met in the sixties. Subsequently, we travelled from San Francisco down to Tijuana in Mexico, living as cheaply as we could.

We spent some time camping out in the San Bernardino Mountains where we found that the seasons change very quickly. A park ranger we met the day we arrived warned us that the season had ended, but we didn't take him seriously, having been driven up in beautiful weather with bright blue skies and temperatures in the low seventies. We then woke up to a fresh morning with all our kit frozen in situ. Fortunately I had a warmish sleeping bag. Slightly less well-equipped, Jim spent the whole night shivering and no doubt dreaming of the missing pair of pants which might have kept him just that little bit warmer.

We hitchhiked down to San Diego but arrived too late to find any accommodation. We headed to the beach where we camped out on a coastguard platform, waking to a beautiful sunrise and the waves of the Pacific gently lapping on the shore. The same couldn't be said of Venice Beach where, finding ourselves in a similar predicament, we headed to one of the coastguard platforms only to fall asleep to the distant sound of gunfire and sirens. We were then woken up at two in the morning by a huge cop who pointed his gun at us and shone his flashlight in our eyes whilst asking if we had a gun.

I assumed I was having a dream and peacefully nodded off as soon as he'd departed. Jim, however, was a little spooked by the incident, lying awake and wide-eyed all night wondering if we'd live to see another day. LA, and Venice Beach in particular, was full of all kinds of weird and wonderful people, many of whom were looking for their big break in Tinsel Town. One of the most memorable was a lass from Barnsley who had two false legs and was looking to make a name for herself as a dancer. You couldn't help but admire her for her self-belief and confidence to pursue a lifelong dream where others may have given up.

After eight weeks of travelling and smelling to high heaven, having run out of money and not had enough for accommodation or a shower for a few days, we headed back home with quite a few stories to tell.

By the time I got back, there was a letter from the London Fire Brigade telling me that I had got through the preliminary stage of selection and was required to attend a medical examination. If I passed this, I would be given an interview followed by a physical test after which a final decision would be made.

Whilst I waited for the application process to run its course, I took a job as a busboy clearing tables at TGI Fridays. The less said about this episode the better, though it gave me a valuable insight into the psychobabble of large corporations – even in the humble job that I was doing, I was made to learn the 'Bible' that was the company policy. I found it to be in the most part complete bollocks, but it must have made an impression as over the years I've caught myself reciting a few of the gems gleaned from it. The 'swan theory', the 'praise-burger theory' and the 'full-hands-in, full-hands-out' mantra were three of my particular favourites, though come to think of it, I can't remember if, in the praise-burger theory, you were meant to put praise (the burger) between two buns (the not-so-positive bits) or the other way around. I guess it depends if you're a vegetarian or gluten intolerant.

At the end of that summer, I finally got the notification that my application to join the London Fire Brigade was successful and I would be joining Squad 10/93 in November. I gladly handed in my stripy shirt, zany hat and badge-adorned (minimum of ten according to the dress code) red braces and headed off to get a whole new uniform.

The day I arrived at the training school at Southwark in London I walked through the archway into the main courtyard and was amazed to see a full-scale drill going on. It seemed like complete chaos with hoses, ladders and crews wearing breathing apparatus going everywhere and I didn't have the slightest clue as to how this could all be orchestrated or, more to the point, how I was expected to be able to do it myself in just twenty weeks.

I nonetheless threw myself into it wholeheartedly and, being fairly fresh out of school, cruised through all the theory, from fire prevention regulations to building construction, chemistry and 'firemanship'. I loved the physical side of things from day one, though I was surprised to find myself outclassed in strength by some of the older guys. Apparently, rowing up and down the Thames countless times doesn't necessarily help you to haul a ladder up the outside of a building or give you any edge when it comes to pull-ups! I was still rowing at the time and training pretty hard and vowed to keep it up whilst at fireman school when time allowed.

I rarely drank due to my training regime for the rowing, but as the first Friday of training school came to a close, I headed to the pub with the other lads from Squad 10/93. It was an early knock-off so we got there at around four, having had a week of hard graft in the yard learning the basics. We'd already lost one bloke, Bob, who on the second day of training decided that it wasn't the life for him. The task that pushed his button involved not much more than rolling out length after length of hose on a snow-covered parade ground and then rolling it up again.

Five pints of Guinness at the Blue-Eyed Maid effectively put paid to the idea of getting up at six next morning for the bike ride to training at my club in Chiswick.

Though briefly resurrected a few years later, my days of competitive rowing soon came to a close in favour of going out and chasing members of the fairer sex. This proved a far more entertaining sport, and, it turned out, was a lot easier when you were a firefighter rather than a busboy at TGI Fridays.

Being the only guy in my squad to have gone to a grammar school and achieved A-Levels, and having had a father in the Fire Brigade for over twenty years (Dad had unfortunately had to leave the year before I joined on account of his motorbike accident), I have no doubt that I was a bit of a smart arse. When we were told to do something one way, I would often look to do it another in the belief that my way could be better.

I distinctly remember doing a drill practicing knots and lines. A searchlight had to be hauled aloft. This required a line to be thrown out of a fourth-four window where the ladder crew had entered; it would then be attached to the searchlight so they could haul it up. According to the firefighters handbook, a guide line was meant to be attached to the searchlight to help keep it away from the building, but I reckoned I could simply tie the power cable to it and use that instead, saving precious time and effort. A shout from the sub-officer in charge of the drill put a halt to that and in the debrief one of my exasperated colleagues commented, 'For f**k's sake, Delstanche, why do you always have to do things differently?'

Funnily enough, I've found myself uttering those same words to myself, having tried to do things differently and ended up in a bit of a pickle on a number of occasions since.

The twenty weeks passed in no time at all and, shortly before our passing-out parade, we were given our postings. They tried to put you somewhere geographically close to your home. As I was from South West London and having heard Dad's tales of daring-do at stations he'd served at, I was gagging to get to a 'busy ship', as they were known, to put all my training into practice. Brixton would have been my first choice, as that's where Dad ended his career, but I'd have been equally happy at any of the stations located in the grittier parts of London. As my name was called I listened eagerly to what exciting posting I would get.

'Delstanche, Blue Watch, Chiswick'.

I'd managed not to land a job where Dad had ended his career, but rather on the same watch, at the same station where he'd started it, in one of West London's sleepiest hollows. Amongst Chiswick's claims to fame was that for two years they had come runners-up in the 'Best Fire Station in Bloom' competition for their flower garden, which with its picturesque fish pond and lovely shrubbery certainly was a sight to behold, particularly in summer. I'm not sure where Brixton came that year but something tells me that they might have been a bit too busy to prune the roses.

My time at Chiswick can be best summed up by one particular story.

For the first year of service, you are considered to be on probation. You cannot put in for a transfer to another fire station until you have passed this period and an assessment has taken place. During the initial part of this period, I was put on watch-room duties. Amongst other things, this meant that for the first part of the day following the handover from the previous watch you had to do all the various log bookings. You also had to be there in the hour preceding the end of the watch to make any bookings that may be necessary.

During my second tour of duty – which consisted of two day shifts, 0900–1800, and two night shifts,1800–0900 – I was approached by one of the old hands. I was absentmindedly looking out the window at the time, willing the time away. Seeing me, Mick said, 'Do me a favour, son, don't look out of the window.'

Not knowing any better, I turned my chair around to look at the map on the opposite wall. Sometime later, one of the other lads walked in, a fellow called Nigel. 'Have you had any complaints from the neighbours?' I asked him.

He said that he wasn't aware of any but why was I asking. I repeated what Mick had told me, to which he replied, 'Ah yes, now I know why he asked you not to look out the window. If you do that in the morning, you'll have f**k all to do in the afternoon.'

Sadly, it wasn't too far from the truth.

It wasn't until my seventh shift – the first night duty of my second tour – that I actually got to go out 'on a shout'. An automatic fire alarm had gone off at a local hotel. Unable to access all the rooms and with no key holder or manager in sight, the 'guvnor' asked me to take a look around the back to see if I could see anything. Stumbling upon an open window, I climbed in only to find a couple otherwise engaged and somewhat oblivious to the fire alarm going off. They didn't seem to be too perturbed by my presence so I made my excuses and climbed back out of the window.

That year went by inexorably slowly with very little other that the occasional car fire, the odd cat up a tree (yes, that is a thing) or a person stuck in a lift to raise any level of excitement. It did, however, produce one of the more surreal jobs that I ever experienced. A family had brought back from their holidays, of all things, a small embalmed shark in a glass jar. One of the kids had knocked it off the shelf, spilling the contents and the embalming fluid onto the carpet, to which the mum had then applied various cleaning chemicals. Two of the chemicals had reacted, incapacitating the mother and triggering a full-scale chemical incident that could have just as easily been dealt with by opening a window, but when you've got that much time on your hands, it's quite easy to get excited about actually doing something.

We occasionally got called to the grounds of other stations to assist when they needed additional help and it was there that I set my sights on my next posting the moment my probation was done.

Having served a brief stint at Kensington as a stepping stone to bigger and better things, I finally got an opportunity to go to Paddington, one of the busiest stations in London. At the time, they were experiencing over seven thousand calls a year, or about twenty a day, as opposed to Chiswick's five hundred a year. Even though a lot of these calls were due to fire alarms going off or other minor requests, around 15 per cent were fires involving an insurable loss – or 'Code Ones', as they were known – meaning that we would be fighting a fire of some form or another on most days.

The mindset of the guys there was in stark contrast with those at Chiswick. For instance, any spare time was taken up cleaning and maintaining gear, playing sport or conducting drills to keep themselves well-trained and ready for anything, which was just as well as 'anything' was exactly what you were dealing with on a weekly if not daily basis. Part of that was down to the ground that the station covered, from some of the most prestigious addresses in London in St John's Wood to some of the roughest estates in London where the police preferred not to go after dark. On numerous occasions on these estates, we'd have to put ourselves in harm's way to tackle incidents as any blue light was seen as the 'enemy'. From having fireworks shot at us to items thrown at us from overhead walkways, it certainly kept you on your toes. Cars and large bins were set alight on a fairly regular basis and at times you'd have to contend with abusive kids whilst trying to put the blazes out.

Furthermore, the station had one of the main arterial roads in London running past it and traffic accidents were commonplace. Nearby too were a series of canals from which we'd occasionally be tasked with pulling dead bodies, while in the vicinity lay five Tube stations where people would unfortunately decide to take their lives from time to time.

Though it may sound fairly horrendous to the uninitiated, I felt that I was in my element. The esprit de corps that existed amongst those I had the privilege to work with during those years was unparalleled and a constant inspiration. The common bond forged by having to deal with all kinds of adversity at a moment's notice was a real wake-up call for me and certainly showed me how thin a gossamer thread between life and death we all hang from, the Sword of Damocles never being far away.

All in all, those days are some of the best I have had and I can say with hand on heart that, in my case, they made a boy into a man.

Station life was pretty much focused on taking the piss out of each other at any given opportunity and having a thin skin was never an option. Mick Connolly, Piss-Taker-in-Chief, was always looking for a chink in people's armour and, though a pain in the arse, I had a lot of respect for him. He was every guvnor's worst nightmare as he was very much a 'get the job done' type irrespective of what command and control might want him to do. My dad had the same attribute, for which he was revered by the firefighters under his command and frowned upon by his superiors.

On one occasion, we were called out to one of the nicer blocks of flats in St John's Wood. There we found a man who was threatening to blow himself and the entire block of flats up by turning on the gas and lighting a match. To give the fellow his due, he wasn't mucking around – there was a strong smell of gas coming from his flat and he could be seen through the letterbox slot flicking a lighter on and off. Contrary to popular belief, the mixture of gas and air has to be just right to cause an explosion. The block was duly evacuated and we set up a perimeter and had emergency crews on standby.

Mick and I were tasked with laying out a hose line to the front door to allow the fire-fighting crew quick access should everything go bang. This we set about doing, but when we were alone on the second-floor landing Mick had an idea. Whilst the police were arranging a negotiator and all hell was breaking loose outside, he asked me to see if I could get the guy close to the door.

I engaged the guy in conversation but pretended not to be able to hear him on account of there being a lot of noise outside. I asked if he could come closer to the door and, once he was just the other side, I gave Mick a signal and he came hurtling down the corridor, crashing through the door and knocking the poor chap for six. Much to the bemusement of everybody else, we then simply walked in, turned the gas off and opened the windows. This taught me a valuable lesson – namely, that there are times in life for procrastination but sometimes you just have to take a good run-up and kick the door in!

There are so many tales to tell from my time at Paddington, such as attending Queen Mary's Hospital, helping to unshackle a gentleman who seemed to have taken something of a fancy to a stainless steel curtain ring, rescuing a pigeon from a tree (yep, even better than a cat!) and so on. It would take almost an entire book to cover them, but some of the best times were simply sitting around the mess table with the other guys on the watch, having a laugh.

Dave Burden was one of the most respected men in the watch. Though he was an older guy (he'd both served and rowed with my dad twenty years previously) he was incredibly strong and a great sportsman. More than that, he was one of the most gentle and steady blokes that I came across during my time in the job and seemed completely unflappable. One of the anecdotes told by Dave during a game of cards would stick with me throughout my subsequent travels and I would like to share it for the benefit of others.

A farmer had a herd of cows. He wanted to increase productivity and decided that, in addition to the old bull that he had, he'd introduce a new bull to the farm. When the new bull was let out of the trailer, he stared up at the field full of cows on the hill and said to the old bull excitedly, 'Wow, look at that field of cows, let's run up there and f**k a few.'

The old bull slowly turned to the new bull and said, 'Let's walk up there and f**k em all.'

Whether Dave was likening me to the young bull or not I'll never know, but I'd like to think he was trying to impart a bit of wisdom.

Though Paddington was one of the busiest 'ships' in London, after seven years in the job I started to get itchy feet. I had a growing sense of life passing me by and despite working my balls off doing building work and landscape gardening on my time off, working eighty to a hundred hours a week, I felt that I was going nowhere fast.

There were guys (not on my watch, I hasten to add) who had already served fifteen years and were marking time, waiting another fifteen for their pension, and I didn't want to get caught in that cycle.

One evening, I struck up a chance conversation with another colleague whom I'd served with at Chiswick but who was now an officer at one of the adjoining stations. He knew that I really enjoyed sailing but he was also aware that I was getting a bit disgruntled with the job. He told me that you could actually be paid to sail boats, something that I knew nothing about and which thus took me by surprise. The idea stayed in the back of my mind, quietly stewing, but a single incident on a warm summer night had quite an effect on me. I wouldn't go as far as to say it was the final factor that drove me to leave the Fire Brigade, but it certainly stuck in my mind as poignant.

We were called out to a road traffic accident in one of the more affluent areas of our ground, just off Queensway. There wasn't much to see other than a crashed black Mercedes, a man standing in shock nearby and a girl lying on the pavement. There was little we could do as the occupants of the car were nowhere to be seen, having fled, the guy was in shock and being comforted by the ambulance crew and the girl was dead.

The story, we learned, was simply that the guy and girl were recently engaged and had decided to go out for a romantic stroll on a balmy night in London. Just after they'd left their flat, a car had come around the corner too fast, mounted the curb and killed the girl outright.

As I mentioned, this was not the only factor that made me decide to leave the Fire Brigade, but seeing such a stark example of how you can be on cloud nine one moment and dead the next meant that when my circumstances changed it was a much easier decision to give up the security of everything that I knew and follow a different path, reassured that none of us knows what is just around the next corner so you need to live your life whilst you can.

Another moment that had an effect on me occurred when I was cycling home one evening. It was dry and bright as I travelled along the A4 out of London. I'd be the first to admit that I always cycled fast and aggressively, often throwing caution to the wind. Had I done this twenty years later I'm sure that I'd have appeared at least a few times on YouTube, attracting some rather disparaging comments!

Anyhow, on this occasion, I was flying along the A4 at about twenty-five miles an hour, on the inside lane but getting ready to turn right to head up to Ealing where I was living at the time. The lights turned to amber and I knew that there was a long wait for the next filter so I pushed hard and skipped the lights as they turned red, swerving over to the right to make the turn.

Unbeknownst to me, a driver had spotted the green light from a long way back and had sped up to catch it. He must have been doing sixty or seventy as the lights turned amber. As I swerved over to the right, I felt the whoosh of the car as it passed centimetres in front of my front wheel. I remember getting to the other side of the lights, climbing off my bike and, though not a religious man, looking up and thanking my Uncle Bert and Cousin Jason (my go-to guardian angels) for looking after me and keeping me alive.

It had been a close shave and I was once again reminded of how fine a line we tread between life and death and how we should take every opportunity to enjoy life whilst we can.

Meanwhile, I can't say that I haven't jumped a red light on a bicycle since, but I've almost certainly taken a longer look behind me first!

Come the turn of the new millennium, the relationship that I had been in for the previous four years started to break up, which although upsetting, was the catalyst that I needed for change. I'll always be eternally grateful for my time in the Fire Brigade, the camaraderie and the life lessons it taught me. However, it was time to grab life by the balls and give them a good squeeze.

4

Make Like Enya

I quit the Fire Brigade in February 2000. Then, deciding that it was going to be a sailor's life for me, I headed down to the Isle of Wight to a sailing academy to complete a number of qualifications which I hoped would give me a leg up into the yachting industry.

Over the following months I completed my Yachtmaster offshore certificates and a whole host of other water-sports tickets including dinghy sailing, windsurfing and kayak instructing, culminating in my Yachtmaster Ocean ticket which I attained in the Caribbean.

The courses were great fun and none more so than the Ocean course which involved spending four weeks cruising around the Caribbean, including a four-day non-stop passage to obtain all the necessary 'sights' using only a sextant to locate our position. The skipper of the boat (who shall remain nameless for reasons that will become apparent) was a lovely guy, very dapper and a proper 'salty sea dog'. Unfortunately for him, one of the other crew members was a guy with whom I'd struck up a friendship during our time on the Isle of Wight and who was of a similar ilk to me and equally fond of a bit of mischief. We were also accompanied by a Finnish couple who were incredibly boring, which seemed to encourage us to behave even more badly. Sadly, my friend's time onboard culminated in an incident after a particularly boozy night in Antigua when he mistook the entrance to the Finnish couple's cabin for the toilet door and proceeded to alleviate his bladder in their cabin. On account of this misunderstanding he was asked to leave the boat prior to the end of the trip.

As mentioned, the captain was a very dapper chap, always smartly turned out; even his stripy pyjamas were always neatly ironed. It being rather sweaty below decks, I opted to sleep in the boat's cockpit, from where I would often see the skipper wander out on deck to go for a wee off the back of the boat in the middle of the night. More strangely, sometimes he would come up on deck, go to the transom and stand there. A few minutes would pass before he would turn around and go back to his cabin without urinating.

After this had happened a few times, I noticed that on the occasions that the captain didn't urinate the pipe that he always carried was unlit. One day, unable to help myself, I quizzed him about this. In reply, he quietly pulled me aside and let me know that he was prone to sleep walking but would rather that I kept that under my hat as he wasn't sure how well the sailing school would take the news.

Sworn to secrecy but unable to resist a small prank, the next time it happened I waited for him to wander past me to the transom of the boat, then after checking for the smell of pipe tobacco to ensure that he was asleep, went to his cabin and locked the door from the inside, climbing back out through the deck hatch and getting back into my sleeping bag. The skipper, pipe still unlit, returned to his cabin, whereupon I could hear the rattling of the door handle. This stopped suddenly and moments later he reappeared on deck and stood at the back of the boat for a while before returning below, whereupon there was more rattling.

After this had happened three times, the pain at having to stop my sides from splitting became unbearable and, relenting, I got up and slid back through the hatch and unlocked the door. As far as I'm aware, the skipper remains completely oblivious about this to this day.

Bearing in mind that we were learning the finer points of boat handling and management, we had an interesting incident whilst passing through the narrow canal that separates the two halves of Guadeloupe. Here there was a lifting bridge that only opened at certain hours, which meant a very early start that morning to make the transit.

We slipped lines in the wee hours, whilst it was still pitch black, and made for the bridge which was plainly closed with the traffic lights showing red. As we got closer, we were amazed at the confidence of the skipper who obviously had done this a lot of times before and knew exactly when the bridge would open and how long it would take to do so.

We found ourselves moving ahead of a queue of boats which were all at a standstill, waiting for the green light. Fifty metres out from the bridge, travelling at about four knots, it was looking like a very ballsy move indeed, so I thought I'd ask if all was well, at which point the skipper woke up. Somewhat confused, he spun the helm hard over but unfortunately it was a bit too late and, with a following current pushing us towards the bridge, the port quarter (back left) collided with some scaffolding that had been erected for maintenance. This put a hole in the side of the boat, although fortunately above the waterline.

As luck would have it, the prevailing wind meant that we could sail to Antigua for repairs with the boat healed over the right way, keeping the hole well clear of the waves. Apart from the prop shaft falling off in the middle of the night and disappearing out of the back of the boat in a large swell, flooding the engine bay and threatening to sink us, it was an uneventful trip and, in comparison with my previous sailing trips with Dad, fairly tame.

It was my aim, upon stepping off of the boat in Antigua, to secure a job on a superyacht. Sadly, however, one wasn't forthcoming and, as I was running out of money, I decided to head home and try my luck again in the South of France in the spring.

Before leaving I did manage to secure a bit of 'day work' on a boat. This is casual labour, paid cash in hand on a daily rate, and turned out to be a great introduction to yachting. Basically I'd turn up first thing in the morning and help set up the boat for a boat show. Normally, just after doing so, there would be a short sharp shower meaning that I had to start all over again. It was thus a cycle of rinse, dry, repeat that would recur four or five times a day throughout the four days that I was onboard.

When I wasn't drying the boat, I was asked to help conduct tours. No problem in itself except that I knew nothing about the vessel or indeed how to find my way around it. I'm not sure what the brokers whom I was showing around thought of the tour, but if they were anywhere near as confused as I was, their subsequent representation of the boat to clients may not have been entirely accurate.

I should add that, prior to going out to the Caribbean, I had never seen or even heard of such a thing as a superyacht. If you saw a fifty footer in the UK, it was quite something. Arriving in Antigua and finding yachts that were a hundred feet or more was therefore startling, filling me with the same sense of awe and wonderment as the first day I walked through the archway at Southwark Fire Station.

After returning to the UK that winter, I picked up some casual work to put a bit of money in my pocket before heading out again in the spring. As with most yachties, I headed down to Antibes in the South of France which is the epicentre for most of the crewing agencies in those parts. I caught the train from Nice airport which runs parallel to the coast. It gave me a good view of the port entrance in Antibes and what I could only assume was a miniature cruise ship on its way out of the harbour. By this point I'd seen plenty of superyachts, but if they were super, this craft was super dooper!

Whilst walking along the quay on my first morning in Antibes, I was blown away by the size of these things. My hopes and expectations upon leaving the UK were geared to, if possible, getting on a boat more than a hundred feet long, but now it looked like I'd struggle to find anything smaller than that.

For the next eight weeks my mornings were taken up walking the docks, joining hordes of wannabees calling at each boat at ports anywhere between Cannes and San Remo to see if they had any work going or would like a copy of my CV for future reference. It was a fairly dispiriting time, watching funds slowly diminish while daily hearing of people far less qualified than me getting their break and being offered a job.

I realised that, at twenty-seven, despite having been a sailor since the age of fifteen and holding a load of useful qualifications, my chance of getting a job was far slimmer than that of a fresh-faced, unqualified twenty-one year old. It seemed rather unfair but I knew for a fact that it was the same in the British military which did not recruit anybody over twenty-six and for good reason. Quite simply, by that age you are far more likely to have formulated your own opinions and thus far less likely to simply do as you are told. To this day, I tend to shy away from more mature candidates for junior roles as they are less malleable and, in the past, this has often led to problems.

Fortunately, just as it was looking like I had missed another season, I was picked up by somebody looking for help in finishing a refit on a boat in La Spezia, Italy. This would then lead to the offer of a deckhand position. The boat had been involved in a major collision some years beforehand and had to have the entire bow (the pointy bit at the front) rebuilt. I was entrusted with repainting the engine room and was told by the captain that he wanted it to look 'like a Swiss clinic'. I'd not spent any time in a Swiss clinic and the only one I knew of by name was Dignitas. If the inside of that clinic was anything like the result of my efforts, patrons wouldn't need any assistance with suicide. They'd do it there and then.

That said, I stuck to the design brief given me by the captain. All diesel pipes should be painted yellow, he said, all seawater pipes green, cooling water pipes blue, poo pipes brown, firefighting red, etc. etc. until what I ended up with looked like the London underground map might after you'd taken a hit of LSD. It was an absolute abomination!

The crew were an interesting bunch too. The captain remained in charge after it had been established that he'd been nowhere near the wheel at the time of the accident. The chef, who *had* allegedly been at the wheel at the time of the accident (and who had suffered major neurological damage and was prone to blackouts and was blind in one eye due to the injuries sustained), was back onboard. The chief engineer liked to start the day with a mug of whisky, 'just to sharpen me up a bit', he said. The chief stewardess had never worked on a boat before and got seasick sitting in port. The second stewardess they found was equally inexperienced and apparently teetotal, admitting that she much preferred cocaine and ecstasy to pep her up of an evening.

The first officer was a nice enough guy but couldn't stand the chief engineer who walked off during fuelling just before the first charter in Napoli leaving the first officer to do it. Either through deliberate sabotage or an accidental cock-up, the bilges were filled on this occasion with 5,000 litres of fuel which caused a huge amount of work to clear up.

It was quite an introduction to the world of 'super-yachting' but fortunately I was plucked from there in the nick of time with another job offer coming along as a deckhand on another boat. This outfit was more professionally run, although it wasn't without its peculiarities, and I came to learn that the kicking-the-door-down approach to problem-solving and the constant sarcasm that I'd honed to perfection in the Fire Brigade had landed me with a skillset not entirely suited to the superyacht industry. In addition, to say that I was clumsy is probably a bit of an understatement and I spent more time in the first three or four months of that job repairing stuff I had broken than I did doing anything else.

Apparently, sarcasm is the lowest form of wit, but I still found it pretty funny. Unfortunately, however, after a while there was little sport in it as the rest of the crew weren't as well versed in it as me and made for all too easy pickings.

One masterstroke was to alter the crew profile which was left in the cabins of the charter guests to tell them a little about the crew. Nobody picked up on it for a good four or five months and the captain, a trained concert pianist who hated playing for the guests, wondered why he was called so often to tinkle the ivories (I may have put something in there about him liking nothing more than playing requests). Other japes included sending the first officer to a plumber's merchant for some 'pump-priming water' ('like normal water but a bit thicker'); convincing the chief stewardess that the Atlantic is roughly one metre lower than the Mediterranean so you could usually feel the bump as you came out of Gibraltar; and telling the deckhand that due to the sanctions on Cuba they were only allowed to export small amounts of motor oil, which was named after the then leader Fidel Castrol (his middle initials being GTX).

The owner of the boat loved sea fishing and spent thousands of pounds on all the latest gear and gadgets to help him land a fish. Countless hours were spent with lines out the back, trolling along coastlines at eight to nine knots (about ten miles per hour), never with any success. Whilst anchored off a beach in Dominica in the Caribbean, a couple of local guys came alongside in a tatty dugout canoe with bamboo poles asking to speak to the chef to see if he wanted any fish. When asked what they had, they pulled alongside with a marlin which must have weighed over two hundred pounds, filling the entire canoe. Thinking it best to get them away from the boat before the owner came out and had his already bruised fishing ego battered more, we promised to come to the beach later to buy some.

Dominica is one of my favourite islands in the Caribbean or at least it was last time I was there as it was still very authentic and felt like the proper Caribbean. It was used in a lot of the scenes in *Pirates of the Caribbean* movie franchise, probably as it needed far less editing to try and cut out the occasional KFC sign or other signs of modern times in other, more commercial islands. It is also home to the last tribe of Carib Indians, the original settlers of the Caribbean, and boasts beautiful rainforests, natural hot springs and a whole host of tropical wonders of the natural world (for the pub-quizzers amongst you, it is also the only nation to have the colour purple in its flag). Sadly, on my last visit, a cruise-ship dock was being built so it'll probably become just another destination. Anyhow, going back to the fish story, it was one of the more bizarre things that I have seen during my time at sea.

When the fishermen returned from their time at sea, If they had anything to sell conch shells were blown to let everybody locally know. Hearing the noise, I went in with the chef to see what was up for grabs. As we approached the rickety dock, intent on getting some fish directly from the fishermen, we saw a wizened, mahogany-skinned old man standing on the dock. Next to him was a decent-sized fish, probably half a metre in length, that had been rigged up to a huge bait hook and a wire trace line. The trace line was attached to a spool of fishing line which was then tied to a soft rope which was in turn attached to the old man's ankle.

As we stepped onto the dock, the fish was thrown in. followed by the old man (just to clarify, he wasn't thrown in, he opted to dive of his own free will) who swam off out to sea. To this day, I have no clue if this was a regular thing or whether it was a rustic Caribbean version of the aforementioned Dignitas but the chef and I just stood there agog as the old boy disappeared off towards the horizon.

Having spent just over eighteen months on the boat and crossed the Atlantic twice, visiting all the usual places on the yachting milk run, as well as Cuba, Mexico, London and even a delightful trip to Lowestoft, it was time to move onwards and upwards. In short, I secured a position as First Officer (second-in-command) on a thirty-four-metre motor yacht owned by a very flamboyant gentleman.

My new boss required a cruising itinerary to be submitted to him before the start of each season. This would normally mean poring over charts and pilotage guides to find out the best spots to take the boat. However, this fellow had something very different in mind with regard to 'cruising' and our main point of reference was something called the *Spartacus Guide*. It's not always easy to park a superyacht outside a public toilet block in a foreign town but we did our best to entertain his wishes.

For legal reasons, I think that it's probably best to leave most of the shenanigans that went on to your imagination. However, I think it's worth saying that, when the boat sold, I was tasked with inventorying everything onboard and clearing the files off the computer. Some of these things were of a personal nature and proved quite an eye-opener. In fact, afterwards I was not sure that I would be able to look at him, his guests or a number of the crew in the same way ever again, having found quite a few intriguing photographs and some very imposing toys!

That said, we went to some fantastic places during my two years onboard. Most notably, we once had to pick my boss up in Beirut, which still qualifies as one of the craziest but friendliest cities that I have ever visited. The food and nightlife was amazing, the climate was great and the people could not have been nicer which was made all the more incredible given the recent history.

The urban landscape still bore the scars of the civil war that raged from 1975 to 1990, many of the buildings covered in pock marks and holes from the shelling and gunfire that occurred during this period and there was an almost anarchic and lawlessness though friendly air to the place. Though only my interpretation, it felt as if the people, wounded by the events of the past, were so relieved to be living in peace again that they had a very laissez faire attitude to life, much as I imagine was the case in post war Europe leading to the 'baby boom'.

Driving in the city was very interesting with traffic lights seemingly there just as an advisory or maybe even for decoration as nobody seemed to pay any heed to the signals, even at the largest of intersections. The familiar red disc with a white line through the middle, commonly seen in most countries as a no entry sign was interpreted as a handy short cut if the traffic was too heavy. Despite the constant cacophony of car horns, no manoeuvre, regardless of how dicey, was greeted with any animosity from other drivers, the honk of a horn being more of an acknowledgement rather than a means to express disdain.

We had a 400cc motorbike on board the boat which was in need of a service however none of the crew had a license but, this being Beirut, it didn't seem to matter so I volunteered and after craning it on to the dock, I had a few trial runs, familiarising myself with how to ride a bike with gears and a clutch, my only previous experience only being on a moped.

After 5 minutes or so and with our local agent becoming impatient as I stalled and kangaroo hopped my way out of standing starts, we set off to the Romanian quarter on the other side of the city which was quite the adventure. Nabil, my guide, weaved his way through the traffic with reckless abandon as I struggled to keep up but he was apparently keen to take me for a culinary tour of the city. The journey involved several stops along the way to various street vendors to sample the local delights which, if this was his average journey, would certainly account for his physique, under which his tiny moped seemed to be enveloped and was groaning with the considerable strain.

Having stopped for tea, baklava, ayran (a popular yoghurt based drink) and pastries at separate street vendors and café's, we pulled over one final time in a grimy back street when he spotted a guy walking along with a tray on his shoulder. Given the 42 degree heat and blazing sunshine, I was a little dubious of the fare on offer however, when presented with a tray of oysters by Nabil who was obviously very proud of his city and keen to show me the best it could offer, it would have been rude to have said no.

I gulped three down with a squeeze of fresh lemon and can honestly say that they have never been bested to this day. Whether that was from the flavour or the sheer relief of not getting an immediate bowel wrenching bout of 'Beirut belly' I couldn't tell you but they certainly left their mark.

After a few weeks here and with the boat ready for departure, having secured all of the necessary visas for our onward travel, the boss and his entourage embarked and we headed up to Latakia in Syria.

From the brochures that we had seen, it looked be a picturesque, typically Mediterranean port from which to explore this historic country, known as being the cradle of civilization. However, the camera angles used in the photos seemed to be somewhat 'sympathetic', and as we passed the rusted out hulks of long abandoned ships in the entrance to the harbour, we were busily checking the charts to make sure that we were in the right place as It seemed that the place had been in steady decline in the intervening few millennia since its heyday.

Upon arrival at the dockside, it took five hours to complete entry formalities so that the boss could go for a thirty-minute cycle ride – only to declare it 'shit' – before spending another four hours doing more paperwork so we could leave. With Syria officially 'done' we continued on to Turkey, Greece and then Turkey again where, very fortunately for us, one of the generators blew up whilst we were in Istanbul giving us ten days to explore that beautiful city.

Once the generator was fixed, we headed up the Bosporus into the Black Sea for a whistle stop tour of Bulgaria and Romania where we travelled up the Danube. The boss liked to sit out on deck for dinner of an evening but there were a lot of bugs about on the delta so he asked us to fit some of those UV bug zappers that you sometimes see in a butchers shop. Dinners were then accompanied by the constant buzzing, crackling and burning of the hordes of critters unfortunate enough to come on board, while the morning set-up literally had us shovelling piles of fried bugs off the deck.

It was onwards to Ukraine after that. The architecture there was stunning, exactly how you would imagine it in the post-Soviet era with huge imposing buildings. One day in Odessa, I went to post a birthday present home to my niece. Entering the post office was like stepping back in time – it was a massive, very austere and cavernous hall reminiscent of the Cold War movies that I've seen. There was endless queuing at different counters to get stamps, envelopes and clearances, all involving a level of bureaucracy that would make the Italians blush and which added to the feeling of having stepped back into a different era.

After a few days there and a few tips ashore for some great sightseeing (and a chance to sample a genuine chicken Kiev, I'm cultured you see), we moved on for a short stay in the Crimean resort town of Yalta.

Yalta was the scene of the 1945 Yalta Conference where the then Allied leaders, Churchill, Stalin and Roosevelt effectively drew the lines of the post war landscape. Although not the intention at the time, it set the stage for the cold war between East and West which would pitch the communist regime of the East against the predominantly capitalist ideals of the West which would last officially until 1991 though echoes of it remain to this day.

Being a resort town, there was much fun to be had here and with vodka at eight dollars a bottle, it would have been a travesty to not at least try to get out, meet the locals and experience the culture. I'm not sure how much culture we absorbed but if the amount of vodka consumed was anything to go by, I'd probably have qualified for a passport by the time we left.

Russia was next on the boss's list and, as a matter of protocol, we had to put into the first port of call which happened to be Novorossiysk. It wasn't exactly how we'd imagined it and the guides that we had read didn't really tell the whole story. It is one of the biggest ports on the Black Sea and home, as we were proudly informed, to the second-biggest cement works in Europe – just what your average billionaire wants to see on their hols!

Undaunted and excited, what's more, to set foot in Russia, we called the pilot station (major ports employ professional pilots who are master mariners trained to guide ships to their berths) and were informed that the pilot was on his way. Upon boarding, however, it turned out that he was utterly legless and stinking of booze. He insisted on taking the controls of the boat and motoring us to our berth which is very unusual. This the captain politely refused, asking instead for another pilot to be sent out to replace him.

When the next pilot arrived he could hardly make it onto the bridge. Clearly they must have done some kind of sobriety test before sending out the first one to see who was the least drunk. Thankfully, the new fellow was too pissed to do anything and was quite content to sit on the couch at the back of the bridge and cuddle a bottle of whisky. As it happened, we were informed that the visas that some of us had were single entry. This meant that if we set foot on land we'd have to turn around and leave Russia immediately afterwards so sadly we never got a tour of the cement works and instead headed back out of port and up to the picturesque town of Sochi, home to the 2014 Winter Olympics.

We were there for several days so I decided that, with a few thousand miles to travel back to Barcelona afterwards, it would be a good idea to put some scuba gear on and give the props a clean before departing. I'd almost finished when I heard a lot of banging on the hull. I surfaced immediately only to find a lot of men in enormously brimmed hats and lots of braiding in a very agitated state. Apparently, the boat on the other side of the dock belonged to a certain Mr Putin and they were a little upset at my presence underwater in such close proximity.

I stayed with that owner until the boat sold in 2005, transferring to another boat of his that was being built in Plymouth, but delays in the process meant that she wasn't going to get her bum wet any time soon and the sea was once again calling.

My first five years in yachting seemed to pass in an instant. Time onboard was interspersed with a good amount of generally booze-fuelled shenanigans and all my time off was taken up doing courses in order to obtain further qualifications and further my career.

My next job was once again as a First Officer, albeit on a forty-eight-metre motor yacht whose captain was keen to bring me up to a level where he could take leave and hand over command to me. It was a thrilling prospect and reminiscent of my final weeks of training school in the Fire Brigade when

I actually realised that all that seemed daunting at first was now almost within reach. The captain was a really nice guy and the man I credit the most in teaching me how to drive a boat and bringing me up to speed on the overall management of a vessel. (Apologies to Captain Ian on the previous boat but, let's face it, we were too drunk most of the time to learn anything. You still qualify as the most fun by a country mile though.)

After a busy season in the Mediterranean, we headed over to the Caribbean but started to get overheating issues on one of the prop shafts. After many exhaustive hours of scuba diving, trying to rod out a gooey rubber substance from the bearings, it was ascertained that somehow one of the prop shafts had become bent and the boat would not be able to travel back across the Atlantic.

By now, I had completed all my courses and could do no more other than accrue time at sea in order to sit my oral examination for my Master's licence. I would therefore be at a bit of a loose end during the three weeks it would take to transport the yacht back to Europe on a huge, semi-submersible vessel. One of the deckhands, 'Boy Band Dave', was very well-travelled so I decided to pick his brains as to where I might go during this unexpected break. Knowing that I was very active and enjoyed adventure, Dave suggested that I head to South America for some backpacking. There, he assured me, adventure could be found and he gave me a bucket list of things to do.

Staying in backpackers' hostels was a great way to get hints and tips on some of the best things to do. But whereas a lot of the seasoned backpackers would do these things over four or more months, I was on a tighter time schedule. Whilst in Peru and Bolivia, I managed to squeeze in, amongst other things, white-water rafting, canyoning, a five-day trek on one of the Inca trails (the famous Inca Trail is booked up way in advance, this was the Salkantay which is a bit longer and a bit higher and far less travelled) leading to Machu Picchu, a three-day mountain bike ride across the Andes, a visit to the floating islands on Lake Titicaca, a two-day climb of Huayna Potosi and three days in the Bolivian rain forest, swimming with the pink river dolphins amongst other things. Of these, the most memorable were the mountain-bike ride and the climb of Huayna Potosi for very different reasons.

The mountain biking was incredible with stunning scenery and empty trails, all at high altitude, above 3,500 metres, which made for hard work but it was enjoyable nevertheless. Just as memorable was the bus ride there. I was paired up with a rather large American who started telling me how good a biker he was, how much training he'd put in and how much he was looking forward to 'smashing the trails'. Even more interesting however was him telling me what an expert sommelier he was and how he had an incredible 'one in a million' sense of smell that could discern the subtlest of aromas.

Meanwhile, as the bus filled up, it became apparent that it doubled as the preferred means of transport for the local farmers and their families, livestock and various other paraphernalia of their lives. We were in an incredibly poor part of South America where, it is fair to say, personal hygiene took a back seat to just getting by from day to day. Thus as the bus filled up with people and their belongings, the olfactory assault on Mr Supernose grew.

The final straw was when, into what we thought was an already packed bus, they squeezed one more farmer along with a goat and two chickens. This forced the chap standing next to my portly American friend to reach for the overhead bar, directly in his nose-line, whereupon he visibly gagged and turned green.

The American remained blissfully quiet for the rest of the three-hour journey. Whilst the beautiful Andean scenery passed by the window, he wept gently into a hankie held over his nose and mouth.

The trip that made the largest impression, however, was the climb of Huayna Potosi. Apart from being very exciting, this experience sowed the seed for all the adventures I undertook over the following four years.

Huayna Potosi is located twenty-five kilometres north of La Paz in Bolivia. It stands at 6,088 metres and was my first real taste of high-altitude mountaineering. Though considered a relatively easy climb with only fourteen hundred metres from the trailhead to the summit, it did nevertheless introduce me to glacier travel and the challenge of steep climbing at altitude, as well as the effect this had on the body, slowing everything down to an inexorable crawl.

I found it incredible how the smallest of exertions required so much effort that left you feeling that your lungs were going to burst out of your chest. I remember extreme effort required on the summit day, trying to climb a six-foot ice step with crampons and ice axes, the lack of oxygen at that altitude making the mountain feel ten times the size and the sheer relief of overcoming this smallest of obstacles. It was upon summiting this mountain, while sitting of a ridge of ice and rock looking up at a star-filled sky and the luminescent peaks of the mountains around me, that I experienced such a feeling of awe that I was hooked.

The descent flew by with my mind preoccupied with thoughts of *what's next?* which was when the first spark of an idea to summit the highest mountain in the world entered my mind. Returning to work, still half-dazed by the adventures of the previous weeks, I started planning my strategy of how I could make this possible.

In the autumn of 2006, I sat my oral examination to obtain my Master 500 GT ticket. This gave me the certification to captain yachts up to five hundred tons and allowed the captain to take some much-needed time off. His intention was to ask the owners to grant increased leave in recognition of his ten years loyal service onboard, which they did in the spring of 2007 only to ask him not to return.

Sadly, the yachting industry can be incredibly fickle like that. I was duly asked to step up into the captain's role. It was a pretty big step for somebody who'd only been in the industry five years but it was too good an opportunity to pass up. In hindsight, I'd have done better to refuse and get a few more years of tutelage from another experienced captain under my belt, but my self-confidence overrode my actual ability and I took on the role.

It was certainly a baptism of fire, during which I became tangled up in a couple of incidents which did me no favours in the owner's eyes. First up was buggering a brand-new paint job on a dock in Mallorca. This came about because I'd never previously had to deal with something called 'bank effect' where you effectively get sucked back onto a dock due to the effect of shallow water, and the more beans you give it with the engines, the worse it gets.

But the incident that still ranks as my worst experience in yachting (so far) was when the guests asked to go ashore in Ibiza for a few hours. The weather was terrible with large swells pushing through so that we could not launch a tender. I formulated a plan to nose into the inner harbour, drop a tender there and then potter around for a few hours until they were ready to be picked up, whereupon I'd repeat the procedure to get them back onboard. I contacted the port notifying them of my intention and, with the guests dressed in their finery and ready to go, I made my approach.

The tender was launched, the guests disembarked and I made preparations to leave until required for the pick-up. The first radio message that I had was from the first officer who was driving the tender to tell me that the engine had cut out and that he was drifting. I asked him to anchor whilst we prepared to launch the other tender with the remaining crew that I had onboard. The next message was that there was smoke coming from the engine hatch, to which I replied by asking him to get the anchor down and keep the smoke away from the guests, activate the fixed firefighting system and reassure the guests that all would be OK.

Apparently, the extinguishing system failed to trigger and the principal guest, not sufficiently reassured by the first officer, ordered his entire family to jump in the water. This would have been OK had it not been for the swarm of jellyfish that they jumped into, but as it was they started to panic. At this point, I had limited crew onboard, having sent three of them off in the tender, so was unable to launch another tender. I therefore took the decision to drop anchor in the outer harbour, which was strictly forbidden but I was running out of options.

Within two minutes, the port police and coastguard were at the boat shouting and screaming at me and threatening to impound the vessel due to my actions. To give them credit, when I explained the situation they were pretty understanding. Unfortunately, however, the guests were less so.

Though not specifically cited in my subsequent dismissal from the boat, these two incidents certainly didn't help my cause. The actual reason given was my 'unique' sense of humour and honesty which wasn't always appreciated by the guests.

The principal of the family who owned the vessel liked nothing more than being taken out in the tender and looking at other boats. One day, whilst at a busy anchorage in the British Virgin Islands, we spotted the yacht *Rising Sun*, which was the new biggest boy on the block at the time at 138 metres long. The boss commented to me that 'though big, you would be surprised at how efficient these new boats are', to which I replied, 'Indeed, about as efficient as you can get for pushing eight thousand tons of steel around the world for the enjoyment of one man.' I thought this was a fair comment but, judging by the all-pervading silence that ensued, I'm not sure that he saw it the same way.

The death knell was apparently sounded in Cannes early the following summer when sitting in harbour. A rather large female guest came teetering down the *passerelle* (a posh gangplank) in a ridiculous pair of shoes and a diaphanous gown. Unfortunately, one of her heels caught in the grating and she took a bit of a tumble. I offered a hand to catch her but, no doubt embarrassed and seeking somebody to take it out on, she screamed at me, 'Have you ever tried walking down here in a pair of high heels?' The correct response would of course have been, 'No, madam, I will do everything I can to make sure it doesn't happen again.' However what came out was, 'Yes, once or twice but only at weekends and I've never had any trouble.'

Come the following week, I had plenty of spare time to plan my next adventure.

Part III

Time to Get High

My plan was simple: to cut my teeth on mountains of ever-increasing size and to learn as much about mountaineering as I could until I felt ready to tackle Everest.

I landed my next job on a boat based in Monaco and the owner did not use it during the winter so I had the opportunity for weekend trips up into the French Alps to hone my winter mountaineering skills and to take advice on correct kit to equip myself with. The sheer physical effort of overcoming the elements during those weekends was something that really appealed to me and I had some terrific mixed- and ice-climbing experiences whilst up there. Mixed climbing, by the way, is classed as technical mountaineering on rock and ice whereas ice climbing is purely on ice, relying solely on ice axes and crampons to scale vertical ascents. Having gained invaluable experience in the Alps, including mastering the exaggerated gait needed to walk in crampons without tearing holes in your over-trousers (I was told to imagine I had a nasty rash on the inside of my thighs), I felt ready to tackle my next challenge.

5

Aconcagua

Standing at 6,962 metres, Aconcagua is the highest mountain outside Asia. It is one of the Seven Summits, the highest peaks on each of the seven continents, and has the greatest vertical ascent of any of them, the climb starting as it does way down the valley at 2,400 metres.

By winter 2008, I felt suitably prepared for the climb and at the end of January flew out to Mendoza, Argentina to join an expedition which was to start on 1 February. I'd chosen to tackle the Polish Glacier Traverse, a well-trodden path to the summit that would afford some stunning views of the mountain as well as an ever-changing landscape as the altitude increased and the flora and fauna changed with it. Typically for me, I chose this route because it was considered harder than some of the others which started at higher elevations and could be tackled in fourteen days rather than the twenty-three that I had signed up for. With a bigger goal in mind, I was keen to push myself as hard as I could.

Having previously travelled in South America and heard stories from other backpackers, I knew that the overarching theme of Argentina was 'incredible steak and red wine' so I decided to get there a few days early to sample the delights.

Well, the reports weren't wrong! The steak and red wine were incredible. However, as big a fan as I am of these things, after two days of being served nothing but cow (at one restaurant I was actually given a complimentary starter of deep-fried bulls testicles just in case the huge steak that I was about to receive wasn't enough to fill my bovine quota for the day) I was really craving some fresh vegetables or a nice salad. Thus, conjuring up my best Spanglish and adding a few vowels to the English words that I didn't know the translation of, I asked the waiter, '*Tienes una alternativa vegetariana?*' or, in other words, roughly, 'You have a vegetarian alternative?'

The guy looked at me a little quizzically and replied, '*Si, pollo*', which is to say chicken. And so it was that a few hours later I waddled my way back to the hotel and fell into another protein- and fermented-grape-induced coma for the evening, only waking occasionally to the rumble of thunder under my duvet as my body tried to process the food in time for breakfast when, no doubt, if they could have got cows to lay eggs, they'd have served them for breakfast.

Mendoza is a great city with beautiful Spanish colonial architecture and wide shady avenues. It is also the base of many expeditions to Aconcagua and the other magnificent mountains in the Andean range and thus equipped with a plethora of mountaineering shops. My first few days were spend popping in and out of these for any last-minute essentials and quite a few non-essentials.

One of the things that the expedition recommended was to get a supply of Diamox, an over-the-counter drug that can assist with the effects of altitude sickness which include headaches, nausea, vomiting, tiredness, dizziness and shortness of breath. Determined to 'tough it out' and somewhat full of my own hubris, I resisted the temptation. When the expedition guys came to my hotel to do a kit inspection, it was pointed out that I hadn't bought any, but this wasn't a problem because, though advised, it wasn't compulsory. A few weeks later, however, lying in my tent with a banging headache, it seemed like Diamox wouldn't have been such a bad idea after all.

The other members of the expedition began to assemble and, as is always the case with me, being a little competitive, I started to weigh up the group that we had. There was a usual sprinkling of different nationalities, several Americans, three South Africans, three Canadians and a couple of other nationalities but just one other Brit, Peter Kinloch, who looked like one of the more unlikely mountaineers that I had come across.

Hailing from the Isle of Skye, Peter was six foot two, stick-thin and pale with goofy glasses and a grin to match. Turning up in a matching bobble hat and a scarf of his favourite football club, Kilmarnock FC, he looked more like Scotland's answer to 'Where's Wally' than a serious mountaineer. He wasn't somebody whom I would normally be in a hurry to buddy up with, but with our bond of both country and time in the emergency services, we became Base Camp tent buddies. Rather surprisingly, he was a chief inspector in the Merseyside Police Force, but then again, if you were ever wanted somebody to go undercover, he'd be the last person you'd spot in a crowd if you were looking for a policeman!

With gear checked, double-checked and packed, we got onto the minibus and headed for the trail head at Punta de Vacas (Cow Point, in other words, and I thought I'd seen the last of cows for a couple of weeks!) where we strapped on our daypacks and began our hike. Base Camp was a three-day hike. We had some mules which would bear the majority of the load for this part of the journey with the muleteers helping to set up camp each night. These first three days were a gentle acclimatisation hike taking us from 2,400 metres up to the Base Camp at 4,200 metres. The scenery was ever-changing from lush green woodlands, following a meandering river, to the stark greys, browns and whites of the rock and ice at Base Camp.

Day one was a gentle four-hour hike up to Pampa de Leña, but even at that altitude, it was good to get into the slow mechanical plod that would have to be adopted at higher altitudes. Though it's not really in my nature to follow the crowd, I resolved to do so in the name of group harmony. That evening we camped at 2,800 metres and I fell into a blissful sleep in the cold crisp air.

Camp life starts fairly early, which suits me, and as the mules began to stir I was ready to get up and face the new day. Morning poo had, breakfast eaten, teeth brushed and gear packed and loaded onto the mules, we headed on up towards Casa Piedra at 3,200 metres. This day was a little longer, taking six hours to reach camp, and I became a bit fidgety with the pace of the rest of the group but stuck with them, the wise words of Dave Burden and the story of the two bulls resounding in my head every time I wanted to speed up. We camped on the stony floodplain of the river where the huge boulder that gives the place its name stood and from there had our first glimpse of the huge mountain that we would be climbing and got a real sense of the enormity of the task ahead.

Undaunted and excited at the prospect of heading up to Base Camp the next day, my night's sleep was a bit broken but I nevertheless woke up keen to crack on. The mules and their muleteers went on ahead as we removed our boots and crossed the icy river which flowed directly from the mouth of the glacier above us barefooted. We emerged both numb and refreshed from the cold, calf-high water, dried our feet, hurriedly donned socks and boots and were off.

The landscape had now completely altered from the beautiful greens at the start of the journey to the muted tones of rock, only changing as the sun passed over the valley. Moreover, the sounds and smells that you normally encounter in the lowlands had all but disappeared with the climate unable to sustain flora or fauna. Even after this small gain in altitude, the air had become noticeably thinner and drier and breathing, though still comfortable, was becoming harder.

Shortly after setting out, my nature got the better of me and, tucking Dave's mantra into the bottom of my pack, I decided to crack on at my own pace to show the rest of the group how big and tough I was. About an hour later, having set a blistering pace, I was surprised not to come across the mules who had set out a little earlier. However, these incredibly tough, sure-footed animals were in their element and definitely had the edge on me.

Half an hour later, the terrain became increasingly steep and, as I scrambled up scree and rocky steps, my admiration for these animals grew. It was upon reaching a particularly steep section that I started to ponder that normally, following a group of twenty or more mules, you might expect to see a bit more evidence of what they'd had for breakfast littering the trail, but I hadn't seen anything for quite some while. Standing still and listening very carefully, I could just make out the faint tinkling of the bells that they wore, carried on the wind in a valley about a mile to my right. Bugger! Dave Burden 1, me 0!

Scrambling back down the slope, I managed to just get to the head of the group of climbers that I'd left in my wake an hour and a half beforehand. Waving a cheery hello to them all and commenting on the wonderful view from the head of the valley I'd just gone up mistakenly and, feeling like a bit of a tit, I forged on, this time checking with the guide if there were any forks in the track that I should know about.

The rest of the day was uneventful as the track narrowed, zig-zagging its way along the ever-steepening valley sides and affording some spectacular views of the summit. I did end up catching those bloody mules in the end and showed them who was boss, arriving at camp an hour before them with no additional kit, nowhere to hide from the wind and nothing to eat until I'd helped the muleteers unload the mules, put up the tents and find my gear. The others arrived just in time to be presented with a nice cup tea and a warm meal after which they grabbed their gear and settled into their tents after a lovey day's hiking. I had a crap sleep that night with a thumping head, sore feet and a dry mouth. Dave Burden 2, me still 0 and probably earmarked by my companions not as being the biggest, toughest guy in the group but as the idiot who was most likely to either fail on the way to the summit or die trying.

The next two days were put aside for acclimatisation and rest. During this time we were also briefed on the probable schedule, park regulations and, most importantly, where and how to have a poo. With thousands of climbers arriving every year and a dry, cold climate in which things take a lot longer to decompose, there being very few bugs or bacteria to aid the process and very little rain to wash anything away, it was very important that there was a procedure in place for dealing with human waste not only for hygiene reasons but also to preserve the pristine environment.

Though as I write it, it doesn't seem as funny, the briefing had us all chuckling at the translation from our guide who kept referring to the act of having a poo as 'you go to make po-po', the Spanish word for 'to do' being the same as 'to make', and the phrase became somewhat of a catchphrase of the rest of the trip. Thus if I asked someone where they were off to, the answer would invariably be, 'I go to make po-po.'

For those of you who haven't had the pleasure of camp life, going to make po-po at this camp basically required us to find a convenient rock to squat behind and then bag our waste up and put it in a huge drum. The drums were helicoptered off from Base Camp every week or so and, as you can imagine, were pretty ripe by then, so that it required taking a deep breath before lifting the lid to deposit your detritus.

To this day, one of the things that I really look forward to when returning from an expedition is sitting on a proper loo and relaxing for my morning ablutions. After just four days on the trail, you could see the eyes of our group looking on enviously as another group of climbers set up next to us and one of the guides unstrapped a plastic patio chair with a hole cut in it from his backpack and placed it on the edge of a precipice with magnificent views down the valley.

Camp life is for the better part a great experience with people of many different nationalities and from all walks of life joined together by a common goal. I don't consider myself as particularly sociable, but it is easy to fall into conversation with people when your goal is the same, particularly on a 'beginner's hill' such as Aconcagua where most climbers are first-timers and very few people barring the guides really know what to expect. There is always a bit of 'dick swinging', with people comparing previous climbing and trekking experiences, but on the whole the atmosphere is very good-natured.

High-altitude mountaineering involves a lot of acclimatisation to prepare the body as much as possible for the increasing altitude and the ever-thinning air. Though the percentage of oxygen in the air doesn't change with altitude, the air is less dense so there are fewer oxygen molecules inhaled in every breath. By spending more time at altitude, the body can adjust to this by producing more red blood cells, which provide what oxygen there is in the atmosphere to your muscles and vital organs more efficiently.

Elite athletes are known to train at altitude or to recreate thinner air in a training facility in order to produce this same effect prior to a race. When you return to normal altitude your body will continue to produce increased levels of red blood cells and therefore be able to supply a greater volume of oxygen to your muscles. Back in the bad old days, with the Cold War raging and the battle for political supremacy spilling over into the sports arena, there were even stories of female Olympic athletes purposely getting pregnant prior to the games as pregnancy has the same effect on red blood cell production. Fortunately or not, illegal steroids were invented which put an end to this practice.

Feeling refreshed after two days and getting a bit fidgety, on day eight we made our first push up the mountain. Base Camp, known as 'Plaza Argentina', was the end of the trail for the mules so from now on all gear would have to be man-hauled (apologies to the woke community, it's just what it is called, though I've probably offended you sufficiently by now anyway with previous phraseology).

Gear was weighed and distributed evenly amongst the group for the haul up to the next camp. Each person was carrying around twenty-three kilograms, which I'd been forewarned of and subsequently trained with. We donned our packs and headed to the track leading out of Base Camp at a snail's pace which was fairly apt given that we were carrying our homes on our backs. The trail was a single track over loose moraine and was very dry and dusty. With every footstep taking a big effort on legs and lungs alike, it was a good idea not to fall behind as the few additional steps required to catch back up with the pace would cause you to hyperventilate and that wasn't funny.

It is hard to explain why, but everyone seemed intent on walking bunched up together. This led to frustrations amongst the group when a loose rock would slide from under someone's feet causing them to bump into the person either ahead of or behind them. Given that the track was very narrow, there was only one way to go and we would all reach the same point at some stage. It was completely illogical but I guess that none of us wanted to be considered the slow one who couldn't keep up.

Despite constant reminders from the guides, this continued to happen throughout the morning. Along with the exertion required to haul ourselves and our loads up the mountain, it made the mood among us a bit tetchy. At our lunch stop, grumbles were aired and everybody agreed that we had to space out a bit more. The situation improved slightly, but there was still the odd clash all the way up to Camp 1, which was at just over 4,800 metres. Here we were relieved to cache a lot of the gear including tents, cooking gear and other items needed for camp, lightening the load before returning to Base Camp that afternoon having had our first real taste of hauling heavy loads at higher altitudes.

Due to a combination of the dry air, heavy breathing, exposure to sunlight and lack of personal maintenance, my lips started to crack which was uncomfortable but not unbearably so. Otherwise I was in good shape and, after a good dinner, we all settled down for the night, knackered from the day's exertions but happy that we were underway and looking forward to the next stage.

One of the benefits of acclimatisation is familiarity with the route and, though it can be fairly featureless at higher altitudes, your mind has little else to focus on other than the next step in front of you. You thus begin to recognise features as small as a particularly steep switchback or a funny-looking rock, things that in everyday life you would pass by without a second thought. This is undoubtedly helped by our pace (and anyone who has small children will know the exact pace I'm talking about) when every step revealed a new fascination and to get the shortest distance took seemingly forever. Fortunately, the pace was pretty much dictated by the amount of oxygen we were able to get into our lungs. Though there were exceptions, everybody moved at roughly the same pace the higher up we went. The closest thing I can equate it to is being stuck in rush-hour traffic on a motorway.

Anyhow, with the familiar route markers up to Camp 1, the day passed relatively quickly and we were all relieved to get there for some rest. We erected the tents that we had cached the afternoon before and boiled water for some dehydrated meals that we had brought with us. Unfortunately, the cracks on my lips had started to develop into ulcers and open sores making it painful to eat. However, keeping up calorific intake and fluids at altitude is incredibly important as you burn through ever-increasing amounts, so it was a matter of simply putting up with the discomfort.

At over 4,800 metres, the air is much thinner and has less ability to hold heat. As a rough estimate, temperature will drop at a rate of about 1 degree Celsius for every hundred metres gained in altitude. It is down to something called the adiabatic lapse rate but, for fear of wandering way off topic, I'll leave you to google that one.

When the sun disappeared that day, it was bloody cold! We tucked up in our sleeping bags for the night and got what rest we could, though sleep was becoming increasingly difficult. Worst of all was waking up in the middle of the night and needing a wee as it meant opening the top of your lovely snuggly sleeping bag and exposing previously warm bits to the bitter night air. (It wouldn't be until two expeditions later that I would perfect the lying-on-your-side-and-keeping-the-sleeping-bag-closed method, during which you ran the danger of either overflowing the bottle or spillage, but it was well worth the risk.) Strangely, despite the incredibly tight proximity in which you live to others on this kind of trip, it's not something that you generally discussed. No doubt, any ladies reading who have found themselves in a similar predicament will be groaning, 'Oh, you poor soul, try using a Shewee!'

After a fairly uncomfortable and restless night's sleep, I awoke to find that unfortunately my cracked and ulcerated lips had stuck together. As with any wound, the body's natural response is to open blood vessels to bring oxygen and nutrients to it to help the healing process, which is very handy if you have an open cut but not so helpful if they are on opposite lips. Sadly, I had no choice but to simply pull my lips apart, tearing off all the scabs and opening new wounds in the process. This made eating from there on in somewhat less pleasurable which, for someone like me who has a large calorific intake, was a bit of a pain in the arse.

The next day we donned our fully laden packs to haul gear up to Camp 2 which would be our final staging post before the summit push. By now, we had all got used to the trudge and thankfully bunching up and colliding with each other was becoming less frequent, though when it did happen it was twice as annoying, with the ever-thinning air increasing the effort required to put one foot in front of the other. It was a long hard slog over steep and sometimes loose terrain which sometimes gave way underfoot, meaning that the effort you had just put into pushing your own bodyweight and the heavy pack up had just been wasted and would have to be done again. Needless to say this was incredibly irksome and avoided whenever possible.

Eventually we arrived at Camp 2, much to our relief, having climbed almost a thousand metres to 5,760 metres above sea level. Having lightened the load by caching some of the gear that we were carrying and had a short break, we headed back down the mountain, all the way to Plaza Argentina for a well-earned rest. As I was learning, though easier, going downhill at high altitude is no cakewalk, exercising as it does already sore and tired muscles and increasing the chances of slipping on the loose ground. As such, it can be incredibly energy-sapping.

Three hours later, we shuffled back into Base Camp, much relieved, for a few days of relative comfort and pampering with three meals a day and the luxury of thicker sleeping mats that were too bulky and heavy to take to the higher camps.

These days at Base Camp passed pretty quickly, sitting out in the sun, playing cards and reading books whilst tending to any blisters and sores. My lips had started to heal a little, making eating and drinking a bit easier but still uncomfortable.

Interestingly, during this period we had our blood oxygen levels monitored twice a day in order to make sure that we were recovering well and ready to push on when the time came. In a healthy person, levels should read between

94 and 100 per cent and guidelines suggest that, under normal conditions, if your oxygen saturation level drops below 94 per cent you should go to hospital immediately. This would have required quite a rescue operation as nobody came off the mountain after the acclimatisation hike with saturation levels above 92 per cent. One guy measured a staggering 78 per cent!

As the days rolled by and we slowly recovered, the readings went up. It was fascinating to see how quickly the human body reacted to the change in circumstances. The expedition leaders had a rule that nobody would set out for the summit with a reading of less than 94 per cent, and though a few only scraped over the threshold on the final morning, come day thirteen, we were ready for the big push.

The mood in Base Camp was that of excitement and mild apprehension as we packed up for the final time. Most of us were relative mountaineering novices. The level of effort required to get to Camp 2 had therefore come as a bit of a shock. As I prepared, there was a quiet voice in the back of my head wondering whether we as a group and I as an individual would be able to make it. I reassured myself by saying that if other people had managed it, so could I, and that regardless of how tough the challenge, all I had to do was put one foot in front of the other until I got to the summit. Though maybe a little perverse, I also took comfort in knowing that the others around me were suffering from the same aches, pains and anxieties as I was and all I had to do was push through this in order to succeed.

Passing over now familiar terrain, we headed up to Camp 1. This was markedly easier than our first two climbs, our bodies having become accustomed to the workload and the thinner air. As night crept in, we bedded down to get some rest and I drifted off, pondering what lay ahead. In the morning I awoke to find myself mummified and stuck to the floor.

During the previous day, it had warmed sufficiently to melt some of the ice in Camp 1 and, unbeknownst to me, my tent was in a puddle, some of the water from which seeped through the groundsheet. I was only carrying a narrow roll mat to save space and weight. Overnight, the sides of my sleeping bag had draped off the sides of my mat into the water which had then frozen, making me truly one with the ground around me. Fortunately, I was able to wriggle out of the top of my sleeping bag and eventually managed to pry it off the floor of the tent.

The push to Camp 2 was hard but doable and we all bedded down early that afternoon in anticipation of the following day's 2 a.m. start, necessary to reach the summit and get back down to safety. Sleep did not come easily with my mind abuzz with thoughts of the climb ahead but, in spite of this, I eventually managed a few fitful hours of rest.

The camp started to come to life at just after one in the morning. Suddenly I heard low murmurs and the glow of head torches was visible through the thin walls of the tent, followed by the sounds of zips undoing and the general clatter of preparation as stoves were lit for warm drinks and gear donned. I was glad to be awake and finally up, having nursed a splitting headache for much of the night and, prying my lips apart once again, I started to prepare for the day.

With everything at this altitude taking increased effort, camp routines should be carried out as smoothly and efficiently as possible. This I was beginning to learn – something as simple as not being able to find an additional pair of socks or finding that the spare batteries for your head torch are stuffed right at the bottom of your pack can cause a huge amount of frustration when your body is already under duress. It was a lesson well learned on this mountain that good organisation of your kit is essential in order to reduce overall stress at times when you need to keep effort levels to an absolute minimum in order to focus on the job in hand.

Fortunately, I'd had the time in the French Alps to carry out some winter training and practice the donning of clothing; getting on the various layers and hardshell boots in the confines of a small tent is a skill in its own right and bending down to fit crampons on your own whist restricted by all the layers is nigh impossible so is an exercise best undertaken as a group.

To this day, I love the buzz of setting out on an adventure. Suddenly, after months of preparation, all the work and training comes down to a single moment when you realise *this is it, I am actually doing what I set out to achieve*. More often than not, this is closely followed by the realisation of the enormity of what lies ahead, but that too is natural and it has never quelled my excitement of taking the first steps.

The first part of the climb required us to traverse the Polish Glacier. We were therefore harnessed and tethered together in case one of us misplaced a step in the darkness and slid off the trail. We had practiced ice-axe arrests in the event of this happening and all carried walking axes, but thankfully nothing of this sort was required. We seemed to start incredibly slowly but, tethered together as we were, there was little point in worrying about it. The pace was dictated by the expedition leader who probably had a pretty good idea of how fast we should be travelling.

The mountain was bitterly cold with light winds and snow as we made our way across the glacier, the crystalline flakes dancing in the light of our head torches. Undaunted, we plodded on, slowly dragging the tips of our crampons across the ice and planting the front foot before repeating with the trailing foot in order to conserve as much energy as possible. At first, I found the pace frustrating but after a while it became rather hypnotic and incredibly relaxing.

To this day, whilst waiting for my kids to catch up on a walk where they've no doubt found a muddy puddle to try and push each other into, I sometimes feel myself lapsing straight back into that rhythm and am instantly taken back to the crossing of the glacier which I find remarkably soothing. My mum and dad once told me a story about seeing hippies on a beach in Goa moving incredibly slowly. They found this very odd (one of our family traits is that we don't hang around or sit still any longer than is absolutely necessary), but following my experiences on Aconcagua I was able to totally get why they were doing it as it is very meditative. Admittedly, my deliberative gait was enforced by the circumstances I was in at the time and I can't say that, other than when waiting for my kids to catch up, I make a habit of it nowadays, but it did at least allow me to see the benefit of such a practice.

The snow stopped falling just before dawn and the skies soon cleared to reveal a beautiful morning with astounding views of the surrounding peaks. I'm not much of a night person and, despite having seen more sunrises than I care to mention, I always feel a renewed sense of vitality and excitement at the start of a new day. No matter how bad the night before might have been, I always feel that the new day is going to be fine and this day fortunately was no exception.

Once off the glacier, we untethered and carried on slowly and steadily towards the Piedras Blancas camp at 6,030 metres. Here the Polish Glacier traverse route met the normal route and we could see a lot of other climbers on the mountain up ahead. Feeling uplifted but cautious, we took a short break to regather our energy for the ongoing ascent.

My hands had become a little frost-nipped so I decided to take my gloves off and put a pair of liner gloves and warmer mittens on. After about five minutes of struggling, I realised that I was trying to put a pair of gloves on over my mittens. Being at altitude affects different people in different ways. The lack of oxygen induces a sort of temporary brain damage which in me resulted in a sense of mild delirium in which I didn't really know what was going on. Giving myself a mental slap in the face, I speedily got my gloves on in the right order and continued.

The rest of the ascent from then on in was a bit of a blur. Putting one foot in front of the other and following everybody else didn't seem beyond me so on I trudged. It was only on the final push up to the summit where a queue of climbers had formed on a seemingly never-ending set of narrow switchbacks across loose scree that I was able to get enough oxygen back into my body to start to regain my wherewithal and, whereas some people were moaning and grumbling about the wait, I was very grateful for the chance to recover.

Due to the traffic on the mountain and the varying pace of our group, we had become separated. However the group leader had said that this was OK and that we should continue at our own pace as the trail was fairly obvious and, with only one route up and down, there was no fear of getting lost. This last bit was prolonged but eventually I crested the summit plateau and felt an incredible sense of relief and achievement looking out at all the surrounding peaks that were now below me and the amazing vista that my efforts had rewarded me with.

The three South Africans in our group arrived shortly thereafter and, after the congratulatory handshakes and photos, it was time to head back down.

Still a little fuzzy-headed, I struggled at first to reorientate myself and find the path down, but after a little wandering, I got my bearings. Rather stupidly, not content with simply reaching the summit, my competitive nature kicked in and I decided that I wanted to be the first one back to camp so set out at as brisk a pace as I could muster wearing crampons on loose rock. Quite how I didn't take a tumble I really don't know but I was determined to come first in a race that nobody else was competing in.

As the day wore on, I became increasingly fatigued, to the point where the simple act of putting one foot in front of the other began to prove difficult. I suffered no pain or discomfort, but I was utterly exhausted. At one stage, just before recrossing the glacier, I sat down to recover and muster up the energy I needed to continue. It was at this point I realised that, in my delirium, I had forgotten to eat or drink anything so was severely dehydrated and weak. This was pretty dumb given that I was carrying a pack full of snacks and drinks.

It was another important lesson learnt in the art of self-preservation. I began to refuel and, after twenty minutes of stuffing myself with calories and drinking some much-needed electrolytes, I was back on my feet and heading down the mountain. I was to learn later that one of the effects of being at altitude is the suppression of appetite. This is obviously dangerous as your body requires vast amounts of energy to survive up high. On subsequent expeditions, I was sure to make an effort to take on calories at regular times in order to avoid this problem.

My mood and well-being improved as the fats and carbs worked their way into my system and before long I was back at Camp 2. We had packed everything away prior to leaving so it was just a matter of picking up what was needed and continuing down the trail, past Camp 1 all the way to Base Camp. Exhausting though it was, each step into the ever-thicker air was a step closer to a hot meal and a good night's sleep. Thirteen hours after leaving Camp 2 that morning, I made it back to Plaza Argentina to be greeted by the cook brandishing a mug of the most delicious orange squash that I'd tasted in my entire life.

Up until then, climbing Aconcagua had been the hardest thing that I had ever done. Never before had I reached the point where I had found myself on the descent, sitting at 6,000 metres groping for the strength to continue. I'd been totally exhausted and wanted to give up, wishing only that somebody would come and take me off that bloody mountain. Now, however, sitting at Base Camp having overcome that and learned some very important lessons along the way, my resolve to conquer Everest was only strengthened.

Meanwhile, apparently I wasn't the only one who was in a race. The Canadians were gutted when they arrived back to camp twenty-five minutes after me to see my grinning face!

That winter, for a bit of extra acclimatisation, I took Dad out for a wee stroll to celebrate his birthday at the end of November. He was turning sixty-three and the plan was to summit Mt Kilimanjaro with him. Kilimanjaro is another of the seven summits, the tallest mountain in Africa standing at 5,895 metres and the largest free-standing mountain in the world (i.e. not part of a mountain range).

It was great to spend time with Dad up on the mountain and the trip was fairly uneventful apart from me getting a hacking chest infection just before we left which had me coughing, spluttering and wheezing my way to the top wearing all my fancy climbing gear while Dad strolled up there in his gardening jacket and Fulham Football Club tracksuit. The trip should have taken eight days in order to acclimatise, but he found it a bit too easy so we skipped one of the camps in order to be back in time for a few beers and to get the football results. Bloody legend!

6

Venezuela

I'd set my sights on Cho Oyu, the sixth-highest mountain in the world, as my next goal. It is apparently one of the 'easier' eigth-thousand-metre mountains to climb and I saw it as a good stepping stone to Everest, giving me more experience of the difficulties of surviving at these extreme altitudes.

Standing at 8,201 metres, it was going to be a big upgrade from Aconcagua. Among the lessons I had learnt on that expedition, it was apparent that, if I was going to tackle bigger mountains, I would have to have a far better level of mountaineering fitness.

Training started in earnest and when the owner of the boat was not onboard, I'd get up at four-thirty in the morning and either cycle the eighty-kilometre round trip to San Remo in Italy or the same distance to Antibes. Alternatively, directly behind Monaco is a mountain called Tête du Chien, or Dog's Head, which at 450 metres was an ideal training hike with varying terrain and inclines.

Initially, I'd just take a small pack with some water and do the round trip in about two and a half hours. As time progressed, I increased the weight until I was carrying a full pack of twenty-five kilograms and running most of the way (apart from the tarmac bits where my knees soon let me know that it wasn't the best of ideas), trying to beat my previous time on each occasion.

Monaco is an odd place with everybody living on top of each other in very controlled circumstances. The break out of town to the tranquility of the mountain was therefore as cathartic as it was great exercise. I remember always feeling a slight sense of loss when returning back to the boat, watching the morning traffic build and losing that connection with nature and the solitude my morning routine afforded me.

During that summer, the owner of the boat decided that he would like to spend winter in the Caribbean. We readied ourselves to go and, as the boat did not have the fuel capacity to make the Atlantic crossing, we loaded it onto a ship transporter and met it in Martinique. We travelled over Christmas and New Year; then the owner asked us to standby in Venezuela where he would meet up with us at a later stage. Not knowing anything about the country or its customs, I enlisted the help of an agency which was to prove invaluable as a number of problems that we came across whilst down there needed somewhat creative solutions.

Firstly, as a matter of safety, the owner asked me to source some firearms for the vessel as there had been incidences of piracy close to where we would be cruising. Apparently, this was mainly opportunistic and generally easily repelled by simply firing off a couple of warning shots. Having never fired anything other than a .22 rifle during my time in the Air Cadets, I was somewhat lacking in knowledge but I had watched enough action movies to settle for a handgun and a shotgun which I figured would do the trick.

Procuring them was very easy. The only question was whether I wanted to pay two thousand dollars or two hundred dollars. The price was for the same guns, the only difference being whether they came through the front door of the government armoury or the back. Well, I've never been one to turn down a bargain so, two hundred dollars later, we drove away from the back of the armoury with a large shopping bag of goodies.

Obviously I didn't have a clue about how to use these guns and would have probably shot myself in the foot before I managed to deter any pirates. The chef and I were therefore driven to a training establishment out of town with our local fixer where brushed up on our weapons handling. Well, when I say 'training establishment' I used the term lightly. The place where we found ourselves was a disused industrial complex with lots of fun stuff to shoot at. After a solid hour of blazing away, we were highly efficient marksmen or at least proficient enough to pick a gun up and not kill ourselves in the process. As long as the thing I was shooting at remained perfectly still and gave me plenty of warning, they were in serious trouble!

Next on the shopping list was oil. As you may know, Venezuela has lots of oil, but the oil we required was a specific lubricant from a specific manufacturer that had to be used in order to maintain the warranty on the main engines. One of these blew up, twice, so I was glad we got the right oil!

Due to trade embargos imposed upon Venezuela, it was illegal to import this particular oil. However, as I was beginning to learn, 'illegal' is a somewhat more flexible term in Venezuela than in other parts of the world; some things just took a little more time and money. The solution was to source the oil in neighbouring Trinidad, pop it on a fishing boat which would then land the booty ashore in the dead of night, local law enforcement being paid to rather handily find something far better to do at the time. It was then loaded into the back of a cab with blacked-out windows and driven to us. We'd receive it at

2 a.m., pump the contents of the steel drum onboard and then give it back to the guys in the cab to dispose of; a gaily painted, red-and-yellow 210-litre steel drum with 'Shell' painted on the side being a bit too obvious to just leave beside the bins apparently.

It was all very clandestine and made a pleasant change from simply buying stuff. At this rate I was thinking of getting my own eyepatch and a parrot.

Lastly, we needed to fuel up. As with the guns, there were two prices, one being the full tax rate for foreign vessels which was just over a dollar a litre, the other the local rate, which was a dollar for fifty litres. We needed approximately forty thousand litres so you could say that the saving was worth thinking about.

I'd been talked through the whole process by our fixer. It involved more nighttime ops whereby we'd slip lines in the dead of night, pop over to the coastguard dock and fill up there. I'd asked about the depth on the quayside and was assured that it was at least three and a half metres at all states of the tide. Having cleared that, we waited till well after darkness when all was quiet before carrying out our plan.

I was just making my final approach and was about two metres from the quay when there was a bang and a thud and one of the main engines shut down. Assuming that I'd hit something underwater, I asked the crew to get torches to see if they could see anything. A few minutes later, the deckhand reported that there appeared to be a large concrete block just off the stern which we must have clipped with one of the props. Fortunately, we were at least now clear of the obstruction but, as you can imagine, I wasn't best pleased with the agent and was thinking of putting my firearms training to good use on one of his softer dangly bits.

We tied up anyway and began fuelling. We had strict instructions to be off the dock before sunrise but the business was painfully slow and, as the sky began to brighten, we had only taken on ten thousand litres of fuel. I protested to the agent that so far it had all been a bit of a cock-up and might end up costing me a lot more than I was saving, particularly as we had only taken on a quarter of what we needed, but this didn't get me anywhere. He insisted that we stop fuelling straightaway before the coast guard woke up and wondered what the thirty-seven-metre superyacht was doing on their dock with something resembling a fuel hose hanging out of the side of it. He did however re-assure me that another solution would be found so lines were let go and we slipped back to our berth, avoiding any further collision with the concrete block.

On the way back, a slight vibration came from the port engine and I assumed that we had bent the prop. This was later confirmed by a diver. Fortunately, it was just the tip of one prop blade which, though not ideal, could wait for repair when we were back in the Mediterranean.

Still thirty thousand litres short of being full – far from enough should the boss turn up – the next plan was to head offshore into international waters to liaise with a fishing boat which would supply us with the rest of the fuel. We waited for a calm day as we would have to raft up with the other boat and, having seen the state of some of these, I didn't want to risk bouncing alongside one for too long in lumpy seas. We were given coordinates to go to and standby and, after about an hour and a half of waiting, an old and battered trawler, belching smoke and sitting very low in the water, approached.

If you could for a moment picture in your mind what this might look like in a Hollywood movie, right down to the crew, I reckon you could pick these guys out in an identity parade! They were to a man dark and swarthy, wearing grubby, oil-stained vests and shorts, with cigarettes casually hanging out of the corners of their mouths and smelling of a heady mixture of booze, sweat and diesel. Flipflops seemed to be the go-to safety shoe and the only feature that distinguished the captain was that he had some teeth.

Undaunted, we tied them up alongside us and commenced fuelling. I was assured that this was straight from the refinery but the chief engineer was taking no chances, testing regular samples. To give them their due, the fuel was actually very good, but once fuelling had finished, we still seemed to be five thousand litres short. I speak very little Spanish but I tried to communicate the problem with the captain who became very agitated as more crewmen started to appear on the deck and the situation grew increasingly tense.

Making an excuse to go to the bridge to phone the agent, I removed the handgun from the safe and tucked it very obviously into the back of my shorts before heading down to the aft deck where the captain could see me. I turned my back to him, finding something to say to the chef who spoke much better Spanish than I did. The sight of the gun seemed to work as miraculously they found another five thousand litres in their hold and the captain calmed down.

It was just as well he didn't call my bluff as I'd have had to throw the gun at him, having put no bullets in it for fear of jagging the safety catch on my belt and shooting myself in the arse. The cold beer that I had upon tying up back in port that afternoon tasted very good indeed.

I was keen for myself and the crew to explore some of the country and also to do a bit of a recce for the owner who was a very fit and active guy. Through our agents, we had some incredible trips to the interior of the country.

On one long weekend, we visited Angel Falls, a three-day trip that involved planes, cars and dugout canoes however one of the most memorable parts of the trip was a rather exciting journey there which involved a leg of the journey in a light aircraft.

After a long ride in a 4x4, we arrived at reasonably large airport and were given directions to the gate we would need to embark. As we strolled through the terminal, it seemed that we were going to run out of airport before we found it with the size and condition of the aircraft seeming to dwindle as our journey went on.

Eventually we reached the gate at which stood a small 6 seater aircraft which looked as if it had seen better days but, excited at the prospect of going to see the falls, we were ushered out on to the apron and on board undaunted, going on the rationale of 'what's the worst that can happen, you don't ever hear of these falling out of the sky' (we were to later find out that apparently Venezuala 'bush service' has one of the worst records for air safety in the world and apparently, though you didn't hear about it, planes falling out of the sky was somewhat less uncommon than we had assumed).

We were crammed on board, the Chef getting the seat next to the pilot and the rest of us huddled in to the back and, after some gesticulations made by the pilot, who spoke no English, which we assumed was the safety brief. It was time to go

To give the pilot his due, despite the protestations of the old aircraft which twitched and rattled its way along the tarmac as the engine revved, all went smoothly and we were soon airborne and at our cruising altitude, affording us great views over the surrounding landscape.

I was sitting directly behind the pilot and after a few minutes of flying straight and level, I noticed him having an involuntary spasm causing his neck to crane down and to the right but assumed that it was just a shiver. A minute or two later, the same thing happened, this time accompanied by a noise following which the Chef looked at me quizzically before returning his eyes to the front of the plane. A few minutes more and the same thing happened, this time with an even larger twitch, spasm and utterance which I at first thought was garbled communication with air traffic control but it became fairly apparent that this was not the case.

Thereafter, the twitching became ever more frequent and pronounced as he twitched, gurgled and shouted out a stream of unintelligible noises towards our destination and we discovered that he suffered from Tourette's Syndrome, fine if he was a passenger on board but slightly disconcerting if it's the guy in charge of flying the plane.

The flight was just under two hours by the end of which, the pilot must have been utterly exhausted from his near constant movement in the flight seat and what at first seemed mildly amusing, became a little worrying as we circled over the airstrip which amounted to not a great deal more than a dirt strip in a clearing in the jungle requiring a steep descent and what seemed like pinpoint accuracy.

As we made our final approach, there was a hushed silence from all of us as we anticipated an ill timed expletive from the pilot slewing us in to the jungle, never to be seen again but fortunately, the increased concentration on his part seemed to steady him as we headed earthward and we were soon on the ground, much relieved to be so and thankfully in on piece before our onward journey.

We were loaded in to shallow draft skiffs with outboard engines which were skilfully navigated up river which proved lumpy but quite tame in comparison to the thrill of the journey there. The trip was great fun as the pilots bumped and scraped their way up the rapids simply changing propellers every time they dinged one on a rock and at times, we had to get out and help drag the boat when the going was too shallow. We camped overnight, sleeping in hammocks on a sandy riverbank before getting back into the boats the following day and going to the base of the Falls which lay amongst some of the most spectacular scenery that I have seen in my entire life

Another weekend we travelled to the Orinoco Delta where we spent a couple of days with the indigenous people. They showed us some of their bush craft as well as how they fished for piranhas and dug for turtle eggs in the riverbanks. On our final day there, we were taken to swim with the pink river dolphins.

We were a little surprised when the boat stopped at the exact spot where we'd been fishing for piranhas the day before. However the guide reassured us that they weren't interested in biting us and we were safe to go in the water. The pink river dolphins arrived and were beautiful and playful creatures who liked nothing more than sneaking up on us in the murky water and nibbling our toes. Occurring in piranha-infested waters, this took some getting used to and we didn't stray too far from the boat.

On our final weekend away we went to Los Llanos, a vast tropical grassland of almost 400,000 square kilometres spanning Colombia and Venezuela and home to an abundance of wildlife. One of the stranger things that we did there was to hunt anacondas which involved wandering around in thigh-high swamps in bare feet, poking the bottom with a stick and waiting for something to slither under our feet. The week previously, we were told, they had pulled a five-metre-long snake out of the swamps but we were happy (and relieved) to catch a 'tiddler' a mere two metres long.

Having previously spent some time in South America, I had come to love the slight lawlessness of the place and my time in Venezuela reinforced that. The people's healthy disregard for red tape and health and safety was refreshing compared to the nanny states we often found ourselves in. The countries I have visited there all seem to have the same attitude to safety in that they'll tell you it's dangerous and then let you make the decision if you are going to do it or not. This really appeals to my sense of adventure and is far preferable to constantly being told what you can and can't do, which leaves no room for learning from your mistakes.

The owner of the boat never did turn up and so in spring we headed back to Martinique to load the boat for the return journey home. This development gave me a few extra weeks of leave so, once the boat had been safely strapped onto the deck of the colossal transport ship, I flew straight back to Venezuela for some more adventures.

I had been training as and when I could, mainly on a turbo trainer (a device I mounted my bike that enabled me to put in the miles without actually going anywhere) to keep up my cardio fitness but, having booked my next big climb in just two months, I was in need of some serious conditioning.

Our agent in the port also had a language school and agency in a town called Merida in the Andes which happened to be a major centre for adventure sports. He hooked me up with two guys who were Venezuela's current mountain running champions but also raced mountain bikes as well as offering guide services so I was in very good hands to be put through my paces.

We devised a plan of activities which involved a six-day hike that would start in the lowlands and take in Pico Bolivar, Venezuela's highest peak, and a three-day mountain-bike trail with a few days in between for a bit of rest and relaxation (I'm not very good at rest and relaxation so went canyoning instead).

Due to the nature of the hike, we had to take a lot of kit. We needed enough food for the whole trip, as there was nowhere to reprovision en route. We also had to carry all sorts of clothing to suit everything from the tropical lowlands to the high altitudes on Pico Bolivar which stood at a shade under five thousand metres and was often capped with ice. Our packs weighed in at a pretty hefty thirty-two kilograms which was not too bad for me, but for the mountain runners who were used to travelling fast and light it was a bit of a struggle.

The head guide, José, stood almost a foot shorter than me and, when he donned his pack, it looked like if he fell backwards he might never get up again. He and his colleague, Jesioto, also a lovely guy, were great companions and the hiking was spectacular, starting off in rainforest which gradually gave way to the cloud forests and subtle changes in plant life until we emerged out onto the higher plains.

I was amazed at just how quickly the scenery changed with the lush vegetation and thick air of the cloud forest suddenly giving way to a rocky and barren landscape within the space of fifteen minutes. The pace was a little slow for me to start, the two guys struggling with a heavier weight than they were used to carrying, so I asked them for directions whilst in the rainforest and headed out alone, keen to push myself hard ahead of my next big climb.

Upon emerging onto the barren plains, I could see the track heading towards a distant jagged ridge which we would have to cross. There were three possible routes up by the look of it and I had been warned that it was a bit of a scramble so I headed for the middle of the three for no other reason other than it *was* the middle one. Having come out of the cloud forest, the skies were clear blue and the sun was high as I made my way towards the ridge. I could see the crest of it towering above me and what I thought looked like a possible route up so I began to climb.

As the gradient increased, the route became more of a scramble and then a full climb until I found myself on almost vertical rock about ten metres from the top of the ridge, with a thirty-two-kilogram pack trying very hard to pull me back down the mountain. By now, I was past the point of no return, it being more dangerous to climb down than continue, so I gingerly clawed my way to the top and was mightily relieved when I pulled myself over the lip of the ridge.

I decided to take a break there as I was pretty shaky from the climb. From the valley below meanwhile came distant shouts. The guys had just emerged from the cloud forest to (as I found out later) see the crazy gringo heading up the completely wrong valley which they knew to be an impasse. They were waving to the right which was where I then headed along the ridge and, within twenty minutes, I was back on the path which gave spectacular views down into the adjacent valleys.

About an hour from there we reached our camp stop for the night, a tranquil spot nestled between the peaks. Whilst there José introduced me to a plant they called *feiderhorn*, which had beautiful large soft leaves that had a slight lemony taste and was apparently medicinal and delicious when steeped in boiling water and made into a tea. Alternatively, it made the most wonderful loo paper (not to be used in the tea afterwards).

The guys prepared a fantastic and unforgettable meal that evening with a succulent smoked pork chop cooked on an open fire that's not been bested to this day and so it was with a full stomach and a wide smile that I settled down for the night for a wonderful sleep. The next day was another stunning hike towards our next camp at 4,600 metres. From here we would make the final push to the summit early the following morning.

The final push was a technical climb with sheer drops and some tricky sections. However, we were carrying light loads and, with less than four hundred metres of vertical ascent, we made pretty short work of it, reaching the peak a little early and having to wait for half an hour for the sun to rise. It was an incredible moment as the sky turned pale and beautiful views opened out over the other Andean peaks and valleys below. Most beautiful was the feeling of isolation, we being the only people there, able to sit in a comfortable silence and appreciate the awesome spectacle unveiled with the first light of day.

We were back at Base Camp early that afternoon, the round trip having taken about nine hours, and settled down for a well-deserved rest before descending the mountain over the next two days – back to a hot shower, some good food and a comfortable bed. I was really happy with my performance overall and very happy that the training I had been doing was paying dividends. The rest of the trip in Venezuela was fantastic with some of the best canyoning and mountain-biking that I have ever done, never with any crowds and always just on the right side of danger.

7

Cho Oyu

There are quite a number of companies offering guided climbs in the Himalayas with prices varying depending on the level of support that is being offered. Some I encountered offered luxuriously heated mess tents with a one-to-one sherpa-to-client ratio and so much oxygen that you would be climbing as if you were at sea level.

Though I wanted some support, I felt that to sign up for a 'Carlos Fandango expedition' (i.e. one that was overly stage-managed) would take away from the sense of achievement. I wanted a 'purer' experience, but I also didn't want to pay for all the bells and whistles, so I opted for a company called Summit Climb which was at the more budget end of the scale and required input and assistance from the climbers and a great deal more self-reliance than some of the other companies which appealed to me.

Though still classed as a fully supported expedition, with everything logistically taken care of and the Sherpas doing a lot of the hard work with regard to camp life, fixing ropes etc., above Advanced Base Camp you would effectively be on your own and allowed to make your own decisions.

I flew out to Kathmandu at the end of April 2009 to join the expedition which was scheduled to last for thirty-eight days including transport to and from the mountain – effectively double the time required to climb Aconcagua, which was only twelve hundred metres shorter, such is the effect of altitude on the body and the additional acclimatisation required to push that much higher.

Kathmandu is an incredible city, a bustling, noisy, dirty metropolis where every one of your senses is constantly assailed from the moment you step outside your door. The all-pervading and near-constant blare of car and motorbike horns is enough to drive you crazy. As well as being a major trading point where tiny stores all crammed together compete for business, it is also the very heart of exploration into the Himalayas and has a unique buzz about it which can be quite infectious despite the grime and noise. Every street seems to have at least one shop or travel agency dedicated to the various activities in the mountains.

Having cut my teeth on other peaks, I had a good idea of what additional kit I would need to tackle Cho Oyu and spent a couple of days wandering the labyrinthine streets visiting various shops. This time I'd be taking plenty of Diamox to counter the less pleasant effects of being at altitude. I also needed to have made a down suit - effectively an adult-size, fully insulated romper suit – for the higher camps where temperatures could fall as low as minus 40 degrees.

The hardshell boots that I had previously used in the Alps and the Andes were not considered enough for the extreme altitudes and temperatures that I would have to deal with so I purchased a pair of La Sportiva Everest Mons boots which were more suitable for the climb. I also bought extra-thick bedrolls for the time spent at Base Camp where I wanted to be as comfortable as possible and an additional 'lighter' sleeping bag (only rated to minus 20) that I could leave in Base Camp whilst taking my minus-40 bag up the mountain with me. All this needed to be transported so I purchased another huge duffle bag that could be strapped to a yak.

Pretty soon my hotel room started to look like one of the shops that I'd just left. It seemed I'd accumulated a colossal amount of kit but none of it was superfluous – it would all be necessary on the mountain. Of great importance was the medication that each climber was supposed to supply for themselves and there was no question this time around of me scrimping on this or deciding to 'tough it out'. As I'd learnt, self-maintenance was one of the most important aspects of mountaineering and being well-equipped could easily mean the difference between success and failure.

It was very apparent from the briefings and warnings we were given that we would be exposing ourselves to a whole new level of risk. Rescue might not be an option and therefore the expedition organisers would have the final say as to whether we would have a chance to summit or not. Obviously they did not want to risk losing anybody so, in order to maximise your chances, maintaining your health was essential. Fortunately, everything needed was readily available over the counter in Kathmandu. Everything from simple cold remedies to broad-spectrum antibiotics and prescription pain killers was purchased, re-packed and labelled for ease of use.

As the team assembled, it was interesting to see the difference between this group and the one that I had met in Mendoza for the Aconcagua ascent. Though of equally varied nationalities (Greek, Italian, Romanian, Spanish, British and American), we were all of a similar ilk, having far greater overall experience in surviving at higher altitudes and with a number of tough climbs under our belts already, but all wanting to push our limits a bit further.

I Immediately warmed to Rick Wilkerson whom I nicknamed 'Doc' as he had served as a surgeon in the US Army for many years and done a huge amount of humanitarian work since. Another favourite, and the eldest of the group, Stewart Barbour (later named 'Irish Stew' by most but I called him 'Catweazle' due to his slightly mad and unkempt appearance) was also one of the sprightliest, always smiling and laughing. His positivity was infectious and you couldn't help but like him – unless, that is, you were waiting for him to put his hand in his pocket to buy a round of drinks!

It took a few days to arrange visas, travel permits and the all-important climbing permits whilst in Kathmandu. This gave us enough time for final shopping and gear checks before loading up the bags to go on the bus. On the evening of 23 April, all kit was brought to the hotel where the majority of the climbers were staying in order that it could be weighed to ensure that the yaks would not be overloaded upon arrival at Base Camp. Leaving the kit there, I headed back to my hotel for the last night of comfort before departure early the following morning.

Once aboard the bus, there was a hushed air of excitement as we headed out of the city and into the Nepalese countryside. It was everything you might expect, with lush green terraced slopes in the foothills, where farmers used oxen to draw their ploughs, slowly giving way to evermore impressive peaks and stunning, if not daunting, terrain.

The original plan was to cross from Nepal into Tibet and then head up to Nyalam. However the road was temporarily impassable due to one of the frequent landslides that occur in the region. With everything clinging so tentatively to the steep-sided valleys and the terrain being almost impossible to tame, rain often sends huge boulders crashing down onto the road, more often than not blocking the route and sometimes claiming casualties with it.

As we picked our way along the narrow mountain roads, we saw evidence of this with the carcasses of vehicles way down in the valley below. It was a sobering sight as we headed ever upwards, but by the end of the afternoon – and after a slight delay at the border whilst permits and visas were checked and double-checked – we entered Tibet and the border town of Zhangmu.

Though I had not visited Tibet prior to its annexation by China, I would like to think that it used to be a lot nicer. I am sure that the Chinese have brought benefits in trade and infrastructure, but the atmosphere was mildly oppressive with Chinese border guards in most of the bars and bored, depressed-looking women occupying red-lit, window-fronted rooms to entertain the troops. Now

I know that there is somebody for everybody in the world, but I'd like to know what would drive a person to frequent one of these squalid establishments where a large elderly lady sat in a stall, illuminated by a dim red light, wearing a housecoat and smoking a cigarette whilst doing her knitting. Maybe she could knock you up a nice warm hat for the long winter evenings whilst you were there?

The following day we were given the all clear to head further up the valley. By this time a lot of traffic had built up in both directions and we inched our way up the road, sometimes hanging right onto the edge of it as we negotiated the lorries, busses, bikes and cars coming the other way. The driver must have had balls of steel, but eventually we made it to the affectionately named 'Rat Hotel'.

I say 'affectionately', but the fact was the place stank of fresh human sewage and all you could hear all night were huge rats scuttling about the floors and in the ceilings. Needless to say, it wasn't one of the best night's sleep that I've had, crammed into a dormitory with seven others and being next to the toilet where every time the door opened I'd be exposed to a waft of the foul stench coming up from below. On the plus side, the following day brought clear blue skies and wonderful fresh mountain air, made all the fresher from our night in the hotel. The chance to stretch our legs after the two days on the bus was welcome and we took in a few of the small hills around the town before getting back on the bus for our last stop at Tingri before heading to Base Camp.

We had long since left the lush valleys behind and were now in a barren landscape devoid of any vegetation which was unable to sustain itself in the cold dry air. Houses were constructed of mud, as were the ruined forts dating back to the Mongol Empire of the thirteenth and fourteenth centuries that we occasionally caught a glimpse of crumbling into the dusty brown earth. Life here must have been incredibly tough, yet people survived, managing to live off the land somehow. The only fuel source was dried yack dung, though quite what the yak found to eat in order to produce the dung was a mystery to me.

In mid-afternoon we pulled into Tingri. This was to be our home for the next two days whilst we acclimatised to the altitude. The town stands at 4,350 metres above sea level and has a population of about five hundred people. Many of these serve the mountaineering community during the short climbing seasons, Tingri being the last town before the base camps for both Everest and Cho Oyu.

Though it has little to offer in the way of sightseeing (unless you enjoy the sport of avoiding the packs of scraggly stray dogs that roam the streets),

Tingri does offer incredible views of Cho Oyu and Everest which loom huge and foreboding in the distance. The sense of awe we felt at seeing these giants and the realisation of the magnitude of the task ahead of us was quite humbling and the group was pretty quiet as we wiled away our time in the local tea houses, playing cards and chatting.

To say that the dining arrangements were 'rustic' would be something of an understatement, as the kitchens were filthy and contained very few things that we recognised as edible. What was served up however was delicious and we spent our days snacking on *momos*, a sort of *gyoza* dumpling stuffed with god knows what which was very tasty. Remarkably, nobody came down with 'Tingri tummy'.

One 'highlight' was trying yak butter tea, a delicacy in the region which, according to the locals, helps you sleep, makes you strong and increases your libido. It's a creamy concoction made from fermented black tea and brewed with salt. As a 'special treat' a dollop of fermented yack butter is added which sinks underneath the surface and slowly melts into the tea – at least it does until you get to the bottom of the cup where there's a lovely blob of it waiting. The flavour was interesting, warm, salty and cheesy at the same time, and, though it was offered to me, I politely declined seconds for fear of not being able to avoid gagging and upsetting our hosts.

That said, it was incredibly generous of them to invite us in to try this, in a land of such scarce resources, and I was enormously grateful, if not for the flavour itself, at least for the opportunity to try it.

Six days after leaving Kathmandu, we finally arrived at Base Camp, relieved to be out of the dusty town and in glorious fresh air. We were one of the first groups to arrive and the day was spent erecting tents and sorting out our 'home' for the next month. It was great to finally get off the road and into the vast landscapes that we'd been watching out the windows of the bus for so long and we all felt very revitalised to be there, despite the altitude, standing as we were now at 4,800 metres.

After sorting out our tents and gear, we spent another day of relaxation getting our bodies used to the altitude. I had started taking Diamox to help with being up this high. It worked a treat but had the unfortunate side effect of making me pee like a racehorse so there were regular trips to the little boy's rock.

Drinking lots of water also helps with acclimatisation. A combination of the two didn't lend itself to prolonged periods of rest. Unfortunately, I had also started to develop a 'Khumbu cough', a dry rasping cough brought on by the cold temperatures and dry air which irritate the lining of your lungs. The cough generally abated during the day when the temperature rose, allowing me to go for a little stroll up a nearby valley to a rock outcrop which gave me a great view of Base Camp (and a welcome break from being around the other climbers in which to enjoy some quiet contemplation), only to come on again at night. Consequently, I spent the first few nights in the dining tent, propped up in a chair, drinking ginger steeped in warm water (I'd stocked up in Kathmandu prior to leaving). Thankfully, this and a course of antibiotics seemed to knock it out after three or four days which was just as well as each coughing fit would bring on a splitting headache.

On 3 May, we started our push towards Advanced Base Camp, referred to as 'ABC'. The initial plan was to go straight past Interim Base Camp, but by the time we got there we were happy to stop, as we had all found the ascent to be unexpectedly hard, zig-zagging through the moraines parallel to a glacier. Accordingly, the yaks who bore the brunt of the heavy lifting were unloaded and camp was set up for the night.

The following morning, after breakfast, we broke down the camp and loaded up the yaks ready for the push up to ABC at 5,700 metres. The going was hard but bearable with light loads in glorious weather and the well-practiced routine of putting one foot in front of the other seemed to go just fine. Sadly, I'd still not completely learnt my lesson and wanted to be the first one into camp every day, but I was quite happy to stay behind the yaks this time!

I reached ABC at around two in the afternoon and helped to set up some of the tents with the last of our group arriving a few hours later. The Sherpas were incredible and in the time it took me to put up a couple of easy-to-erect dome tents, they had the twenty-person dining tent up and dinner already on and everything else in order. The camp was blissfully quiet with very few other teams on the mountain at that stage, although over the coming days numbers would swell as a dozen or so teams of varying size arrived.

The following days we engaged in the usual cycle of rest and acclimatisation hikes to ever-increasing altitudes to prepare us for the next push. Though we were all reasonably experienced outdoorsmen and women, it was necessary to assess our abilities as mountaineers so an exercise was set up not far from ABC which allowed us to both practice and demonstrate our prowess in ice climbing, rappelling and the use of a jumar, a sort of non-return device for climbing ropes –basically, if you're attached to a rope and fall, you only fall as far as the length of the leash tied to your harness.

As previously mentioned, this particular operator left a lot of the decision-making to the individual climber. Thus a lot of the group were organising their own acclimatisation, heading up to different heights at different times in smaller groups as suited their needs and the way they were feeling. On 6 May we held a *puja* ceremony where prayer flags were hoisted, offerings made to the spirits of the mountain and traditional songs and dances, led by the yak herders and Sherpas, were performed. This was done in order to bless us with good luck on the mountain and marked the beginning of the next phase of the climb.

Camps 1 and 2 were the next targets and getting to them proved to be very tough. The trail to Camp 1 involved a steep climb over very loose terrain, often resulting in your foothold giving way and sliding back from whence it came. Under normal circumstances, this would be mildly irksome. However, with just under half the oxygen available in the air at 6,000 metres to power your muscles, it was a bit soul-destroying, particularly knowing that we would have to tackle 'Horrible Hill', as we named it, three times during the course of the expedition.

As with all high-altitude climbing that I have done, regardless of how fit and strong you are, there is always a sense of relief at reaching camp. Essentially, the human body isn't designed to be up at such heights, particularly those of us who do not live at altitude and have to rely on just a few weeks of acclimatisation to take us 'from zero to hero'. Upon reaching Camp 1, I was very happy to find that the tents had already been erected by the Sherpas who had even managed to establish a small kitchen and started making food for us.

It's hard to quantify the effort that these quiet and often unsung heroes put into an expedition. Most simply, without them climbers wouldn't stand a chance of success. For every climber who summits, there is a large group of yack herders, porters, kitchen staff and Sherpas who are there to support, always with a smile on their faces despite the conditions they endure. The Sherpas also act as a vanguard on these expeditions, going ahead of the climbers to set up camps and fix ropes which act as a guide and safety line for the groups as they ascend.

As an example, the first people credited with summiting Everest, Sir Edmund Hillary and Sherpa Tenzing Norgay, were part of the 1953 expedition led by Sir John Hunt which totalled 350 porters, twenty Sherpa guides and four and a half tons of equipment.

Though equipment and access to the mountains has improved greatly over the years, the logistical and human effort required for a successful expedition is huge and to say 'I summited such and such mountain' is a bit of a misrepresentation in my eyes unless you have done everything yourself. That said, even with support it's still bloody hard work!

The night at Camp 1 was fairly uncomfortable, sleeping on ice with only a thin roll mat and the inevitable need to pee every few hours. The temperatures plummeted as soon as the sun disappeared and I was very happy to see the first vestiges of light so that I could get up and start moving once again. The other problem I was having whilst trying to rest was sleep apnea, again a fairly common ailment at altitude. As you start to fall asleep, your body relaxes and your breathing slows. This is all well and good whilst at home, but with only half the oxygen available, I'd invariably wake up gasping for air as my body attempted to counteract the oxygen deficit.

From here on in, we were climbing on snow and ice all the way so needed our high-altitude boots and crampons which are fairly bulky but do the job. Another long day's arduous climbing got us to the ice wall between camps 1 and 2 at an altitude of over 6,700 metres, after which we turned back for another night at Camp 1. The wind picked up in the afternoon making it fairly uncomfortable and causing many of us to return to our tents with ice beards caused by the tiny windblown particles of ice in the air mixing with the vapour in our breath and instantly freezing to our chins.

The climb down Horrible Hill the following day was not any easier as snow had started to fall making the trail very hard to find and footholds impossible to spot. In some areas, the snow had drifted to a couple of feet thick, which was incredibly energy-sapping to negotiate but after seven hours or so we arrived back to the relative comfort of ABC. Some digging was necessary to get to the entrance of our tents, although the snow banks that had developed around them did at least give some very good protection from the wind.

The snow and strong winds did not abate for a further two days. Then finally on 13 May the skies cleared and preparations were made for the next push. During this time, we were given training on the use of the Gamow bag, a portable inflatable pressure chamber used to treat climbers with acute pulmonary oedema (a condition brought on by the effects of altitude which results in a build-up of fluid on the lungs and can be fatal). We also received training and information on HACE, high altitude cerebral oedema, which is a build-up of fluid on the brain leading to confusion, hallucinations, irrational behaviour and, if left untreated, death. Sadly this isn't an uncommon condition among mountaineers, claiming the lives of numerous climbers every year, and there is no rhyme nor reason as to who will get it and when. There are plenty of stories of climbers ripping off their oxygen masks and protective clothing and being very combative when offered assistance which makes any rescue attempt incredibly difficult, being, as you are at extreme altitudes, at the very limit survival yourself, never mind having to look after somebody else.

That afternoon whilst relaxing around the camp we were suddenly hit by a huge cloud of ice crystals and a brief spell of high winds which flattened a number of tents and knocked people off their feet. It was my first experience of a pressure wave pushed up by a distant avalanche and, along with the training and information that we received that day, provided a sobering reminder of the environment that we were in and the potential dangers we would be exposing ourselves to.

On 15 May, myself and three other climbers made the long slog up Horrible Hill to Camp 1 in calf-deep snow. Fortunately, a group of Sherpas had headed up earlier that day so some of the route was already compacted making the going a lot easier. Nevertheless, we were pleased to reach the camp and spent the rest of the day relaxing in preparation for the following section of climbing. The next day was the toughest so far, taking us seven and a half hours to reach Camp 2 at 7,100 metres and involving a long traverse across a 40-degree slope in knee-deep snow, concentrating most of the exertion on one side of the body and sapping energy with every step.

It is hard to explain the effort required to do the simplest of things at this altitude to those who have not experienced it. The closest I can equate it to in terms of the oxygen deprivation is trying to breathe through a drinking straw whilst exercising. At best, you can take two or three steps before stopping to hyperventilate for thirty seconds to catch your breath before taking the next few steps. The steeper the slope, the less steps you take and the longer the recovery period.

This is repeated time and time again over many hours until you reach your destination. Then you either turn around and do it again or set up camp and look forward to doing it the next day.

One of the stranger ailments that I had picked during the day's effort came from the constant need to gulp lungfuls of air whist travelling across the sparkling ice and snow. When trying to eat that evening, I realised that I had sunburn on the roof of my mouth! I didn't see myself reaching for the factor 50 to smear in there every few minutes so it was more a matter of putting up and shutting up. After a restless night, I and my now high-altitude tent buddy, Urs Jaggi, headed all the way back down the mountain to ABC for the final time before the summit push. We were both dead on our feet by the time we reached camp and very grateful for a hot meal and the chance to rest.

The weather reports were not great and the conditions up on the mountain were at best marginal for our summit push. The best we could hope for was to push up to the higher camps and hope that a small window of opportunity would open up at some point.

On 20 May, the whole group – less Doc who sadly had to abort his attempt due to a recurring knee injury – set out. It was our last time up Horrible Hill and, as we had already pushed ourselves much harder further up the mountain, I downgraded it to 'Not So Horrible Hill', though I'm not sure everybody else would have agreed.

The following day we pushed up to Camp 2 at 7,140 metres. The effort took between seven and twelve hours, such was the mixed pace of the group. The weather was overcast and a little windy with some snow showers, but the forecast was not good so we hunkered down to let a storm pass through, occasionally poking our heads out of our tents to see clouds racing across the summit, creating a spectacular plume as they did so. As the afternoon wore on, the temperature fell to minus 20 plus wind chill and whiteout conditions prevailed so we stayed tent-bound.

The atmosphere in our tent was at first fairly convivial, but it began to get a bit strained due to our inability to rest with the tent constantly battered by high winds. To compound matters, my tent buddy Urs was, it turned out, a habitual nose picker and continuous farter who would snort and sniff every few minutes to clear his sinus (apparently congested by using snuff). At Base Camp, he was a really nice guy, but after forty-eight hours of having my personal space constantly invaded by his noises and smells and nasal cavity excavations, with my patience further stretched by sleep deprivation and lack of oxygen, I was ready to put my ice axe through the top of his head.

The constant flapping of the tents and discomfort proved too much for one of the team who decided to head down the mountain with his personal Sherpa. The rest of us stayed to wait out the storm which seemed to be forming a pattern of blowing up at around nine-thirty in the morning and then dying down by eight in the evening, driven by the warming and cooling of the surrounding mountains, creating areas of low and high pressure which would then be amplified by the gradient winds.

On the evening of 22 May, one of the climbers, Fernando, decided to make a break for Camp 3 with his personal Sherpa, against the advice of the team leader. He returned twelve hours later having taken a fair battering.

By the following evening, having been confined to our tents for three days, the winds had died down and the news from Base Camp was that there might be a small weather window to make the climb before conditions deteriorated once again. My tent buddy, Urs, was getting conflicting reports but the decision was made to push upwards at eight-thirty that evening. Unfortunately, the three days spent at such high altitude had taken their toll on Urs whose heart no longer seemed to be in it and, despite my efforts to gee him up, he abandoned the climb.

We set out in the early evening under a beautiful moonlit sky with zero wind. The plan was to reach Camp 3 by around one the following morning and, after a short break there, make a bid for the summit. Having already had some pretty tough days climbing and knowing from previous experience that summit days are considerably tougher, I was resigned to the fact that I was going to have to push myself both physically and mentally harder than ever before.

I arrived at Camp 3 just behind Dan, the expedition leader, but the rest of the group were nowhere to be seen. I'd passed all of them on the way up after starting at the back waiting for Urs to get ready. All of them had looked pretty tired despite the fact that most were using oxygen, but I'd assumed they were just pacing themselves.

Dan and I waited in the tent for them to arrive but, to cut a long story short, some went to the wrong tents whilst others took as long as seven hours to reach Camp 3. Dan became rather agitated and told many of the group that they should not attempt the summit; most in any case were too tired to do so. Much to Irish Stew's credit, he decided that he wanted to go and, seeing that he had a personal Sherpa, Dan agreed. Together Stefanos, Stewart and I, along with Dan and the Sherpas, set out for the top, albeit three hours late at five in the morning.

From then on, it was simply a slog to the summit. There were a few technical sections which involved a bit of climbing but nothing too difficult. I can't say that there was much enjoyment in this part of the climb as I was fairly exhausted and concentrating solely on making my every movement as efficient as possible to preserve what energy I had left – stopping to enjoy the view was just not an option. My mind, however, remained focused on my goal and I kept telling myself to keep moving, taking one step at a time until I got there.

We ran out of fixed rope shortly before the 7,800-metre mark so Dan and one of the Sherpas adopted a system whereby they'd go ahead to fix the ropes whilst we waited. Once the rope for a section was in place, we would advance to the end of it before settling down to wait whilst they repeated the process. It was pretty time-consuming but, with the wind now gusting up to forty to fifty knots, it was for the best.

At around 8,000 metres, the rope ran out again, but with less than two hundred vertical metres to the summit, we decided to carry on up roped together without any fixed rope to go by. This turned out to be a real pain in the arse as we failed to work as a team, with everyone moving at different speeds and not seeming to give a rat's arse about the people in front or behind. It was inevitable perhaps, since we don't all work on the same wavelength, particularly at altitude.

At 8,050 metres, Irish Stew collapsed in the snow, unable to continue. Despite coaxing from us and with just 150 metres of vertical ascent to climb, his attempt was evidently over and so we left him there with a view to collecting him on the way back hoping that by then he would have regained enough strength for the return journey. He was not showing any signs of the aforementioned sicknesses that tend to be the main killers at altitude, but was utterly exhausted, not even his constant positivity being enough to pull him through. He decided to let his own Sherpa summit which was fairly gracious of him. This would give his Sherpa greater kudos and allow him to charge a higher fee for subsequent trips but would leave Stew stranded alone on the mountain for a few hours.

The rest of us carried on up as the wind grew stronger, reaching the summit plateau about an hour and a half later and getting some great views of Lhotse and Everest in between storm clouds.

Far from the elation that I'd felt on previous climbs, my mind was already on the return journey. Knowing how deep I'd had to dig to get to the summit and having experienced how exhausting the climb down was on past expeditions, I knew that this climb was far from over. It might sound stupid but the simple effort of taking my glove off to unzip a pocket and get my camera proved too much and, to my regret, I didn't take a summit photo. Much to my chagrin at the time but ultimately to my benefit, Stefanos was apparently feeling in better shape or just had better mental discipline and was able to take a photo of us.

I don't have much recollection of the summit other than the frustration of not having the energy to do anything other than stand there and wait to get going again, not wanting to give in to the temptation to rest any longer than necessary and not wanting to show any weakness to Stefanos, whom by now had really started to irritate me for no other reason than he was fitter and stronger than I was and was forcing my pace, roped together as we were.

Leaving the summit behind us, we started making our way back down the mountain, stumbling every now and then on tired and shaky legs. A short while later, we arrived at the point where we had left Irish Stew; he was still sitting on a rock, exactly as we had left him. He was fairly delirious from hypoxia and moving him was very slow going, as we were only able to manage a hundred metres or so at a time before he would collapse again and need a while to recover. This went on for a few hours which was difficult as the clock was ticking with both the continued exposure at this altitude and the weather forecast playing against us and our chances of survival.

I hung back with Stew to help him where I could but, after an hour or so, he called to me to let me know that he was in trouble. I talked with Dan and we agreed that it would be best if he and Stefanos went ahead, leaving myself, Stew and the two Sherpas to make our own way down. Sometime later, after ever-faltering progress down the mountain, the Sherpas went on ahead, no doubt exhausted themselves from all of the additional duties that they had carried out on the mountain.

I in no way blame them for doing so. They were experienced mountaineers with families of their own to support so there was little point of them risking their lives any further. Part of me hopes that they felt that we were close enough to camp and I was strong enough to get Irish Stew down from there on my own. I also know from having spent time with them that they would have done anything they could to help until they couldn't help anymore so their decision to carry on without us was the right one.

By now, Stew was fairly incoherent but, remembering my experience on Aconcagua, I managed to find out that he'd not eaten or drunk anything for twelve hours. His drinks were frozen and he couldn't remember if he had any snacks so I delved into my pack and gave him the last of my supplies which left me feeling like I was swallowing razor blades for the rest of the journey to Camp 3, such was my dehydration. He also complained that he couldn't see; it turned out this was due to his goggles freezing up so I gave him mine.

After ten minutes or so, he perked up a little as the food I had given him started to take effect. Falteringly, over the next three and a half hours, we made our way back to Camp 3 below in the fading light, although by now I was basically supporting Stew and it took us ages to reach it. Darkness had fallen by then which made our original plan of carrying on down to the relative safety of Camp 2 no longer possible.

I had assumed that the rest of the team had retreated to Camp 2 with the deteriorating conditions. However, it turned out that everybody had decided to stay, hoping for a weather window the following morning in order to make another attempt. It was pretty cosy, to say the least, with five of us sardined into a two-man tent, but the other team members – a Romanian couple and Urs – were fantastic, assisting Stew out of his gear and getting him some fluids. Somehow we all managed to survive a very uncomfortable night with me lying at everybody's feet by the door of the tent.

At around one in the morning, the wind having dropped a little, one of our group, Zsombor, received a call on the radio from one of the other climbers, letting him know that they were kitting up for a summit attempt. He duly got ready and slipped out half an hour later to give it a go.

About fourteen seconds after he'd left the tent and before he had a chance to change his mind, I snuggled in between the other occupants and was mightily relieved to get off the icy ground and into a much more comfortable situation on a mat, albeit listening to the wind build once again outside. Shortly after leaving, Zsombor returned, having wisely decided to turn back with the conditions rapidly deteriorating, but I was buggered if I was going to give up my spot between Urs and his fiancée!

I had a crap night's rest, partially due to suffering from snow blindness; every few minutes it felt like I was having red-hot needles poked into the pupils of my eyes. The others fared little better (apart from Stew who apparently had a wonderful sleep!) and we awoke to blizzard conditions and slowly prepared to leave. Unfortunately, with the conditions being as they were and with only two Sherpas, we had to wait until everybody was ready and the camp dismantled prior to heading down the mountain. My hat goes off to Eva, Zsombor's fiancée, who was the first to get ready and hence the first out of the tent and had to endure the terrible conditions for well over two hours prior to us moving down the mountain, in typical fashion, without a murmur of complaint.

We finally got underway and almost immediately another of the climbers, Fernando, developed some kind of a problem which I think may have been the onset of frostbite in his fingers. Fortunately, his personal Sherpa took care of him whilst we carried on down the mountain. The winds had not abated and we were soon into knee-to-thigh-deep snow which, after the efforts of the past month, was incredibly tiring. I stuck with Stew who had difficulty keeping up and was experiencing trouble with his vision, suffering as was I with snow blindness, but we trudged on undaunted into the white-out conditions.

Unfortunately, we traversed too far towards the end of our journey, but were much relieved to hear shouts and whistles guiding us into Camp 2. The tents slowly drifted in and out of focus as the snow storms howled around us and it seemed to be a long haul to finally get back to our tents where we settled in for the night. The whole journey had taken about seven hours rather than the one hour it would take if the conditions were good.

The tents flapped and banged all night in the wind which was pretty constant, gusting up to fifty miles per hour, finally dying down at about five in the morning when I managed to snatch an hour or so of sleep. I was keen to get going the following day before the winds picked up again, but everybody else seemed to be quite happy to stay in their tents to wait for the day to warm up a little and get something warm inside them before committing to the conditions.

With the additional tents at Camp 2, we had a bit more space and Urs and I tried to get the stove lit for a cup of tea and a little breakfast. Unfortunately, the matches were damp and the fuel too cold. After many attempts and with us down to the last few matches and conditions deteriorating outside, we decided to use the last of the chemical handwarmers to get everything as dry and warm as possible before the final attempt (the prospect of drinking the only thing fluid left in the tent which was rather yellow and smelly not being overly appetizing) to light the stove and melt some ice.

I decided to guarantee the attempt by calculating the interior volume of the tent before releasing a few litres of the oxygen I'd brought down from Camp 3 to aid combustion. We listened to the oxygen hiss into the tent for a few minutes at the prescribed rate of four litres a minute before I got bored and cracked open the cylinder, super-oxygenating us and the tent and making us feel a lot better!

The match unsurprisingly lit on the first go, burning my fingers pretty quickly, and the accompanying flash blinding anyone within a two hundred-metre radius, but the good news was that we were able to make a lovely cup of tea and any thoughts of having narrowly avoided shrink-wrapping ourselves into our own tent were quickly forgotten.

Zsombor and Eva were not quite so lucky in their attempts and soon ran out of matches. Given their kindness the previous day in helping Stew and me, I tried to find some for them as well as taking their stove to one of the Sherpa tents to light it and get back to their tent before a gust blew out the flame but sadly the gaps in between gusts were not long enough for me to succeed. They were delayed in leaving but assured us that they were OK and would be following us shortly.

The going was fairly tough as we were once again forced to make our way through increasing winds and knee-deep snow but progress remained steady, the only hold-up occurring while trying to find the fixed line just below Camp 2 which had become buried. The Sherpas searched for fifteen minutes before Fernando dropped his pack, picked up his ice axe and started digging, finding the line in about thirty seconds two feet from where he was standing.

About halfway down and after a good few hours of alternately walking and abseiling, we came across a small camp that some Austrians had left. The tents were now buried under snow, but the decision was taken to dig them out so we could take a break as everybody was feeling pretty tired. After we'd been resting for about an hour, Zsombor and Eva joined us, much to our relief as we were a little worried about them. They seemed pretty fresh and together we carried on toward the top of the first ice step. The only event worthy of note was watching Zsombor disappear up to his armpits in a crevasse about the width of a size-nine boot, which was pretty unlucky but I figured that would teach him a lesson for being short and having little feet!

Whilst at the ice step, we heard reports of an avalanche over the radio. It sounded a little confused but it transpired that some Sherpas we'd met at the Austrian camp, on their way up to retrieve the gear left at Camp 2, had been caught in an avalanche on the slope that we had come down just two hours previously. One had fallen a hundred metres and the other twenty metres but thankfully there were no serious injuries and the Sherpas were told to retreat to Camp 1. The incident was a timely reminder of how, despite all the training and planning in the world, sometimes you can just be in the wrong place at the wrong time.

Meanwhile, Stew and Fernando had started to drop off the pace and at one stage, in winds that were gusting at over a hundred miles an hour, we were forced to wait without shelter whilst they were located. Fernando appeared first, after what seemed like ages, but there was no sign of Stew or the Sherpa who had been dispatched to get him. I guessed that his personal Sherpa was still with him but thought that maybe he was struggling also. Eventually the decision was made that we must carry on so, with no fixed line, we roped to one another and set out the best we could until we came to another fixed line.

By now the mountain had taken on a very different form, scoured down to bare blue ice by the wind's roaring gusts. It was an incredible contrast to the slopes we had encountered just a week before and a good lesson learned in just how bad things can get in a short space of time.

Our instructions were to carry on to where the fixed rope ended and to wait as the way from there on in would be too dangerous. Thus we carried on down, Urs leading, me second and Zsombor and Eva following.

At one stage, Urs on the fixed line seemed to stall. However, he kept disappearing from view in clouds of spindrift whipped up by the now constant gale, so I abseiled down to him to see what the problem was. I found him in the relative shelter of a rock pinnacle and could not see any more fixed line more than ten metres below which would leave us on a very exposed col over which the winds were charging.

I had a bit more energy than him at this stage and he was starting to get cold so I agreed to go ahead and see if there was any more fixed line. Fortunately, the line continued out of sight and we were able to progress albeit slowly due to the wind constantly knocking us over on the abseil despite our legs being spread three feet apart.

Eventually we came to the end of the fixed rope. However, given the conditions and the known proximity to camp, we decided to carry on, reaching the camp about one hour and twenty minutes later.

The majority of the tents had been ripped apart by the wind. Fortunately for us, however, one of the Sherpas had been left at the camp to maintain what was left of it, which included four tents that could be used, at least for the time being. After a very welcome cup of coffee, I headed out of the Sherpa tent and started making myself comfortable in one of the storage tents. By now, I was wearing a chest plate of ice where the winds and cold had frozen the moisture in my breath, which had to be chipped off before I could get inside as I couldn't bend to undo my crampons. Urs joined me shortly after and we tried to make ourselves as comfortable as possible for another long night.

Sleep was impossible as the wind continued to roar, each successive blast leaving us wondering whether the tents would make it through the night without being torn apart. The gusts were getting under the tent and literally lifting me off of the floor, which was a tad disconcerting.

Most of the tents were damaged during the night, but thankfully none of them were made uninhabitable and it was a very welcome respite when the winds started to die down at around six in the morning.

Upon waking, we regrouped and prepared for the leg back to ABC where we were all looking forward to the relative delights of a thick foam mattress and being served a hot meal that didn't consist of the porridge, cheese and spam that had been our staple over the past few days. The weather was much improved with the wind having died right down with just the occasional snow flurry. However, on Not So Horrible Hill conditions were not so easy, a mixture of snow, ice and scree which sent me flat on my arse cursing and swearing on more than one occasion.

Urs and I caught up with Fernando, Stuart and their Sherpas at the bottom of the hill and from then on led the charge through the moraines, often thigh-deep in snowdrifts blown in by the wind of the previous days which was pretty exhausting. Fortunately, halfway between there and ABC, we came across the porters coming the other way to clear Camp 1; their footfalls had compacted the path which made for much easier going. We also came across quite a few other climbers on their way up who would unfortunately have to abort their attempt due to the fact that their camp and supplies had been redistributed halfway across Tibet by the storm of the past three days.

Urs was by now getting tired so I bid him farewell and trudged back alone to ABC, spurred on by the thought of a cold beer! Upon arriving there

I was met by Dan, Stefanos and three other climbers whom it was great to see back in such 'comfort' – on reflection, it was the first point at which I felt that I'd actually made it. Much back-slapping, hand-shaking and photo-taking followed, the excitement of which was surpassed only by the hiss of escaping gas from the top of the can of beer.

Eventually everybody drifted back in and after a great dinner (probably not that great really, but trust me it was truly ambrosial at the time!) I settled into my sleeping bag on top of three mattresses and slept like a baby protected by high walls of snow from which our tents had to be dug out.

The following day came and we started packing the camp away. I set to carefully and diligently digging out the rocks holding the guy ropes of the tent in order that we could take the it down. It wasn't until after forty minutes of digging with my ski pole (my axe was already packed and yak-bound) and down to the last guy that one of the Sherpas appeared and chopped through it with his ice axe. Bastard!!!

All was packed away and most of the group had left, three of us staying back to assist in any way before heading down ourselves. We arrived back at Interim Base Camp for a spot of lunch before heading down to Base Camp which was a much longer slog than I remembered.

About five hundred metres from the camp, a 4x4 stopped and the driver tried to usher us in. The only words he spoke were 'Tingri, Tingri', which didn't make for much of a conversation. We also weren't sure of what arrangements had been made and whether this guy was a private cab driver after a fast buck. OK, on reflection I realise that four thousand metres up a mountain in the middle of nowhere would be a strange place to hang out in the hope of picking up a fare but unfortunately I'm a little suspicious! I was also intent on walking back to the point from which we had started and reaching the tea tent where I had a date with a cold beer in my mind.

After a little conversation, the driver went off and we continued on foot for the final furlong to the awaiting tea tent which was closed with no sign of a porter with my beer. Fortunately, the representative from the Tibetan Mountaineering Association was at the Chinese Base Camp just over the road and explained that the 4x4 was indeed for us and that we were to go to Tingri. As for the beer, the TMA rep went to the Chinese army tent and appeared with six beers, one for now and five for the road which raised spirits immeasurably and did more for international relations in a single gesture than ten years of a hearts-and-minds campaign could ever do!

The rest of the group arrived a little later having met several 4x4s at IBC and saved themselves the eight-kilometre walk back to Base Camp.

Meanwhile, though it was dearly tempting, I refrained from a lift and thus could claim that I was the only member of the group to have walked from Base Camp, summited the mountain and walked all the way back – sad, I know, but hey, it's things like that that make me tick!

The storms that we had encountered whilst on the mountain had also battered the lower slopes and much of the roadworks that we had seen on the way up the mountain had been smashed to pieces by falling boulders. Thankfully, we were now being transported in 4x4s which were a bit nimbler and had us back in Kathmandu within two days.

Irish stew made a full recovery and was soon back to his usual self, bouncing around like a twelve year old on a bucket of smarties within a few days. It was only when we went for a few beers in Kathmandu with a couple of other climbers and they explained what had happened – and what he'd been blissfully unaware of – that he realised the precariousness of his situation at the time. To this day and without fail, he phones me every Christmas Eve to thank me on behalf of his family which is more than I could ever have asked for. Moreover, upon completing the London Marathon in 2022, he was able to come and stay with us and I can honestly say it was one of the proudest moments of my life when he turned to my sons over dinner and told them that he would not be alive today if it wasn't for me.

That year was one of the worst on record with only one other climber from all of the teams on the mountain managing to summit due to the weather conditions. Sadly, one Dutch climber who we had met at base camp was to succumb to H.A.C.E. during his summit attempt and did not return. Despite the discomfort and trials of the climb, the fact that I had succeeded where many had failed only made me surer that I'd be able to summit Everest and, within a week of returning, I had paid my deposit with Summit Climb to join an expedition starting in April 2010.

8

Everest

Standing at 8,849 meters tall, Everest is the highest mountain in the world. Its status was first established in 1852 by the British government's Survey of India. At this time it was known simply as Peak XV, but was renamed in 1865 by the Royal Geographic Survey in honour of George Everest, a Welshman employed in 1823 as the superintendent of the Great Trigonometric Survey which surveyed the meridian arc from the southernmost tip of India to Nepal (a distance of 1,500 miles which took 35 years to complete, starting in 1806 and ending in 1841). Everest's named was put forward by his protégé and successor Andrew Scott Waugh, but Everest objected on the grounds that he had nothing to do with the mountain's discovery and that his name wasn't easily pronounceable in Hindi (His name was actually pronounced 'Eeverist') but the name was adopted nevertheless.

Maybe more fittingly, in Tibetan the mountain is known as Chomolungma, meaning 'Goddess Mother of the World'.

As previously mentioned, Sir Edmund Hilary and Sherpa Tenzing Norgay are credited as being the first men to summit Everest in 1953. They climbed via the South Col route, but almost thirty years before, during the summer climbing season of 1924, two British climbers, George Mallory and Andrew Irvine, attempted to summit via the North Col route. It was Mallory's third attempt and proved to be his last.

According to Noel Odell, a support climber on the Mallory expedition, camped at just below 8,000 meters, Mallory was last seen surmounting a 'prominent rock step' (which could have been the Second or even the previously unknown Third Step) at around one o'clock in the afternoon on 8 June. This was the last sighting of him before he disappeared, swallowed up by clouds of mist swirling around the peak.

Circumstantial evidence argued that Mallory may have summited but this was mainly based on a pledge he made that he would leave a photograph of his wife at the summit. When his body was found, well-preserved in 1999, no such photograph was found upon his person. The other piece of evidence was the discovery of Mallory's unbroken goggles which suggested that he had made a push for the summit and was descending after sunset. Whether Mallory and Irvine did in fact summit or not may never be known, although analysis of their bodies and the points where they were eventually located suggest that they did not.

Nevertheless, upon the news of the eventual discovery of Mallory's body, Sir Edmund Hilary described the possibility that Mallory might have summited Everest decades earlier as 'very appropriate'. 'He was really the initial pioneer of the whole idea of climbing Mount Everest,' Hilary said in tribute.

The North Col route was first officially climbed by a Chinese team in 1960.

Both the north and south routes are accessible to climbers so a decision has to be made on which route to take. On the Nepalese side the weather is generally better due to it being south-facing. The northern, Tibetan side, on the other hand, is colder and more exposed. Due to its orientation, the Nepalese side is the more popular route with climbers and trekkers alike. When people say that they have been to Everest Base Camp, they are usually referring to this approach.

The downside of this is that the southern approach is far more populous. In addition, exposure to the sun can make the icefalls and glaciers less predictable, particularly later in the day when the sun has been on them and there has been some melting. Of particular renown is the Khumbu Icefall (after which the cough is known), a four-kilometre stretch of glacier which is constantly in motion (more so given the effects of climate change) and is considered the most dangerous part of the climb on the South Col route. Keen to avoid both this and the crowds, which have gained a lot of public attention in recent years, and in part fuelled by my desire to do it the 'tougher way', I opted for the North Col route from the Tibetan side of the mountain.

I was pretty happy with how I'd trained for Cho Oyu, but felt that I could further improve my general strength and fitness. I was still based in Monaco on the same boat. So now I supplemented my morning cycles and treks with gym sessions in the evening and on weekends I'd either get dropped fifty kilometres or so into the Alps Maritimes with a heavy pack and make my way back or I'd go for long cycle rides in the mountains, clocking up two hundred kilometres or more in a day.

I've mentioned before that there are a few instances in my life when I've felt utterly content and some of these training hikes were definitely amongst them. Being out in the mountains for a few days by myself, setting up camp next to a stream and settling down to sleep after some food with just the sounds and smells of nature and unspoiled starry skies to keep me company was, without wanting to sound too corny, incredibly fulfilling for my soul. Whether this was due to spending my life constantly around others and all the trappings of modern life, or simply a personal predilection for solitude, I don't know. All I know is that in those moments I felt completely at one with the world.

The feelings upon cresting the last mountains and being once again exposed to people in an urban environment only heightened the sense of loss that I'd originally felt on those early morning hikes and the last hour or so into town was something that I never looked forward to. That said, once I was back onboard and had dumped my pack, had a shower and headed out for a beer and something to eat, I generally felt much better about living amongst the trappings of modern life!

Going somewhat off subject but nevertheless an important part of my tale, during my time in the Caribbean on the boat and prior to our trip to Venezuela, we'd entered a yacht show to drum up some potential trade for charter. We had a succession of lovely charter managers onboard the boat, three of whom were very good friends with one another. In various conversations with them, some more drunken than the others, I'd promised each of them a special gift for their efforts.

One was to receive a photo of me semi-naked; another who suffered from cold feet at work was to receive a heated mono-slipper (something I'd seen in the classified ads in the back of the papers) that you could plug in and put both of your feet in to keep warm; and the last I'd promised to retile her bathroom when I was back in the UK. Just to clarify, I'm not a vain man and the semi-naked photo that I sent was actually a poster of me dressed as a Smurf at a fancy dress party.

With the first two taken care of and admittedly with an ulterior motive, I went on a few drinks dates with the third woman, a gorgeous lass named Helene, reiterating my pledge, and subsequently met up with her again whilst in London in October 2009. I'm glad to say that the bathroom did get done and, obviously impressed with my DIY skills, she agreed when I suggested something a little more romantic. We have been together ever since.

My new status brought a slightly different dynamic to my way of thinking as up until then, despite a few dalliances, I'd been free to do pretty much whatever I wanted. Now, keen to spend time with Helene, I had to do a bit of juggling. Fortunately, she was a pretty decent skier, a very good sailor and an excellent drinker so, apart from the drinking, my training schedule didn't suffer too much. Furthermore, she was very independent and understanding of my goals and aspirations (as I was of hers) and to have somebody that I considered my equal and to be in such a symbiotic relationship was quite a revelation to me.

Helene was also one of the poshest people my parents had ever met and I remember being in a pub when we first started seeing each other and Mum remarking, 'She's a bit special' when Helene popped to the loo. After ten years of playing footloose and fancy free, that was me pretty much sold so when I left for Everest, it was a lovely feeling to know that I had somebody to come back to, that there would be somebody thinking of me and willing me to come back in one piece.

Now, back to the story. With an eight-thousander already under my belt and hundreds of hours of training and preparation done, I was feeling confident as I flew out once again to Kathmandu to start the expedition.

Upon getting there I settled into my hotel and went for a stroll around town and, though it felt familiar, it also felt slightly different to be back just under a year later. My time spent there previously meant that I was familiar with the city and I knew where all the climbing stores that I required were. This allowed me to help other members of the team but, more than that, my success on the mountain the previous year and struggles through adversity made me feel that I had earned the right to rub shoulders with some of the more experienced mountaineers at the various hangouts in the city, no longer having to hang onto their every word and feeling experienced enough to being taken seriously.

I guess it reminded me of a time of life, probably when I was twenty-four or five, when I suddenly realised that people were interested in what I had to say rather than simply humouring me, being as I was up until then the smart arse with all the answers and not enough questions.

This expedition was scheduled to last around two months and, given the deprivations of the previous campaigns, I was determined to make it as comfortable as possible. One of the biggest motivators for me is food and, despite the best efforts of the camp cooks, after a while you do start to miss the comforts of the things you really enjoy, so stocking up with them prior to departure can really help you on the days when you need a bit of a pick-me-up.

The hardest part is rationing them to last. My mum was keen to help out and, having always been a feeder, she was tasked with constructing a 'hamper' for the expedition. Since I was a kid, I've always loved *kabanos*, a long, thin, dry Polish sausage. I remember every now and then when I was young Mum would bring me one home as a treat which I'd eagerly devour. I was very happy therefore when she presented me with a 3.5-kilogram pack of them along with another childhood favourite, sesame snaps. As luck would have it, as well as tasting great, both are packed with the good stuff you need for long expeditions rather than the empty calories provided by other, less nutritional snack foods. The extra weight did mean some additional charges when I went to check in at the airport, but it was well worth it.

Time was pretty limited with only three days in Kathmandu before we loaded up on the buses, but it being a pretty well-trodden path by now, there wasn't a huge amount to do, the main delay being obtaining all the necessary visas and permits. One big change I wanted to make to my kit this time around was the procurement of a big thick mattress for Base Camp. Having been careful not to take too much gear on Cho Oyu, I remembered looking on enviously as people appeared at the weigh-in with huge, four-inch-thick rolled foam mattresses. This proved better than my stack of three normal foam carry mats which tended to slide off each other and were only the width of a sleeping bag anyway, meaning that you had to spin on your own axis to stay atop of them. Now I found myself a particularly pretty one, three foot wide and covered in pink and white flowers. I turned up with it without a hint of shame or remorse, knowing that I'd be one of the comfiest guys on the mountain.

As an aside, my purchase started something of an avalanche of mattress-buying that evening as some of the other climbers scurried around town looking for their own little bit of base-camp luxury.

We were going to be a very big group on this trip, twenty-three climbers in all. Among them was Pete Kinloch, the 'unlikely' climber I'd met on Aconcagua a few years previously. He'd not changed one little bit, still sporting the same scarf, bobble hat and goofy grin. Dan Mazur, the leader on Cho Oyu, was also in charge of this expedition.

With regard to organisation, it was going to be a similar climb to the last with climbers given a fair amount of autonomy once on the higher slopes of the mountain. It was also expected that we would do a lot more of the heavy lifting ourselves, the logistics of having others do it for you at higher altitudes being prohibitively expensive. I learned that allowing climbers autonomy was the way that Dan – a highly experienced climber but far from dictatorial leader – did things. His style was to give you the information you needed and let you make up your own mind. This could be a bit frustrating at times, such as when you asked him a direct question only to receive his standard response in his laidback drawl, 'Well, ya know, it's kinda…' leaving you none the wiser. That said, his method put the ball firmly in your court to make a success or failure of whatever you were trying to achieve.

There were other operators on the mountain offering 'five-star' expeditions in which each client had two Sherpas who would erect tents and feed and water them all the way up (pretty much everything apart from wiping your arse) and provide supplemental oxygen from Camp 1 at 7,000 meters upwards. However, I felt that this would completely denude the whole experience and didn't really rate in terms of actually conquering the mountain. Some of the climbers taking this option were paying up to $100,000 to get to the summit, whereas we paid less than a quarter of that.

Each night prior to departure we got together for kit checks and briefings. It soon became apparent that we were quite a mixed bunch with regard to ability, experience and personality and I found myself subconsciously picking out my 'dream team' knowing the group would be way too big to move as one on the mountain and so we'd be required to split into smaller units. Instinctively I gravitated towards four guys: Laval St. Germain, a Canadian ultramarathon runner and serious outdoorsman; Gavin the 'big bopper' Vickers, a huge, loud Australian who worked in mining; Tom Janvrin, a music and drama teacher from London; and Dave 'Gandalf' O'Brien, the assistant team leader. I'd singled them out, rather pig-headedly, as the climbers that I gave the best chance of succeeding and was thus most keen to associate with. Given the time, effort and money that I'd put in to get this far, I didn't want to be in a group with any lame ducks.

Given that Dave would have to spread himself thinly across the whole group and Tom's aim was to get to Camp 1, it left three of us to form a climbing group. As luck would have it and unbeknown to me, Laval and Gavin had come to the same conclusion.

We loaded up as before and headed the same route to Tingri. Thankfully, the Chinese had made huge improvements to the road and what had previously taken five days now only took three. We still had to stop in Zhangmu to cross the border and have a night there to help acclimatise and I was pleased to see that the ladies there had not lost an ounce of their charm or allure and the knitting seemed to have progressed nicely.

The next day we headed up to the 'rat hotel' in Nyalam only to be greeted by the owner who had just opened a new rat hotel! It was literally brand-new, fresh and cleanly painted with only the faintest hint of human excrement emanating from the bathrooms. That evening, the owner threw a huge party to celebrate the opening of the hotel with a big bonfire, fire crackers, dancing and much merriment had by all. I'm not sure quite how well the hotel will have withstood the rigours of time, the bonfire and fire crackers from the evening before seemingly enough to crack the concrete that the hotel stood on!

Next morning, after an un-traumatic night's sleep, we made the rest of the journey in good time to Tingri for our last stop prior to Base Camp. Visiting the tea houses was somewhat of a homecoming from the previous year. The *momos* hadn't lost any of their flavour and were just as delicious when washed down with a bottle of the local 'Everest beer', although maybe due to the size of the group and the popularity of this snack, it did seem that there may have been one or two less stray dogs on the street the following day (the contents of the *momos* being something of a mystery).

Whilst there, Dan and Dave liaised with the yak herders (or 'yakpas' as they are known) and arranged the yaks that would carry most of our gear up as far as ABC. Astonishingly, we would require 168 yaks to do the job.

At the entrance to the valley, eight kilometres from Base Camp, lies the Rongbuk Monastery, which has become synonymous with images of Everest due to the spectacular views of the mountain to the south. We had been catching excited glimpses of the mountain through the windows of the bus on the way to Base Camp, but the view from here was breathtaking and something that photographs alone cannot even begin to depict. I was incredibly excited to be there, as an experience that had only been in my dreams up until now was becoming a reality and to be in the valley, looking up at the Goddess Mother of the World and the signature plume of cloud racing across the summit, whipped up by hurricane-force winds, is something that I will never forget.

Rongbuk Monastery was built in 1902. It is an important pilgrimage site for Buddhists who come from Nepal and Mongolia to spend time in the meditation caves which dot the cliffs in the area. Surprisingly, to me at least, sky burials still took place here, a fact I learned upon seeing a large flock of circling vultures, which prompted me to ask someone what the hell was going on. The practice, whereby the deceased is placed on a mountaintop to decompose and be taken by scavengers, may seem a bit macabre to Westerners but it serves a number of purposes, both practical and religious.

Tibetans believe that, after your death, your body is an empty vessel, your soul having already transcended. Sky burial is considered the final act of merit, feeding the birds and giving back to the earth what you no longer need. It is also practical with the ground in these parts often being too frozen to dig up and the terrain so far above the treeline that the fuel required for cremation is unavailable. Interestingly, it can only be used for those Tibetans who die of natural causes and not from infectious diseases or poisoning for fear of infecting the birds and harming the environment.

Early expeditions in the 1920s and 30s often visited the Monastery and reported that there were hundreds of lamas and pilgrims engaged in meditation in a cluster of brightly coloured buildings. One expedition commented that they did not meet the head lama as he was on a year-long meditation in a cave, subsisting on water and barley brought to him once a day. Quite an incredible feat given the environment he was in and highlighting the discipline that the must have had to exercise. It would be nice if we all could take a bit more time to just sit and think rather than flying into a blind panic every time the Wi-Fi goes down.

Unfortunately the Monastery was razed to the ground in 1974, its practices and principles not in alignment with China's Cultural Revolution. Furthermore, its vast treasury of teachings and costumes – smuggled out prior to the destruction and deposited in Tengboche – were lost in a fire in 1989. The Monastery has since been rebuilt and is once again home to a small number of monks and nuns. We would come back to the monastery later during the expedition for the *puja* ceremony, but now we headed on up the valley to settle in to Base Camp which a group of Sherpas and porters had gone ahead of us with the supply trucks to set up.

Everest Base Camp in Tibet sits at 5,150 metres at the base of the Rongbuk Glacier in a dry and dusty valley through which a glacial meltwater stream runs. Small scrubby plants dot the landscape that is otherwise featureless other than the brown rock walls that enclose the valley. For two months every year, it is transformed by the many groups of climbers who come here to attempt the ascent of the mountain and a colourful tented town springs up to service the climbers. A little further back down the valley a smaller village also pops up, servicing climbers and tourists alike in traditional Tibetan tea tents made of thick yak hair and equipped with yak-dung stoves. They offer a welcome change from sitting around the camp itself and are a good excuse to go for an acclimatisation hike.

We were one of the earlier groups to set up. However, ahead of us there was a group of eighty Chinese climbers, porters and photographers on an expedition to capture the mountain in all its glory. I was astonished at the amount and size of the equipment they had brought with them, all of which would have to be ferried up to the higher camps on the backs of porters and yaks.

Over the coming days, more and more people arrived, swelling to a crowd of some three hundred or more. A lot of noise has been made in the press in the past years over the amount of litter this caused, but thankfully I saw little evidence of it with every team stressing the importance of respecting the unique environment we were in. I know that I've already talked about the procedure for using the loo on Aconcagua and you may feel that I dwell on the subject a little too much (there are going to be at least three other references after this in the book so you can skip the next paragraph if you want), but pooing up high does come with its own unique set of challenges that you don't face in normal life so here goes:

Toilet blocks had been constructed, away from the main camping area for sanitation purposes. The toilet block was effectively a two-storey building with an external staircase leading to the upper floor where there were four wooden partitioned cubicles for doing your business. In each cubicle was a hole in the floor which went directly to the floor below so over the course of a season, the pile of poo would gradually grow but would be cleared out by the Tibetan Mountaineering Association when required. (Quite who got tasked with that job, I don't know but if working for the TMA, I'd certainly make sure I was one of the first to work every day just in case!) The structure had large wooden doors on it to keep the poo and paper in which then could be opened to facilitate the removal of the poo when the time came.

All good so far? You'd have thought so but there was a slight design flaw. The doors had fallen off quite some time beforehand by the looks of things and not been replaced, leaving the large aperture open to the prevailing wind which came down the valley with some force and became concentrated through the holes. Not only did this make the procedure pretty unhygienic (face masks were always to be worn way before COVID) but upon completion, when trying to wipe, the sullied toilet paper would be blown back up through the hole and chase you around, these becoming known as 'poo fairies'. More often than not, the updraft would be localised and, if dodged, the poo fairy would land in your stall but on days of stronger wind, you might receive a visit from an adjoining stall requiring cat-like reflexes at a time when you really would rather not have to worry about such things.

We set up our camp, which consisted of the tents of the individual climbers, Sherpa tents and our mess tent which could seat all the members of the team, and spent the next few days acclimatising with short walks up the smaller adjoining valleys and the occasional trip to the aforementioned tea tent down the valley. During this time, I got to know the rest of the team and gauged their strengths and weaknesses, trying to work out whether I'd want to team up with them if push came to shove.

I was pleased to find that my original choice seemed to be the right one that suited my pace and personality. That's not to say that the other climbers were any stronger or weaker than me, or any less able, just that the guys that I'd chosen suited my way of doing things. You have to take into account the fact that you will be spending a heck of a lot of time in a very confined space with somebody that you've never met before so ascertaining exactly who this might be fairly early on is quite important. The last thing that you want is to be stuck in a tent for two months with somebody who really gets on your nerves!

Gradually we began to pair off and to form groups and, within the first four days, we'd pretty much found our places. At Base Camp we had the luxury of having a tent to ourselves so if needed you could simply go to your tent and have some peace and quiet, only popping out for meals if you wanted them. I was particularly glad of this when tucking into the contents of Mum's food parcel; I found out that dried apricots metabolise somewhat differently at altitude, a handful of them creating the largest, smelliest and almost constant bout of flatulence that I've ever had the displeasure of having endured. I put this down as a one-off, but trying it again at Camp 1 where I had to share a tent with Gavin I experienced the same thunderous results and my stash was begrudgingly handed over to the Sherpas as a gift. I was hoping that they metabolised them differently as they were in the cook tent with a naked flame, which could have led to disaster.

In accordance with tradition, we attended the *puja* ceremony at the Rongbuk Monastery in order to get the blessing of the mountain before beginning the climb. Each climber had to take an item that they would carry to the summit with them – this was blessed by the lama along with the climber themself.

I'm neither a religious nor a superstitious man but there was no way in hell that I would leave the golden prayer shawl that I was given at the ceremony behind. It stayed securely packed in my rucksack from that day until I returned home at the end of the expedition. As per the previous ceremony, but I'm sure not exactly in line with tradition, a few bottles of whisky were circulated, just in case there were any other spirits that needed appeasing. The lama seemed to have adapted very well to this addition to the traditional ceremony and toasted our good health repeatedly which must have been a good sign.

I realise that I have talked a lot about acclimatisation, but I should add that it is something of a misnomer, or certainly it was in my case. Yes, it does have the physiological effects that I talked about some time back and, yes, the incidences of headache, nausea and dizziness ease with time. However, it is not some cure-all in the sense that one day you feel rough as guts and a few days later you're bouncing around like a puppy without getting out of breath. At this altitude, everything that you do leaves you short of breath; all that the acclimatisation does is allow you to do things a tiny bit more easily and quickly at the altitude you are at until you get to the next stage whereupon you are pretty much back to zero ('easily' and 'quickly' being very relative terms, nothing happening particularly quickly or easily unless you fall off something and let gravity do the work).

Anyhow, we were now eleven days into the expedition and 'acclimatised' enough for the next part of the journey: the trip up to Advanced Base Camp. As on Cho Oyu, those who wanted could stop at Interim Base Camp, while those who felt fit and strong enough could bypass this and go straight to ABC.

The slow trudge began up the left-hand side of the glacier in beautiful weather. Yaks and porters were sent ahead with the heavier high-altitude gear meaning that all we had to haul was enough gear for a possible overnight camp at IBC. I was really glad that I had taken every opportunity to gain experience in mountaineering over the past years. The going was tough, but I was now used to the idea that, regardless of the climb, it was always tough but as long as you could endure you would get there.

It helped immensely having Laval along. Being accompanied by somebody so supremely fit and well-conditioned meant that there was absolutely no point in trying to get into camp first as he'd win hands down every time. Gone was my instinct to try and prove that I was the fastest or the strongest on the mountain.

As I had learned the hard way on Cho Oyu, the mountain would always win if you tried to take it on and pursuing pointless short term personal goals at this stage of the game was futile. Instead I maintained my own steady pace and concentrated on making every movement as efficient as possible in order to conserve valuable energy.

On reaching IBC, I almost carried on, once again a victim of my own hubris, knowing that Laval had gone on, but fortunately I checked myself thinking, *Why not stay here? Though I can probably make it to the next camp, I'm a bit tired so what's the point in pushing it? There's always tomorrow.*

Adopting this attitude was quite a big step for me and it created – rather stupidly it seems twelve years on – quite an internal conflict but at the time it was the essence of who I was, always wanting to beat the person ahead of me. On the other hand, I guess that if I hadn't had that attitude, I may not have accomplished the things that I did.

That night, we camped on the glacier at 5,800 metres and, internally conflicted or not, I slept pretty well, not dreading the next day's exertions due to having already overdone it, but looking forward to the next step. Sleep was frequently punctuated by the eerie cracks and bangs of the glacier as millions of tons of rock and ice made its way incrementally down the mountain. The following day brought about more spectacular conditions as we made our way to ABC through the ice flow and moraines, following a narrow path through towering pinnacles of ice known as 'pilgrims' and over loose rock scoured from the mountainside by this colossal icy serpent.

Upon arrival, we found the camp already starting to fill with other teams and most of the prime spots had been taken. However, the Sherpas and porters had gone ahead and set up the mess tent so at least we were welcomed with drinks and snacks. Laval had arrived the night before and set up his tent and I was one of the first of our group to arrive from IBC, just ahead of the yaks, so after a short break I was able to grab a tent and erect it on one of the flat(ish) sites next to the mess tent. Clearing and flattening the site as best I could at 6,400 metres was slow and exhausting, but after about half an hour of methodical movements, I was ready to pitch my tent.

I'd gained a lot of experience with this design of tent when on Cho Oyu and was familiar with how best to put it up so it didn't take long before I was ready to move in. Grabbing my kit, I had started to make my house a home when I heard a commotion outside. Popping my head back out of the tent, I saw that one of the yaks had gone berserk and was bulldozing its way towards me. I leapt out of the way and down the slope (refer to my earlier comment on speed and gravity) just in time to see the yak flatten all my hard work and disappear down the mountain trailing half my kit behind it.

Rising from a rather ungainly position, I dusted myself off and checked for lumps and bumps, but apart from a few scratches on my legs, all seemed to be in working order. I then set off down the mountain in the wake of the crazed yak, collecting my bits and bobs as I went. Fortunately, there were spare tents so I grabbed another and started again, this time thankfully without a rampaging hairy cow to destroy it. I had at least nabbed the same spot close to the mess tent so I didn't have to go too far for my meals and, within an hour or so, I was settled in.

The rest of the group arrived later that day and I was amazed at the difference in pace. I'd taken about four hours to get from IBC to ABC yet some took double that. They made it, at least, which I suppose was the goal, but I did start to worry about their performance at the higher camps.

Tom Janvrin, who was on a pretty tight time schedule due to work commitments back in the UK, spent one night at ABC before going straight up to the North Col the following day and then turning around and coming straight back down again. It was a pretty Herculean effort and one that I didn't envy him in, particularly as the weather wasn't great with strong winds and snow showers. He was also one of the first climbers to ascend to the North Col so the trail had not been particularly compacted making the going even more difficult.

We waited for his return in the mess tent, but he didn't make it back until well after dark at around ten o'clock that evening. Our jubilation in his success was in marked contrast to his reaction, such was his level of exhaustion, appearing as the hollow shell of a man on the edge of delirium. The following day he had to make the long trek all the way back down to Base Camp to get into a car and return to civilisation, so rather understandably he was in no mood for celebration.

Having seen him, we were all very grateful for the fact that we didn't have to rush. Ironically, as he was heading back to Kathmandu, there was a massive volcanic eruption in Iceland, halting all air traffic to Europe, so he ended up stuck in a hotel for another week before he could return to work.

Advanced Base Camp sits at the foot of the North Wall, a 600-metre rampart of ice and snow which marks the first major obstacle on Everest and is where the trek turns into a climb. We spent the next two days there, making the short hike across the smooth ice of the glacier in boots and crampons to the foot of the Wall where we practiced ice-axe arrests, ice climbing, rappelling and jumar techniques (going up and down ropes) on a convenient ice pinnacle just below the camp. Again, it was fairly apparent that the group was of very mixed ability, ranging from the completely competent to a chap who gained the unfortunate moniker of 'Carl the Squid' on account of his attempts to climb the slope – akin to throwing some uncooked calamari at it and watching it slide down again.

Having gained 1,200 metres in two days, we were all feeling the effects of altitude to different degrees and were very happy to have a few days' break to recuperate, with only light exertion which would invariably bring on a thumping headache at first but would subside pretty quickly. Due to the tent incident upon arrival and keen to reserve the spare tents for when they might be needed, I'd buddied up with Gavin and was sharing with him. We'd set up quite the cosy love nest, both of us having brought thick mattresses up the mountain. Gavin had even hauled up a duvet which made the cold nights ever so snuggly, wrapped up next to a six-foot-six Aussie and feeling something of a little spoon.

It was also at this time that I realised that I didn't have to undo my sleeping bag and get on my knees to have a pee. The second time I did this whilst sharing a tent with Gavin prompted the response, 'What the f**k you doin', mate?' My tent-mate then taught me the finer points of relieving oneself into a bottle, thankfully without an actual demonstration – you've got to draw the line somewhere, after all! This method had the added benefit of providing an immediate warm water bottle for my feet which was handy as I suffer from the same unfortunate affliction as my Mum, in that I can't get to sleep if they're cold.

After a few days at ABC, it was time to tackle the climb to Camp 1. Apparently, the Sherpas had already set up the fixed rope that we would all be depending on. However, they reported that, unlike in previous years, there were problems with crevasses which had opened up en route – which was a little ironic given that one of the reasons behind my decision to climb via the North Col was that it would avoid icefalls and crevasses. To try and solve the problem, the Sherpas had set up bridges across the crevasses with aluminium ladders with two guide ropes acting as both makeshift handrails and safety lines. We had been warned about this and subsequently trained in full kit including boots and crampons to get across these bridges.

Given my time in the Fire Brigade, I was probably more familiar with ladders than most. I knew that the weakest plane of a ladder was when it is horizontal so practicing on these thin aluminium jobs lashed together at ABC was a very worthwhile exercise in saving me having to carry additional underpants to the higher camps. Once again, we were pretty lucky with the weather which seemed to be holding quite well, cold enough to prevent sweating but warm enough to maintain feeling in hands and feet. Due to it being a steep slope on the north side of the mountain, this face did not receive a great deal of sunlight. However, it was still preferable to be past the worst of the icefall prior to early afternoon to minimise the chances of a further collapse as the slope heated up.

From ABC we could see a huge serac hanging over one of the traverses that we would have to take, and a mental note was made to get clear of that section as quickly as possible. Incredibly, we had seen other teams take this traverse with no such caution, instead seemingly taking breaks underneath the ice column (although to be fair it is often hard to judge given the incredibly slow pace that is maintained at these altitudes). To give some idea of the pace, I once showed Helene footage of the team advancing up to Camp 3 and she was startled after about fifteen seconds when somebody moved as she had assumed it was a photograph rather than a video.

By now, we'd pretty much established our own individual pace within the group and there was no animosity when I asked to be closer to the front in order to be able to travel at my own speed. We set out across the smooth surface of the glacier to the base of the Wall and began the climb. Unlike Cho

Oyu which was effectively a high-altitude trek with only one small technical section, Everest was a very different animal with much steeper slopes which at such altitude required a great deal more effort with each step taking longer to recover from.

As mentioned, we had practiced crevasse crossings at ABC but tackling the first bridge was a very different experience with crosswinds gusting and the dark blue mouth of a seemingly bottomless chasm gaping below. Clipping in and double-checking the safety lines, it was just a matter of trying to forget about the danger and trusting in the kit; there was no other choice. Trying to control breathing is difficult at these altitudes at the best of times with the heart hammering away, trying to send what little oxygen there is around your body, and this certainly didn't help matters. We made it across, however, step by step, only to have to perform a difficult dismount followed by a four-metre vertical section before the incline evened out giving us the chance to catch our breath.

Given the mental and physical stress that everybody is under on the mountain, climbers are remarkably good-natured and there is an unspoken attitude between them of mutual cooperation which is particularly necessary on these sections where there is only one route and different groups on different schedules. On any given day on Everest, there may be as many people going up as coming down. The tracks are no wider in places than a single human being and priority is generally given to those descending on account of the fact that they have expended more energy to get to where they are and thus have a greater need to return and recuperate than those going up.

As the day wore on, we made our way gradually up the Wall, finally reaching the North Col seven hours after starting out. Laval had arrived about twenty minutes before me and after a short break we started setting up camp, not only for ourselves but also for the other climbers. Though exhausted from the climb, there was a bit of me that wanted to prove that I was still capable of more. I also felt that if I could exert myself now, it would stand me in good stead as the expedition went on.

Laval and I managed to set up three tents in the ever-dwindling space on the Col before some of the Sherpas and other members of the team showed up and took over responsibility, leaving us to get some well-earned rest and sustenance as the weather started to close in. All the group made it up that evening, the slowest taking thirteen hours. Thankfully, the winds were pretty light – albeit with the occasional huge gust as katabatic winds raced down the mountain – and we managed to get some rest before descending the following morning to ABC and thereafter all the way back down the valley to Base

Camp for a well-deserved break in relative comfort.

For the most part, we were really happy with our performances and the organisation as a whole. As always within a large group, there will always be whines and moans but there is little place on the mountain for negativity and persistence with this generally leads to marginalisation. There was one couple consisting of a hen-pecked husband and his particularly vociferous wife who were quickly becoming 'those people' but she was easily ignored and he wouldn't say boo to a goose.

Helene had bought me an iPod to keep me company on the way up, as I had found twiddling my thumbs for hours on previous trips a little tiresome at times. Though they'd been around for almost ten years by then, I hadn't had one for long and rather than download tunes onto it, I'd diligently loaded my CD collection into a library and uploaded it to the device. With forty-five hours of music, I was already listening to the same albums repeatedly by week two and I vowed to take more time to get that sorted prior to departure on future expeditions. (Truth be told, I have since done so and yet I still listen to exactly the same albums as I did then.)

There were a few books doing the rounds and Gavin had also brought a portable DVD player with him so evenings were spent in relative comfort in the mess tent at Base Camp, sipping tea and eating popcorn whilst watching a seemingly endless number of episodes of the TV series *Entourage*. Between this and card nights, we were fairly well entertained.

Days were spent resting or washing and preparing kit. I'd only brought the bare minimum of clothing with me so it was a good opportunity to clean T-shirts and underwear to prevent them becoming too ripe over the course of the two months we were on the mountain. The only downside was that, due to the cold dry air, any washing would come off the line frozen as stiff as a board. Conditions were such at the higher camps that you rarely stripped to less than two layers so whatever you left Base Camp in was pretty much what you would return in.

By 24 April, after three days' rest, we were ready for the next push. As previously mentioned, familiarity with the trail is a huge bonus as you are no longer left pondering how far, how long or how hard it will be. Indeed the only consideration you need to factor in is the weather which thankfully was still kind to us. This time we pushed straight past IBC, stopping only for a quick spot of lunch as the expedition had kindly left a cook and a porter there for us to refuel on the way up. Our small group arrived in good time having taken just seven hours all the way from Base Camp and, though tired, we were in good shape. The slowest member of the group took thirteen hours to reach us and subsequently had a unit of speed named after him, the 'Marino', which was best expressed as going only just faster uphill than the glacier moving downhill.

Dave was in charge of these back-markers and must have had the patience of a saint as he felt the seasons pass by during his plod up the hill.

The next day was designated as a rest day so we relaxed as other teams departed. The North Wall was easily visible from our camp and we'd track the progress of other climbers as they headed up. Once again, we were astonished to see people loitering underneath the serac which all teams were now well aware of and must have notified their climbers accordingly. However, once having left camp, you are pretty much on your own to do what you will. That said, if I was anywhere near as knackered as I had been on previous climbs and someone had told me 'You can't stop there', I think I'd have mustered the energy to tell them to go screw themselves!

Sadly, later that day, the inevitable happened and the serac split away from the Wall. Miraculously, given the amount of people up there, only one climber from Hungary was killed and a few others injured but no more than battered and bruised. Amongst them was Jordon Romero who, unfazed by the experience, would go on to become the youngest-ever person to summit Everest at the age of thirteen. We met him later in the trip when he told us that the icefall was so close to him that his ascending device was bent in half by the ice as it passed. Given that it would have been attached to him on a leash no longer than a metre long, he had a very lucky escape indeed.

Most of the fixed ropes covering the traverse had been destroyed in the icefall so there was a further delay of a day whilst a new route was made and new protection installed. The mood in the camp was a little sombre as we all knew that it could have been us caught in the collapse. However, my gallows humour learnt in the Fire Brigade lightened the mood a little when I suggested that this part of the climb should become known as 'Goulash Point' in recognition of our lost Hungarian colleague. Word spread fast in the tight-knit community and within a week it was commonly known by this name throughout the camp.

By 28 April, a new route had been found, ladders repaired and fixed lines installed so we headed up once again, this time the entire climb from ABC to Camp 1 taking just over five hours. It wasn't any less exhausting, but I was just able to make better speed, my body having had time to adapt to the thinning air. Upon reaching Camp 1, it became apparent that there had been a huge storm at some point as at least half our team's tents lay in tatters. It looked as if the yak who had been my undoing when I first arrived at ABC had donned a pair of crampons, scaled the Wall and run amok once again, flattening everything in its path.

We dug out and salvaged what we could before helping set up some of the spare tents which thankfully had been stashed there in case of such an eventuality. Some of the other teams had not been quite so lucky and had taken the full force of the storm as it passed through, destroying everything in its path and taking a lot of their essential kit with it. The forecast for the next day was marginal, but our way was to be a non-technical and pretty straight slog up a 40-degree ridgeline that would eventually lead into a rocky section where a camp had apparently already been set up.

Laval had shot off out of the blocks the day before with the intention of staying the night at Camp 2 and then carrying on halfway to Camp 3 before turning around and coming back to Camp 1. I therefore agreed with Gavin to head to Camp 2 and spend the night there. The following morning we split what gear we needed between us to share the load before kitting up and heading out. I'd decided to take a lot of my hamper including the *kabanos* that I'd been saving so that I could stash them at Camp 2 for the summit push, lightening the load for when I would need the most energy.

Again the altitude slowed our movements, so that it took almost twenty minutes just to get out of the tent and ready to go, but eventually we headed upwards. As the day drew on, Gavin began to drop back so, rather than wait for him and have to travel at his pace, we agreed that I'd head up and meet him at Camp 2, which enabled me to maintain my own rhythm.

As with every climb that I'd done up until now, every step on the mountain required a greater effort than the last. The snow slope was seemingly endless and the rock band that I could see in the distance seemed to get no closer, regardless of how much work I put in. However, after a huge effort I finally made it, much to my relief as the rocks offered some respite from the winds which were building from my right, whipping up ice crystals and making life fairly uncomfortable. Looking back down the slope through the spindrift, I thought that I could just make out Gavin who was a tiny dot way below me.

Camp 2 is fairly exposed with very few places to pitch a tent so the word 'camp' doesn't really describe the reality. It is rather an area of tiny rocky footholds spread over about a kilometre on an ascending slope of some three hundred metres between 7,500 metres and 7,800 metres.

We'd already been told that our camp was towards the top of the area so, in deteriorating conditions, I carried on looking for signs of it. After two hours more of thigh- and lung-burning effort, I finally caught sight of one of our tents on a rocky outcrop ten metres above me and just to my left. Already fatigued, it took me a further twenty minutes to make those last few metres, whereupon I collapsed, hyperventilating, into the tent, relieved to have made my goal.

As yet, I hadn't summoned the energy to do so much as take my crampons off so my feet were still outside the tent (it's a bit of a golden rule to never enter a tent with them on for fear of ripping through the material) but slowly I recovered to the point where I was able to get them off along with my boots which allowed me to finally zip the tent shut providing a wonderful respite from the howling winds.

Gradually, I sorted my kit out. Each little job required a ridiculous amount of effort, the difficulty compounded by a fuzziness in my head caused by oxygen deprivation. Once set up, I eagerly awaited Gavin's arrival as he was carrying the stove and fuel which would enable us to melt some ice for both drinking and cooking up the dehydrated meals we had brought with us.

As the afternoon wore on and eventually turned into night, the winds increased and it was apparent that Gavin was either in serious trouble or had turned back.

(As it would turn out and much to my relief, it was the latter. Two hours behind me, on the exposed ridge, he had been battered by the storm and was making increasingly less progress. Upon seeing me enter the rock band, he had realised that I was in a more sheltered spot but had doubted his ability to make it so decided to turn around and descend to the relative shelter of Camp 1.)

Once it became apparent that Gavin would not be joining me, I unpacked my supply of snacks and greedily chowed down two of my *kabanos* and a chocolate bar, hugely grateful that I had decided to take them with me. I had very little water left so I reached outside and balled up some ice to suck on to slake my thirst and lubricate my throat which in the cold dry air had started to feel like sandpaper.

Resigned to the fact that I was going to get no rest that night due to the storm-force winds, I made myself as comfortable as possible. Unfortunately, however, within half an hour of my having done so, an almighty gust collapsed the tent, breaking one of the ridgepoles in the process and pinning me to the floor of the tent with its force. Almost suffocating with the wind knocked out of me, I required all my energy to push the tent material away from my face allowing me to breathe. Kidding myself that this was just a one-off, I tried to make the most of the situation by pinning my back to the windward side of the tent, effectively supporting it against the force of the wind. But I had no sooner done this than another gust, roaring like a jet engine, knocked me flat on my face and I found myself pinned to the floor again.

Clearly, it was time to get out of there as quickly as possible before the situation worsened. In rapidly fading light, with only my head torch to make sense of the situation, I gasped for air as I hurriedly repacked my rucksack with everything that I could. By now the gusts were coming thick and fast, each one picking up the floor of the tent and re-distributing my gear, always it seemed just out of arm's reach. Still I did what I could, thrashing away in the storm like my life depended on it.

I was nearly finished and fully rigged when another almighty gust tore the tent to pieces around me, sending any remaining bits of gear into the air and over the precipice into the void hundreds of metres below. Among the treasures lost, I was devastated to realise, were my much-loved *kabanos*.

In the relative lulls, when the wind dropped from a hundred miles per hour to about sixty, I rechecked my kit and prepared to leave. It took me two or three attempts but eventually, with my head torch on but frequently blinded by spindrift, I clipped on to the fixed rope and started my descent. Though the rock band offered me some protection, once out on the ridge I was fully exposed to the fury of the storm which lashed me relentlessly, knocking me over time and time again. I was wearing a full hood and goggles, but the force of the wind found tiny apertures through which ice crystals would blow, filling my goggles and blurring my already poor vision. Powered by not much more than pure adrenalin, I slogged on through the night, cursing with every new gust that knocked me to my knees and swearing not to let it defeat me.

Eventually, to my relief, lights in the tents at Camp 1 hove into view. Encouraged by this, I continued descending until, some two and a half hours after setting out, I reached camp and collapsed into my tent. Laval was there and he gave me one of the most wonderful cups of tea that I've ever tasted. At the time, I wasn't best pleased with Gavin for leaving me up there, but I didn't have the energy to remonstrate with him. This was just as well as, come the morning, all was forgiven. Unfortunately, the night took its toll and I started to go blind in my left eye with a large grey dot in the centre obscuring about 40 per cent of its sight. We had been prewarned about the possibility of this and I knew that the only remedy was to head down the mountain to a much lower altitude. However, I had come too far to do so and, knowing that we would be returning to Base Camp for a final rest, I decided to keep it to myself.

Upon reaching ABC, I found out that two of the other climbers had suffered from the same plight and, upon telling Dan, were promptly sent down the mountain, not to return. The constant struggle to achieve the simplest of tasks had also got to Carl the Squid, who decided to call it quits.

Meanwhile, Laval had made it past Camp 2 and continued all the way to

Camp 3. He had passed my tent whilst I was in it, not knowing that I'd made it that far (while a number of other climbers who had decided not to tackle the climb to Camp 2 that day did so over the following days in better conditions). Following an overnight rest in ABC, I headed back down the twenty-eight-kilometre route to Base Camp for a good break before the summit push.

With a lot of spare time on my hands and surrounded by other adventurers, each with their own tales to tell, I started to wonder, *What next?* Lying in my tent pondering, I started to come up with a bucket list. I enjoyed the challenge of surviving in extreme conditions and pushing myself to the limit, but much though I was enjoying the climb, I wasn't sure if mountaineering would be next on my list.

The Seven Summits appealed to me, having already scaled two of them and hopefully crossing the big one off my list in the near future. But if I succeeded on Everest, would I be suitably motivated to tackle the other four lesser mountains, particularly since the Vinson Massif in Antarctica was horrendously expensive due to the logistics of getting there. The poles really appealed to me and Dave and Laval were also interested in skiing across Antarctica, so that was a possibility, but my yearning was to do something solo so that I alone could stand up at the end of it and say, 'I did that.'

The seed was sown on that day to row solo across the Atlantic. I'd read a little about other adventurers doing it and decided that I would row from the Canaries to the Caribbean upon returning back to earth.

The trip up to Camp 2 and back down again had taken a hell of a lot out of me so I was very happy to have a minimum of four days' rest before even having to contemplate putting on my boots and going back up again. Obviously, you want to be in the best possible shape when taking on such a challenge as this, but by now all the training that could have been done had been done so it was time to kick back, take afternoon naps and do as little as possible other than eat and rest.

Being at altitude is a sure-fire way to lose weight and it was fairly apparent that this was happening to me with my trousers getting baggier by the day. Our bodies are just like any other systems in that the more you ask of them, the more energy you require. My resting heart rate was normally around fifty-two beats per minute, but now, even lying down at Base Camp on a sunny day, it was beating at eighty in order to get the depleted oxygen around my body supplying vital organs and muscles. When the temperature drops, your body has to work harder to keep you warm, expending more energy. The combination of these two factors means that you end up burning a hell of a lot of calories just to stay alive.

When you throw into this mix a long walk up a big hill, the calorific deficit is huge and you simply cannot shovel in as many calories as you are burning which can be as much as twelve thousand a day. This makes the rest-and-relaxation days important to try and pile on a few extra pounds. Unfortunately, a side effect of altitude sickness is appetite loss which increases the higher up you go. It goes without saying, therefore, that it's essential to maintain discipline and remember to feed yourself even when you would really rather not bother.

Whilst sitting and chatting with Laval at Base Camp, he wondered what my thoughts were about him attempting to summit without supplemental oxygen. He was very much a purist and was thinking about achieving the goal of becoming the first-ever Canadian to achieve this.

Of course, in his mind, he was already doing it. However, he wanted to go over it with me as I was the only climber in the group who could get anywhere near his speed and we planned to buddy up on the mountain. After he had gone over the cons of the idea – including the increased risk of failure, frostbite or succumbing to one of the altitude-related illnesses and dying – we agreed that he would try but that we would carry a spare mask and bottle between us in the event that he should get into difficulty. Laval had spoken to his wife about the idea and she was supportive as long as this condition was held and I assured her that I would not come down without him. This was quite an onerous responsibility, but given his physical prowess, he'd probably be the one bringing me down!

As the days passed at Base Camp, we were constantly looking up at the plume on the summit which could extend as far as twenty kilometres and gave us a pretty good idea of the conditions up there. The forecast wasn't great with reports clocking wind speeds of over ninety miles an hour meaning that any exposed flesh would freeze solid within one minute and standing up would be impossible. The weather had been pretty nasty as far down as ABC with tents frequently getting blown away. Only the efforts of the Sherpas in staying there and maintaining the camp for us guaranteed that our kit would still be there when we returned.

The prevailing winds blow pretty much all year long across the summit, sitting as it does in the upper troposphere and being subjected to the jet stream, a powerful stream of air that races around the globe from west to east. For a short period most years, monsoons over the Indian Ocean deflect the stream of air away from the summit, giving far lower wind speeds and creating conditions possible to climb in. The weather this particular year was not looking good with no sign of the usual two-week window of opportunity appearing and, as the days rolled by, tension grew as to whether we would get the opportunity to make the ascent.

The problem was that the smaller the window, the more crowded the slopes would be due to everybody making their summit bids on the same day. The congestion that this causes can lead to increased exposure at altitudes that we're simply not built to be at, which increases hypoxia and leads to a greater chance of errors being made. Sadly, most climbers die on the way down from the summit, not going up, largely due to these factors and subsequent mistakes made in their dilapidated state.

There was some light on the horizon with a small window opening up on 15 May which would allow the Tibetan Mountaineering Team to advance above Camp 3 and set up the fixed rope toward the summit and another chance on the twenty-second when the wind might drop enough for two or three days enabling us to make our attempt.

With that in mind and in coordination with the other teams on the mountain, we split into two separate teams in order to try and reduce congestion. Laval, Gavin and I would form part of Team 1, with Dave bringing up the rear with Team 2. Dan would come up to ABC with us but would stay there to coordinate movement on the mountain.

Much relieved at having been given the green light, we prepared to depart on 18 May. There would be no rest days this time, just a straight shoot all the way to the summit once we left ABC. Needless to say we were excited to start moving towards our ultimate goal.

The weather was cold and windy as we set out on the now familiar trek to ABC with a stop at IBC. Although I had enjoyed trekking through the monumental landscape, I was happy that this would be the last time that I would have to travel this route, though it had become markedly quicker now to do so for all the climbers. Reaching ABC, we waited in anticipation for the weather report to confirm whether or not all the years of preparation and training had been worth it and, much to our relief, the forecast that we had received at Base Camp held and we would indeed be setting out on our summit bid.

The mood in camp was very buoyant as we made our final preparations for departure. By now, the grey blind spot on my left eye had shrunk and was hardly noticeable and I was feeling good about the task ahead.

The morning of the twenty-first came and, following breakfast, we headed to the North Wall. The weather was fair though overcast with a few light snow showers as we made our way up towards Camp 1. This time, Laval and I made the climb in just three and a half hours. Upon arrival, we found that the storms had wreaked havoc, but fortunately splitting into two groups meant that we only needed half the tents so we were able to use what was left without having to put up any others.

I shared a tent with Gavin who wasn't far behind. He'd suggested that I take a few Imodium that evening as the last thing you wanted to be worrying about on the summit push was needing to go for a poo, the sheer physical effort of disrobing and squatting at altitude being exhausting. We settled down to get as much rest as we could and tried to squeeze a few calories down us. Amazingly, as we were settling in, there was a knock at the tent flap – it was one of the Sherpas bringing us some hot food. Not having any appetite but knowing that I needed to consume any food that I could, I gratefully accepted the bowl from him.

For me, food is one of my real pleasures in life. I love both cooking and eating it and I'm always keen to learn new tips and techniques. What I didn't know is that if you leave a sack of porridge oats in a Sherpa cook tent for long enough, it'll become infused with the aromas within the tent. Thus as I accepted the bowl I got a waft of the wonderful smell of sweat and mothballs just before the slice of fried spam and processed cheese slid beneath the surface of the grey splodge, only reappearing as a special treat as I got to the bottom of the bowl. It was all I could do to hold it down but I was nevertheless thankful for the effort that these guys were going to.

After a relatively comfortable night, we headed out of camp towards the long slope up to Camp 2, not knowing if there would be any shelter left there. There were quite a few people on the mountain, but with a wider slope here, it was easy enough to pass if necessary, albeit at a snail's pace. It was a bit embarrassing if you were nipping at the heels of somebody and they were polite enough to let you pass, which involved them holding still whilst you unclipped from the fixed rope and then shimmied past them to clip back on and then set off again at a crawling pace, looking back fifteen minutes later to see that they were only five metres behind you. Yet maintaining my own pace and rhythm was really important to quell any frustration and conserve energy.

Thankfully, a Sherpa team had already been up to Camp 2 and replaced the tents so upon arrival we once again settled in, sharing duties of collecting ice to boil for drinking water and food as well as topping up water bottles for the following day. It was pretty arduous work, chipping away at the incredibly hard ice with our axes at this altitude, trying to get bits big enough to make a difference. I'd tried snow but, as most of us know, it's mainly air so a pan full of melted snow equated to next to sod-all once boiled down so wasn't worth the effort of collecting it.

We did however have a visitor stop by on the way down: Jordon Romero who had just set the new world record becoming the youngest person to have summited Everest. It was a pleasure to share a cup of tea with him, along with his dad and stepmum, the three of them having summited together.

With water boiling at far lower temperatures at this altitude (I'll not bore you with Boyle's law but feel free to look it up), dehydrated meals took forever to rehydrate but eventually we were fed and replenished, with water bottles kept in our sleeping bags to warm our feet and stop them from freezing overnight. We were now up at the upper end of Camp 2, close to 7,800 metres, so it was a fairly restless and uncomfortable night, far away from the big comfy mattresses left behind at ABC to save on weight.

The key to mountaineering at this altitude is to climb fast and light, carrying as little as possible and staying at altitude for the minimal amount of time. By now, therefore, packs were stripped back to around fifteen kilograms, carrying only the essentials for survival. That said, we were also wearing another fifteen-odd kilograms of clothing – boots, crampons, harnesses, down suit etc. – so were still hauling a good amount of weight.

We were relieved when dawn finally came and we were able to press on for the last stop prior to the summit bid. This was new territory for me and would take us well in to the 'death zone' above 8,000 metres. Some of the group had opted to take supplemental oxygen from Camp 1, but I felt good enough to continue without it until the final push. The pace was excruciatingly slow on the climb, with each step taking between thirty seconds and a minute to recover from, with my lungs feeling like they were about to burst out of my chest with every new exertion. However, step by step, we made our way.

The vertical ascent between camps was only five hundred metres, but it may as well have been five thousand, such was the effort required. Still, eventually the camp hove into view. Though the gradient for the better part was fairly even, I clearly remember a small step of snow and ice, no higher than a metre, just below the camp and how deep I had to dig into my energy reserves to get over it. It took what seemed to be an inordinate amount of time to do so and the feeling of having surmounted it was one of sheer relief.

Looking up at Camp 3, we could see that it was just a slope of rock and ice with very few places to pitch a tent. After some searching, we found about the only place possible which was on a slope of about 20 degrees and had a footprint about two-thirds the size of our tent. Finding the stash of gear that had already been laid for us, we got about setting up the tent which we had done many times before but which now seemed to be a very different animal with the wind constantly flapping the nylon as we tried to slide the ridgepoles through the narrow sleeves and the extreme altitude taking its toll. However, there was nothing we could do other than persevere.

We were now at 8,300 metres where the effective oxygen levels were around one-third of that available at sea level. This meant that, rather than a single lungful of oxygen necessary to perform a particular task, we had to take three making every movement extremely hard work. In my mind, however, I was glad to be doing this without supplemental oxygen – having got this far without it, it would hopefully give me a boost when I used it to continue to the summit.

With the tent finally erected, Laval, Gavin and I agreed that it was best for the three of us to share, saving the energy involved in putting up another tent and making it warmer with us all together. We then settled into a rota of harvesting ice and boiling water – one would do the work whilst the other two rested, then we would change over. This way, it took three hours before we had managed to replenish both ourselves and our supplies for the next day, but once completed we were prepared. Shortly afterwards, we collected the oxygen cylinders that we would need and set about fitting the masks and regulators, as we had practiced previously.

Upon checking the pressure gauge, I was dismayed to find my bottle was only two-thirds full but, after some back and forth with the Sherpas, it was found to be something of a Hobson's choice, by which I mean I could either like it or lump it! I was assured, however, that a further stash was available at Mushroom Rock, at 8,500 metres, where bottles could be exchanged if required.

The plan from here was simple. Laval, being without oxygen and having to travel more slowly than a lot of the other climbers, would set out at 23:00 that evening. The rest of the group would kit up and get ready to go at 01:00 the following morning.

Rest was impossible that night with a mixture of nerves and excitement along with the tent being pitched on a slope that required us to caterpillar back up the tent in our sleeping bags every fifteen minutes or so as we kept sliding down. Times that by three, one of them being a six-foot-six Aussie in a two-man tent, and you can imagine the scene. All wearing manmade fibres in sleeping bags, it was a wonder that we didn't electrocute ourselves from the build-up of static alone.

Laval 'Little Spoon' started getting ready at around ten that evening and, after a few manly hugs and backslaps, he was off and on his way, hopefully into the record books. Two hours later, it was Gavin's and my turn and, with the familiar effort and contortions, we got out of our sleeping bags, donned our boots and crampons and prepared for our departure.

The camp was now alive with the glow of head torches illuminating the coloured tents across the slope. The temperature was around minus 20 degrees and there was slight snowfall but thankfully only a light breeze. Once assembled, our group headed towards the trail, along with all the other groups converging with us into a single line as we exited the camp. Stupidly, I had forgotten to change the batteries of my head torch prior to leaving and knew that my spare batteries were back in ABC. I felt a wave of slight anxiety pass over me as I realised my error in the dimming torch beam, wondering if my summit bit would be thwarted by two triple-A batteries!

Fortunately, Gavin was carrying spares and disaster was averted! As previously, the 'conga line' out of camp was very well-ordered and mannered with a hushed silence as each climber concentrated on the crunch of their own boots on the snow and ice, no doubt all wrapped up in their own thoughts and dreams of the summit as I was.

In the slow mechanical march that I'd now become so accustomed to, I was surprised at what little difference the oxygen was having. When I first put it on, I assumed that I would be able to pick up the pace without the hyperventilating that I had experienced on the way to Camp 3, but it was not the case. Any exertion, as before, would still have me gasping for air, needing to rest in between taking each step. It was not the elixir that I was hoping for, but with everybody else in the same predicament, all of us moving at the same pace, there was nothing else to do but shuffle onwards.

Making way steadily through the icy cold night, we reached the First Step about two hours after leaving Camp 3. The North Col route has three such steps, a mixture of rock and ice vertical ascents which have to be climbed in order to reach the summit with a mixture of fixed rope and ladders for assistance. Given that the pace is slow, progress grinds almost to a halt at these vertical sections where each climber faces a head-on battle with gravity, oxygen deprivation and fatigue so bunching up is inevitable at these points. Happy with progress so far and grateful for an excuse for a short rest, we patiently waited our turn at the bottleneck that had formed, although the biting cold soon had us wanting to move on.

Being so early in the morning, no climbers had yet made the summit so there was no problem with people coming back down. Slowly but surely, I edged my way to the bottom of the first ladder in the slow procession of climbers, careful not to get too close to the climber in front lest they should slip and fall – an event which could prove very nasty for both of us, despite being clipped onto a safety line. At this level of fatigue, simply taking one hand off the ladder to move the jumar device upwards was exhausting and the temptation was always in the back of my mind to simply unclip it and work my way up the ladder, clipping back onto the fixed line once I was at the top. Fortunately, however, the voice of reason cut in and told me to not be such a bloody idiot!

The next stop was Mushroom Rock, the outcrop which is the 'oxygen depot' for most of the teams. Only fifty vertical metres above the First Step, it was a welcome landmark to head for, finding – as I do with any large task – that it helped to break the ascent into little bits and take each one as a small victory as I completed it. As you can imagine, a huge effort on the part of the Sherpas goes into caching these stocks so the oxygen supplies for each team are carefully looked after.

Upon approaching the Rock, I asked where the oxygen for our team was, but there seemed to be some confusion. The Sherpa that I approached checked my gauge. It was now showing under half and he explained, in broken English, that I had more oxygen in my tank than any of the other bottles that were available and that I should carry on as I was. To say that I was furious is a bit of an understatement, as I felt that it could jeopardise my attempt to summit. However, you can only argue so much through an oxygen mask, when even talking uses up precious oxygen, causing you to have to catch your breath every second word.

The Sherpa waved me on, saying that I had enough and, with the precession building behind me, I decided to stop wasting what oxygen I had, turn the supply down a little to conserve it and carry on.

I rejoined the line and we made our way towards the Second Step. This is the largest of the thee consisting of a thirty-metre vertical climb up fixed ladders. Any mistake here would be fatal as was evidenced by the bodies of at least two climbers, frozen in time as they were, victims of a previous expedition.

Much has been made of the number of corpses on Everest. There are now over two hundred and the question that I get asked most frequently about my experience on Everest is, 'Did you see any dead bodies?'

The simple truth is that, despite huge improvements in equipment, safety and climbing standards, Everest remains a savage, unforgiving and unpredictable environment where people push themselves way beyond their physical and mental limits in a way they have never previously done. Inevitably accidents happen. People die and, when that happens, there is little that can be done to retrieve the bodies, as even the most experienced Sherpa teams are unable to haul a body from the higher altitudes.

There was a story of a wealthy Japanese climber who sadly lost his life at around 8,500 metres. His body was very close to the trail and his family, desperate to get it home so that they could bury and grieve him properly, hired a team of twenty-three Sherpas to do the job. Yet while these guys are naturally adapted to high altitude and supremely tough and competent, they were able to move the body only two hundred metres before exhaustion set in and they had to abandon the retrieval. Meanwhile, helicopters cannot be used for rescue at these altitudes because the air is so thin that there is simply not enough for their rotor blades to push against (in the same way that we can tread water but struggle to tread air).

By now it was roughly five in the morning and we'd been on the go for four hours. Though tired, I was still feeling good and able to continue. As the queue for the Second Step shuffled slowly forward, I could see the lights of the climbers as they disappeared upwards into the inky blackness of the night sky. It was a pretty awesome sight – it looked like they were literally ascending to the heavens. My turn eventually came and, step by step, I scaled the ladder, conscious of but not thinking about the three-thousand-metre vertical drop to my right. About halfway up, I began to really struggle with my breathing, getting ever more breathless and light-headed as I climbed. I put it down to the adrenalin kicking in and tried to control my breathing as best I could, but to no avail.

Gasping for air, I was tempted to rip the mask off my face, but common sense dictated otherwise. The climber ahead of me, though moving slowly, was starting to edge away from me, and though it may have been my imagination, I felt that I could sense the frustration of the climbers below me. I then remembered that I had halved the flow rate on my regulator to conserve my oxygen supply, but I couldn't adjust the flow whilst hanging from the ladder and made a mental note to do so when I got to the Third Step to give me the boost I needed for the vertical sections. After what seemed like an eternity of gasping and wheezing, I finally made it to the top of the ladder to huge relief.

I found a spot where I would not be in the way of other climbers, sat down and ripped off my mask so that I could gasp in what little oxygen was there, unencumbered. My breathing slowed and I could no longer hear my heart pounding in my head. But I also realised that I could no longer hear oxygen coming out of the mask. The gauge was still showing above one-third full and the regulator was set to two litres a minute but still nothing was coming out.

It took about ten minutes but eventually I found a blockage where part of the regulator had frozen, cutting off my oxygen supply. I assumed that this had happened halfway up the Second Step, which was about the worst place you could imagine. Relieved to have found and fixed the problem, I donned my pack and continued onwards.

The first light of day was starting to break and with it I felt a huge sense of relief and reinvigoration kick in. The Third Step was at 8,690 metres and was the final obstacle before the summit pyramid. After this, it would be a straight shot to the top, a non-technical section that would take around two hours of continuous uphill walking on a 30-degree slope.

Again, there was a little bit of a queue to get to the bottom of the Step, but with the string of climbers having thinned out due to their varying speeds and this being the shortest of the three steps, it wasn't long before it was my turn to climb. The day had now dawned which further increased my spirits. Just being able to see what lay ahead of me made the obstacle far easier to rationalise – I knew that when I got to a certain point, I would be into the home stretch and, with this in mind, I decided not to turn the oxygen flow up on my bottle, partly to conserve the dwindling supply and partly because of the effort required to do so.

Climbing the Third Step seemed a lot easier than the previous two despite the fact that I'd been on the go now for seven hours. Shortly after reaching the top of it, I came upon a bit of a queue. This didn't make any sense as all thee bottlenecks had been passed; stepping out of line, I was delighted to see that the hold-up was so that people could get past Laval who was moving slowly without the aid of oxygen.

I can't express the joy I felt upon recognising him and I'll be the first to admit that I welled up with tears of relief and happiness. Strange really given that there was only one way up and down and we were attached to the same bit of rope so there was a pretty good chance that I'd see him at some stage! We were into the final furlong and, though still a long way off, the summit was within our grasp.

Eventually it came into view, a tiny pinnacle of ice and snow dotted with prayer flags and eight or so climbers sitting atop it. Then in what seemed like an eternity but – oddly enough – passed in a flash, we found ourselves standing on top of the highest mountain in the world.

Learning my lesson from Cho Oyu, this time I did manage to get my camera out of my pocket and take various photos of Laval and myself. I also took a picture of me holding a passport photo of the deckhand on the boat I was currently captaining and which I'd promised him I'd bring along (not exactly the stuff of Mallory but he was mightily pleased with it). I had hoped to find a small stone up there that could be made into a ring for my then girlfriend, but sadly everything was frozen firmly in place. On reflection, I'm happy that I didn't take a bit of the 'Goddess Mother of the World' as she should be left exactly as she is. Unfortunately, the weather had closed in by now so my view from the highest point on earth was restricted to about two hundred metres, but it was of minor concern, my thoughts turning to us both getting back down safely.

After about twenty minutes at the summit, Laval and I donned our packs once more and headed back down the way we came, meeting the other climbers in our group on their way up as we did so. Fortunately, the four hours between us ascending the Third Step and reaching it upon our return allowed the majority of other climbers to pass so there was no queue. Upon reaching the top of the Third Step, Laval informed me that he was losing sensation in his fingertips. I therefore said I would go down first and stand by on emergency belay so that I would be able to stop him from falling by pulling on the rope should he lose control. He started to argue that he would hand-rappel down in order to save time and energy – true, but ridiculous, as a single slip would mean certain death. Between gasps of breath, I reminded him of the promise that I had made to his wife and I'm glad to say that he relented and agreed to go on belay.

Shortly after leaving the obstacle behind, my oxygen tank ran out but, with nothing I could do about it, I simply carried on. I quickly became hypoxic, my mind hazy but my body on automatic so my recollections of the journey down are somewhat fuzzy. I remember the effort it took to cajole myself into taking each step and also remember trying to shout to Laval from the bottom of the Second Step as he was once again threatening to hand-rappel. I only remember two other things vividly, one of trying to have a wee about a hundred metres above Base Camp and being confused when it came out looking like hot chocolate due to my severe dehydration (my supply of water having long since frozen), the other of being on the final approach to camp and deciding to slide down on my bottom as I was too fatigued to walk any further. Unfortunately my crampons caught in the snow and I just flipped over, headfirst into a snow drift, and lay there unable to move for a few seconds due to my exhaustion.

The plan upon reaching Camp 3 was to continue all the way down to Camp 1 as remaining in the death zone any longer than necessary is a very bad idea. The problem was, however, Laval and I were simply too exhausted to face the descent even as far as Camp 2 so elected to stay there. It was now around four in the afternoon and I'd been on the go for fifteen hours solid. My head was still fairly fuzzy and I literally had nothing left in the tank.

The second half of the team had now started to accumulate in Camp 3 for their attempt the following day. This made things a bit tight as we weren't meant to be staying there the night but Laval and I made ourselves as comfortable as possible. The difficulty was compounded a few hours later when a rather large Australian stumbled into camp in a bit of a bad way and was also unable to make it further down the mountain. Between us, we managed to get Gavin's boots and crampons off and shovel him into a sleeping bag before getting some hot drinks down him which revived him a little.

Gavin still had some oxygen left in his bottle so once he'd settled in we zipped up the tent and cracked open the bottle to try and enrich the atmosphere. This seemed to help and before long I drifted off into a fitful sleep as night drew in, waking regularly to check on Gavin who appeared to be recovering and was just in need of rest.

Come midnight, the next wave of climbers were getting ready to depart and, though uncomfortable in the tent, I was mighty glad not to be amongst them. We could hear a bit of a kerfuffle from the tent next door and it turned out that one of the climbers, Frank, a German physiotherapist, was having difficulty with his hands and feet to the extent that he did not feel that he could make the climb as he was reliant on them for his work. As the rest of the team left, it was agreed that his personal Sherpa would take him down the following day. However he spent the whole night crying out for somebody to help him because his hands were very cold.

As you can probably imagine, I didn't take too kindly to this, having already been to the top and back and not really in the mood to nursemaid him in my exhausted state. A few suggestions of where he could put his hands to warm them up were forthcoming, but the whining didn't stop and after some reasoning with him, possibly followed by threats of physical violence (that I would have been utterly incapable of carrying out), he seemed to calm down and was further placated when we gave him the last of our chemical handwarmers.

Next morning, we were keen to get going early to reach the lower altitudes that we should have been at the night before. Having re-packed our kit, the three of us headed out, moving at a snail's pace but downwards nevertheless. We stopped at Camp 2 for a break, arriving there at around one in the afternoon and, having got a brew on and still feeling fairly knackered, decided to stay there for a while. Gavin had a radio so he let Dan at Base Camp know of our intentions.

It wasn't recommended, flying in the face of the climbing fast and light principle, but we felt OK in ourselves other than the fatigue. I can't remember the exact chronology of events, but during the course of that afternoon it became apparent over the radio that one of our second climbing group was in trouble and that they were in need of assistance. Again, I don't know the full circumstances, but Peter Kinloch had succumbed to high altitude cerebral oedema and exhaustion after summiting. Dave O'Brien and two Sherpas had stayed with him for twelve hours in order to try and effect a rescue, but their efforts were to no avail, almost claiming their own lives in the process.

I'd become close to Dave over the course of the expedition and was devastated when I heard what I thought was going to be his final message over the radio with his voice barely audible and faltering. My immediate thought was, *What can I do to help?* but the simple fact of the matter was that, although they were only five hundred metres above me, I was in no position to assist in my depleted state.

The feeling of helplessness was horrible and is something that sticks in my mind to this day. Many years later, whilst watching *Everest*, a film about the 1996 tragedy on the mountain when a violent storm killed eight climbers, a cold chill ran down my spine in a scene where one of the climbers radioed back to Base Camp knowing that he was going to die. The timbre of his voice was exactly like Dave's had been and sent unpleasant memories flooding back.

Fortunately, unlike those in the 1996 disaster, Dave made it back. He later told me a story of being overcome by exhaustion and feeling totally at peace as he lay down in the snow, effectively to die, but he dreamt of his sister coming to give him a shove and telling him to carry on, whereupon he revived himself and made it back safely. Interestingly, all the bodies that I saw on the mountain, discounting the ones that had obviously fallen, were in a very peaceful repose and looked like they had simply curled up and gone to sleep which I hope, for their sakes, was the case.

Obviously upset to hear about Pete, but hugely relieved that Dave had made it back to the relative safety of Camp 3, we headed to Camp 1 for a final night. The journey was an unimaginably hard slog after the exertions that we had all been through. Laval referred to it as a 'death march' in his journal, but thankfully it was uneventful. Upon reaching Camp 1, Laval continued onwards to seek medical attention for the suspected frostbite in his hands.

Next morning I woke up, as I often do, with a nice big fart (not when I'm at home with my wife, I hasten to add, but I didn't think Gavin would take offence). I was facing Gavin at the time that I let out my second early morning bugle which was abruptly truncated; at the same time, my eyes widened and a look of stricken panic spread across my face. It being extremely cold and still a huge effort to put all my gear on to go outside, a full ten minutes elapsed before Gavin said in his Australian drawl, 'Y'alright, mate?'

'Yep,' said I.

After a brief pause Gavin asked, 'Have ya shit yerself?'

'Yep,' said I.

After another ten minutes, the not-so-comfortable silence was broken by Gavin advising, 'D'ya think ya should g'aan sort y'self out, mate?'

To which I said, 'Yes, indeed I should.'

After ten minutes of dressing in various layers and donning boots and crampons, all the time clenching my buttocks for fear of the Imodium plug giving way any further, I left the tent for the last trip to 'Poo Point', a small col just outside Camp 1 where I completed my business (in the white landscape, this feature was visible all the way from Camp 3 by the end of the climbing season).

In no particular hurry to get down with only the final climb to ABC to go, we slowly packed up and got ready to depart. Frank, the guy who had problems with his hands, had made it from Camp 3 along with his Sherpa carrying most of his gear. However, the Sherpas who were not involved in the rescue were now required to help break down the various camps so we split Frank's gear between the two of us and set off down the North Wall for the final time.

Upon reaching ABC, we found the mood understandably sombre, having lost one of our climbers, and nobody was particularly keen on celebrating with a few muted handshakes and slaps on the back all that was deemed appropriate in the circumstances.

Laval had made it back down the day before and was being treated for hypoxia and frostbite. Upon returning to Canada, he had the tips of three of his fingers amputated, down to the first knuckle, and was not allowed to go back to his job as an airline pilot for some time due to the hypoxia having caused temporary brain damage and subsequent loss of motor skills.

Of the original group of twenty-three, nine of us made it to the summit and sadly one did not return. Only three climbers died that year, all of them on the North Col route.

After the camp at ABC was packed away for another year and loaded onto the yaks, we said our final farewells to the amazing support crew and headed back down the mountain for the last time. Within half an hour of arriving at Base Camp, we were put into 4x4s put on by the Tibetan Mountaineering Association and taken back down the long road leading to civilisation. It was a strange feeling, having become so attached to this landscape over the past two months, living within this community and suffering the trials and tribulations of the trip, for it to be over so suddenly. Even stranger still was the sudden sensation of speed; having grown accustomed to travelling at no more than one or two miles an hour, I was overwhelmed at seeing the scenery racing past at lightning pace.

Not only that, but as we descended the valley, we started seeing greenery again. After the monochromatic landscape of rock and ice, the sight of so much lush vegetation and the smells that it produced were quite intoxicating. Crazy though it may sound, even the rubbish tips outside the villages were fascinating with all the different hues of the various detritus.

The trip back to Kathmandu was thankfully very quick and I was incredibly grateful to get to my hotel room and close the door behind me for some peace and solitude. After a long hot shower, I dressed and went out looking for a barber to have a haircut and shave, but within ten minutes I was back in the hotel as I found the noise and chaos on the street too much to bear. Instead, I adjourned to the tranquil hotel garden to sit and relax for a few hours whilst downing a few medicinal gin and tonics. Comfortably numbed, I was eventually able to venture into town but I didn't want to see any other climbers from my group for now, being happy to just process the events of the past two months in my head.

It's a strange thing but I felt no jubilation or sense of achievement at the time, or indeed for quite a while afterwards. Whilst in Kathmandu, I was amongst other climbers, all of whom had a story to tell, having achieved pretty much the same as me. Every day on the expedition, you just do what you had trained to do, putting one foot in front of the other, so it was a bit of a comedown when that stopped suddenly and I found myself amongst all these other plodders who had made it to the summit.

I was desperate to get home to people who thought that what I had done was incredible and would give me the due adulation, which really surprised me as I don't consider myself a braggart. I have never sought recognition for what I do and have only ever done the things that I have done for a sense of personal achievement, so this was a bit of a shock, but I guess it was as much to do with the people I was with as any personal hubris.

As luck would have it, I did return to a hero's welcome from Helene and my immediate family, all of whom played their part in helping me gain back some of the sixteen kilograms I had lost during the previous two months!

Overcoming Everest and triumphing in all my previous challenges had an effect on my psyche, making me feel, for want of a better word, invincible. I knew that I could succeed where others might fail, which helped me to grow in confidence about my own ability to endure. With the idea of the transatlantic row still fresh in my mind, I immediately started planning for that. However, fate would intervene and skew me onto a different path.

PART IV

Back on the Water

Upon returning to the UK at the end of May 2010, I was staying between my parents' place in the New Forest and Helene's in London before I was due back to work in the middle of June. Helene had very kindly booked a sailing holiday in Greece for a week which I was really looking forward to for some much needed R&R, but whilst at Mum and Dad's I received a phone call from the Russian manager of the vessel on which I was employed informing me that my services were no longer required. It came as a bit of a shock as I'd really enjoyed working for the family and was under the impression that they quite liked having me as a captain, but with little else to do other than accept it, I put the phone down and told everybody the news.

Though I got on really well with the owner and his family, I didn't have the same relationship with the manager and had made the error of questioning his authority. In addition, I probably didn't do myself any favours in taking the opportunity to wind him up. I knew that he was surreptitiously reading emails sent from the captain's account so, every now and then, I'd send a false one out, knowing that if he were to react to it, he'd have to admit that he was intercepting the emails.

I took great delight in doing this, once asking one of our suppliers how quickly they could deliver five thousand litres of jelly as, knowing that the owner was away, I was thinking of holding a wrestling competition on the sundeck that coming weekend. A day later, I received an out-of-the-blue phone call from the manager (which was unusual), asking what my plans were for that weekend. He followed the call with an impromptu visit on the Saturday when he found me onboard reading a book. This highly amused me, as I knew that he'd flown in from Moscow specially to do it.

The news of my job or lack thereof put a bit of a dampener on my homecoming, but I was confident of being able to find another role. It would however delay my plans to row the Atlantic as it took time to build a relationship with an employer to be able to ask them for the time off to complete such a challenge.

During my sailing trip in Greece with Helene, I received a call from the owner of the boat asking me why I had left which was a little confusing. I explained what had happened and it transpired that the manager had taken it upon himself to fire me. Strange as this was, in the event the manager's decision stuck and I remained out of a job. Unfortunately, this was just after the market crash of 2008 so where there had once been a plenitude of jobs working for the ultra-wealthy there were now very few, with captains happy to hang onto their jobs rather than swapping and changing and opening up new opportunities.

I'd been pretty fortunate in my career up until now and was still footloose and fancy-free so I thought that maybe now was the time to take a bit of time out and attempt to row the Atlantic that winter, getting a major item off of my bucket list without disrupting my career and hopefully returning to a more buoyant job market. Helene was very supportive and Mum and Dad, though questioning why anybody would want to do it in the first place, were behind me. In hindsight, it was rather short-sighted of me, not appreciating the amount of training and logistics that went into such a challenge let alone the amount of cash it would require to get me to the start line. However, I bought a second-hand plywood boat and did a few training runs along the South Coast, enjoying the sense of freedom that it allowed me, but dismayed at just how bloody hard the boat was to shift when fully laden, leaving my hands completely blistered and ripped to shreds.

As I was about to find out, despite my yachting connections, fundraising for such an endeavour, particularly after the Financial Crash, was a very dispiriting business, most of the requests I sent out being either rejected or completely ignored. After one month of trying, I'd managed to raise £500 in a single cash donation and some new cushions made free of charge.

Having no income and chowing through my savings (mainly spent on wooing Helene) it looked unlikely that I'd make it to the start line that year. Whilst browsing ocean-rowing websites for tips and used gear to put on my boat for the crossing, I stumbled upon an announcement for the Row to the Pole expedition, an attempt to take a rowing boat to the magnetic North Pole for the first time in history during the summer of 2011. My interest was immediately piqued, particularly when I recognised the expedition leader, Jock Wishart, whom I'd known when he used to row out of Kingston Rowing Club .

I wrote to Jock excitedly, and sent him a CV of my past achievements, and was overjoyed when he replied to say that he was interested in meeting me. My plans for a solo row across the Atlantic would go on hold for now.

9

Row to the Pole

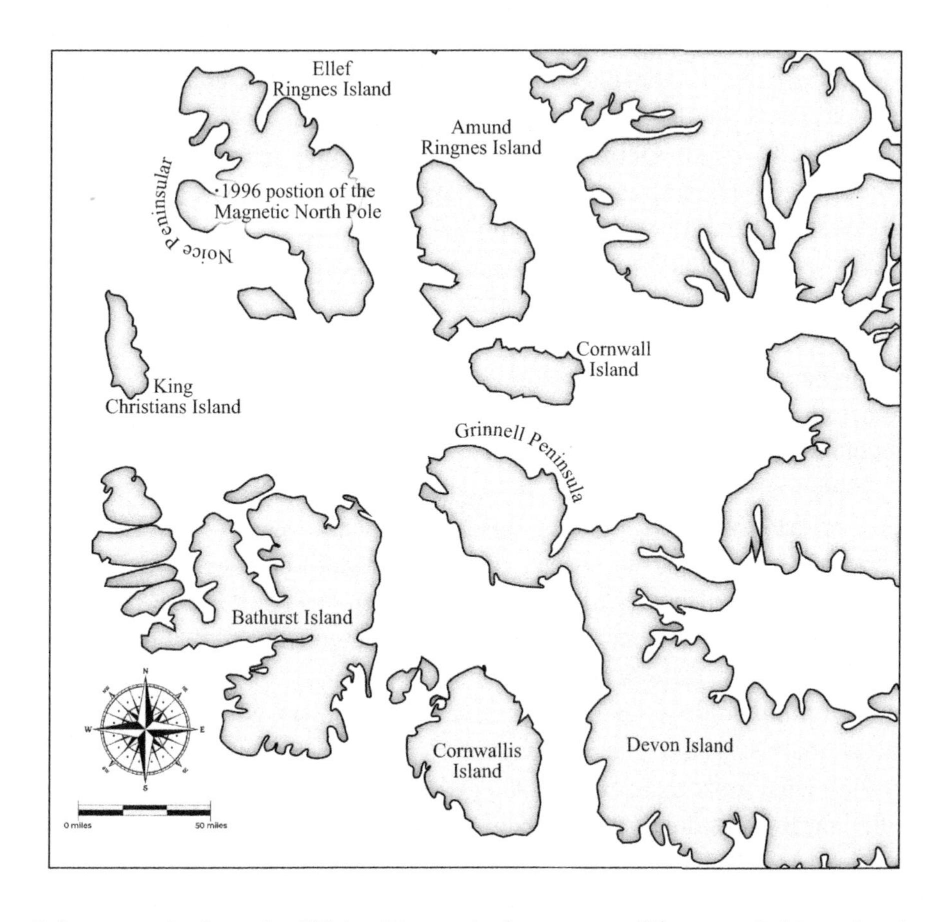

I first met Jock at the White Hart pub, just across Kingston Bridge, South West London, in early July 2010. As we chatted, I learned that he was a bit of a legend in his own right.

Claiming to be a direct descendant of Robert Burns, amongst other achievements he'd taken part in the America's Cup, was part of an expedition in 1996 that was the first to pinpoint the magnetic North Pole, skippered the vessel *Cable and Wireless* in 1998 when they broke the world record for a circumnavigation of the globe in a powered vessel, rowed across the Atlantic from east to west and in 1996 ran the Polar Race (a bi-annual race across the high Arctic to the aforementioned Pole), completing the journey twice himself.

As the story goes, whilst in Resolute Bay in the Canadian Arctic, Jock was waiting with the other competitors taking part in the Polar Race. To alleviate the boredom, he decided to take a rowing machine from the gym at the only hotel in town and put it out on the ice for a bit of exercise. Upon seeing this, one of his colleagues asked, 'What are you going to do next, Jock, row to the Pole?' This planted the seed of an idea in his head and in April of 2010, as I was heading up Everest, he announced his intention to do just that.

He had a major sponsor already so the building of the boat began. He needed somebody with nautical knowhow to oversee this whilst he attended to other business and, as luck would have it, it was being built at Rossiter Yachts in Christchurch only twenty minutes or so from where my parents lived. The crew at that stage had not been decided so I gleefully took on the role in the hope of securing a place on the expedition. Being somewhat of a tinkerer and an avid amateur engineer, I relished the role of trying to produce something to carry out a task that had never been attempted before and had about as blank a canvas as you could get.

The basic design had already been agreed upon and the brief was that the craft had to be both a rowing boat and a sled, capable of being dragged across the ice and housing the six crew in all conditions for a minimum of a month. It would also have to be of exact dimensions to fit it into the back of a de Havilland Buffalo aircraft that would take it on the final leg of the journey to Resolute from Yellowknife.

With my cold weather experience, I was also tasked with sourcing all the kit that we would need for every eventuality including manoeuvring the boat on land, trekking across ice and getting through anything that the Arctic could throw at us during the expedition. The basic design was good with the plywood hull being sheathed in Kevlar to resist scraping should we end up having to make our way through narrow ice leads and the bottom was fairly flat, albeit with sled runners attached for when we needed to drag the boat over ice. But this flat hull design had a major problem – namely, if we were in crosswinds, the boat would have a lot of leeway, meaning that rather than going forwards, it would skid sideways.

On modern ocean rowing boats, this is countered by having a dagger ard, a big fin that you can place into a slot that runs down the centre of the boat and helps you go in a straight line. However, with the likelihood of bumping into ice, I discounted this as a possibility as there was a chance that the force of any collision could crack the hull and sink the boat. Instead, I took inspiration from the Thames sailing barges that I'd often see close to where I was living with Helene in Battersea. Being also flat-bottomed to allow them to navigate in shallow waters, they faced the same predicament so were fitted with lee boards, big planks of wood that could be lowered into the water on either side of the boat depending on the wind conditions which helped to stabilise their direction. Outriggers for the rowing boat were thus designed and fabricated with slots, just forward of the rowing deck, that the board could be fitted into. The daggerboard board could also, with a bit of imagination, be used as an emergency rudder.

Next was the rudder itself. Once again, on a standard ocean rowing boat, there is little chance of bumping into anything so the rudder is fixed through the hull. However, this sort of design would be asking for trouble so instead the rudder was mounted on the transom (the flat bit at the back) and a quick-release system installed that would allow the rudder to pop up in the event of collision. This wasn't fitted until later but deemed a necessity after one of our training sessions but we'll get onto that later.

There were loads of other tweaks made and obstacles to overcome including how we would drag the boat onto and over the ice, how we would we beach it in the event of emergency, how we would we store gear on deck safely, what we would do to overcome the inevitable condensation problem, what the best method would be of generating electricity etc. One by one, the problems were discussed and solutions found until, by early November, the boat was almost ready for its first outing.

In the meantime, the crew was being assembled. To my relief, my place on the team had been secured and I would be responsible for the boat, the kit and the training of the crew. This included Rob Sleep, an experienced yachtsman and marine electrician, Billy Gammon, a sports marketing executive and ocean rower and Mark Beaumont who held the world record for the circumnavigation of the globe on a bicycle. Mark was also being employed by the BBC to capture the trip for a documentary. This left one position available and a national competition was launched to find the person who would fill the sixth seat onboard. There were over two hundred applicants for the position which was whittled down to forty who would attend a series of trials in order to ascertain the best fit for the team with a second place reserve position being available in case one of us became injured.

The last forty met at Dorney Lake in Buckinghamshire and were split into two groups to undergo both physical and psychometric testing throughout the day. The physical consisted of what was meant to be a three-hour session on the rowing machine split into 3 one-hour sessions with a five-minute break in between, although time constraints reduced this to two and a half hours.

Most if not all the guys assumed that we were looking for the strongest rowers, but what we really wanted were people who were willing to push themselves hard and would not crack under pressure. To ascertain this we casually walked around the room, asking the guys questions whilst they were slogging away on the ergos. A few of them snapped; one even told me to f**k off. He was only about thirty minutes into the first session but it seemed a shame to let him know that he wasn't going to make the cut at that stage so I let him enjoy the rest of the afternoon slogging away on the rowing machine for another two hours.

Others put in incredible distances and splits, but without pushing themselves to their limits. I wasn't involved in the psychometric testing, but it was very interesting once we had the results from both sessions to see that the candidates who impressed me in the rowing hall with their attitude were the same ones who came up trumps in the latter with about an 80 per cent correlation. This left six candidates who were on both lists and, after much deliberation, the sixth person was chosen – Dave Manns, a serving captain in the British Army and decent club rower.

With the team now fully selected, training began in earnest. Though we couldn't get anywhere near replicating the conditions that we would be facing in the Arctic, it was important that we bonded as, once there, there would be no turning back. Over the weeks and months that followed, we spent a lot of time out on the water, getting familiarised with the boat and its systems as well as developing as a team. The boat was kept at the far end of a big basin which emptied out in to the English Channel through a narrow inlet which became unnavigable at low tide so it was also imperative that we got the tides right.

On one particular training outing, we knew that we were cutting it fine and the swell had been building throughout our time at sea. As the tide went down the waves coming toward the shore were being amplified and the approach meant that we had to make a sharp turn to the left once over the sandbar. Unfortunately, just as we were making our approach, a large set of waves came through sending us surfing over the bar which was fine until the rudder caught the seabed which snapped off its mountings leaving us at the mercy of the waves. The boat went broadside to the waves and we were all thrown off our seats as it skidded sideways down the front of the wave, almost capsizing in the process.

Thankfully, once over the bar, the conditions eased, but trying to row against the tide through the narrow inlet without a rudder was impossible so we made for the shoal, jumped into the water and towed the boat to shore. Unfortunately for us, a journalist was on the shore watching events unfold and we took a bit of a slating in the press along the lines of 'British Adventurers hoping to go to the North Pole cannot even get past the Isle of Wight'. This stung at the time, but what they didn't report was that we regrouped, dragged the boat along the far shore to a point we calculated to be a suitable spot, jumped in and rowed our socks off for a good few minutes, gliding to a graceful halt right outside our 'office', the Haven Inn which just so happened to be a pub where we stayed until the tide changed which we took as a big win in terms of team morale.

Meanwhile, on the home front, Helene and I had been humming and hawing about having kids. We both loved our lives as they were, but neither of us was getting any younger and for Helene, having turned a very youthful forty earlier that year, matters were a little more pressing. She was away at a boat show in the US when I came to the conclusion that maybe we should just throw caution to the wind and see what happened and I resolved to discuss it with her when she got back.

Once she was home, we went out for a meal and a few drinks and upon getting back to her flat I thought that I'd broach the subject. Before I could say anything, however, she emerged from the kitchen with two glasses of wine and suggested that we threw caution to the wind and see what happened, stealing my big moment!

That was that settled, but I warned her that if she fell pregnant straight away I would not be there for the birth as I had committed to being on the expedition. She assured me that she had spoken to the doctor about it and that, due to her age and the fact that she had been using contraception for many years, it would not happen for at least a few months. It was therefore a bit of a shock when, a few weeks later, I entered the bathroom to find her sitting on the loo saying 'f**k, f**k, f**k' and brandishing a pregnancy test stick. Not exactly the reaction I was expecting, but I was mighty glad that it was her and not me who made the suggestion to 'see what happened'!

The tweaks on the boat were going well and we were all becoming dab hands at our various roles with all the necessary drills being carried out as time allowed. One glorious January day, we took the boat out to try the recently procured dry suits and practice man-overboard drills. It was a bright crisp sunny day with hardly a breath of wind nor a ripple on the water as we set out.

Once a couple of miles offshore, we decided it was time to commence the drill and simulated getting an unconscious casualty out of the water. Being one of the heaviest onboard, I'd opted to be the crash test dummy and asked Billy to zip me up. Once ready, I jumped over the side only to find that the zip wasn't properly fastened and went rigid as the 8-degree Solent water ran down my back and filled my not-so-dry suit. I learnt an important lesson that day and never let Billy near my dry suit again.

One part of the preparation that I found quite interesting was working with the BBC. They had a camera boat that would follow us for the first week or so to capture images of us as we made our way from Resolute, around the southern tip of Cornwallis Island and across the Wellington Channel to Devon Island. After that, however, it was deemed too unsafe for them to continue, being as they were in the only boat available, a twenty-six-foot open aluminium skiff. Even the local Inuit were nervous about going this far and never ventured beyond this point by boat.

What was most interesting was the number of hoops the film crew had to jump through to get there with a seemingly endless amount of risk assessments. I found this hilarious, it being an expedition to achieve something that had never been attempted before and therefore no precedent had been set. No accurate charts exist for the area north of Cornwallis Island and nobody had a clue what the tides did. I had been asked to help fill out the myriad of forms for risk assessments and when I got to a section in the paperwork about the risk that musk ox might present to the expedition, I pretty much gave up, there being much bigger stuff to worry about.

I had managed to secure pretty good discounts on a lot of the gear that we would be taking and, given that I'd done a fair bit of research on the best stuff to take, the camera crew were keen to equip themselves similarly. However, being the BBC, they were not allowed to accept the discount that I had arranged as they could not be seen to curry favour with one particular supplier so had to pay the full price. The last 'big corporation' that I'd worked for was the London Fire Brigade, ten years previously when a lot of time and effort went into everything from procurement of gear to risk assessments and command-and-control procedures and the decision-making process became overly complicated by lots of people all of whom felt they had something to contribute. This generally led to confusion and inefficiency. The beauty of it, however, was that once an incident was in progress, you could generally just get on with the job.

This situation was to be very similar whereby once the boat left the relative safety of Resolute all the risk assessments and round-table discussions would be meaningless. We simply could not foresee some of the hurdles that we would have to overcome and we had to pretty much make it up as we went along. This reminded me of a rather amusing quote that was taped to the wall in the office at Paddington Fire Station:

'We trained hard – but it seemed that every time we were beginning to form up into teams we were reorganised. I was to learn later in life that we tend to meet any new situation by reorganising, and what a wonderful method it can be for creating the illusion of progress while actually producing confusion, inefficiency and demoralisation.'

Petronius Arbiter 52 AD, London Fire Brigade 1998 AD

I considered myself very fortunate in my career that I was not subject to corporate culture and subsequent decision by committee which drove me nuts at times when seeing the amount of dithering that could occur over the simplest of decisions, preferring my own style of 'caring dictatorship' to make things work. It was one of my concerns about being on this trip and having to work as a team of six in very close confines and not being in charge. However, given Jock's wealth of experience in all matters polar, I was more than happy to bow down to him. With two 'Marks' onboard, we were out on a training row and Jock mentioned that this might become a bit confusing at some stage and asked what they called me whilst at work. 'Simple,' I said, 'captain'. I was Mark D from that day on.

As time went by and we became increasingly exposed to each other, we settled naturally into our roles. Mark B was in charge of camera work, assisted by Billy, who would also deal with media and marketing. Rob was technical; Dave and I were effectively the donkeys who would do the day-to-day physical stuff and Jock was there to organise the breaks every twenty minutes of rowing due to his weak bladder and to ensure that we didn't get too much sleep due to his monstrous snoring.

Jock had managed to convince a management consultancy firm to get involved with the project to assess each individual and propose ways of overcoming any potential friction or conflict, an approach called a Belbin test that I knew of but had never taken part in. Though the team was already picked, it was seen as a worthy exercise as once we left Resolute, we were pretty much on our own and would have to rely on each other for everything.

Each of us had to fill out a questionnaire. We also had to nominate two other people to act as referees; they had to have known us well for at least two years but could not be family members or colleagues. I found this to be a bit of a struggle as I'm not particularly sociable and don't really take time to foster relationships outside of work. I had to ask for an exception to be made and felt like a bit of a sad sack when I nominated my mum as one of my referees and Dave O'Brien – whom I'd only met the year before – as the other. All the questionnaires were gathered and a 'map' of personality types was made while our strengths and weaknesses were assessed. However, Jock, quite wisely, kept the results close to his chest until we were already in Resolute and about to set out.

Finally, Jock read the results out to our group. It proved greatly amusing hear what our friends (and family in my case) thought of us and to have our peculiarities and foibles as seen through the eyes of others laid bare. The overarching message of the assessment was that we formed a team that would either thrive spectacularly or go down in a ball of flames.

As for my own assessment, I learned that I may have been overestimating my own prowess and that a bit of humility and empathy for others every now and then wouldn't hurt.

One thing that it did throw up was that Rob and I would be designated the role of watch leaders, in charge of the day-to-day stuff in our separate watches of three, allowing Jock the freedom to keep an overview of the expedition and strategy. This would also ensure that it wasn't felt that there was only one 'Master and Commander' which was deemed as essential with quite a few alpha males on the boat.

Getting the boat to the start line was going to be quite a logistical problem, a supply ship only arriving in Resolute a few times a year when the ice conditions allowed. Unfortunately, those timings did not tie in with our plans so it had to be flown on a small transport plane from Yellowknife in Canada. That still left one hell of a gap between the South Coast of England and the North of Canada to fill. Trying to keep costs to a minimum was essential as Jock was increasingly out of pocket and I was subsidising a lot of the kit purchases out of my own finances which were also dwindling, as I had failed to secure any short-term roles as a relief captain. I'd taken on a labouring job in the meantime, installing bunkers on golf courses. This helped to keep the wolf from the door but didn't leave me rolling in funds.

The first part of the boat's journey was to be easy enough, shipping it in a container to Halifax, Nova Scotia, but that still left over six thousand kilometres by road to get it to Yellowknife. I volunteered to hire a pick up-and tow it there which I thought would be a great road trip. But offers of trucks capable of doing the job were not forthcoming. Even if we had managed to secure a truck to do the job, it would mean that we'd have a trailer and a truck left in Yellowknife that needed returning afterwards which just didn't work.

We also looked at the possibility of flying out to Canada, buying a truck and trailering the boat all the way to Yellowknife and trying to sell it upon arrival, but we simply didn't have the time or finances to arrange all that. In the end, the only way was to put the container on the back of a low loader and truck it all the way to Yellowknife which was the sensible option but nowhere near as much fun.

With the boat nearing completion and with obligations to our title sponsor, we had a couple of press launches to attend to, one of which was at the ice rink outside the Natural History Museum in London which had been booked out especially for the occasion. My dad, now having retrained as black cab driver and therefore very familiar with London, was the nominated driver and, though it was tricky, he made easy work of getting the boat to the venue. Shifting the boat off the trailer and onto the ice was a bit of a mission, but once we had it there we set everything up, wearing our branded clothing and harnesses that Jock had previously used to pull sleds during the Polar Race events.

All harnessed up and camera rolling, we were asked to pull the sled across the ice so on three we all leaned into the harnesses and… well, we didn't actually go anywhere. Having not been able to test the boat out on ice previously, it became apparent that due to its weight, any movement generated enough friction between the surface and the nylon sliders to melt a thin layer of the ice which, as soon as you stopped, would instantly refreeze, gluing the boat firmly in place.

After our embarrassment with the press when coming into Christchurch Harbour, it wasn't exactly the image that we wanted to present to the media. I could almost imagine the headline: 'British crew hoping to reach the magnetic North Pole struggle to get across an ice rink', but after a bit of waggling from side to side, the bond between the boat and the ice rink was broken and we got the shots that we needed.

By the end of May 2011, we were confident in our ability to function as a team and conduct all operations onboard. The boat was complete and ready to ship with all the logistics to get us there sorted. Laval had come up trumps with getting discounted flights for most of the crew to Resolute through the airline that he flew for, Canadian North, and we were ready to rock and roll.

In the middle of June, I dropped the boat off at the shipping company in Norwich. It was fully packed with everything I thought we might need and so that was that, there was nothing more we could do to prepare until we arrived in Resolute.

Dave and I were the first to leave in mid-July, flying up to Yellowknife to oversee the loading of the boat onto the aircraft. Along with us was Tony Woodford, a long-term friend of Jock's who had previously assisted on the Polar Race events and knew the lay of the land in the Far North. We were also to do some last-minute shopping whilst there, procuring amongst other things bear flares and other pyrotechnics that couldn't be shipped with the boat.

We were in Yellowknife for three days and I was blown away by how helpful and friendly the people were. If we couldn't find what we wanted in the store, somebody else there would and were more than happy to help out. I'd been used to living in London where if somebody struck up a conversation, you'd immediately assume that they were a lunatic or wanted something from you so to be in this close community was a welcome change. With a population of twenty thousand people, Yellowknife is the largest town in the Northwest Territories, a province of Canada covering 1.35 million square kilometres, over five times the size of the UK. It probably shouldn't have come as a great surprise, therefore, when on our second night we went to a bar and ordered a couple of beers and the lady behind the bar remarked, 'Ah, you must be those crazy Brits rowing to the North Pole.'

By day three we were pretty much locals and seemed to be always bumping into somebody that we had already met. But it was now time to depart so we went to the airport to supervise the loading of the boat onto the de Havilland DHC-5 Buffalo aircraft. The latter was first produced in 1965 and, while I don't know how old our one was, they stopped producing them in 1986 and it didn't look as if they'd updated much in the meantime.

They were, however, very reliable aircraft, used for servicing the small communities dotting the remote region, and ideal for the purpose due to their extraordinary short-takeoff-and-landing performance, requiring a runway of less than four hundred metres when fully loaded with up to eighteen tons of cargo and only three hundred metres to land with a similar payload.

When the boat was unloaded from the container and brought to the aircraft, it didn't look feasible that it could possibly fit, but as the day progressed, by jacking different parts of the aircraft up to change angles of approach, we inched it into the fuselage. The only thing that I can equate the process to are those scenes on wildlife programmes where a snake swallows a buffalo. We boarded the aircraft shortly thereafter and perched on the jump seats behind the pilots, separated by the bow of the boat which stuck into the rear of the cockpit. Following the safety briefing (which was the equivalent of 'in the event of emergency landing, tuck your head between your knees and kiss your arse goodbye') we were shown the facilities should we need to use them which consisted of a funnel poked through the fuselage. I didn't ask but I assumed that there wouldn't be any snacks or light refreshments served during the flight.

As luck would have it, I got a window seat though, in retrospect, there probably wasn't a huge amount of luck involved, there being a rather large boat taking up the centre and aisle seats. The views out the window, though fairly uninspiring, gave an idea of the immensity of this complete wilderness as it passed below us with mile upon mile of what looked like marshland that would undoubtedly be frozen for much of the year. We were routing through Iqaluit where we would stop for a bit of fuel before continuing to our destination and after roughly four hours we touched down at around nine o'clock in the evening with the sun still high in the sky. A quick refuel and we were off again, this time to our final destination.

Landing in Resolute just after midnight, we immediately got a real sense of just how remote this community was. It felt like the modern equivalent of a frontier town with not a great deal to see and wind whipping up the dust from the surrounding plains. It is one of the coldest inhabited places on earth with an average yearly temperature of minus 15.7 degrees Celsius. However, this was mid-summer, where the sun would not set for another month and a half, and though brisk, the air temperature was comfortable enough.

Though desolate, the place did have a strange beauty, to me at least, but I realise this was a tourist's impression and that having to live through its harsh realities and deprivations all year round would be something else again. Upon meeting one of the locals, he quipped, 'It's not the end of the world but you can see it from here.'

Though there are signs of sporadic habitation as far back as 1500 BC, modern humans did not inhabit the area until a program called the High Arctic Relocation was initiated by the Canadian government in the early 1950s at the start of the Cold War. Due to its strategic location and proximity to Russia, Canada was fearful of a land grab or argument over the sovereignty of the area so Inuit from Nunavik territory in Northern Quebec were forcibly relocated to these remote outposts. The community of Resolute, named after an Arctic exploration vessel, HMS *Resolute*, was established in 1953.

The first people (including one Royal Mounted Police Officer named Ross Gibson, who later became the community's first teacher) were promised homes and game to hunt. However, upon arrival they discovered no buildings and no wildlife that they were familiar with hunting. They were equally unaccustomed to the winter months of constant darkness which did not occur in the lands that they'd been uprooted from. They were promised that they could return home after one year if they wished but this offer was rescinded on account of Canada's fear of losing claim over sovereignty. Over time, the local population started to learn the annual migration patterns of the Beluga whale which allowed them to survive, but what hardships the first settlers must have endured is beyond the comprehension of most of us.

In 1994 the Royal Commission on Aboriginal Peoples issued a report acknowledging that the Inuit had not consented to the relocations and decreed that the Canadian government owed them an apology. This finally came in 2010 whilst in 1996 a fund of ten million Canadian dollars was created that the relocated families could claim on albeit with the caveat that they must acknowledge the honourable intentions of the government.

The year that we were there, the national census put the population of Resolute at 214 people and, though I couldn't exactly say that they were thriving, they certainly lived in far greater comfort than their predecessors must have done.

Once the boat had been unloaded, we headed to the accommodation that had been allocated to us. However, despite it being two in the morning, I was unable to rest, so excited was I to be in such an alien landscape. Whilst everybody else slept, I headed down to the waterfront where huge icebergs littered the bay which was otherwise perfectly flat and calm. Teams of husky dogs, tied up outside, were the only ones to break the silence of an otherwise tranquil scene with the occasional howl as I looked out upon the sea bathed in the midnight sun. It was a fantastic feeling to be in an environment that I had never been in before and it made me all the keener to start the expedition and delve further into the unknown.

The following morning, we spoke with the town mayor, Rudi Pudluk, who kindly offered us the use of one of the insulated hangars on the edge of the community where we could store and work on the boat so we arranged delivery there. Money for the expedition was tight and food fairly expensive at the accommodation so the first priority was to set up a kitchenette in the hangar. We had a stove and a load of out-of-date dehydrated meals, leftovers from previous expeditions, so we were OK for rations.

Given the weight loss I'd experienced on Everest, I'd bulked out prior to the expedition, gaining twelve kilograms and a belt size in the process, which I'd thoroughly enjoyed doing. Fortunately, my weight would be for the most part supported by the water around me and I didn't have to drag it up a mountain so there was plenty to spare when the boil-in-a-bag meals didn't quite meet expectations.

Once the kitchen was set up, we had to figure out a way of getting the boat to and from the water. We were a good few hundred metres along a gravelled road from the nearest slipway and the boat had been delivered on its cradle. Rather than employ a crane, we set to work building a trolley suitable to do the job.

For those of you who remember, there used to be a program on TV called *Scrapheap Challenge*. I used to enjoy watching the two teams battle it out, having been given a task to complete and a whole scrapyard full of stuff to build it with. Admittedly, they had chop saws, welding gear and a whole workshop of tools, as opposed to my hammer and adjustable spanner. However, we had a whole field full of stuff that had been accumulating since the community had first come into being so I was happy as the proverbial pig in shit, wading through mountains of discarded parts from the past decades.

We finally found all the bits we wanted, the front of an old trailer and the back axle and wheels of a long-discarded quad bike, and got on with mounting them to the bottom of the cradle which seemed to work well enough apart from the fact that one of the tyres had a major puncture and so needed to be reinflated every five minutes with a small bicycle hand pump. The process itself took about ten minutes, which was a grind, but given the generosity of the community thus far, I didn't want to push my luck by asking if anyone could repair it.

With all fettling on the boat complete and the stickers of all the various sponsors applied, we were pretty much ready for our maiden Arctic voyage by the time the rest of the crew arrived. They too had been busy shopping and came with arms full of trail mix, nuts and other treats that would be rationed out daily to supplement our dehydrated rations and were portioned into easy grab bags that could be taken out on deck for some quick calories whilst rowing.

I wanted to go through some final stuff with the guys before we set off, most importantly the effects of cold-water shock. One afternoon we headed down to the waterfront with our dry suits, donned them and swam out to the nearest iceberg and tried to climb out. After just one or two minutes in the water, our hands were completely numb while climbing out on the berg was difficult but doable. We then swam back to shore and disrobed, allowing anyone who wished to skinny-dip in the Arctic Ocean a chance to do so.

I was glad to see that, to a man, the crew ran into the beautiful clear and icy cold waters with reckless abandon, swam a few metres and then returned to shore, half the men they had been just a few moments before. A few of the locals were watching and that evening apparently one of the elders approached Jock and commented that the water was probably a little warmer than usual where we'd decided to go for our skinny-dip due to our proximity to the town's sewage outlet. Ah well, what doesn't kill you and all that!

Another part of our training was a requirement handed down by the Canadian Royal Mounted Police. This entailed what to do in the event of being approached by a polar bear and the rules of engagement thereafter. There are very strict regulations about this as polar bears are now sadly considered an endangered species. Their number one prey are seals and thousands of years of evolution have made them into incredible hunters who employ sophisticated tactics to stalk and capture the animals on the ice, allowing them to stock up on the fats that they need to build up in their bodies to survive the winter hibernation. Sadly, however, climate change has altered their natural habitat much faster than they have been able to adapt and there no longer exists the ice pack they used to rely on as their hunting grounds, making their skills increasingly obsolete. Starving, the quest of these magnificent creatures for survival is bringing them increasingly into contact with humans with predictably dire results.

Whilst we were in Resolute, a polar bear entered the bay looking for something to eat, having smelt the promise of food from many miles away in the form of dog food put out for the huskies. As it approached, the dogs went crazy, alerting the Inuit of the danger. The regulations are that every attempt has to be made to deter the bear and scare it away which was done by firing bangers close to it. This worked but two days later the bear returned, obviously starving.

This elicited the same response by the townspeople and the bear once again fled. However, tragically, it returned one more time. The law dictates that if continued attempts had been made to scare a bear away and there was a credible threat to human life, lethal force could be used on the third occasion and the bear was subsequently shot dead.

We weren't there to witness this but it upset me deeply. Firstly I felt angry and dismayed that this beautiful apex predator should have to resort to trying to feed itself by scavenging dog food. But far worse was that it was then killed by the species that had put it in that situation in the first place. After it had been killed, it was found that it had a tracker fitted and had travelled over fifteen hundred miles from Greenland to Resolute only to meet its demise at the hands of humans. Though at the time it seemed utterly unjust, we had to accept it as the way of life in the Arctic. We were no less guilty of destroying the planet than the Inuit, but we were shielded from the brutality of it.

The training video that we sat and watched was based upon lethal force being the very last option and would be part of a four-stage process. Firstly, if we were approached by a bear, we had to make ourselves appear as large as possible, slowly raising our hands above our heads and back down to our sides whilst shouting in an even tone, 'Whoa bear'. During this time, another of the group who had hopefully been alerted could fire off a cracker shell, a shotgun-launched banger. Should that not work and the bear continue to approach, a non-lethal round could be used to hopefully give the bear enough of a whack to make it change its mind. Finally, if all else failed, a lethal round could be used.

One useful tip was to make sure that, if using a cracker shell, the shot should be fired in a manner that, when the bang went off, it was somewhere between you and the bear rather than behind the bear as it could end up scaring it towards us rather than away.

We were carrying two stainless steel shotguns (regular steel shotguns not being deemed appropriate for a sub-zero marine environment) onboard to facilitate this, each with three rounds loaded in the prescribed order in case of an encounter. As an essential part of the training, each of us had to get used to firing the guns. It was pretty good fun, too, shooting at various objects out in the open, but the truth was that none of us wanted to have to use the guns in anger and they would only be employed as a last resort. Bears are naturally curious but generally easily scared away. Just like with the human race, however, it is generally the adolescent males who are cockier and more aggressive and are the ones likely to cause more of a problem, though if it came to it, I'm not sure I'd want to get close enough to ask its age or gender.

With our training complete and the boat fully stowed, it was time to say our goodbyes and head off. Conditions were looking good for departure on 26 July, but a subtle change in wind direction overnight meant that by the time we woke up next morning, the bay was choked with thousands of tons of ice – a stark demonstration of the dynamic environment we were now in. We were getting satellite imagery of the ice every few days so the journey was always going to be tactical, made in short dashes from point to point as the conditions allowed. This gave us a pretty good idea of the major ice movement, but, as we discovered, it did not account for the smaller local changes which would have just as much of an effect on our progress as the mass sheet ice.

A band of smaller icebergs could easily be wind-blown or moved by the current, bunching up at points and pinning us in in a matter of minutes, so it was essential that we remained on guard at all times. This was going to be demonstrated to us very early on in the trip.

Our first goal was to be a 'shake-down' row, just six hours of rowing in our two teams of three, progressing along the south coast of Cornwallis Island and finding somewhere to anchor the boat up for the evening to rest before pushing further along the coast next day if the conditions allowed.

By 28 July, the ice had silently slipped out of Resolute Bay overnight, leaving just a few of the huge bergs stranded on the shore, and we were ready to go. Waved off by a small group of local well-wishers, we pushed off from the small wooden landing stage and paddled out in flat calm water. The original intention was that whilst three people rowed, the other three would rest, the steering being carried out using a moveable footplate operated by one of the rowers who would be able to see any oncoming ice using a large mirror mounted on top of the aft cabin. It had worked very well in training, but there weren't many obstacles or lumps of ice to dodge in the Solent and this soon proved impossible in the ice-strewn waters.

The smaller the iceberg, the lower it would sit in the water. Even something the size of a washing machine would only just bob above the surface and was impossible to spot in the mirror. Even though it was freely floating, hitting something the size of that which weighs around a ton could do some serious damage so a better technique was needed. Eventually we boiled it down to the guys on rest taking turns doing hour-long shifts standing in the stern of the rowing deck and steering by hand, calling out if the rowers needed to watch their oars on smaller bergy bits. We had taken the precaution of cladding the edges of the oars in Kevlar, but if an oar should get stuck under one of these bergs the momentum of the boat, which weighed nearly two tons fully laden, would snap it in two. We carried two spares, but even so, we would rather not break anything so soon in the expedition.

The first day on the water was beautiful. It felt very special being out in such a pristine environment with not another soul or hint of human life around. We made our way through narrow leads in the ice, bumping and scraping our way between it before entering areas of beautiful clear water with the sun shining, stripped down to shorts and long-sleeved tops. At times fog banks would drift in, obscuring the sun, but they never stuck around for long and visibility remained good enough for us to pick our way through the labyrinth of ice as we followed the coast.

After six hours of rowing and thoroughly pleased with our first day's progress, we looked for a suitable spot to go ashore to cook some dinner and settle down for the night. Our first intended spot was choked with ice so we carried on. It was about eight in the evening when we finally spotted what seemed like a suitable place, a shallow-angled pebble beach in a slight indent in the coast, so we dropped the anchor off the bow and backed down the boat to shore.

This was done as we had previously practiced – to wit, two guys donned their dry suits and a pair of wetsuit booties, waded ashore and hammered in a metal stake to which a stern line was fixed and the boat secured, effectively stringing it between sea and shore. The guys were all keen to stretch their legs ashore so we decided to take the stove and cook dinner there, those in dry suits piggy-backing the others through the shallow water.

Being on a beach in the middle of nowhere, with so much unknown ahead of us, was a wonderful feeling and we were all in great spirits and looking forward to the adventure. We had pre-portioned the freeze-dried meals into packs of six which were chosen at random. All kinds of convoluted methods would develop over the coming weeks as to who got what, as some were more highly prized than others, but the lottery was always conducted in good humour. As with most expeditions, meal times were one of the highlights of the day, generally marking the end of the work, and the comfort of getting some warm food inside our bellies was always good. After dinner, we headed back to the boat and settled down for our first night onboard.

Strangely in hindsight, we had not spent a full night onboard together so it was all a bit of a novelty when we squeezed into our various compartments. Jock and Rob, being the shortest of the group, were in the 'matrimonial suite' in the bow cabin, along with the majority of the gear, while the rest of us were sandwiched in the stern cabin. The accommodation certainly wasn't for the claustrophobic, with two 'coffin bunks' which went beneath the rowing deck, and a double bunk right in the stern of the boat above further storage compartments.

The two guys assigned the coffin bunks, initially Dave and Billy, would slide into them. Once they were in, supports would be swung out and a flap lowered, extending the upper bunks to a man's length but effectively pinning in the two guys below who now had about four inches of headroom and just enough space to rotate their hips should they wish to turn over. It was far from comfortable, but the dimensions of the boat had been restricted by the transport aircraft, so we had to make do with what we had. After much shuffling and giggling, we settled down for our first night's sleep of the expedition.

About an hour and a half after settling in, having just nodded off, we were awoken by the sound of the anchor dragging. Inside a small boat this sounds very dramatic, shaking and juddering the vessel and making an awful grinding noise. We were quickly up and out on deck to find that our quiet and tranquil bay of just a few hours ago was now the thoroughfare for some huge icebergs coming back to reclaim their territory with the turning of the tide. The stern of the boat was still firmly tethered to the shore but an iceberg weighing hundreds of tons, carried by the current, had snagged the anchor chain and was dragging the bow, putting everything under immense strain in a tug of war with the stern line.

Unfortunately, we only had one anchor so simply cutting the rope which fastened it to the boat would only be done as a last resort as there was every chance of the anchor and chain being carried off, snagged as they were on the underside of the berg.

If cutting the line allowed the berg to untangle itself and drift past, it may have been too deep for us to dive down to retrieve the anchor. As far as I could see, if we were not to jeopardize the expedition by losing this essential bit of kit, there was only one solution so I donned my dry suit and leapt into the water, diving down so see where the chain was caught. It was a bit of a shock going from a cosy sleeping bag into freezing cold water with only minimal underclothes and a dry suit, but something needed to be done quickly before the situation worsened.

Having seen that the chain was twisted around the front of the berg and snagged on an underwater ledge, I climbed onto the berg, got to the other side and dived back in. Having attained a better angle from which to lift the anchor, I was able brace myself against the berg and haul it free of the seabed which was thankfully composed of loose stones and didn't offer a huge amount of resistance to a near-vertical pull. I was then able to climb back onto the berg, lift the anchor and loop the chain back around the leading edge of the berg and free both it and the boat, whereupon the crew were able to get the chain and anchor safely back to shore.

Lesson one for the trip learnt, we now had to decide how to moor the boat safely on a tidal coastline prone to passing ice floes. Foreseeing this problem, I had purchased three inflatable sausage fenders that we could use as rollers to haul the boat out of the water. We thus set off to find a suitably shallow-angled bit of beach, where we once again hammered in a metal stake and attached a block and tackle to the bow of the boat. The rollers were inflated beneath it and the strain taken up but, despite all of our efforts, even this relatively shallow incline of around 20 degrees was too much and we simply couldn't get the boat up the beach to a flat platform where we might rest.

Conscious that the more work we put into getting the boat up the beach, the more work it would be to get it back down again, we settled on a new scheme and, using a pickaxe that I'd brought for the purpose, we levelled out a platform only twenty centimetres above the waterline and parallel to the shore which would give us enough protection from the ice floes. With no tidal information available, I had taken the precaution of observing the tidal range (i.e. how much it went up and down) prior to leaving Resolute and could only detect a vertical change of about one metre. As we'd been working for about three hours by now, the tide should have only had another three hours to run so I figured we should be fine where we were. It was all pretty much based on guesswork but, taking no chances and no doubt to the amusement of some of the others, I took the anchor and walked up the beach where I buried it in the stones as a precaution against being carried away on an ice floe in the middle of the night.

After the euphoria of our first landing on the beach, this was a real wakeup call and I kicked myself for not having trained for the beach landing beforehand. However, this was a world-first expedition and there were bound to be some situations that we would just have to overcome and learn from as we went. We finally got to sleep at around one in the morning in bright sunlight, tired and feeling a little humbled by the experience but ready for whatever the next day would bring.

News from Base Camp that morning was good with more light conditions, both wind and ice, enabling us to carry on along the coast to the southeast tip of Cornwallis Island. The latter would act as a jumping-off point for crossing the Wellington Channel – one of the longer open-water passages of the trip – over to Devon Island, the largest uninhabited landmass on earth.

The day passed relatively uneventfully, though at times fog closed in and we found ourselves trapped in ice leads that went nowhere, which meant having to double back to find clearer water. At other times, we had to use the two aluminium scaffold poles that I had brought with us to help lever the boat out of the ice and push some of the smaller bergs out of the way in order to make progress. We confined ourselves to a relatively short hop as it was imperative that, even though the conditions looked good for crossing the Channel, we picked the exact right moment for departure as the fickle winds and ice conditions could put us in a lot of trouble very quickly.

In the afternoon, we dragged the boat ashore, this time with a great deal more proficiency, and settled in to await the forecast. Being on the southeast tip of the Island meant that there was far less protection from the currents which tend to slow as they run along a shoreline; we had been sheltered during our voyage so far. I was stunned to see the speed at which towering blocks of ice silently glided past our new vantage point. The thought of having to try and make our way through and across such floes only reinforced the need to pick the right moment to leave.

Sitting on the shoreline watching these monoliths pass by filled me with a sense of awe. Just being up here, looking at the charts and seeing the names of places which were so evocative to me, made me feel very privileged.

Having read about numerous expeditions launched in the 1800s by the British Admiralty to chart the fabled Northwest Passage – a sea lane between the Atlantic and Pacific which dramatically reduced the time it took to ship goods around the world – I knew that we were treading in the footsteps of giants. Of the charts that we had available to us, much of the data with regard to the depths and the coastline was collected during surveys carried out in those pioneering days. There has been no commercial value in updating them for modern use since.

The most famous of these pioneers was Sir John Franklin who led polar expeditions over a period of thirty years, mapping the coastlines and hugely expanding our knowledge of the area. Sadly, his last expedition was to be his most famous with the loss of the ships HMS *Erebus* and HMS *Terror* and 129 crew members after suffering for two years in the ice. No less than thirty-nine successive expeditions were sent out to find the remains of the expedition and any survivors, but to no avail. To this day nobody knows what truly happened to him, though it is believed that he died on 11 June 1847 near King William Island, approximately three hundred and fifty miles south of our current position.

We were well aware that Franklin had sailed in the precise waters where we were currently and must have witnessed the same coastlines, nothing having changed since.

The following morning we awoke to cold and fog, making departure too risky, but as the day wore on and the sun climbed into the sky, this burned off giving rise to more beautiful still and sunny weather. Though keen to get on the oars and make the most of these conditions, we awaited the forecast before preparing to get underway as these waters were known by the locals to be incredibly treacherous. The smallest of pressure changes funnelled winds from the north directly between the two landmasses, bringing with it fast-moving and massive bodies of ice broken off the main pack. The wind might be just about survivable if you were running with it, but rowing as we were directly into it would only end one way.

By the shortest distance, it was only thirty miles due east to Devon Island. However, wanting to make it as far past the narrowest part of the Channel and therefore a potential choke point for the ice should the conditions change, we set our sights on a sheltered bay fifty miles to the northeast.

With our forecaster giving us the green light, we set out across the Channel just after lunchtime. The weather was stunning with a bright blue sky and only the occasional iceberg drifting by on the otherwise glassy sea. On a few occasions, a light breeze stirred and we braced ourselves for conditions to deteriorate, but mercifully the wind invariably died down just as quickly as it rose. Being so close to sea level, the visible horizon was only about seven miles away so for long periods we were well out of sight of land and the feeling of being the only ones out there was beautiful. As the sun dipped close to the horizon, we experienced the magic of the midnight sun with not a breath of wind and just the sound of the oars dipping in the water to break the silence. Despite the fatigue of another hard day, it was a moment that I would gladly revisit.

By eight o'clock the following morning, we were once again in sight of land having made great time overnight. We pushed on and by ten were safely tucked up in a small, enclosed and ice-free bay. With the winds forecast to pick up from the north later that day, we were extremely thankful to have made it to this place of safety in such comfort, overcoming one of the more worrying parts of the voyage with such ease.

As we approached the Island, it became obvious why it was uninhabited as it was completely barren, low-lying and rock-strewn with no discernible features. Somebody commented that it looked like how one might imagine a Martian landscape, which proved a more accurate statement than we first thought upon later discovering that a team from NASA was testing a Mars rover not fifty miles from our current position! With a gentle breeze already rising from the north, we rowed as close to the gently shelving coast as we could, dropped the anchor and waded ashore with the wind holding the boat comfortably off the coastline.

We were all fairly tired after rowing through the night and, having been cooped up for so long in the close confines of the boat, it was a treat to lay out on the shore in our sleeping bags in the morning sun as we rested. This was to be the last stop for the camera crew who had been following us and getting some amazing shots for the documentary. Their fuel supplies would only take them this far and, with the weather set to worsen over the coming thirty-six hours, it was time for us to say our farewells as they headed back across the Wellington Channel.

Unbeknown to us, they were to face their own trials on the way back in rapidly deteriorating conditions and heavy pack ice, but at least it left them with their own tale to tell.

In our 'ration-pack roulette', the king of the puddings was the chocolate chip biscuit pudding so I was blown away when I found that the lads had been saving theirs to make me a birthday cake to celebrate my thirty-seventh year of successfully not having killed myself despite my best efforts. Presented in a mess bowl and adorned with peanut M&Ms, wine gums, jelly babies and even a few minty mentos to freshen it up a little, I was very grateful to them all for their sacrifice. Sadly, I couldn't do it justice and only finished about half of the two-thousand-calorie bowl of delicious chocolate goop. Given its consistency, I imagine that there may still be some there that we left behind.

As per the forecast, the winds freshened that afternoon and into the evening and we were very happy to hunker down in our safe spot with additional lines put ashore as the gusts built to over forty knots, accompanied by sleet and snow showers. Each of us had our own large dry bag for our belongings which could be taken off the boat and stowed ashore when we landed or stowed on deck to allow additional space in the cabins when we weren't rowing. Given that we knew we would be here for a while whilst the weather blew through, we'd also erected a tarpaulin over the rowing deck to provide a bit of shelter should anybody require some fresh air. By now, after three nights in the coffin bunk, Dave (roughly the same height as me)had had enough of the cramped conditions and opted to rest out on deck.

I'd brought waterproof bivvy bags to put the sleeping bags in should things get a bit soggy. It was perfect for him who, being a British Army man, was more than happy to be out in the elements rather than cooped up with us and it gave us a bit more room to manoeuvre within. The wind howled, the tarpaulin flapped and the boat swung around as we were battered by the weather; the idyllic conditions out on the water that we had experienced only that morning suddenly seemed a long time in the past, yet Dave stayed steadfastly on deck, happier out there than he would have been in the claustrophobic confines of the cabin.

The opposite shore of the bay we were in was only about five hundred metres away and I was wary of us breaking our mooring at some stage during the night so getting up to do regular checks meant that my rest was only fleeting. However the winds did subside eventually allowing me to get some shuteye. The next leg of the journey would take us northwest, following the coast of Devon Island until we reached its north-western tip, 150 miles away as the crow flies but considerably more in our case due to our need to keep close to points of refuge should the weather and ice conditions turn against us.

The strong northerly winds had broken up the edge of the main pack ice which was still sitting just to the north of our final destination and was heading down the Wellington Channel. Satellite imagery showed that it would not be advisable at this time to head out of the bay that we were currently in, although the forecast showed that wind from the south was due and would change this situation. Being anchored off the shore with the current winds keeping us that way, a 180-degree swing in wind direction would put us on a 'lee shore', meaning that we would be blown onto it which would be suboptimal to say the least. A decision was therefore made to ready ourselves for departure and, at the first sign of the wind changing, off we would go.

This proved to be a prudent decision as a few hours later the wind suddenly dropped, which was a precursor of the change. In the ten minutes or so that it took to remove the ground tackle that was holding us fast, the wind was already up to fifteen knots from the south, making the crew row just to keep the boat in position whilst the rest of us retrieved the metal spike and rope from the shore. By the time all equipment was aboard, the wind was up to twenty knots, with the gusts reaching twenty-five knots.

Rowing a heavy boat into strong winds is like rowing through concrete. Every stroke strained muscles and sinews as we fought what at times seemed like a losing battle in the larger gusts which brought the boat to a complete standstill. The five hundred metres to the opposite shore took just over twenty minutes rowing at full tilt which was pretty exhilarating and great to blow off a few cobwebs, but we were glad to land and get our ground tackle reattached to sit out the southerly blow which was only due to last half a day before calming down again. The weather was still a bit grotty with sleet and snow showers, but we did what we could to amuse ourselves as the hours passed by.

Come the morning of 2 August, the weather had eased and the winds were due to swing back to the north in the next few hours. Given the lull in conditions, Jock was keen to press on, though I argued that it seemed to be a bit pointless given that we would only be making twenty miles at best into the wind before we would need to hunker down on a lee shore compared to the protected bay we were in. However, he was determined to continue in order to make up the miles whenever possible as ice conditions might not allow us to do so in the future. It was a minor disagreement and quickly forgotten once we were underway and back on the oars.

With good conditions once again, we came out of the bay and resumed our northerly course along the coast. Picking our way between the loose icebergs, we came across a huge one standing approximately fifteen metres high. Keeping about twenty metres from it, we were surprised when the water turned suddenly from dark to iridescent blue – we were above a shelf connected to the base of the iceberg, which caught the helmsman unaware and clipped the rudder. It duly popped up as it was designed to do, though it took one of the locking cleats with it.

Not long afterwards, an eerie calm set in and a flock of birds that was resting on top of the berg suddenly flew off in unison. Moments later, the entire iceberg rolled over raising the enormous shelf that we had just passed over from horizontal to vertical and showing us it's true size. Had this happened minutes earlier, we would have been scooped into the air along with the shelf, the boat smashed to pieces and goodness knows what would have happened to us. It was a magnificent sight to see from our vantage point but we were reminded once again that we were totally at the mercy of nature out here and that the success or failure of this expedition would be down as much to good luck as to knowledge and expertise.

Twelve hours later, with the northerly winds starting to build, we decided that we would look for a place to stop and wait for the predicted ice to pass through before we got caught in it. A decent enough spot was found and, though not particularly protected, the water shallowed a long way out meaning that any larger blocks of ice would ground before hitting the boat. We were able to beach the boat very close to shore so once again we tethered it and set up camp. The forecast wasn't great and we knew that we'd be stuck here for at least forty-eight hours so we made the most of our time, using an iceberg rather handily stranded close by to do some training with the kit that I'd designed for getting the boat out onto the ice.

Basically, I'd had two metal fulcrums fabricated with large spikes on the bottom. They were hammered into the ice and had pivots upon which the two large scaffold poles could be rested. The scaffold poles had hooked ends which hooked under a nylon roller which had been fixed through a strengthened point on the bow of the boat. The two poles were then locked together at the ends, keeping them parallel allowing the bow to lever up clear of the edge of the ice and then slide down the scaffold poles, assisted by tension on the block and tackle which was fastened to the ice via a pair of ice screws.

That was the theory anyway and, given my vast prior experience of lifting one ton rowing boats onto ice floes, I was mightily relieved when it worked… well, sort of. It worked exactly how I imagined it might, it just took a darned sight longer than anticipated; the whole operation required more than an hour to complete and even then we only got the boat half out of the water. At least we knew we could do it in an emergency, but the reality was that if we had to do it repeatedly, we'd be better off finding a different method.

Whilst there, we also found out that our demand for electricity was far outstripping our supply. At first, we assumed that we had 'sprung a leak' and that something must be draining the battery. But after Rob had been through everything, he discovered that we were simply not getting enough electricity from the solar panels to power the equipment. We had done all of the calculations before we left, taking into account everything fitted to the boat as well as Mark's filming gear, and even then had increased the required solar panels by 50 per cent. As a 'belt and braces' approach, we'd even added a wind generator to supplement the supply to allow for the days when it was overcast.

However, despite having twenty-four hours of daylight, the batteries were still running down. We surmised that a lot of time the angle of the panels to the sun was not good enough to supply the equipment we had onboard so we had to start rationing, using only what was essential for communication, navigation and filming (the latter might not be deemed by most as essential but we had obligations to both our sponsor and the BBC who were partly funding the expedition). Billy wasn't even allowed to charge his mobile phone which was particularly galling as I'd just been introduced to a game called 'Angry Birds' which he'd downloaded and was keeping us amused with.

One of the biggest power draws, as on any ocean rowing boat, was the water maker, but luckily we had some quite big ice cubes floating by that we could harvest. This sounds pretty easy but it proved to be slightly more work than we imagined. At first, we just hacked off lumps from the nearest berg and melted them. However, the smaller lumps, which we could get closer to shore, tended to be younger sea ice and the water was still quite salty – it is only as the ice ages that the salt leeches out of it making it drinkable. It took a bit of trial and error to pick a good berg from a bad one, but the general consensus of opinion from our panel of expert tasters was that the bluer the ice, the fresher it tasted. Unfortunately, these tended to be the bigger lumps lying much further out which, during their ageing process, had become rock-hard. The only solution was for the donkeys (i.e. Dave and me) to head out to sea in our dry suits with a pickaxe and a sled, going as deep as we could reach and still touch the bottom, and hack lumps off the iceberg which we'd load onto the sled and bring back to shore raised above our heads to stop any contamination from the ocean.

Again, perverse though it may seem, I actually really enjoyed this work and it certainly kept us occupied, as we had to do it at least once a day to make sure that the technical and media teams had enough water to have a nice cuppa and wash their hair.

By the afternoon of the fourth, it looked like the ice was starting to clear and, with a bit of cabin fever setting in, we decided to set out along the coast to try and break the deadlock. Prior to departure from the UK, we'd studied trends in ice formation over the past five years. Though fairly unpredictable on a day-to-day basis, we knew that if we did not reach our objective by the end of August, we would not stand a chance as the sea would start to freeze over once the sun was dipping below the horizon. Making continual progress, therefore, regardless of how incremental, was essential to success.

The weather was fine with plenty of sunshine and blue skies as we set out in the early evening. The water was stunningly clear, enabling us to see the bottom ten metres below us as if we were looking at it through a glass window. After twenty minutes or so, we were stunned when a huge pod of beluga whales joined us on our journey, passing all around us and seemingly chaperoning us on our way north. There must have been at least forty of them as we glided through the crystal-clear water, swimming within metres of the boat. They provided an incredibly uplifting sight after our confinement of the previous forty-eight hours.

The whales stayed with us for almost two hours before disappearing, much to our disappointment. Yet what an incredible experience! I'd seen a lot of dolphins and the occasional whale whilst at work, but to have such a close encounter with these beautiful creatures for so long was another experience of a lifetime and once again I felt amazingly fortunate to have witnessed it.

We made good progress overnight, clocking up another thirty miles north. However, by five o'clock the following morning, the weather had once again turned against us so we looked for somewhere to put in whilst it passed. The waters were clear, with no threat of ice coming into the bay, so we anchored about fifteen metres from the shore and ran out a line so we could pull the boat in when needed for a stroll on land or to have a bit of food.

We had been onboard for just over a week by now and it was becoming clear that the imposed restrictions on the size of the boat were suboptimal when it came to shoehorning six hairy-arsed guys into it for any long periods of time. We had tents with us so upon reaching this stop Dave and Mark B took the decision to camp ashore to give themselves as well as Billy and me a bit of space. Jock advised strongly against this noting that the winds were slightly onshore and informing the guys that polar bears had an extraordinary sense of smell, able to sniff out prey from over ten kilometres away. The pair took this into consideration but decided to camp anyway, albeit with a loaded shotgun.

The beach that we were anchored off shelved fairly steeply so we all mucked in, clearing stones to make a horizontal platform, and pitched the tent before the boys settled in for the night in comparative luxury. There's a lovely bit of footage in the BBC documentary with Mark B interviewing Dave about the situation when the subject of Jock's warning comes up. 'Not a chance,' Dave says in relation to being approached by a bear.

Just before ten in the evening, Billy was sitting at his laptop updating the social media side of things when he suddenly blurted out, 'Bear!' I assumed that he was looking at something on his laptop, but as I glanced over at the screen he said, 'No, BEAR!!!' and pointed out the hatch at a huge polar bear cautiously approaching the tent with the guys inside completely unaware. The animal was about ten metres away, but by the time I had sprung out of the hatch wearing nothing but a pair of pants, it was within three metres of the tent.

With the instructions from the video in mind, I stood on the deck of the boat, fifteen metres away, and slowly raised my arms while shouting in a low voice, 'WHOA BEAR', thus also alerting Jock and Rob in the forward cabin.

Apparently, the bear had not seen the video or possibly did not speak English. Either way, upon seeing me on the deck, he decided that I was a much more interesting proposition, turning his attention away from the tent and heading directly for me. I can't say for sure, but I've got a vague recollection that the arm-flapping may have become a little more frenzied and the low calm voice may have gone up a few octaves as the bear approached. Fortunately, Rob was quick with the gun and a couple of cracker shells were enough to convince our furry friend that maybe we wouldn't be on the menu that evening.

Following the close encounter, Dave and Mark B seemed to think that sleeping onboard wasn't that bad after all. Jock was suitably amused!

The following day, we set out and headed to a bay to the north which would give us excellent shelter from any passing ice. Our copy of the Admiralty chart showed it as an inlet only open to the southwest which was perfect for the weather conditions with the forecast showing more northerly winds due. Upon reaching the spot where we planned to stay, however, all we found was a straight part of the coastline with no protection whatsoever and no sheltered inlet.

Having double-checked our position, we decided to land anyway and hike to the top of a large hill to have a break from the oars and get a better vantage point to see the ice conditions further out to sea. Sitting on the bluff overlooking the coastline and comparing it to the chart offered some explanation as to how the mistake may have been made.

In days past, prior to the invention of sonar, depths were gauged using lead-line surveys whereby a lead weight was lowered on a piece of string to the seabed and the depth ascertained from this once brought back to the surface. The measurements would be recorded and plotted on a chart, accounting for any tidal differences, and eventually a map of the seabed was made. This had the disadvantage that a big rock or anomaly could be missed, although this would be more problematic in tropical waters where coral reefs can grow over ten centimetres in a year than here in the Arctic where the seabed was scoured by glacial action and the water temperature made it impossible for coral to grow.

With the pressures of modern commercial shipping, popular sea routes are surveyed regularly and extremely accurately as the potential for loss in revenue due to inaccurate chart information is huge. However, in parts of the world such as this where there is no commercial value (yet) in surveying the sea bottom data remains based on lead-line surveys made a hundred years ago or more.

Furthermore, if a bay was choked with ice, lead lines could not have been used so a best guess would have been made using the contours of the surrounding landscape to gauge how the coastline might look. After all, who would be stupid enough to take a boat up there to refute the measurements?!

Standing on the hillside, we could easily see how this mistake might have been made if the bay had been ice-bound at the time of the survey and the mapmakers had been forced to resort to assumptions as to where the underlying coastline might be. In much of the surrounding landscape, the contours of the land continued at a fairly steady angle into the sea giving a pretty good idea of where the coastline might be, even if choked with ice. In the position we were in, the coast formed more of a shallow river estuary, familiar to temperate climes and incongruous with the surrounding landscape so, if covered with ice, it would be an easily made assumption that there was water where in fact there was coastline.

I'd been explaining this to the guys and Mark B looked a bit dismayed once I'd finished. He'd been filming at the time and was a bit peeved as he'd have loved to have caught it for the BBC documentary were it not for the fact that, whilst giving my wee diatribe, I was chowing down trail mix which didn't make for great viewing as bits of chewed peanut got stuck in my bushy ginger beard and the sound was a bit muffled by the happy sounds of mastication.

Mark was the consummate professional, employed by the BBC to make a documentary, and he knew a good shot when he saw one, whereas most of the rest of the team were there to get to the Pole (Billy being the exception and a lot more media savvy than the rest of us). There would be other moments where there was a slight conflict of interest in our goals, but we all accepted that and carried on regardless. Fully sated, I did offer to go through it again, but apparently the moment had passed.

From our viewpoint, we could see a good twenty miles ahead where an increased amount of ice was building. We weren't in a great position, but if we got the boat out of the water we would be safe from any ice that might come down the coast. Upon getting back to the boat, therefore, we once again beached her and hunkered down until we could next get moving. As luck would have it, that wasn't to be long and twelve hours later we were back on the oars and working our way northwest following the line of the coast.

The west coast of Devon Island forms a back-to-front crescent with a big knobble at the top called the Grinnell Peninsula which narrows the gap between it and neighbouring Bathurst Island to less than twenty miles with a couple of smaller islands in the middle of the channel, which is known as the Penny Strait. Given the large amount of open water to the north of this, the Strait acts like a huge funnel through which ice passes and was thus another of the choke points which could well put an end to our ambitions if conditions were not in our favour.

Satellite imagery from previous years confirmed that potentially this was one of the most dangerous points of the expedition. The good news was that if we were able to get through here we should have at least one hundred and fifty miles of relatively open water that would enable us to make some serious miles closer to our ultimate goal. The leg of the journey that we were currently on would take us to the last point within the protection of this crescent before rounding the peninsula.

The winds seemed to be settling into a pattern whereby they would die down in the afternoon and pick up again mid-morning. This meant that generally we'd set off late each day and row through the night. Initially, this had messed with our body clocks and, while the twenty-four hours of daylight allowed us to adjust to some extent, it became a little more difficult as the days passed and the sun got noticeably closer to the horizon, bringing colder temperatures and heavier eyelids towards the end of the three-hour shifts.

The novelty of the one-hour steering watches was also starting to wear off. Initially, it was great being out of the cabin with free rein to marvel at the splendour of the Arctic landscape. However, as time went by it became a bit more of a chore, particularly on passages of open water where there wasn't much to see. The worst watch to cop was the first one as you would come off your shift on the oars, often a bit sweaty and tired, then have to stand still in the cold for an hour, after which you would go and sit in the cold damp interior of the boat and never fully warm up again until it was time to go back on the oars. After some discussion, therefore, we agreed that we would take turns and rotate the shifts around. I had lined the cabins with foil-backed insulation in order to try and reduce the amount of condensation, but the outside water temperatures meant that my effort was largely in vain.

We did at least have synthetic down sleeping bags which offered some thermal resistance even when damp, but after a while even these became fairly saturated and offered little comfort, particularly in the coffin bunks where the cold and damp seemed to accumulate. Dave really struggled with claustrophobia in these bunks, but I thought they looked rather cosy, having dry-tested them when in the shipyard. I therefore offered to swap bunks to give him a bit more breathing space which he appreciated.

Keeping the boat on an even keel where possible was also important for the rowers on watch as rowing whilst the boat constantly leaned to one side was really uncomfortable. 'Human ballast' was used to keep us upright, which meant that the two coffin bunks had to be occupied rather than the comparatively sumptuous upper bunk in the aft cabin. Though bumping into bears remained a constant possibility, our stops ashore were becoming increasingly important for a chance to warm up, stretch our legs and give each other a bit of space. Having rowed through the night, we reached our next stop around eighteen hours after setting out without incident and, as had become our modus operandi, headed up to the nearest high point to assess the ice conditions further out to sea.

Meanwhile, back in the UK, Helene was on one of her regular trips from London to visit her friends in East Sussex when she heard on the radio that a group of explorers in the Arctic had been attacked by a polar bear who'd killed one member of the expedition and left four more seriously injured. I can only imagine what went through her mind upon hearing this, particularly as she was now eight and a half months pregnant, but she calmly pulled over and called our communications manager in the UK who gave her the news that fortunately it was not us but a group in Svalbard in Northern Norway.

Though suitably reassured by this, I can't imagine that it did a great deal for her nerves at hearing that a well-organised group who had set up a camp complete with tripwires to warn of the approach of bears could still be caught out, but in her usual stoic manner she accepted the information knowing that there was nothing she could do to improve my safety so there was no point in worrying.

We'd made good progress on this leg clocking up over forty miles in open seas. At times, the wind started to blow, pushing up a short chop which made rowing a little difficult as often one of our oars would catch the top of a wave putting us out of sync and slowing progress. However, these periods didn't last for long as we regularly approached bands of ice which soon broke up any swell that was forming. The leeboard that I'd had fitted also seemed to work really well in helping to stabilise the boat, not only allowing us to maintain a straight line but also keeping the boat upright which improved rowing conditions.

By 6 August, we'd made it to the base of the Grinnell Peninsula and, amazingly, the conditions were set fair for a push through the Penny Strait with the satellite imagery showing broken ice and the forecast still in our favour with only light winds predicted. As before, over the following days we made short hops up and around the bottom of the peninsula, edging ourselves towards a point where we would have to commit to a long and exposed passage around it.

On the afternoon of 7 August, we rounded a part of the coastline that led to a large bay where a colony of walrus were sunning themselves on a beach approximately five hundred metres away. We were all excited to see the creatures and edged into the bay for a closer look. About three hundred metres out, we saw a few of the bigger creatures lollop across the beach and slide into the ocean. We thought nothing of it until, a few moments later, three huge-tusked male bulls surfaced close to the boat, snorting and barking at us, obviously not best pleased about our proximity to the colony of females and pups.

Given their agility in the water and immense size – male bulls growing in excess of three and a half metres long and weighing over one and a half tons – we took their increasing aggression as our cue to turn around and get out of there, fairly briskly as it happened, and though our curiosity was sated, we made a note to keep a rather more respectful distance in the future.

By 8 August, we were in a good position to round the top of the peninsula and, after a short stop for some food and to gather all the possible meteorological and ice information that we could, we decided to make the big push through the Strait and around to the northern tip of the island. It appeared that we had a forty-eight-hour period in which to make the sixty-mile passage which, if all went well, was well within our capabilities as we had been clocking up averages of over two knots on all other clear passages. We had made excellent time up until then and were well ahead of where we expected to be so Jock insisted on stopping off at a rock cairn, erected in the name of Sir John Barrow, a geographer and very influential figure in polar exploration in the early 1800s.

Born in 1764, Barrow was not from a wealthy background, being the only son of a tanner in a village in Lancashire. Fortunately for him, he was a gifted pupil and gained a place at a local grammar school where he excelled in mathematics. Yet he left school at the age of thirteen to found a Sunday school for poor local children, during which time he also served as a clerk at an iron foundry in Liverpool.

At the age of sixteen, he joined a whaling expedition to Greenland. Four years later, he took a job teaching mathematics at a private school in Greenwich. One of his pupils at the school was the son of Sir George Leonard Staunton whose influence helped him gain a position in the first British embassy to

China in 1792. During his time abroad, he acquired a good knowledge of the Chinese language and was frequently consulted by the British Government on Chinese affairs.

In 1797, he took a post in South Africa and was later appointed auditor-general of public accounts for the new colony of the Cape of Good Hope. In 1800, he bought a house in Cape Town, planning to settle there, but political unrest would dictate otherwise.

He returned to Britain in 1804 and was appointed as Second Secretary to the Admiralty, a post that he held for a further forty years. It was a time of relative peace for the British Navy and there were a lot of boats and men to spare. Barrow was a great advocate of exploration and, having gained a huge amount of respect from the eleven chief lords who presided successively on the Admiralty board and indeed King William IV, he promoted many now legendary names in polar exploration including John Ross, William Edward Parry, James Clark Ross and the aforementioned John Franklin.

Nowadays, Barrow receives mixed reviews. Some claim that his thirst for exploration led to the loss of the lives of many men in the quest of a pointless dream, but one thing that cannot be disputed is the fact that his belief led to a far greater understanding of these regions. Not bad for the son of a tanner!

Upon visiting the cairn, we were treated to an incredible view of the Arctic Ocean, stretching out in every direction, a vast deep blue expanse interspersed with thousands of icebergs, all illuminated by bright sunshine beneath clear blue skies. Moved by the sight, Billy commented, 'There in front of us lay two very different sides to the Arctic, on the one hand calm turquoise water, on the other menacing-looking ice fields which we'll shortly have to navigate through.'

Returning to the boat, keen to push on, we cast off for the next leg, past Spit Island and around to the north of Devon Island. We knew from the forecasts that though the winds would be light, the ice would be starting to accumulate on the shore here so it was imperative that we made good progress before our window of opportunity closed. Opting not to stop, we carefully navigated our way through the ice leads which became narrower by the hour.

The greatest danger for us was closer to the coast where the ice would concertina with the potential to crush us if we were caught in a sudden change in wind direction or current. Increasingly, ice leads that we had passed through began to close behind us. The problem was that though we had made great progress and were very close to where we wanted to get to, we were still a mile off the shoreline and the entire coastline was becoming choked with ever-larger pieces of ice, affording us little chance of landing there. We would see potential leads open up, only to be thwarted by the movement of the ice as we approached. However, eventually we made our way though and reached land two days after setting out.

It was with a small amount of relief when we heard that the weather and ice conditions were set in for at least the next thirty-six hours. This would allow us a bit of time to recuperate, though in the back of my mind was the thought that we were on a lee shore with the ice constantly piling up upon it. Despite all the historical records, there was really no telling what the Arctic might have in store for us. All we could do was sit and hope for a change for the next leg.

Our final destination now only lay one hundred and fifty miles to the northwest of us as the crow flew. However, we would have to take a circuitous route to get there, first heading northeast before making a large arc back to the northwest and heading around the Noice Peninsula which would present a final obstacle, giving a total journey distance of two hundred and fifty miles.

The good news was that with two hundred and fifty miles already behind us, we were already past the halfway point and all still in good spirits with the kit holding up well also. The weather here was decidedly colder and more changeable and, as the sun dropped lower in the sky each night, temperatures fell towards zero, exacerbated by the northerly wind which blew directly off of the polar ice sheet. Reading this back to myself now, I find it quite funny to think that in the UK during a cold spell when the northerly wind gets up everybody puts on their woolly hats and comments that the gale has come 'straight from the Arctic'. Yet here we were, in the Arctic feeling the effects of the same wind coming pretty much from the other side of the hill.

The enforced forty-eight-hour sojourn had us marching up to the top of the surrounding peaks at least three times a day, looking wistfully out to sea in the hope of seeing an easing in the conditions which would allow us to make the next short hop to Table Island, twelve miles to the northeast. Though not ideal for any kind of protection, this would at least get us clear of the coast of Devon Island and provide a much better springing-off point if and when the conditions cleared.

It was incredible, sitting on top of a hill and watching how quickly the ice leads changed. We'd pick out potential leads which looked really promising only to return our gaze ten minutes later to find that they had disappeared; certainly not the conditions we wanted to be setting out in. The walks did do us good, however, allowing us to get out and away from the boat for a bit of personal space and experience more of the terrain. On one of their treks, a couple of the guys even found a den of Arctic wolves.

By the end of the second day, some of us were getting restless and becoming keen to press on, badgering Jock to see what we could do. We agreed that conditions were marginal, but with the ever-present clock of the changing of the seasons ticking away in the background, we were very reluctant to sit still for too long. Accordingly, seizing what we thought was an opportunity, we got into the boat and headed for Table Island. We made it about a mile offshore before encountering the first band of ice through which, we were dismayed to see, there was simply no passage.

Rowing up and down it in the hope of finding a lead yielded no success so we continued east in what water we could find. Pretty soon the whole ocean started to close up around us and to compound matters a heavy fog enclosed us meaning that we now had no sight of the land and no real idea of which direction to travel. We battled on for six more hours, finding ourselves in dead end after dead end, at times caught in pools where the leads had closed up behind us. We also spotted a large polar bear on the ice, no doubt hunting seals, which put us all on high alert. But it seemed that whichever direction we tried to go in, we found ourselves stuck fast.

I wasn't too worried as I knew that if necessary we could haul the boat out onto the ice and just have to go wherever it took us. However, this feeling was short-lived as we travelled further east and heard the distant cracking and grinding of ice as the bergs collided with one another, piled up we assumed against some uncharted shoal or headland. In the fog, the noises sounded quite uncanny if not a little disturbing.

With the limited visibility compounding our concerns, we decided to give up on the idea of Table Island and get back to shore by whatever means we could, preferably away from the noises we could hear ahead of us. There was a moment of brief comical respite when a ringed seal popped up onto the ice just ahead of us and looked at us quizzically as if to say, 'What do you bunch of idiots think you're doing out here?' The same seal (or so I assumed) popped up a few more times with the same expression and, if that was indeed what it was thinking, I'd have been inclined to agree.

Eventually we got back to shore having spent ten hours making the magnificent total of three miles' progress and putting us in a much worse mooring spot than we'd been in previously. Though no one expressed any dissatisfaction openly, it was a bit of a slap on the wrist for me, being the main instigator of the 'let's get going' movement, and rightly deserved though truth be told I was quite glad to have had a bit of excitement.

It was another two days of waiting in grey and changeable weather before we got the break we needed. It was only a little one but we decided to make the most of it and were grateful to finally be leaving Devon Island behind us. As we'd headed further north, the landscape had been changing from low-lying barren landscapes to higher, more dramatic cliffs and valleys. After eight hours of weaving between icebergs and frequent diversions around huge islands of pack ice that stood in our way, we were therefore a bit disappointed to reach Table Island and find what looked like a big lump of mud in the middle of the ocean.

We made several attempts to land, each time ending up to our knees in thick, cloying alluvial deposits and covering everything onboard in the same stuff as we did so. In the end we found a suitably lodged iceberg to tie up to which was big enough to stroll around. Due to our power generation or lack thereof, we were still having to use the ice as our water supply and were pleased to find that pools of meltwater had formed on top of the berg we were attached to. This allowed us to replenish our supply and, though the water was still a little brackish, it was at least drinkable.

Time was marching on and there had been a definite change in temperature over the past week as we headed towards the first days of autumn. Even though we had only been away for just over two weeks, the difference in seasons at these latitudes is very much more marked. Inevitably, this led to greater anxiety over our chances of success, knowing that we only had a few more weeks before the ice conditions would make success impossible. Thus sitting there tied to the equivalent of a cow pat in the middle of the Arctic Ocean didn't do a great deal for morale, even though we all knew that there was nothing we could do but hope for better weather.

We were stuck on Table Island for a further two days before we received the news we had been waiting for, with a window of opportunity for further progress opening up.

We'd had plenty of time to discuss the plan ahead and had already decided that, should the opportunity arise, we would try and make a large push across the Belcher Channel to Cornwall Island and then continue on to Ellef Ringnes Island, just off the coast of which the 1996 position of the magnetic North Pole lay.

Just after breakfast on 17 August, we set out towards Cornwall Island. The winds had changed direction and the ice that had been plaguing us for the previous week had all but disappeared. We made the relatively short hop in great time, arriving at the Island in mid-afternoon. One of our sponsors was a golf club in Cornwall that Billy had strong ties to, so, as promised to them, we had a quick stop on a sandy beach for a bite to eat and for Billy to pull out a golf club and a makeshift pitch and putt was set up for possibly the most northerly game of golf ever played. I didn't quite make the cut due to the proximity of bunkers and water hazards which seemed to be quite prevalent on this particular course but a few of the other boys made a much better go of it. With no clubhouse at the eighteenth to celebrate in, we pressed on, this time to tackle the largest stretch of open water to date, the seventy-mile stretch to Ellef Ringnes Island.

The waters were thankfully fairly ice-free with only a few small isolated patches to negotiate. This didn't stop a few of the crew colliding with the occasional lump, just to keep us on our toes, while Jock seemed to have developed an uncanny sixth sense, able to find the smallest berg in the clearest patches of sea and subsequently hit it. What little wind there was only formed small waves which were little impediment to us. However, it did give us great early warning as to approaching ice bands as the waves would quell upon approach, not having had any distance to build up in.

By midday on the nineteenth, relatively unimpeded, we'd managed to take a massive chunk out of the journey having covered 105 miles in the fifty-two hours since leaving Table Island. Our original plan was to make landfall on the southern tip of Ellef Ringnes and rest before heading up the west coast, but as we approached the island it seemed that the whole coastline was choked with ice pushed up by southerly winds. We therefore took the decision to continue on to King Christian Island whose north-facing coast would hopefully offer some refuge.

It wasn't an easy decision to come to as we were all fairly knackered from sleep deprivation from the past two days' rowing and constantly being uncomfortable onboard. We were also only guessing that this plan would be any better and had no real idea whether we would be able to land, but the Island did lay in roughly in the right direction and we were pleased to be making good headway.

Six hours further on, we were much relieved to find a relatively ice-free coast. The gamble had paid off and we were all able to have a decent break. As with every stop, a phone call was made to base to let them know how things were going and to find out what the weather and ice would be doing over the coming days. This time the news was not good.

For the better part, the weather had been exceptional this year with record temperatures when we left Resolute helping to break up the ice as well as lulling us into a false sense of security. Unseasonable southerly winds had kept our path relatively clear and also helped to hold the leading edge of the main polar ice cap in the north allowing us to make incredible distances that simply wouldn't have been possible in most previous years.

This however was about to change. With falling temperatures and a cessation of our helpful southerlies, the ice that had been bottled up to the north was now able to creep slowly towards us. The main pack was still to the north of Ellef Ringnes Island, but not by much and in between us and it lay our goal – just sixty miles in a straight line but one hundred miles by sea with the Noice Peninsula in between.

The forecast also predicted strong northerly winds within the next twenty-four hours. This would break up the leading edge of the main pack ice and send it crashing down onto the coastline that we currently inhabited so our only choice was to get back on the boat and seek a better position to shelter in and make a new plan from wherever that might be.

En route to the Noice Peninsula, the last large obstacle before our final destination, was Thor Island. So on the same day we'd arrived on King Christian Island, we once again packed up our gear and headed out for another overnight trip to cover the thirty-six miles in search of some kind of protection from the prevailing conditions.

We were about two hours into the row when I thought that the sleep deprivation had go to me – I was hallucinating that King Christian Island was suddenly upside down and floating in the sky, despite the fact that we hadn't seen it for a while. I didn't say anything just in case the other guys thought I was losing the plot, but when the image persisted despite me blinking and screwing my eyeballs up, I decided to share my vision with Dave. He admitted that he'd been seeing the same thing which was reassuring as either I wasn't going bonkers or we were both going bonkers together.

I guessed it was something to do with layers of cold air refracting the light and making things very confusing, but I was later to learn that I had witnessed something known as a Fata Morgana. It is named after Morgan the Fairy, or Morgan La Fay in Arthurian legend. The phenomena is apparently often seen in the Straits of Messina between Sicily and Italy and have been described as 'fairy castles in the air' or 'false land conjured by her magic'.

Fairy or no fairy, through tired eyes it was very hypnotic as one island would appear the wrong way up, then a few would be stacked upon one another, all caused by light bouncing off air layers of different temperatures. It certainly helped to pass the shift and I was just relieved that I wasn't the only one able to see it after the amount of brackish water we'd all been drinking!

By nine o'clock on the morning of the twentieth, we finally made it to Thor Island. It had been a big push but once again we were filled with a feeling of mixed relief and trepidation. We were now so close to our final goal, but with no sign of a let-up in conditions for at least the next four days, we may as well have been a thousand miles away. By now, the temperatures were dropping daily and the predictable annual freeze was days, rather than weeks, away.

We found a shallow inlet and beached the boat clear of the water's edge on the less preferable western tip of the island as the eastern side was already choked with ice (we guessed that the shore we were currently on would soon be too). With the wind now blowing directly past us over open ocean to the south, hopefully out of sniffing range of any polar bears and knowing that we would be here for some time, we pitched tents to get some much-needed space and rest.

Jock was left in the bow cabin of the boat because if the bears couldn't smell him from ten kilometres, they would have almost certainly heard him snoring from a much greater range. There was a fair bit of 'housework' to be done so, after a short break and with the luxury of having a couple of tents for extra space, we set to organising kit and tidying the cabins onboard. Setting up camp was by now a well-practiced drill and we all set to our various tasks until all was done and we were able to finally grab some rest.

The cold northerly winds had now started to build and we were very grateful for the shelter, which allowed us to get together if we wanted a chat, to play cards or just relax out of the elements and in relative comfort. We took every opportunity to try and dry out damp kit, but the conditions weren't great for that with regular sleet and snow showers blowing through and the cold wind not being overly conducive to drying.

The morning of the twenty-first, we awoke to a freezing day. As forecast, the coastline was completely choked with ice as far as the eye could see. Even upon hiking to a high point overlooking our position, all we saw was the ocean further offshore littered with ice with no discernible way through and, to the north, a lot more ice on the way.

This wasn't unexpected but it was a little disheartening nevertheless, having come this far. Personally, I was starting to feel the strain of being in such close proximity to the other crew members. This was no detriment to them, just my own proclivity for a bit of solitude meaning that some of them were starting to get on my nerves a bit. I was acutely aware that it was me who was the problem and not them and vowed to keep a lid on it as best I could.

The day passed by easily enough and, as is always the case on expeditions when there's not a lot to do, meals tended to dominate the schedule, punctuating the day and giving us something to look forward to. Well-thumbed books were passed around until they were returned to the owner and cardsharps in their respective chosen games would be revealed. Hopeful walks were taken, but it was more for exercise than anything else as current predictions had us marooned here for at least four days until any hope of a break.

Unbeknownst to us, back at Base Camp the mood was not great. Chris Tibbs, our weather forecaster, and Kim Partington, our ice expert, had been liaising and between them they put our chances of being able to make the last sixty miles to the pole at less than 30 per cent. The prediction was that the ice sheet would shift too far south and the freeze begin before we were able to break away from Thor Island. This would leave us in a very precarious position, isolated in a remote place a long way from any feasible extraction point. Quite wisely, this information was kept from us.

On the morning of the twenty-second, the day that my first child was due to be born, I received a call via the sat phone at around nine in the morning from Helene. My heart sank as she spoke to me in tears and a feeling of helplessness suddenly hit me as I assumed that something had gone wrong.

As it turned out, Helene had walked the three miles to the hospital that morning for a routine check-up only to be informed that the baby had twisted around and was now in the feet-first position rather than the way it should be, head-first and ready to pop out. She was upset, wanting to give birth naturally, but after reassuring her as much as I could from three thousand miles away on a faltering satellite phone line, she calmed down and was booked to go in that afternoon for a caesarean section, otherwise known as being 'whipped out of the sun roof'.

Helene's mum had come over from Holland to look after her during this period and was equally reassuring and I was very glad of her presence. By the time they'd walked the three miles back home to collect some bits and bobs on a beautiful summer's day in London, all was alright with the world apparently. Four hours later I received a call to find that I was the father of a healthy baby boy which I was overjoyed at. I'd previously been asked if I wanted a girl or a boy, to which I always replied that I didn't care as long as it was healthy and had a penis.

As you can imagine, the news brightened the mood in camp as good news from home always did and following a round of hearty congratulations and a few nips of whiskey I decided to write my new-born son a letter which I then took to the top of a nearby hill and buried beneath a small rock cairn. It was a lovely moment of reflection for me to suddenly have a very new and very different challenge to look forward to as well as a new sense of purpose to finish what we'd started in order to make my son proud in the future. After all, let's face it, to admit at some point down the track that 'I wasn't there for the birth of my son as I was in the Arctic on an expedition that I didn't complete' would make for a pretty rubbish tale and probably incur a severe tutting from a lot of parents!

The Noice Peninsula lay just ten miles to the north of us, across Dome Bay, and from our various vantage points we could see on 23 August that a crack in the ice had formed running parallel to the shore, east to west, which would allow us to make progress. Unfortunately, however, the route to it was completely blocked with ice for as far as we could see, all the way to Ellef Ringnes Island, covering an area of some three hundred square kilometres.

The wind had changed, now coming out of the east. This was the right direction to clear the huge shelf of ice out into open waters, but whether it would be strong enough or blow for long enough to do so, nobody knew. Satellite imagery showed that even if we were able to make it to the Noice Peninsula, the rest of the route was completely choked and, more worryingly, the main ice front was slowly progressing southwards towards Deer Bay which was our final destination. It had already reached the top end of Ellef Ringnes Island, eighty-five miles to the north of us, and at its current rate would envelop the entire island within the next four to five days.

Once again, there was nothing to do but sit and wait. However, there was a growing sense of anxiety and the urge to just try and crack on was almost irresistible. None of us were ready to throw in the towel and we grasped onto every bit of news from the forecasters as a positive, willing the ice to bugger off and give us a final crack at getting to the Pole. The easterly winds continued to blow at a steady twenty knots throughout 23 August giving us renewed hope, although they were forecast to die down the following day which would then allow any ice that had built up to the west to come flooding back, pinning us in for good. If we had any chance of success, it was very slim.

After a fairly restless night with the wind flapping the tents and the excitement at the prospect that maybe we'd have one final push the following day, we woke to a cold start but the grey skies looked to be gradually clearing. We went to our now well-established lookout points to survey the scene over Dome Bay and were astonished at the damage that the easterly winds had done to the previously impenetrable ice sheet. It was far from ideal, with quite a lot of ice in the Bay, but where there had been a vast sheet of white was now mainly dark blue with only a few narrow bands of solid ice remaining.

Initial optimism was slightly quenched by the knowledge of how quickly the situation could change. By midday, however, the decision had been made to pack up and prepare to depart. The tension was palpable as we packed the tents and stowed the gear for what we suspected was going to be a bit of a rough ride towards the Noice Peninsula. However, by mid-afternoon, the wind had dropped and we were ready to go.

We'd discussed how, given the ice conditions and dire weather forecasts, simply getting to the southern shore of the Peninsula would be a huge success. But there wasn't one of us who wasn't secretly hoping for more. The shoreline was still strewn with ice pushed up over the previous days, but after some careful manoeuvring, we cleared the initial ice band and headed northeast, directly for the nearest part of the Peninsula.

Initially, navigation was tricky on account of the residual large bands of ice, but slowly the picture cleared as we headed further out into the bay and, by the time we neared the southern coast of the Peninsula, it was as if an unseen hand had opened the way for us. In the four hours since we had set out, the marginal conditions had completely abated, the only evidence of the previous week's storms being massive icebergs pushed up against the coast where they lay stranded in the shallow water, the smaller ice having been blown out to the west.

After being stranded for four days and anticipating that this part of the journey would be the toughest, we were flabbergasted to find ourselves on the southern tip of the Peninsula, flying along in bright sunshine and calm, clear seas. At this point there was absolutely no point in stopping and, truth be told, a team of wild horses would have struggled to hold us back as the mood in the boat soared.

We knew that these conditions were only temporary and that we were in a race with both the ice coming down from the north as well as the mass of it to the east that had built up during the past few days, but we didn't care. All that mattered was making as many miles towards our ultimate goal as possible whilst the conditions allowed and preparing another plan should the circumstances change. We continued through the night, marvelling at our good fortune as the sun first kissed and then semi-submerged below the horizon for the first time since we'd arrived. The sight spurred us on, reminding us that both the season and our chances of success were almost at an end.

Jock reported our position and remarkable speed of progress back to Base which, though they had been tracking us, took them a little by surprise, particularly when he told them that we could be at the pole in three to four hours. After a flurry of phone calls, the message came through that we should slow down. Not quite believing our ears, having been out amongst the ice for twenty-nine days, we were told that the rate of our recent progress had been far quicker than anticipated and, as a result, the press weren't ready for the news. In my mind, that wasn't our fault, after all they'd had a f**king month to prepare for it, but Jock and the media department owed our sponsors their pound of flesh so the decision to delay was accepted albeit very begrudgingly by yours truly.

We dropped anchor in a pretty uncomfortable spot between two icebergs stranded on the northwest tip of the Peninsula, just short of the entrance to Deer Bay, and awaited further instructions whilst I silently fumed at the waste of time. In hindsight, it's just as easy to argue that, while the folk back home had been a little casual in their approach, after twenty-nine days at sea a few hours wasn't going to make a lot of difference. But that's hindsight for you and, given that there had been a few other moments when the need to get the right content for our sponsors had, in my eyes at least, conflicted with the interests of the expedition as a whole, I was in no mood for consolation. It also should be remembered that, given the speed at which conditions were changing, a few hours could have made *all* the difference.

By the time the green light was given, I was tearing at the leash. Deer Bay lay just ahead of us and the exact point we needed to get to was approximately three miles offshore, equidistant from both headlands, the exact position being 78°35'42"N, 114°11'54"W, just twelve miles away.

As we rounded the Peninsula and headed into Deer Bay, the ice started to thicken once more and the leads began to narrow. When we were within two miles of the Pole, having rowed up and down the ice barrier for an hour, it became apparent that there was no longer a waterway through the ice and that we would have to make the decision to drag the boat out onto the ice if we were to stand any chance of getting to the Pole position.

Mooring up alongside the ice, we stepped ashore to survey the scene ahead. The whole of Deer Bay, seven miles wide and ten miles long, was, as far as we could tell, completely blocked with one continuous ice sheet. It wasn't smooth either, but rather a labyrinth of hillocks up to three metres high and pools frozen over with ice of varying thicknesses, some of them with ominously dark patches disappearing into the depths of the bay below.

Though fatigued, the crew was fairly pragmatic about it and, having come almost five hundred miles, there was no way that they weren't going to give it their all to make the last two. We all knew how hard it was going to be, having dragged the boat short distances ashore on numerous occasions – by comparison, two miles seemed an enormous way. But this was, after all, what the boat had been designed for.

Our first priority was to get the boat out onto the ice. We therefore scouted out the ice edge to find a suitable slope with a shallow enough angle to allow this. From our experience so far, we realised that there was a design flaw in the runners on the underside of the boat. These consisted of a single skid on the bow and a pair of skids further aft. Unfortunately, there was a gap between forward and aft skids, which meant that if you tried to haul the boat over any sort of lip in the ice, it would go so far and then get stuck. Thus any type of irregularity was to be avoided wherever possible.

Eventually, finding a kind of ramp in the ice, we climbed ashore, tethered the boat to a rope and tried to hauled it up after us. Unfortunately, however, this proved ineffective; we could only get the boat halfway out of the water before the strain became too much and we had to release our hold, letting it slide back down the slope.

Next we tried using a block and tackle secured to ice screws. This was definitely an improvement but painfully slow. As we had experienced all those months ago, as soon as the boat stopped it would freeze to the ice. We then had to expend a huge amount of time and effort to get it unstuck before we could start dragging it again. Like I say, it was inch-by-inch progress, but progress nevertheless. Rob then suggested unloading the boat, which was a definite improvement, allowing us to keep the boat moving a lot more easily. After the first hour or so, we found that maintaining motion was key.

Each movement over the undulating ice required a different strategy, depending on the slope and conditions underfoot, and gains of just a few metres without stopping to unbreak the bond between the boat and the ice were rare. Though having the boat empty was a definite improvement in terms of making progress, it did mean that every fifty metres or so we had to go back and ferry the kit taken off the boat to a new position. We all been awake for more than twenty-four hours by now so, as you can imagine, we were pretty knackered as time crept by and we edged our way across the ice.

Knowing what an effort it was to get the boat in and out of the water, we decided early on to try and avoid the 'puddles' on the ice flow. However, it quickly became clear that easier metres could be gained with the boat in the water. Dave and I scouted ahead to find some decent pools, twenty metres or more in length, which would allow some decent, fast progress to be made.

We therefore decided to switch our strategy to puddle-jumping. This meant that we could leave the boat fully stowed for a lot more of the time and avoid the slog of having to shuttle kit. After six hours of back-breaking work, we stopped for a break and checked our position. To our relief, we were only half a mile from the Pole and heading in the right direction.

Finding ourselves so close gave us a massive boost and, with a renewed effort, we carried on. Two hours later, we were just three hundred metres away from the position and, tired though we were, we knew we were going to make it. By now, we had become a well-oiled machine, scouting ahead for the best routes, getting the boat out of the water and back into new leads with two crew pulling the boat from the bow, smashing the ice with an axe and pick as well as their feet as two of the crew pushed.

At times, we would come across darker patches in the ice where the surface was thinner and more treacherous. Then the guys on the bow would cling to the boat as they passed over and the guys on the stern would push until it was their turn to cling onto the stern and pass over the holes through which they could quite easily disappear. An hour later, we stopped and checked our position, certain that we must be very close if not there. To our dismay, we discovered that the Pole was now two hundred metres to our left despite us having headed in an arrow-straight line for the past hour.

Being on such a solid lump of ice had lulled us into the false impression that it was fixed in place, but of course the whole ice pack was in constant motion. To all intents and purposes, we had made it to the Pole. So, in a final act of defiance to the ice, knowing that the pole was at that time two hundred metres to our left, we fixed a point on the ice and called that the finish line.

One hour later, having spent ten hours making the last two miles, the boat slid down the final slope into the water, much to our relief and huge cheers from the whole crew. So it was that on the 26 August 2011, a new world record was set.

Unbeknown to us, people at home had been watching the tracker live and knew that we'd reached the Pole way before we did, having chased it around in circles for the better part of three hours. It was an immense source of happiness to all of us and any gripes or woes that we'd had over the previous weeks were completely forgotten.

After a short celebration and some photographs, we decided to take a break before continuing on as we'd been on the go for thirty-six hours by then and needed at least a few hours' rest to avoid making any silly mistakes. We had to bear in mind that this might be the finish line, but unlike most finish lines, this one was over three miles out to sea on unpredictable pack ice drifting in god knows which direction in conditions that we knew were about to deteriorate. The sun had set below the horizon that very day as the Arctic summer drew towards autumn and the difference was incredible. Temperatures plummeted and though the sun was only just below the horizon, providing us with enough light to function in, it did nothing to warm us in our energy-depleted state.

After a six-hour break, we scouted out a route to the north where thankfully it looked like there were some decent leads in the ice within a mile of the boat which might then head to open water. The winds were predicted to pick up from that direction so the leads should only get bigger as the day progressed.

We started to move the boat but quickly found that, in the six hours we'd been resting, the sea had started to freeze. Whereas before the guys at the bow could generally break through the ice easily by treading on it or giving it a light tap with the axe, overnight the thickness had increased to ten or fifteen millimetres which meant it had to be broken with a sledge hammer or the pick; no longer could the bow of the boat break through the ice and gain easy metres. We slogged on and, as we approached the edge of the main pack, we were relieved to find the leads getting bigger and thought that we might be able to get in the boat and row though them.

As the pack opened up, the puddles disappeared and there was nothing but deep blue water beneath us. We therefore got onboard and tried to row, using the reinforced edges of the oars to smash through the ice and get some purchase. However, the ice didn't yield, holding the boat firmly in its grasp.

I have spoken about how fast the seasons changed up here. But we nonetheless amazed at how, coinciding with the first sunset of the year, the ice had suddenly thickened to a point where we could neither wade ahead to break it nor row through it.

After some procrastination, I volunteered to try something different. Getting a long line from the boat, I attached it to the bow. I then tied the other end to myself and jumped into the frozen ocean, breaking through the ice. Turning onto my back, I started 'windmilling' through the ice using my elbows to break it, propelling myself forward to the next solid piece of ice; scrambling up onto it, I dragged the boat through it, using the reinforced bow to break the ice whilst Rob, dangling over the bow, helped out with a sledge hammer.

We were still chasing leads through the ice, which required a lot of manoeuvring, so Dave quickly followed suit, getting another line and jumping into the water, swimming to opposing ice floes so that we could manouvre the boat left and right as required. On a couple of occasions, the bends were too tight to get the boat through so we'd spend twenty minutes or so taking turns to swing the pick axe to chisel a new corner that the boat could then get around. It was exhausting work but incredibly satisfying as the leads became larger and larger and, after five hours of swimming, smashing and pulling, we were finally free.

We'd set our sights on the far shore of Deer Bay, which was still two miles away and, to add insult to injury, the predicted north wind now started to kick in with some force. It took us another two and a half hours and a massive effort from the whole crew to cover the distance. We had to regularly swap out due to fatigue, feeling at times like every stroke would dislocate our arms from our shoulders; just to haul the oar through the water and propel the boat into the increasing winds to finally reach the opposite shore was agony.

Finally arriving, utterly exhausted, it was only now that we truly felt that we had made it. Personally, I was glad that we'd had to fight for every inch of those last few miles as, up until the last days, I hadn't really felt that I'd earned the plaudits that we were receiving. Again, it was just the masochist within me telling me that if I wasn't on my last legs, it wasn't a true achievement; but this expedition was always going to be as tactical as it was physical. Fortunately, we weren't at the finish line yet so I still had time to truly feel that I'd earned the victory.

It had always been our intention to leave the boat close to the Pole and to hike out to our extraction point, a disused Distant Early Warning Line station at Isachsen. During the Cold War, these stations were set up in the Arctic, all the way from Alaska to Iceland, to give early warning in the event of Russia launching a nuclear attack. The project included the building of massive infrastructure including the construction of runways capable of taking the huge transport planes necessary to bring in supplies and equipment so it was the ideal point to collect us from.

Ideally, we would have liked to have rowed the fifteen miles or so around the headland and into the bay by the disused station as it would only be a short hike and we had a lot of gear to unload. But the weather and ice conditions dictated otherwise. Upon reaching the shore, first on the list of things to do was to drag the boat far enough up the shoreline to protect it from ice and prevent it from getting dragged back out to sea when the ice retreated. The shoreline we were on was made of a fairly soft material so the inflatable rollers were ideal, spreading the weight of the boat, making a relatively easy job of it. Once that was complete, we pitched the tents and settled in for the night, ready for the first of two hikes out to the abandoned air base the following day.

Well rested, we started dividing kit between ourselves after breakfast. The packs were a cross between a dry bag and a rucksack so great for hauling light loads over short distances, but not exactly suited to what we needed them for now, being pretty uncomfortable with around twenty-five kilograms of kit in each. We'd decided to only take one sleeping bag and a bivvy bag between us, just in case somebody became injured on the hike, the intention being to get to the base, dump the kit that we had and head back later that day ready for the second round of kit. But, shortly after setting out, it became apparent that this probably wasn't going to happen.

The going was far tougher than we'd anticipated with a mixture of uneven ground strewn with mile after mile of ankle-breaking tussocks interspersed with energy-sapping bog. We started out as a group, but I found the pace painfully slow so set out on my own, glad to be free of the others for a bit of head space. I'd experienced the same feeling on other expeditions where the moment I didn't have to spend time in the company of others I would be off like a shot, wanting to have as little to do with them as possible and enjoying my own solitude. Before long, I found myself out on the windswept plains alone with my own thoughts which was wonderful.

Fortunately for me, my own thoughts didn't extend as far as what to do if approached by a polar bear, seeing as I had no gun and was a long way from the rest of the group. The same thought had occurred to Dave who was holding the only gun; realising my error, he sought to position himself somewhere between me and the rest of the guys, but before too long I was over the hills and far away.

My only moment of doubt at having left the team crept in about two miles short of the base when crossing a dried-up river bed I suddenly disappeared up to my hips in thick dark mud. I was unable to move due to the weight of the pack and wondered momentarily if I was going to come to a sticky end, but, ditching my pack, I was able to eventually roll myself out of the bog and onto firmer ground. I decided that it was probably a good idea to reroll the pack, trapping air in it to act as a sort of air bag should this happen again, but thankfully it didn't.

By the time I reached the base, there wasn't a lot left in the tank and it was with sore feet and tired legs that I approached the abandoned buildings. It was only then that I realised how vulnerable I was, the sudden presence of structures that a bear could be hiding behind in complete contrast to the open plains that I had just come from where I would at least have been able to spot danger coming from a long way off (I could start 'whoa bearing' much earlier). Not one to scare too easily, I found this place really creepy. It made me feel like I was on the set of a horror movie.

At the end of the Cold War, these stations were simply abandoned and all the personnel flown out with their kit and anything that was required, leaving everything else in situ, even down to plates on the tables and food on the shelves. It was very eerie as I explored the buildings, gusts of wind causing doors to slam behind me periodically, and me expecting to see a polar bear or something grizzly behind every door.

Knowing that we would not make it back to the boat that evening, I decided to keep myself busy scavenging what I could from the buildings to make us as comfortable as possible. I found some old mattresses which were dry enough to use and started ripping down curtains and collecting any other material I could find for bedding as it was going to be a very chilly night with the temperature dropping already and one sleeping bag between the six of us.

I found the driest room that I could that had no broken windows and set about making it homely for the boys. Still coming close to soiling myself at the banging of every door and window, and having semi-barricaded this wing of the building, I decided to put my big-boy pants on and wandered around the site to find the mess hall to see if there was anything worth salvaging and came across some tins of food which might do if we got desperate. It felt better to be out in the open where I could see something coming than it did inside, but it was getting pretty chilly so I was relieved to see the rest of the team coming over the last hill on the approach to the base.

There was a time for solitude and a time to have others around me, particularly when one of the others was a trained soldier with a loaded gun. This was definitely one of the latter. We'd all been through the same ordeal and arrived filthy and knackered with the knobbier bits of kit having dug into our backs for the past seven hours and all the weight having been borne on our shoulders. It was blissful to ditch the packs and we quickly settled into our humble abode and got the stove on for a cuppa, having found a small stream to refill our water bottles close by. We'd only brought day rations with us, expecting to return to the boat that evening, and though hungry, nobody was quite brave enough to tuck into the tins of food that I had found, it being over twenty-five years since anybody had last inhabited these buildings.

Grateful for some rest, we settled in for the night, sardined together to try and keep some warmth as the night came and the temperatures dropped. Dave and I were on one end, sharing a small curtain, and every half an hour or so, somebody would roll over causing everyone else to do the same. It reminded me of sweaty hot dogs on a rotating rack at a petrol station, the thought of which immediately made my stomach rumble. We were all cold, tired, hungry and uncomfortable, but suffered in silence as the night wore on until the tranquility was broken by Jock letting off one of the loudest farts that I had ever heard, which sent us all into absolute fits of laughter and suddenly made light of what was not a great situation.

I must have dozed off at some stage as I woke up just before 5 a.m. in a very happy place, warm and semi-spooning Dave who looked angelic with his head tucked close to my chest. It felt very odd, but I didn't want to wake him and so let him sleep on for a while longer. It's not happened since (with Dave or any other guy for that matter) but I guess there's a time and place for everything.

Due to the cold, we were all happy to get up next day and start moving. Though our feet protested after the previous day's exertions, we were happy to be carrying very light packs and made much easier work of the return journey. This was the third day since the sun had first set and it was incredible to see how quickly the season was changing. The boggy ground that we had crossed just the day before was now firmer, crunching underfoot as we made the trek back to the boat. This made the going considerably easier with the result that the return trip took two hours less than the trek out.

Water was becoming an issue with no streams on this side of the island and no icebergs present on this side of the bay, but we cobbled enough together for drinks and some much-needed sustenance before settling down for our last night in the wild Arctic, very happy to be reunited with our sleeping bags.

Jock had got through to the base at Resolute and arranged a pick-up by aircraft for the following day, which meant that we only had one more trek to do with the rest of the equipment so we all drifted off peacefully with dreams of a hot shower and a solid meal in our heads.

Waking the following day to a cold and grey start, we laid out all the gear we would be taking with us on a tarp, distributed it between us and duly loaded it into our packs. Our sleeping bags and spare clothing took up any remaining space so it was with some dismay that I turned around to see the water-maker which cost around £6,000 to buy and was only on loan to us sitting there staring at me.

Given that we hadn't even used it, I found it particularly irksome when no volunteers stepped forward to carry it, leaving me to pick up the slack. Any ideas of esprit de corps seemed to instantly vanish when I asked the team to help out by redistributing the gear and I found myself trying to repack my already full bag with a large twenty-five-kilogram piece of rock-hard kit that would have been difficult enough to haul by itself, let alone with everything else. Eventually, the rest of the team did take some of the gear as there was simply no room left in my pack and we set out.

Dave offered to take my pack every now and then, but by then it was a matter of principle and I marched on silently fuming for the next six hours, carrying forty kilograms, often completely doubled over to try and take the weight off my shoulders onto my back. By now, my need to be away from the group was fairly intense so I marched on whenever they stopped, determined to stay ahead of them and away from any offers of assistance as carrying this bloody thing had become a matter to me of telling them to stick their offers up their arses. If ever there was a case of cutting off one's nose to spite one's face, this was probably it! The only saving grace was that, in the hours that had passed since the previous hike, the ground had now completely frozen which made going across the boggier bits a hell of a lot easier, though the extra weight on my back coupled with the thin-soled sailing boots that I was wearing made it very painful on my feet.

As I stomped my way around the shoreline of the final bay, I saw that we had arrived just in time. Ice crystals had started to form all along the tideline, freezing the ocean in place for another year, and it would only be a matter of days before the entire bay was once again encapsulated.

Finally, I made it back to the base. The relief of taking the pack off my back was immeasurable and I was able to just sit and collect my thoughts for twenty minutes before the rest of the team arrived. I was still not happy with the reluctance of anybody else to pick up the load in the first place and pissed off at the assumption that I would carry it. The incident took me back to my early rowing days when I felt I was the one doing all of the work and that nobody was trying as hard as me. I did realise, however, that I was just being a martyr for my own suffering and that offers of assistance were there, but I was too bloody-minded to accept them, once again happier to suffer just to show how tough I was rather than sharing the load and having nothing to gripe about.

The whole expedition had been a huge team effort. In this respect, the Belbin test had been pretty spot on and it was only upon reflection that I came to appreciate that the team had been made up of the perfect mix of individual personalities rather than what I'd thought would be best – another five of me, that is, which would have been a bloody nightmare, with no one talking to anyone else and the boat smashed to pieces from trying to push too hard, too soon.

The aircraft turned up a few hours later and we were all relieved to get onboard into the relative warmth with comfortable seats. I'm not sure what the pilot made of us – we looked like a bunch of dishevelled tramps, covered in mud from the previous day's hikes and no doubt stinking to high heaven. Flying over the route that we had taken during the past month gave us a true feeling of the feat we had achieved; whilst seeing the densely packed ice made us realise how lucky we had been with the conditions – the difference between success and failure really had been balancing on a knife edge.

Upon return to Resolute, we were met by the rest of the team who had been manning the base and after hearty congratulations we headed for a warm shower and a fresh change of clothes.

My new-born son was now a week old and I was desperate to get home to see him and Helene. So after a call home Helene arranged a flight out for me a few days ahead of the other guys and I was duly met by her with our baby boy who still didn't have a name. 'Thor' was bandied about, with him being born whilst I was on Thor Island, but I'd want some reassurance that he was likely to grow up to be a big strong Viking type before committing, as he'd look a bit silly with a name like that if he turned out to be a sixty-kilogram pipe-cleaner.

Coming back from Heathrow on the M4, we discussed 'Heston', though I didn't think that he'd thank us in later life when he asked why we'd decided to call him that and we'd have to reply that this was the name of the motorway service we'd been passing at the time and we couldn't think of anything better. Eventually, we settled on 'Louis' and I settled into a new life as a dad.

Despite having had such an amazing experience in the Arctic, there was still a very big itch to scratch and I still felt unfulfilled in that I had not achieved my goal of a solo expedition. I felt that the cancellation of the row across the Atlantic was a personal failure, though I had really enjoyed the feeling of achieving a world first in the Row to The Pole, which was something that could never be taken away from me.

For now at least, I was content to spend time with Helene and Louis, but the ember lit by having attained a world first and the desire to complete a solo achievement would smoulder for quite a while, refusing to burn out.

10

Back to work

After over a year out of permanent work and with a small baby at home, I was very keen to get a new position onboard a boat not only to provide for my family but also, to be totally honest, to get out of the house. It was all well and good playing happy families, but the truth of it was that my first year as a father was fairly rubbish.

Gone were the good times of going out for impromptu nights in London followed by lazy mornings and weekends away, replaced by structured feeding times, seemingly endless nappy changes and constantly feeling tired and irritable. The focus of our relationship had shifted almost overnight from being about us to being about Louis, leaving little time for anything else. That said, Helene was very strict with his routine so we did still manage to get down to one of our favourite local pubs just in time for him to nod off and us to have a few pints and a decent lunch in peace every now and then.

By now, the markets had started to recover from the Financial Crash and, given my achievements over the past year (now added to my CV), I was confident of securing a great job.

As the weeks passed, there were a few offers but nothing that really tickled my fancy. I was determined to hold out for a dream job which would revive my career and keep me stimulated, preferably a boat around the fifty-metre size, cruising the world and doing exciting stuff with good pay on a full rotation that would give me equal periods of time onboard and at home with Helene and Louis.

A month later, with the pot about to run dry, I was ready to give up those ideals and take the next job that came along. Thus when offered a position on a thirty-seven-metre boat based in Monaco all winter on the lowest salary I'd ever been paid as a captain and offering forty-two days' leave a year, I nearly bit their arm off for it.

The boat looked pretty but was held together with duct tape, spittle and good luck. My brief from the manager was that I had to give the owners the best season they'd ever had, albeit on a tight budget, so I set to work employing as cheap a crew as I could to get the boat ready for the following season.

There were, however, two dangling carrots – these being that the boat wouldn't be used all winter, so I'd be able to commute home at weekends, and that there was a bigger boat within the family fleet with an even bigger one in build and there would be a captain's position available at some stage for the right candidate.

My first trip was to take the boat out of Monaco, down to Viareggio in Italy to carry out a short yard period that winter. We were a little pushed for time and the weather wasn't great, but a window of opportunity opened up which would allow us to make the fifteen-hour trip. The forecast was for one-and-a-half- to two-metre swells on the nose which, though uncomfortable, should have been perfectly doable at a reduced speed on a boat of this size.

We headed out after dark at around eight that evening. The idea was to arrive in Viareggio nice and early the following morning but, having only covered eight miles, things started to go wrong.

Though it was a pitch-black night and therefore hard to gauge the conditions, it felt like we were in much larger seas than forecast with the boat being tossed around like a cork. As each wave hit, it sent judders through the boat that dislodged ceiling panels that I could hear crashing down. It began to rain heavily and, shortly afterwards, I could hear water pouring into the living area behind the bridge. I asked the deckhand to investigate, upon which he informed me that the boat always leaked when it rained and that the solution was to go outside onto the sundeck with a wet vac and hoover out the rainwater from a locker to stop it from filling up.

Faced with another fourteen hours of this, I spun the boat around only to find that the waves were indeed only one and a half metres in height; this boat just handled like an absolute dog and a wet one at that. We headed back to Monaco to lick our wounds and I suggested to the deckhand that maybe it would be a good idea to find the source of the leak rather than keep a vacuum cleaner handy.

A plug, some spray foam and ten minutes' work the next morning resolved the problem and I waited for a forecast of flat calm conditions before we next attempted the voyage. Winter passed and as spring approached all efforts were put to buffing the boat to within an inch of its life to bedazzle the owners and I'm glad to say that bedazzled they were. As the saying goes, 'You can't polish a turd but you can roll it in glitter'.

As I was to find out that summer, one of the greatest things about serving onboard were the owners who were the nicest people I'd ever worked for. Getting money out of them was always difficult, though, and every corner was cut to save money, but the crew were always paid on time and the owners were a joy to have onboard.

That summer we cruised extensively in France, Italy, Greece and Turkey, working 18 hours a day seven days a week which was tiring but fun as there was always something going on and the owners seemed genuinely appreciative of our efforts (not appreciative enough to grant the smallest of pay rises to any of the crew but appreciative nevertheless). At times we would work all day and then travel overnight and, with limited crew and watch keepers, I'd have to go days without sleep, but I enjoyed my time onboard immensely and was well-liked by the family.

It was, however, far from my ideal job and I vowed to keep looking for something else. Thus another year passed and, with Louis growing up, the ability to go home for weekends and keep money rolling in was the priority. By the winter of 2013, I'd just about had enough of life onboard and felt that, lovely people as they were, my career had stalled and I was going nowhere fast. I still had the desire to row an ocean solo, but there was no way that this job would give me either the necessary funds or the time off to do it, leaving me unfulfilled in both my work and personal ambitions.

Fate intervened when the captain of the owners' fifty-two-metre yacht slipped on some ice whilst the boat was in drydock in Marseille, injuring his head and breaking his elbow, and I was subsequently asked to step up, at first temporarily but then permanently, as the captain. Just for the record, I was nowhere near him at the time that he fell down the steps and have an alibi to confirm this.

Stepping up the ladder to a bigger, much better-built boat was certainly needed for me to get some sense of progression in my career as I was starting to get very fidgety. The money was still below par but I retained the ability to fly home at weekends as the boat stayed in Monaco throughout the winter. However, even this started to wear a bit thin, spending four or more months away over the summer and not knowing when I would be able to get back home and only being able to take my forty-two days' leave during the winter. It was also a difficult transition on an almost weekly basis as I was in charge for five days of the week onboard the boat and then definitely not for the other two at home. 'Helpful' suggestions at home with regard to childcare and how things could be done differently certainly didn't go down well and I started to feel more like an encumbrance than a help.

I'd often not return until the early hours on a Saturday morning and have to leave home at three in the morning on a Monday to get back to work. Helene was also now back at work fulltime so weekends were always strained, trying to get as much done as possible. In the meantime, Helene and I had been trying for a second child, but with me being away as much as I was, timing was of the essence, and coupled with the fact that we were either too busy or too tired to make a baby in the normal fashion, everything was reduced to timings and necessity rather than fun and frolics.

We lost a few very early-term pregnancies. This always occurred whilst I was away, which was upsetting for both of us but Helene, stoic as ever, always bounced back, consoling herself that 'at least I can have a glass of wine now'. However, in the summer of 2013, we finally got one to 'stick'.

Work was going well and the owners were happy, but I was still on the lookout for something more exciting, offering more pay and, most importantly, more time off. But nothing was forthcoming and, with the owners' eighty-metre yacht due for launch the following year, I'd decided to stick around as doing a stint on there would do wonders for my CV.

Our second child was born at the end of March 2014 and this time I was at least there for the birth, once again 'popped out of the sunroof', which was incredible to see. I'd been curious and peered over the other side of the curtain to see what the doctor was up to and was fascinated by it. I'd seen my fair share of blood and guts during my time in the Fire Brigade, but it's a bit different when it's your own wife the doctor has his hands inside, having a good old rummage around. When I say 'rummage', I mean rummage, as there was no subtlety about it. I've seen my local butcher preparing a chicken with more finesse!

I was convinced it was going to be another boy, whereas both our families and Helene expected and hoped for a girl. Thus when the doctor grappled the new-born infant out, my fist pump gave the game away. Helene rolled her eyes, not in any kind of disappointment but more for the fact that I'd been right.

We'd moved out of London to East Sussex in the meantime to give us a bit more space and some fresh air, as well as for Helene to be closer to her friends whom she'd grown up with as a support network. Helene was now home alone with two boys, a cat and a dog for the majority of the year which was bloody hard work. It was nice to be home, but I considered myself very fortunate to be able to go back to work for a bit of a break. My hours were long, but nothing compared to those of Helene who had no respite at all.

At the weekends when I was at home, I'd invariably have stuff to fix and we had very little time for each other with Helene looking after the majority of childcare and me resigned to the fact that whatever I did was probably the wrong thing. This doesn't paint the best of pictures and, to be honest, it wasn't the best of times, although with Louis now two and a half, he was becoming a lot more fun so I was at least willing to look after him as well as doing what I could to help out rather than trying to 'run the ship' every time I got home.

Another year rolled around and during the spring of 2015, with the launch of the owners' 'big boat', they decided that they would charter the fifty-two-metre boat out to other people which was great fun. When the owners were onboard, they were always looking at the boat in terms of maintenance and budgets, whereas charter guests were generally there to have a great time.

During the summer of 2015, we had some wonderful guests onboard cruising around the Mediterranean. It was a very successful season culminating in a charter during which a crown prince of Saudi Arabia made me one of his favourite meals, a tomato omelette, in exchange for my mum's sticky toffee pudding recipe which I'd made him earlier that week. It's a boast that I'm proud of to this day and I can confirm that he made a very good omelette!

As previously mentioned, the owners were rather frugal and at the end of the season, having served three years onboard, we were normally awarded an end-of-year bonus. However, this year they argued that the crew would not get one as we had been chartering and had earned tips. It was a bit of a slap in the face, seeing as we'd brought in just under a million euros in charter revenue, but not entirely unexpected.

As usual, we spent the winter in the Mediterranean and I went back to the commute, but I was also now involved with the eighty-metre boat, acting as temporary captain, allowing the permanent captain-manager to take leave himself. She was a much bigger beast than I was used to, but I've always been a pretty confident boat-handler so I didn't have too many problems.

The stopping distance did come as a bit of a shock the first time that I drove her into a dry dock though. (A dry dock is sort of a dead-end road that you drive a boat into after which the gates are closed behind you and the water drained out allowing maintenance on the hull.) I'd been asked to meet the boat in Gibraltar and take it the 1500 or so nautical miles to Trieste in Northern Italy where they were to carry out some modifications and annual maintenance.

The weather was reasonable and apart from one occasion when, due to an electrical fault, the entire ship blacked out in the middle of a busy shipping route with the rudders locked over to one side, almost causing a collision with another vessel, all went quite smoothly. We arrived in Trieste and a pilot boarded. I approached the dry dock, as I had previously on the fifty-two-metre boat, at between two and three knots. Upon reaching the entrance to the one-hundred-metre space, I put the engines into neutral to slow the boat down, which was when I learnt that two and a half thousand tons has a bit more momentum than five hundred.

I could see the pilot start to twitch a little so I put both engines casually into slow astern and marvelled as I looked over the side to see that the dock still seemed to be going past us quite quickly. I waited a few seconds and perceived a slight slowing down so, rather than going full beans astern and letting everybody watching know that I'd come in way too fast, I just left them ticking over. The result was that as the end of the dry dock approached we slowly came to a halt with metres to spare.

There haven't been many times in my career at sea that have had my pulse racing but this was one of them. Thus when the pilot said, 'Very good, captain, I thought you were coming in too quickly but all is fine,' I shook his hand and casually said, 'Thanks, I've done this once or twice before,' giving him an all-knowing nod and a cheeky wink before going to my cabin and changing my underpants.

Having been with the same family for almost five years, captaining the two smaller boats, I was due to step onto the eighty-metre boat permanently the following summer. However, at a meeting with them in the office in Monaco where my terms and pay conditions were discussed, I politely told them to poke it up their bums. They knew that I now had a young family and were offering the same forty-two days off a year, but the proposed schedule was hectic – the boat would do a busy Mediterranean season, followed by a short yard period, then head over to the Caribbean where we'd have a full itinerary before returning to the Med to do it all again, all for the princely addition of one thousand euros a month.

After the meeting, I called Helene and told her what they had offered. She suggested I take it, do the job for a year and move on. Begrudgingly, I accepted the terms, found a replacement for myself on the fifty-two-metre boat and was due to hand over the reins to the new captain by June 2016.

A year beforehand, at the Monaco Boat Show, I'd been introduced to a guy who was managing the build of a seventy-four-metre yacht. He was looking for a new captain for the project and we'd had a long sit down and chat about it. I'd not heard anything since, but at the beginning of June 2016, he called me to ask if I was still interested. The conditions of pay and leave were a huge step up and would allow me to spend a minimum of four months of the year at home so I gratefully accepted the offer.

The owners of the boat that I was on and the prospective new owners were good friends so I thought it best to give my present employer a call, preferring that he heard the news from me. We'd always had a good relationship and, apart from the lack of money and time off, I'd loved working for the family. When I explained the situation, the principal owner asked me what kind of package I was being offered as he was sure that we could come to an agreement.

I told him what I was being offered at which he wished me the very best of luck in my new position and called the owner of the other boat, giving a glowing reference.

When I had spoken with the manager of the new yacht about the job back in 2015, I had explained that sometime in the next four years I was planning on rowing across the Atlantic and would be requesting the time off to do so. He said that he would mention this to the owner but suggested that it was probably best that I got my feet under the table first.

I stepped off the fifty-two-metre and onto the seventy-four-metre on the same day, leaving the first boat in Olbia, Sardinia in the morning and joining the next in St Tropez that evening. Upon getting onboard my new posting, I sensed a very weird atmosphere and almost stepped straight back onto the tender as there was definitely something not right.

Within my first five days onboard, eight of the twenty-one crew had resigned and walked off the boat leaving very few who knew how to manage it. It turned out there had been a huge crew turnover since it launched due to a variety of factors but ultimately due to poor management. The atmosphere onboard was so bad that I was again tempted to take the next tender ashore myself but, not being one to shy away from a challenge, I decided to stay and see what I could do to turn matters around.

The boat was poorly built and the engineers were facing a losing battle most days, but there was little that could be done about that at the time, other than plug the holes where and when they appeared and support the engineers in any way I could. But the rest of the crew were really struggling. The reputation of the boat was so bad that a number of the crew agencies as well as other support services refused to deal with it, but I'm glad to say that over the following years we did manage to turn things around.

After three years onboard, I considered my feet well and truly planted under the table so in 2019 I approached the owner with my intention to row across an ocean and thankfully he agreed. At the time, I don't know how seriously he took me but, good to his word, he stuck with me throughout.

11

NYLON: The Build-Up

With the idea of rowing solo across an ocean as my next goal and a desire to achieve a world first, coupled with my inner penchant for masochism, I decided that the normal trade winds route, from the Canaries to the Caribbean, was not for me. The idea of having to ship the boat to an island only to arrive at another seemed a bit arbitrary so I set my sights on a continent-to-continent row.

I'd read a lot about ocean rowing, enough to glean that the true gold standard was the North Atlantic, statistically the most dangerous ocean in the world to row having claimed more lives than any other and with the highest failure rate. Comparing the trade winds route to the North Atlantic was, it seemed, the equivalent of comparing Everest to K2. Not decrying mine or anybody else's efforts on Everest, as it is still a massive undertaking and achievement, but K2 is a serious climbers' mountain where you must have incredible technical skills as well as the necessary endurance to summit it. To this day, of the people who make a summit attempt on K2, 25 per cent do not make it back.

The attrition rate of rowing the North Atlantic is nowhere near that figure, but there had been twice as many failures for solo rowers crossing the North Atlantic as there had been successes, most of the rows failing within the first four weeks and ending up in rescue. Attempts had been made to make it to the UK mainland, but most fell just short, stopping at the Scilly Isles just off of the southwest tip of England or taking a tow once past the longitude of Wolf Rock lighthouse, at which point you are deemed as having crossed the Atlantic.

Laval, whom I had summited Everest with, had made the North Atlantic crossing the previous year and set a new world record in the process (of course he did!). He'd taken the 'short route' to do so, a mere 2,500 miles from Halifax Nova Scotia to Brest in France, which he achieved in fifty-four days averaging forty-six nautical miles a day.

Speed records will always be beaten eventually (in fact Laval's was beaten the following year) so I decided that, rather than simply follow suit, I would try something that had never been attempted before. To me, it was important to have an affinity for the place where I would finish. It therefore seemed a natural choice to head to London, the city where I'd been born and raised; its river, the Thames, was where I had first learned to row. As for the start point, there seemed only one candidate: New York. This created a route that would link two of the world's most iconic cities, synonymous with the Blue Riband crossings of old when passenger liners would compete to be the fastest ship to make the 3,500-nautical mile crossing. (the record held by the liner *United States* which on her maiden voyage in 1952 maintained an average speed of 34.51 knots).

Silly though it might sound, a sense of national pride played a part in my motivation. Essentially, I wanted the first person to do it to be British. One thing that I had learned from my adventure in the Arctic was the importance of marketing to attract sponsors. Accordingly, I hoped that by choosing these two cities, I would be able to attract the attention of a large sponsor with a foot in each camp to assist with the cost which I'd estimated at around eighty thousand pounds.

Having seen my plans to row across the Atlantic come to nothing eight years previously, I was determined to at least get to the start line this time. After setting out to do so and having told quite a few people what I was hoping to achieve back in 2010, it always grated when they subsequently asked me how I'd got on and I'd had to tell them that I hadn't done it. As the years passed, the enquiries died down but I decided nonetheless that I would use this as motivation. Once I'd decided on the route, therefore, I set about telling as many people as possible about my intention to make the attempt either in the summer of 2020 or 2021 and, in doing so, I created my own wave of peer pressure.

(For anybody considering any challenge, I'd thoroughly recommend this method as I found it to be a great motivating force, rather than just telling yourself that you are going to complete something which is way easier to back out of!)

Given my experience with rowing in open ocean in the Arctic, I'd found that getting power from the oars into the water was quite challenging in the slightest chop and the strokes were often inefficient. I'd had an idea in my mind since that row that if you could transfer the work you put in to a drive underneath the boat you could generate thrust regardless of the ocean conditions. I'd done a fair bit of research, but despite coming up with some pretty funky concepts (one involving a retractable scoop like a duck's foot), it seemed that the most efficient method of propelling a boat through the water was by using a two-bladed propeller. I therefore started looking at how this could be linked to a rowing 'handle'.

Previous crossings had been made successfully in glorified pedalos, but I reckoned that it would be far more efficient to use a rowing stroke, utilising arms, shoulders and back as well as legs to produce power, so I was keen to explore the possibility of linking the two. With this idea in mind, I'd been liaising with two guys since 2017. Phil Morrison was a naval architect who had come up with the original design of the particular boat that I would be using, while Jon Turner was a highly decorated dinghy sailor and boat fabricator; both were based in South West England. They had worked closely together on other concepts as well as sailed together competitively and there was not much about boat fabrication and design that they didn't know. Phil was also a light aircraft pilot so knew a thing or two about propellers. In short, I reckoned that I had found the right men for the job.

Upon talking to them about my project, I found that they were incredibly enthusiastic. Phil had had a similar idea for a smaller coastal rowing boat, but never had the time to put it in to practice so was really pleased to help design the system. Jon was equally keen to get his teeth into building something out of the ordinary that would require a lot of problem-solving and out-of-the-box thinking.

We started building a drive system and by 2018 we had a working prototype that could be married up to a propeller and installed in a boat, although it was pretty rudimentary and needed quite a lot of revision. First of all, it was very noisy, using a standard ratchet system as on a rear bicycle wheel which would drive me nuts over months at sea; I therefore introduced Jon to a sprag clutch found in rowing machines which runs silently. Next we addressed gearing as, if I was going into wind, I didn't want the increased loading on my body, preferring to keep the load the same even if that meant less work went into the water.

We bandied around a few ideas and they came up with a controllable pitch propeller. This would allow me to adjust the amount of thrust generated by feathering the blades which was a beautiful solution and a prototype was made on a 3D printer.

Another thing I'd learned from the Row to the Pole expedition was the power of social media, particularly in generating money for charity, so I was keen to find a way to get people involved. With this in mind, I came up with the idea of somehow incorporating a strain gauge into the system whereby I could upload my data daily so that other people could row with me at home. These were all quite exciting concepts, none of which had been used before, so a lot of time and effort went into research and development at this early stage.

Unfortunately, however, it all took a bit longer than anticipated, not helped by the COVID outbreak which seemed to make everything twice as hard while getting hold of necessary parts took twice as long. With pressure building, I eventually decided to push the start date back to 2021.

By the end of 2019, we'd ironed out a lot of the kinks and had working bench-mounted versions of the drive system. All we needed was a boat to put it in.

I'd already set my sights on a Rannoch boat, known for their speed, as proved by many an ocean crossing. Laval had used a version called the R10, a purpose-built solo boat, for his record-breaking crossing, and an American, Bryce Carlson, had subsequently smashed the record the following year in a boat of the same design. Given that I would be going a much longer distance, I decided to go for a larger boat, an R25, designed for two people, which would give me more space for the extra food and supplies that I would need as well as a bit more weight to hopefully improve stability in rough seas.

I looked at the figures and was banking on being out at sea for around 120 days with upper and lower thresholds of ninety days and 150 days as best and worst case scenarios. I would therefore have to carry enough rations for five months at sea. Another reason I chose this boat was that there is a pretty strong second-hand market for them. I'd been bitten ten years previously when I'd bought my plywood boat just as they were coming to the end of their life cycle, being superseded by faster fiberglass and carbon boats, and subsequently got lumbered with it as it slowly rotted, having eventually to sell it and all the gear onboard five years later for less than a third of what I'd paid for it. I was naturally keen to avoid this, particularly as I didn't yet have any major sponsor and was rapidly chewing through family finances.

Ideally, I'd have ordered a new boat and built it around the drive system. However, one of these fully kitted out wouldn't leave you much change from £80,000, which didn't account for all the other expenses and I'd already spent a fair amount of cash on research and development. Rannoch would not have been able to deliver a boat in time anyway, as they had a lot of other projects on, so I scoured the second-hand market for the best boat that I could find, eventually settling on one called *Dioreann* which had been raced in 2018 and had completed three previous ocean crossings. After my offer had been accepted, I took delivery of her in January 2020.

I'd been pondering what I should call her for some time. There was one name that stuck, a nod to my sometimes non-conformist ideas, which also seemed to tie in well with my plan not to use oars: I duly reregistered her as *Square Peg*.

Now with a boat and at least something to show potential sponsors that I meant business, I started firing off emails to my contacts within the yachting industry to see if anyone was willing to part with some cash to get me going. I really didn't enjoy doing this as, in my eyes, the expedition was something that I wanted to do for myself; asking people to give me money to achieve a personal goal didn't sit too well with me. I was, however, chowing through personal savings and had already spent over £60,000 on the project and was still a long way from the start line. If not for anybody else, I owed it to my family to make an effort.

I know that a lot of other teams are very good at this sort of thing and can get their adventures almost entirely paid for by being able to market themselves in a far better manner than I am, but I really don't like being beholden to anybody so I concentrated on only using the suppliers that we did a lot of business through. I was also very transparent with my boss's office as to whom I was approaching and what, if anything, they had donated as the last thing I wanted was to be accused of currying favour with a particular supplier in exchange for a cash donation.

I also aligned myself with a charity, Global's Make Some Noise, spearheaded by a national radio broadcaster. We'd often listen to Heart Radio on the school run in the morning, which was presented by Jamie Theakston and Amanda Holden. Jamie had done a charity bike ride from Edinburgh to London in 2019 and we'd listen to his broadcasts which gave moving stories of the people that the money he raised went to. It was basically a foundation set up to support small charities that didn't have a marketing budget, all of whom dealt with disadvantaged families in the UK. To hear how the donations could directly change the lives of some of these people was truly heart-rending.

I looked at several other charities that were very close to my heart. However, more often than not, the vast majority of money raised in donations by the bigger charities went directly to the charity itself which I was very keen to avoid. I remembered many years before, being on a superyacht in the British Virgin Islands, when we took the guests out for a snorkelling trip. One of the guests didn't want to go so I stayed on the tender with her and fell into conversation about what she did for a living. 'I work for a non-profit charity,' she told me, adding, 'it's very lucrative.' This flew in the face of all that made sense to me, but each to their own, I guess. Certainly, if you relied on a few little old ladies or well-meaning folk to run jumble sales to raise a bit of cash on a voluntary basis, many of the amazing deeds done by charities would not be possible.

Loath as I was to start cutting lumps out of a perfectly good ocean rowing boat, I now took *Square Peg* to Jon's workshop to start fabrication whilst I went back to work with the aim of hopefully doing some sea trials upon my return. At the time, I was still contracted to the boat that I was working on for eight months of the year and had just taken on the responsibility of managing it which meant that I'd actually only get thee months at home that year and the occasional weekend whilst the boat (the one that I worked on) was in the shipyard. Time at home was very limited as a result, making it tough to juggle with training and testing of the boat.

I'd started training in earnest, clocking up a lot of miles on the Concept 2 rowing machine and seeing considerable improvements in my performance. Ironically, being at work allowed me more time to train and I'd be up at around four most mornings if guests were onboard, ready to train before they were up and about. Fortunately, the owners of the boat were creatures of habit and there was often a lull in the early afternoon where I'd get an hour's break for a 'cap nap' before starting the evening session which generally had me awake until after midnight.

During the times that we were in the shipyard, I'd be able to train at more sociable hours, though I've always preferred exercising in the mornings so was able to push it to five o'clock and at least get a good night's kip.

At home, it was pretty much the same story as having guests onboard, in the sense that I tried to fit my training around the family as much as possible so as not to impact too much on our time together. With the boys now eight and five years old, life was a heck of a lot more fun and, with the new job and increased amounts of leave, I knew when I was coming home and could dedicate time to the family and plan things well ahead which made a huge difference, particularly between me and Helene. Having me come home and upset the apple cart generally caused havoc to the well-rehearsed routines, but this only happened every few months now so a few days' grace before I realised that I wasn't in charge anymore was tolerated.

With the additional time off, I also joined a local rowing club and loved getting out on the water after dropping the kids off at school. Being back in a single scull brought back fond memories of the Thames, but unfortunately health and safety restrictions brought in shortly after I'd joined limited my time on the water as I couldn't go out alone between October and March because the water was too cold. I did try and play the 'rowed in the Arctic, swam naked to an ice berg and stared down a polar bear wearing nothing but a pair of underpants' card, but unfortunately the powers that be at the rowing club were resolute.

I was in constant contact with Jon at the time with regard to how the work was going. The modifications were throwing up problems left, right and centre, but we were always able to figure a way around them. I was a little frustrated with progress, hampered as we were by COVID restrictions in the UK, but as the months went by the boat started to take shape and by late spring 2020 I was able to get it out on the water. I brought it back home to test it on the local reservoir where I'd been training as, with the system being very much in the prototype phase, I thought it best to test on some enclosed water rather than out at sea.

After launching, I pulled away from the landing stage and into clear water. However, there was quite a crosswind blowing. Using the oars, I positioned myself by one of the banks, protecting myself from the wind as best I could, but by the time I'd stowed the oars and got ready to trial the system, I'd be pointing downwind and already going at some speed towards the opposite bank. This was pretty frustrating as I'd only get a very short time to tweak settings before I'd have to get the oars back out and try again, there not being enough water to work up enough speed for the rudder to have any effect using the propeller. After a couple of hours trialling what I could, the good news was that the propulsion system did work and was incredibly smooth.

It was a bit faster using the oars, but I'd always expected that to be the case in flat water. Despite the frustrations, it did highlight that the controllable pitch system needed modifying as the lever that had been installed went from zero to hero with the tiniest of movements and it was impossible to judge what the prop blades were doing. The pulley system which transferred drive from the handle to the flywheel would also have to be changed as after just twenty minutes' use the cord had shredded through two of the pulleys. It was a case of two steps forward and one back which I'd anticipated, though I was a bit concerned over the amount of time the development was taking as there was less than a year to go before I'd have to ship the boat from the UK.

I was hoping to spend some quality time in the boat prior to departure to get to grips with the way she handled and become totally familiar with all the systems. However, with my time away at work, that only left me with four months of potential dates to do this in. Nevertheless, with some important lessons learned, I took the boat back to Jon's workshop for further modification before heading back to work.

At this time, I concentrated on putting in as many hours on the rowing machine as possible, starting at a hundred kilometres and increasing my total by five kilometres each week. Although I enjoyed getting on the rowing machine, getting into the 'zone' and pushing myself more and more every week, I was picking up niggling injuries that wouldn't go away which became annoying. Inevitably, spending nine or ten hours a week repeating the same movement only exacerbated the problem.

After asking around, I got in touch with Gus Barton, a personal trainer and ocean rower himself who had trained a lot of guys for the Talisker Race (an annual rowing race from the Canaries to Antigua) as well as for many other ocean rows. In our initial consultation where we did a live video session of me on the rowing machine, it became apparent where my injuries were coming from as I'd slipped into a lot of very bad habits in my routine. I must admit, I was pretty shocked when I looked at the video which proved to be a very worthwhile exercise!

I explained to Gus that my greatest fear was failing due to injury and he designed a program for me that totally shifted the focus of the training I was doing. Instead of endurance, I now concentrated on building strength and flexibility. It was a very welcome break from the hours of toil at home and at work, doing the same thing over and over again, or so I thought.

The first week was hard but really enjoyable. However, the intensity increased as the weeks passed and, by the end of week three, I'd have given my eye teeth to spend a couple of hours staring into the distance whilst the kilometres ticked by on the rowing machine. Still, I stuck with it, knowing Gus's reputation for preparing rowers for ocean crossings, hitting targets as I went and exceeding my own expectations.

I remembered telling myself when I first started training that if I was able to row sixteen kilometres in an hour and two thousand metres in under seven minutes I would consider myself up to strength and ready for the row. The last time I'd been able to do that was fifteen years previously, so when I hit those targets with eight months to spare, I was elated. Now it was all about just how far I could push myself in the months to come.

In the meantime, I had some fantastic news at work when the owner of the boat generously agreed to grant me a full rotation, roughly a two-months-on, two-months-off basis. It had been a long time coming, having worked almost twenty years in the industry, but it was a huge relief not only for the row but also because it meant that I could spend six months of the year with Helene and the boys and plan well ahead.

Up until then, I knew that I'd been missing huge swathes of my boys' lives, feeling constantly guilty at every birthday, school sports day or any other significant event that I was forced to skip. So, yes, this really was a godsend. Though I would still be away for six months of the year, my six months at home could be completely dedicated to spending time with them. There was one small fly in the ointment, in that the captain I'd be rotating with wouldn't have been my first choice, but he'd been working for the owner for fifteen years and served as relief captain whilst I was away so deserved the role out of loyalty if nothing else.

I was at work for June and July, cruising the South of France and Northern Italy as we usually did at that time of the year and work was continuing on getting my boat ready. I'd decided to repaint the topsides of the boat in luminous yellow, having spent many hundreds of hours staring out to sea whilst at work and knowing that small white vessels tended to get lost amongst breaking waves very easily. Given that there would be long periods during the row when I would not be on deck whilst I was resting, I was determined to make myself as visible as possible for any other passing ships which would hopefully not bump into me. I would carry an AIS (automatic identification system) onboard which would send out a 'ping' to other vessels to let them know that I was there, but these are only mandatory on commercial vessels over three hundred tons so anything smaller than that may well not see me coming.

There was of course always the possibility that the AIS could break so I preferred to stick out like a sore thumb, particularly for coastal navigation. The boat was still down in Devon but needed to be back home where a local guy had very kindly agreed to paint it for free. Chris, one of my friends from the local village, drove the five hours to Devon to pick it and deliver it to the spray shop. He was even good enough to stop off at the local pub for an impromptu 'christening' with a couple of pints of the local brew which would no doubt bring some good luck!

Once I got back from work, further restrictions due to COVID made movement around the country quite difficult and I wasn't sure whether driving to Devon with a bright yellow boat in tow could be classed as essential travel. It certainly wasn't inconspicuous, but I was ready to test the improvements that had been made so headed down to Exmouth with Dad as my trusty helmsman to meet up with Jon and Phil and get *Peggy* out on the water. The main purpose of the trial was to try and finalise the prop size and design as well as checking the improved pitch control system. The plan was to do three trials with differing prop sizes to see which one felt best.

Phil and Jon had secured a boat for the morning so they could chaperone us around and assess the efficiency of the system. It was very much a 'goldilocks' assessment on the propellor, the first being too big, offering too much resistance, the second being too bendy, flexing too much, clipping the rudder and immediately disintegrating, and the third being just right.

Jon and Phil only had the support boat for the first run which was a bit of a shame when the second prop sheared just by the mouth of the harbour with the tide running at full spate. By the time I'd put the oars into the rowlocks to get back to shore, the battle was already lost and, try as I might, the strength of the outgoing tide kept me at a distance. Fortunately, Jon had a local contact who was able to come and give us a tow in or it would have been a very long wait for the tide to change. Though it was a glorious day, I didn't much fancy rowing for six hours in to the current just to hold station whilst waiting for the tide to change!.

By the end of the third trial, we had a much better idea of how the boat would perform, having been pushing out up to three knots with a pretty sustainable effort, and I was really happy with the system overall. The controllable pitch propeller still needed some fine tuning and the strain gauge that I had fitted sadly was not going to be tough enough for the job as well as being overly complicated, so with limited time and a preferred ethos of keeping things as simple as possible we binned that idea. Jon took the boat back with him that afternoon for a final round of fettling and we made a plan for a final sea trial later that year. This would be in Weymouth due to the fact that there is very little tidal flow there so it would be much easier to gauge the actual speed of the boat without having to factor in the current.

By now, the sponsors were starting to trickle in which was quite a relief as I'd already invested a lot of my own money in the project. There wasn't much in the way of cash, but I at least got my food, clothes and satellite phone covered by various suppliers that we used. A few others had pitched in to cover the weather routing and transport out to New York, another couple of looming costs which I was relieved not to have to bear.

With so much now done and the start date fast approaching, my next major concern was simply getting myself to New York. International travel was still in lockdown and there was absolutely no way that I would be able to fly directly to the US. Thus, with eight months to go, all I could do was sit and hope for a change in the laws. Fortunately for me, the maritime sector was considered as essential travel so I was able to get to and from work, though it was a weird feeling strolling through deserted airport terminals with just a handful of flights available.

I rejoined the boat close to Napoli towards the end of September and stayed onboard, finishing up in the South of France two months later. Training had become intense with the programme that Gus had designed for me and every week I'd open the app on my phone with a new sense of dread as the daily torture routine was revealed. In the end, I gave up looking at the whole week and decided to surprise myself on a daily basis rather than spending the whole week in fear of what was to come. There was nothing random about this, however, as the whole programme was based on how far I wanted to push myself, with each increment building upon my previous performance.

I guess I could have eased back a bit but, as you can probably gauge by now, this really isn't in my nature; the suffering that I was going through on an almost daily basis was almost entirely self-inflicted. I was getting pretty used to the pain by now but the short sharp sprint work still killed me. On a number of occasions, the crew were wondering whether they should call for help as they'd find me lying on the deck hyperventilating and unable to move from exhaustion. I'd reached the stage where throwing up and passing out from sheer effort were regular occurrences so, after a while, they got to know better and just left me alone.

Every session pushed me. The numbers were still going up and every time I thought about quitting I told myself that if I failed on the row it could be down to that one time when I didn't give it my all in training, adding that if I couldn't maintain the effort for these relatively short periods of time, what chance did I stand on the open ocean?

On these occasions, I always remembered a parable told to us by my school chaplain, Reverend Evans, or 'Rev Ev' as he was known. I've never been a religious man and most of his ramblings went in one ear and out of the other, but every now and then he'd come up with a cracking story and this one stuck.

It was the story of an important town by a river which was often attacked by raiders as it was known to be very wealthy. Each time raiders approached, the lookouts would spot them and ring a huge bell, alerting the townsfolk who would come in from the fields and defend the town which never fell to the raiders. One night, during a violent storm, the bell tower was struck by lightning and the bell fell into the river, leaving the inhabitants with no way of warning in the event of an attack. They managed to attach a rope to the bell, but despite all efforts to drag the bell from the riverbed, they could not raise it.

Fearing a further attack, the locals consulted the wise old man of the town who told them that they must scour the land for two horses of the purest white and only then would they be able to pull the bell free of the riverbed. Weeks and months passed by and huge efforts were put into seeking out these horses and eventually one white horse was found. People faced incredible hardships as they no longer tended the fields but were out searching high and low for the second horse.

One day, a man came across such a horse but noticed the tiniest fleck of grey under its shoulder. Knowing how the town was suffering, he covered the tiny speck with some chalk and proudly returned to the town to the delight of the people. The horses were harnessed and took up the weight. To everybody's astonishment, the huge bell began to rise from the riverbed and soon the top was visible. The horses were under immense strain and, just as the bell was about to emerge fully from the river, they could take it no more and the bell topped back down into the riverbed, smashing in the process. The people all turned to the old man and questioned why, after all this hardship, his plan had failed, whereupon he inspected the horses and found the grey fleck. The town eventually fell into ruin.

It was a very long tale to just say, 'Don't do things by halves', but it obviously had an effect on me as despite the taste of blood in my mouth and my inability to get enough air in my lungs during these ball-busting workouts, it always came back to me when I was ready to give up.

There was no let-up when I returned home in November. Training would start after I'd dropped the boys off at school on weekdays and at three-thirty in the morning at weekends to enable me to maximise my time with the family. The rest of the time was split doing whatever needed to be done around the house and organising logistics for the row. It was incredible how quickly the weeks whizzed by and I was very wary of the approaching deadlines. I wanted to be out in New York by 1 May in case an early weather window opened up, which would mean getting the boat to the shipping company by 1 April. Suddenly, then, the years of planning and training were down to the last five months, for two of which I would be back at work and I still didn't have a fully functioning boat.

By the beginning of December, Jon had worked his magic and we were ready for what would hopefully be the final sea trial. Everything that we had learned through trial and error had now been rectified and all the modifications that I had requested had been carried out. I'd booked a slot at Rannoch for a final check-up of all the systems for the middle of December and I was due to fly back out to work on the twentieth so time was very tight. There was simply no time for any further fettling so it was essential that everything went well.

Dad and I met Jon in Weymouth as planned and launched the boat down the slipway, Dad helping at the helm once more. The winds were blowing at about ten knots and the sun was shining on a glorious early December day as we coasted out into the harbour. We really couldn't have asked for better conditions.

Jon had managed to use his contacts to secure a support boat to see us safely underway and to carry out tests with us, but all indications were very good. The system ran smoothly and noiselessly and we were making two and a half knots into the wind and four knots downwind, which, though it might not sound like much, is pretty quick for an ocean rowing boat. It was all very eleventh hour, but what had only been a concept in my head for the past ten years was now a reality and I was one step closer to the starting line. I was overjoyed at the work Jon had done and all the worries about whether the propulsion system would work were quickly forgotten.

The following week, as planned, I delivered the boat to Rannoch and gave them my final wish list along with a request for a check-up of all the systems, effectively a pre-departure MOT.

It was a bit of a kick in the teeth when the assessment came through as, in addition to the things that I had requested, they had found a lot of other items that needed to be replaced or repaired. However, I had come this far and there was little point in scrimping now on systems whose failure, should it occur, would mean the end of the adventure.

I had added a few additional comforts, moving the autopilot controls to where I could reach them and installing a chartplotter on deck which would be necessary for coastal navigation, as well as installing a solar-powered vent fan to get some air into the cabin and new deck speakers so I could listen to music whilst out at sea. But apart from that, everything else was deemed essential so I simply had to swallow the £6,000 in extra costs.

One thing that Laval had encouraged me to do was to install a pair of rudder lines that led from the back of the boat, under the deck, all the way to the main cabin. In this way, if I was shut in my cabin during a large storm and the autopilot failed, I would still be able to hand-steer the boat. It seemed a bit of overkill as I was carrying three autopilots, but as they were prone to failure I took his advice and had a simple pulley system installed. A pull of the lines from one end of the boat would disengage the steering ram of the autopilot and give me hand control. It was a simple mechanism but very effective.

I'd also asked the guys at Rannoch to test the output of the solar panels that I'd need for navigation, communication, steering and, most importantly, the water maker. They'd duly done this and, after giving them a good polish, had given them a clean bill of health. I'd have liked to have replaced them as they were already six years old, but time and funds didn't allow this so instead I got them to fit a socket on deck so that I could plug in an emergency panel that was supplied with the boat. It was fairly bulky but fortunately it fitted snugly into the space where the other crew member would normally live.

A few days later, I flew back out to work in the Caribbean for my final stint onboard the yacht. I'd worked out the schedule so that I'd finish up in early February, giving me a few months with Helene and the boys before I set off. By then, my second-in-command had his captain's qualification so, not wanting to burden the owner with any additional costs, I offered to pay the increase in wages for him to step up into my role out of my own salary. This also meant that, when I came back, I wouldn't 'owe' the other rotational captain any leave.

Meanwhile, I'd accounted for all household costs for the period I would be away and I didn't plan on too much internet shopping in mid-Atlantic so financially all was set.

Fortunately for me, that year we were based out of Antigua. Arriving early in the New Year, we were just in time to see all of the crews arriving at the end of the Talisker Race which was a huge morale boost for me. At the time I was struggling a little to motivate myself to train in the heat and humidity, so seeing these guys arrive and just being part of the euphoria as they were reunited with their families at the finish was a wonderful tonic. I took the time to get to know a lot of the teams as they arrived to pick their brains over certain elements of their rows and took a particular interest in how they kept their bottoms healthy. I'd seen a lot of very nasty rashes from sitting on a sweaty bum for hours on end in a marine environment and knew they could be incredibly painful, the worst being salt sores caused by wet, salty clothing rubbing against the skin forcing salt into the pores leading to severe boils.

This could make life an absolute misery so, keen to avoid it, I asked as many people as possible about their bottom routines. Hopefully, I didn't make a name for myself in doing so but it seemed like a combination of seat pads, good hygiene and regularly applied ointment, either Sudocrem or Vaseline, should keep the worst symptoms at bay. I vowed to make sure that I gave myself a wet wipe (biodegradable, of course!) bath at the end of each shift, dry my bottom as best as I could and make sure I stuck to a regime of cream application.

As for a comfortable seat, there was no single solution. Everybody seemed to have their own ideas about this, but the general consensus was that you were going to be uncomfortable whatever. Laval came up with the best suggestion, which was to take a couple of medical sheepskins from which you could cut seat pads, adding one every time you became uncomfortable; amazing as it sounds, the shape of your bottom changes throughout a row like this, putting pressure on different bones and muscles as it does so. The sheepskins also had the advantage of wicking moisture away so hopefully keeping your pores free of infection.

Being a solo rower, without anybody else to tend to my potential woes, I also made sure that a decent mirror went on my kit list!

Another thing that I learned from the solo rowers was their shift patterns. I'd thought that I would row in the two-hours-on, two-hours-off pattern that all crewed boats use, but speaking with Laval and the other rowers, the general opinion was that this didn't work and they felt better rowing according to their circadian rhythm – i.e. the natural pattern of waking and sleeping, by which they'd row during the day and rest at night, unless they felt like rowing for a few hours in the evening. I decided to keep an open mind on that one as some of my miles would be dictated by the tides in coastal waters, over which I'd have no control.

I had a two-week block of endurance training whilst out in Antigua. Among other things, this allowed me to get out of the crew gym which was a space in the bowels of the boat that also doubled as the sewage treatment plant room. It was always fairly smelly down there and rarely below 28 degrees, but the two weeks of endurance work meant that I could put the rowing machine on deck and at least get some fresh air. Still, I like to exercise in the cold and the temperature never dropped below 23 degrees with humidity around 75 per cent which was sweaty to say the least. By the time I finished long sessions, there would be rivulets of sweat running the length of the foredeck as I puffed and panted my way to ever-bigger distances.

The greatest test was to be two 3-hour sets with one hour recovery in between. In order to avoid the heat of the day, I got an early night and started rowing at two in the morning. Unfortunately for two of the crew, they had snuck out onto the foredeck for some 'deep and meaningful conversation' just before I got onto the rowing machine. They were hidden from sight, in a well where we carry out anchor operations, obviously keen not to be seen or get caught. Knowing that I tended to train for quite a while, but assuming they would be able to sneak back to their cabins at some stage, they waited. To give them their due, they did very well and lasted until four-thirty before they had to blow their cover!

By now, I hoped that the quarantine restrictions for entering the US had eased and that the UK was off the 'red' list. Unfortunately, however, this was not the case. I tried using my yachting connections to see if any boat was willing to sign me on as a crew member, thus allowing me to enter the country, but given the strict rules, understandably nobody was willing to do this. My only option was to fly to a third country, one on the 'green' list, and quarantine there before flying into the States. One of the few places I could secure the paperwork necessary happened to be Antigua so whilst I was there I booked a hotel which had a fully kitted-out gym which was perfect.

It may sound idyllic. However, with the cost of the boat and a whole host of other expenses having pretty much wiped out my savings, the thought of having to pay for another two weeks' accommodation when I could be spending it at home with my family was a bitter pill to swallow. Yet the sad fact was, I simply had no other option.

I knew of three other teams setting out to row the North Atlantic in the same predicament, one team of four and two other solos, all from the UK. Remarkably, we had all chosen exactly the same marina in New York to set out from and the goal of all of us was to reach some point in the UK. I was a little bit gutted upon finding out that the team of four was headed for London as my claim of being the first person in history to do so would have to be downgraded to the first solo person, but it was only a small concern. We were in constant contact and, though one of the solos had managed to wrangle a way into the States through one of his business contacts, the rest of us would have to take the circuitous route, quarantining in Antigua for two weeks.

Come the end of my rotation onboard the yacht, I was given a rousing send-off by the crew. This was quite moving and I remember looking back at them thinking, *When I next see you, I will have set a new world record*, which sent tingles down my spine and put a spring in my step as I bounced my way along the dock.

Back at home, preparations continued and there was no let-up in the training. I was fortunate that I had enough covered space outside to allow me to set up a home gym as all public gyms were closed due to the COVID restrictions. With my options limited, I made do with a rowing machine and some weights. The program continued to push me, but it was so nice to be back in the cooler fresh air in the UK and to be in the garden with the smells of spring and the sounds of birds; a very pleasant change from the odours of the poo room and the whir of the macerator pump as one of the crew flushed the loo on the deck above. I was hoping to get at least two more training rows in, one going across the Channel to France and another around the Isle of Wight, but delays due to the unforeseen work on the boat meant that I wouldn't get my hands back on her until the beginning of March, leaving me just one month to get to grips with her before shipping, which caused some concern.

However, I was heartened by a conversation that I'd had with Laval some months earlier during which he told me that he'd spent a total of forty-five minutes in the boat that Rannoch had prepared for him prior to departure and had made up the rest as he'd gone along. If he, a non-sailor and non-rower (he also told me that he only ever spent twenty minutes on the rowing machine before he got bored), could do it and set a world record in the process, I was sure that I could give it a go.

As with most expeditions nowadays, staying in contact with the outside world and having a social media presence is essential if you want to raise money either for yourself or for charity. Having asked around, I couldn't find a definitive answer as to what worked best and the systems that I used in my profession were far too unwieldy to put on a rowing boat. The previous owners had installed a system which, though not receiving rave reviews, was at least in place and compatible with my satellite phone so would save time and money. It could only be used for text and I wouldn't be able to send pictures so I decided to rent a BGAN (broadband global area network) unit to enable me – hopefully – to send images back home.

The unit arrived through the post and, as per the instructions, I had to call the rental company to configure it in order to get it to work. All I needed was a clear line of sight to the sky above me, access to the router that I would be using and a mobile phone signal so they could talk me through the process. This would have worked well in most circumstances, but the only clear skies I could get were quite a long way down the garden as I have a lot of trees which, no matter where I stood, seemed to be perfectly placed between the unit and the satellite it was trying to reach. There is no mobile signal where I live and the home phone didn't reach anywhere near the unit and the router was plugged into the wall inside the house so, with nobody else around to relay messages, I spent an increasingly frustrating hour and a half running between the two units as the person on the other end of the line took me through the process.

At each step, there would be a new hurdle. 'You should now see two green lights on the unit,' the guy would say, whereupon I'd sprint down the garden, find that there weren't any green lights, then sprint back to the phone to let them know that this was the case. We would then have to go through the process all over again. My wife eventually came home to find me with steam coming out of my ears and a garden that was a tangle of cables as I tried to get one thing in reach of another, all to no avail. If you had designed the perfect prank call, this wouldn't have been far off it, while if a film crew had jumped out of a hedge with a presenter shouting, 'Gotcha!' I wouldn't have been at all surprised.

Though I wasn't quite as gung-ho as Laval in terms or preparation, with time rapidly running out and every moment spent with Helene and the boys becoming of ever-increasing importance, I set my sights on a trip around the Isle of Wight. With its tricky tides and the need it presented to row through every point of the compass, this would make a good test for all the navigation equipment as well as allowing me to see how the boat handled in all sorts of winds. Another advantage was that Mum and Dad lived just up the road from my launch point at Lymington, so Dad would be able to drop me off with the trailer and I would get one of Mum's 'Full Monty' breakfasts and a chance to say goodbye to them before I headed off.

Having double-checked with the shipping company, I found they had a sailing on 18 April so I had to have the boat to them no later than the thirteenth for loading and formalities. The weather was looking good for 6 April so I headed down to the South Coast for an early start. We put the boat in via the slipway at Lymington as planned and, after a few adjustments, I was off and away on my own.

Lymington is a very busy little port with lots of boats and obstacles to negotiate. Thus, as I manoeuvred out into the channel under oars, I thought it might be a good idea to go back to the slipway to fit the rudder which might come in handy at some stage and which, in my eagerness to get away, I'd completely forgotten! Fortunately, Dad hadn't quite driven off so we pulled the boat back out of the water and duly attached it. The good news was that I'd only have to remember to do this once more between there and arriving at Tower Bridge so I hopefully I'd be OK.

Once I'd negotiated my way out of the Estuary and into open water, I pointed out toward the Needles Channel and got to work. The wind was blowing at ten to twelve knots from the west, which was where I wanted to go but, with a following tide, I made decent headway; although if I stopped rowing for just a few moments, the boat would spin around and head in the opposite direction. I knew from my earlier experience on the reservoir that this was going to be the case, but it was very frustrating nevertheless as I was keen to play with different systems onboard. Every time I stopped, however, I'd have to unstow the oars to spin myself back into the right direction and then quickly grab the rowing handle to get the propeller spinning. The effect of the propeller pushing water over the rudder was not enough to turn the bow of the boat through the wind without losing a lot of ground in the wrong direction and required me to describe a wide arc which would be fine in an open ocean but was not so good in restricted waters. Yet after a fair bit of cursing and going around in circles, I finally got the hang of it and carried on.

Next on the list of things to sort out was the AIS. Again, in the open ocean it would be a great tool, but here in congested waters I got an alarm every time I came within a mile of another vessel with an AIS system. Though only obligatory to carry one on bigger boats, these systems have become very popular amongst recreational boaters so on a lovely day on the South Coast, there were literally hundreds of boats around equipped with AIS, the bleeping of which assailed me with every stroke. I was mighty glad that I'd requested to have the reset button within easy reach, but this didn't make it any less frustrating. I'd have loved to have paused and found out how to inhibit the alarm, but having experienced what would happen if I did, with the boat spinning around, I was loath to stop rowing.

Another thing I had to test was the autopilot. I'd already put a route into the system and knew the waters quite well anyway, so I booted up the system, plugged in a rough direction and set off. The minute I did so, it threw me 90 degrees off course and the chartplotter in front of me showed me heading the wrong way up the Solent despite the fact that I knew where I was going (or at least was trying to go). The autopilot then went into alarm to accompany the AIS, which was only drowned out by me swearing whilst trying to row and constantly having to press buttons at the same time.

At least the system that I had designed allowed me to row one-handed. This wasn't the original intention, but it did prove to be a very useful function as I cursed my way along the channel. I switched off the autopilot, which seemed intent on taking me straight into the opposite shore, just in time to save myself from having to get the oars out to spin the boat around, and headed back to where I wanted to go, at which point my chartplotter decided that I was in fact going the right way so all was well. However, I still hadn't managed to test the autopilot so decided to give it another go.

According to a quote attributed to Albert Einstein, 'Insanity is doing the same thing over and over and expecting different results.'

Unsurprisingly, despite me having given the thing a severe swearing at, the same thing happened again so, with the tide due to change against me in a few hours, I decided to ditch that experiment until I had a bit more clear water in which to play with the toys. Fortunately, as I neared the entrance to the Needles Channel, the traffic thinned out a bit and the AIS alarm became less frequent. Due to the wind and the rather wobbly route I'd chosen, it had taken a little longer to reach the Needles lighthouse than anticipated but, after three hours, I made it just in time for the change of tide and turned a sharp left to head around the south side of the Island.

As I rounded the corner, the wind that I'd been battling into through the Channel died down to a gentle following breeze, the seas calmed and I was treated to a stunning day. The AIS alarm had run out of people to beep at so I just sat there and savoured the tranquility of being out at sea, just me and my tiny boat without a care in the world. The propeller system was working like a dream and we were making a very pleasant two and a half knots towards St Catherine's Point, the southernmost tip of the Isle of Wight. My plan was to get as far around the island as possible before the tide changed against me and then drop anchor, testing another bit of essential kit against the west-going tide.

The day wore on and I was making great progress. I was getting tired, but I was completely content out there with nothing other than my own thoughts for company. As I had done many times in training, I often visualised the finish, approaching Tower Bridge, to pep myself up. Though it was a long way distant, with each little victory and lesson learnt, it seemed a step closer to reality.

It seemed that on every outing in *Peggy* I was blessed with incredible weather and this day was no exception. I rounded St Catherine's Point bang on time and coped with the overfalls (rough water caused as strong currents interfere with the seabed and rise to the surface) with ease. As the boat was jostled around by the waves, the propeller silently purred away and I smiled to myself, feeling pretty smug about the system I'd envisaged all those years ago and thankful for the work that Jon and Phil had done in bringing the project to fruition.

I was pleased to get past St Catherines Point as this is where the tides are strongest and I wouldn't stand a chance of getting past there if they were running the wrong way, but as the day drew on and a bit of fatigue started to creep in, my pace slowed. I knew that I had a big day ahead of me the next day as the forecast was predicting the wind to pick up from the west by late morning and strengthen throughout the day. This would make it a hard slog to get back to Lymington so I decided to carry on as far as I could.

I'd told myself that once the pace dropped below one and a half knots over the ground I'd look for a place to stop as I would be fighting a losing battle against the current. However, I needed to be as far east as possible to make use of the next tide which would get me around the corner and back west.

By eight o'clock that evening, I was all in having spent, apart from a few short breaks, a solid ten hours at the oars. I glided into a lovely little bay in Sandown, put the anchor down and marvelled at my own good fortune at being here, by myself on this night with a glassy calm sea and stars in the clear sky above me. I was tired and cold due to the amount of effort I'd put in, but just sitting there in the brisk night air with a warm pot of food in my hands, I couldn't have been happier.

The next tide wouldn't be until two the following morning so I settled into my cabin for my first proper night onboard *Peggy* and snuggled up for a few hours' rest. I managed to get some fitful sleep, but I was a little nervous of the anchoring position, not having the data for the range of the tide and being quite close to shore. On each occasion I awoke, I'd take a glimpse out of the hatch to reassure myself that all was well outside.

By one in the morning, I'd become bored with laying around waiting to fall asleep so decided to get up and row slowly towards the eastern end of the Island to catch the next tide. I didn't want to get there too quickly as the tides run swiftly and I would have been taken way too far east before the tide turned, but there were a few spots where I could anchor if the need arose.

After stowing everything away, I proceeded to haul the anchor which had done a great job – so good in fact that it had dug itself into the seabed and was impossible to lift. The water was beautifully clear and I could just about see that it was well bedded-in, about eight metres down, and I didn't much fancy swimming down to try and haul it out in the pitch-black dark, free-diving being something that I've always been particularly rubbish at. After half an hour of huffing and puffing, I took up as much slack as I could and tried rowing over the anchor to get it to topple over and free itself from the sand; but with the only accessible tying-off point being close to the middle of the boat, as soon as there was any tension on the line the boat would just spin around on the spot.

I'd contemplated this happening prior to stopping, but had been too tired to attach a trip line to the anchor. A trip line is a bit of string tied to the head of the anchor with a float on top so you can row to that and drag the anchor out of the seabed by the path of least resistance. That five minutes of extra effort six hours beforehand would have saved me forty-five minutes of puffing, panting and swearing as the rope and chain bit into my blistered hands. The incident was frustrating, but it provided me with an important lesson. I'm sure the Rev Ev would have had a suitably long-winded tale!

Eventually, I decided to give myself as much of a run-up as possible by using the full length of the anchor chain and rope, which was about fifty metres, and then row like buggery straight over where I believed the anchor to be (though on a pitch-black night, it was going to have to be a pretty good guess) in a bid to get it free. Thankfully, after just over an hour of trying, it yielded on the second attempt and I was much relieved when I finally dragged it over the side of the boat. I was also glad that I'd decided to get up early as it had now gone two o'clock in the morning and time to leave anyway.

The tide was still running well and I hardly had to make an effort to make two knots over the ground so I took the time to enjoy the stars and even had a lovely bit of contemplation time, sitting on my bucket having my first boat poo on *Peggy* as the current pushed me towards Bembridge.

In this, I was very grateful for a simple bit of advice from one of the crews I had met in Antigua who suggested that the best method was to fill the bucket one-third. This was enough to help prevent any unwanted adhesion but not enough to cause splashback even in the roughest conditions. The set-up is also important; you need to make sure that everything you need is both to hand and secure as in a proper seaway you're holding on to try and stop yourself and the bucket from toppling over which could have very unpleasant ramifications. On this occasion, the weather was fairly calm, but it was as good a chance as I was going to get to practice this particular drill which would make life a bit easier once out on the open ocean.

I rounded the eastern end of the Island just as the sun began to rise, revitalising me as it always did. Progress was pretty slow, as I was still rowing into the last of the east-going current with a slight breeze from the same direction, but I was happy to be on the way back, making just over one knot. Every hour now would be an hour closer to a nice meal, a few pints with Mum and Dad and a comfy bed, after which I'd get back to see Helene and the boys.

With the tide due to change and start running with me, I tried to settle into an easy rhythm but found the going a bit tougher this morning. I put it down to fatigue but it seemed to take an absolute age to get past the lifeboat station at Bembridge, particularly in light of the progress I had made the day before when the scenery rolled by much more quickly. Eventually the speed slowly crept up to over one knot, but I was hoping for more with the current. In the event, it wasn't until I poked my head up that I found out what was going on.

I had been sheltered by the cabin of the boat from the breeze, while my proximity to shore had kept the swell to a minimum. Unfortunately, the forecast wind seemed to have arrived earlier than expected and I was rowing directly into it, which meant more effort and less speed. Not that I had much of a choice, but I kept on plugging on as the miles ground out over the course of the morning into an ever-increasing wind.

By mid-morning the breeze had built to around twelve knots, and despite putting in increased effort, I made very little headway and any pause from rowing would see me pushed back to where I'd come from. On deeper-draft vessels, a strong current will generally drive the boat in its direction unless the wind is very strong, the reason being that water is a lot denser than air. However, my boat was designed to be slippery through the water – specifically for the trade winds route – so the wind was the deciding factor even in these light airs.

The good news was that I did have the hang of the autopilot and that the boat was now tracking well. It was something to cheer me up at a time when the effort required to make the miles seemed to increase with every stroke. By the time I had reached Ryde, my hands were really starting to blister up from the increased pressure on the handle. Blisters that had formed the day before popped and began to tear off exposing raw skin. I was in desperate need of a break but reluctant to take one. I was faced with a bit of a quandary: looking at the surface of the sea, I could see what looked like calmer winds inshore, about a mile to my left, which would allow me to make better progress, but it would also mean that I would miss out on the advantage of the current which would intensify over the coming hours.

I decided to try and head inshore just to give myself a break and have the possibility of anchoring in shallower water if required. However, with the wind now intensifying to more than fifteen knots, my speed had dropped to below one knot and it would take me an hour of balls-out effort just to go sideways.

Eventually, exhausted, I had to take a break, which was when I remembered that I was carrying a whole range of drogues and sea anchors. These are effectively parachutes which grab onto the water and hold a boat in position against the wind; though designed to stop a boat from drifting too far backwards in open seas, they would be ideal for my situation. My only concern was that I wouldn't have much control of where the boat would be swept, which wasn't great in a congested waterway; but needing a break, I decided to give it a go. In a bit of a rush, I turfed out all the gear from the aft cabin, the drogue that I wanted being right at the bottom of one of the gear lockers. I was losing ground quickly back to the east, but after about ten minutes I was ready to deploy it.

I'd chosen the biggest of the drogues which was about one and a half metres across. It was still small compared to the para-anchor, which is the really big boy, designed to sink further down into the water column and be able to hold against hurricane-force winds. Having never used one before, I hoped that I had rigged it correctly and that it would give me some advantage. Double-checking everything first to make sure it wasn't going to snag anywhere and was indeed tied securely to the front of the boat, I threw it over the side and waited as it drifted past me, thankfully in the right direction.

As it caught the current, the bows swung around and finally we were heading the right way, into the wind at about one and a half knots. This was a massive relief as I was finally able to take a break after a solid eight hours of rowing. I was pretty tired and in need of a decent rest so decided to ride the current for an hour before trying to battle into the headwinds again. It seemed like a bit of a cheat but I reckoned that I'd earned it.

The current was strengthening and it was lovely to see the 'free miles' pass by. However, given the congested waters around the entrance to Cowes on the northern tip of the Island, I knew that I would have to gather in the drogue way beforehand in order to be in a position to avoid a collision if the situation arose. The wind was by now a constant fifteen knots with occasional stronger gusts, but I knew from previous experience that the current around Cowes ran very fast so would hopefully give me the push that I needed. I therefore hauled in the drogue and jumped into the rowing seat as quickly as possible to try and prevent the boat from spinning around but, alas, I was unable to do so; the second the drogue came out of the water, the boat pirouetted and headed off in the wrong direction. I jumped onto the oars, but despite my every effort the boat refused to turn into wind which was immensely frustrating.

The strength of the current did at least mean that I was no longer losing any ground, so I redeployed the drogue to swing the bow back around to reassess the situation. Initially, I wondered if I would be able to row with the drogue attached, but the slow speed of the boat over the water surface due to the headwind meant that the rudder had little effect; as soon as the line to the drogue went slack, the bow of the boat would come around so that was a no-go. By now, I was approaching the entrance to Cowes harbour with a whole host of ferries and other watercraft crossing my path. It was no place to be at the mercy of the tide, attached to a large parachute with little or no ability to manoeuvre, so my choices were limited to say the least.

I decided to give rowing another try and so, with everything set, I gathered in the drogue as quickly as possible and jumped back into the rowing seat. The bow swung around but I was just in time to gain enough momentum for the rudder to work and slowly the direction stabilised.

Having now rowed for twenty out of the past twenty-eight hours, this final slog into an ever-freshening wind was not what I was hoping for. However, slowly, I made my way past the entrance to Cowes harbour and into clearer water. It had been my intention to get back to Lymington that afternoon on the last of the tide, but it had become apparent that this simply wasn't going to happen. I was pretty gutted at the prospect as I only had a week before I was due to ship out, after which I knew that I would be away for at least five months. The idea of missing another day at home wasn't something I relished.

With the wind now up to twenty knots and the coast of the Island exposed, there were no options to anchor so I took the decision to head to the small inlet on the Beaulieu River, just over two miles northwest of my current position.

In doing this I would be able to make my way across the wind without turning too far through it, which would result in me spinning around. I'd have to cross the Solent, exposing me to strong opposing winds, but it would also put me in a powerful assisting current. Hopefully, the latter would help, but as any sailor will tell you, this effect of wind over tide produces steep wave forms and heavy chop. Still, having no other choice if I was to make a safe haven and await a change in conditions, I put my big-boy pants on and got on with the job.

The propeller system worked like a dream through the building seas. Though not big by ocean standards, when you only have twenty centimetres between your bum and the sea's surface, a one-metre wave feels fairly big. Had I been using the oars, I wouldn't have stood a chance of making any progress. I'd briefly tried using them earlier in the day when passing Ryde, but the additional resistance of the wind on the back of the oars meant that I had to literally drag myself back by my feet to take the next stroke, and every time I clipped a wave with an oar the boat would come to a standstill, needing a back-breaking effort to get it moving again.

After two and a half hours of near flat-out effort, I neared the opposite coast. This gave a little protection from the wind, which was now back down to fifteen knots, allowing me to make slightly better progress. However, the river entrance is tricky and the river was now in full ebb, so that the current as well as the wind was against me. Yet having come this far, there was no way that I was going to give up and I could see a mooring buoy just a few hundred metres ahead. I was nearing exhaustion and desperate for another break, but I was fired up by the sight of people passing in their boats, travelling up the river under engine and watching me obviously struggle without stopping to offer assistance.

The truth of it was that I'd have probably said no anyway out of pure obstinacy. However, it would have been nice to have been asked! I was busting my balls for every centimetre and the final approach had to be carefully made as, if I missed the buoy on the first attempt, it would take me about half an hour to get back to where I'd been.

Rowing flat out, I could just about make out the buoy in my rearview mirror. I was having to make constant adjustments on the autopilot to stay on track, but eventually I felt a soft thud as the bow touched it. It took me a further five minutes, struggling against wind and tide, to get the buoy the one and a half metres to a position where I could grab it with my now shredded hands. I had to work very quickly as the boat was about to pivot on me, swinging me side-on to the current which I would be unable to hold against.

As the bow came around, the pressure on my hands quickly intensified. The buoy slid from my grasp, but I managed to throw a final hitch into the knot which held and the boat drifted back onto the buoy. It was far from ideal, but it did at least give me a chance to catch my breath after three and a half hours of continuous effort. The feeling of having achieved this small goal was fantastic and I was suddenly very glad that nobody had stopped to help as I wouldn't have forgiven myself had I given up.

Once I'd tied a more secure line to the buoy, I sat back and took a look at the forecast to assess my options. The wind was due to die down to twelve to fifteen knots in the early evening, while the tide would turn in my favour a little later on. I was so tired at this point that I was sorely tempted to row the hour up the Beaulieu River that evening on the flood tide and get Dad to bring the trailer around in the morning, but I decided to take a break, get some food inside me and reassess later. For now, I was at least safe and comfortable and ready for a well-deserved break.

Though the option of pulling the boat out at Beaulieu was entirely feasible, it was never really going to happen as I would have considered and, after a short rest and some decent grub, I felt refuelled and ready to go. It was then 10 p.m. and the wind was still blowing, but it gradually died down as the evening wore on. It proved a long, slow slog, but the last eight miles back to Lymington gradually passed and I finally made it into harbour where I tied up at two in the morning.

By the time I'd tied up in the sheltered harbour, there wasn't a breath of wind and all was beautifully still and peaceful. I was cold and aching all over and my hands were torn to shreds. But as I sat on the deck clutching a cup of hot chocolate, I was totally content to just take in the moment and congratulate myself on a job well done. In the past day and a half, I'd learnt a huge amount about the boat and how it handled, as well as about how far I was able to push myself when required, and felt that I'd made a huge step towards being prepared for the journey ahead. Ideally, I'd have loved to have more time to get to grips with the boat, but I was happy with everything I'd achieved up to now and felt increasingly confident about my chances of success.

Upon my return, Gus was kind enough to give me a few days' grace from my training. But the week flew by anyway as I crammed every spare minute I could into spending it with my family. As planned, *Peggy* was dropped off at Rannoch for shipping on 13 April, two days before my own departure, and before I knew it I was standing at Gatwick Airport with Helene, my boys and Dad to see me off.

The atmosphere was pretty strained as we sat at a café having a drink, none of us really knowing what to say. Eventually I got up and bid everyone a very emotional farewell. Having little idea what the next months would bring was a strain on all of us. It was a terrible wrench when I hugged them all for the last time and disappeared through the departure gate. A thousand thoughts went through my head, but eventually I calmed down and was able to focus on each step of the days and months ahead, all reaching to the point where I would be reunited with my family again.

12

NYLON: Final Prep

I'd crossed the Atlantic as many as twenty times aboard various boats and at least twice as many times on airplanes, but this time the journey took on a whole new significance as I looked down from my window seat at the sheer scale and emptiness of it. I was daunted and excited in equal measure by the idea of being in the middle of this blue nothingness, completely alone.

Physically, I felt that I had done everything that I could to prepare for it with the arduous programme that Gus had put me through. This was still going, but I was really looking forward to not having to train anymore and simply getting on with the row. The mental side would be a completely different story as I'd never done anything that involved this level of isolation before. I believed that I had the tenacity and level-headedness to deal with whatever the ocean threw at me, but only time would tell. I'd always been very happy in my own company and often craved a bit of solitude. This, however, would be taking it to a rather extreme level.

It had always been my intention to be in New York with the boat for the beginning of May. Weather patterns tended to change for the better from the middle of the month so I wanted to be there a few weeks beforehand for any final preparation and also on the off chance that a weather window would open up earlier than expected. This seemed a possibility with weather patterns becoming less and less predictable, new precedents being set nearly every year.

The two weeks of quarantine in Antigua was annoying with regard to missing out on family time as well as the additional expense. However, with the boat needing to be shipped in mid-April anyway, I was at least not missing out on any time training in it and, let's be fair, there are worse places in the world to be. The team of four hoping to cross from New York to London were also quarantining there so it was a good chance to catch up with them prior to arrival in New York. Though some regulations were in place, it was lovely to have a bit of freedom having been subject to the restrictions in the UK. I was still doing my workouts in the morning, but the rest of the day was spent wiling away the hours. It was a great time to decompress and focus on the task at hand after the frenetic activity in the months prior to departure.

I of course missed my family, but to have the head space to concentrate on the project and think of anything that I might have missed was a huge bonus. There was a growing shopping list to look after upon arrival in New York, but it turned out that I was probably going to have a bit more time there than anticipated.

The previous month (March 2021), the container ship *Evergreen* was transiting the Suez canal when the captain suddenly realised that he'd left his phone charger at the hotel in Cairo so spun his 400-metre-long boat around to go and get it. Sadly, he slightly misjudged the turn and, with the canal only being 250 metres wide at this point, he got a bit stuck, buggering up traffic for six days and causing an approximate US$7,000,000,000 loss in global trade. The funniest part was that his charger was in the side pocket of his bag all along (this may not have been the actual cause which is yet to be determined).

This had huge ramifications for global container transportation, effectively meaning that containers weren't where they were meant to be when they were meant to be there. And as it turned out, included among these delayed containers was the one that my boat was to be loaded into.

The day after I arrived in Antigua, the shipping company got in touch to say that *Peggy* would not arrive in New York until at least the third week of May. This was incredibly frustrating, the worst part having to call home to tell my family that I could have stayed there for a few more weeks. I did contemplate getting on an airplane and flying straight back home, but having already gone through one heart-wrenching goodbye, I didn't really want to face another. Plus, with COVID travel regulations being rather fluid at the time, there was no guarantee that I would be able to get back out to Antigua. Thus there was little I could do other than swallow the news and wait.

The two weeks went by quickly enough and I was both glad and relieved to board the flight for the final leg to New York. Until I got on the flight, I'd had it in the back of my mind that they could change the quarantine status at any time and ban flights from Antigua overnight, as had been the case in so many other countries throughout the previous year. My last hurdle was getting through immigration into the US. I imagined the scenario as they asked me how long I was staying for (I don't know, as long as it takes) and how I planned to return to the UK (yep, you can imagine how that conversation would go). So I was amazed, given previous experience with US immigration, which can be a little officious to say the least, when I turned up to a deserted airport and breezed through without so much as a single 'What's the purpose of your visit?'

There was a small part of me that felt disappointed not to have been detained and subsequently interrogated, upon which I could have regaled them with the entire contents of this book so far, but nevertheless I hurried out of the terminal before they had a chance to change their minds.

As previously mentioned, I didn't want to start and finish at arbitrary points, so starting from the Statue of Liberty and finishing at Tower Bridge, two of the most recognisable landmarks in the world, seemed like a good idea (yes, yes, I know, my French Friends, you've got that big radio mast thingy in the middle of Paris and there are a few others around the world so maybe 'amongst' the two most recognisable landmarks might be a little more accurate!). I'd therefore booked a berth at Liberty Landing Marina just around the corner from the monument. Coincidentally, the team of four and the other two solos from the UK were also setting out from there and we'd almost certainly get together before departure.

I don't doubt that there are plenty of New Yorkers out there who would dispute that I set out from New York at all, given that officially I set out from New Jersey. There is equal hubris on both sides, with each not wanting to be confused with the another, but I think that coming within touching distance of the Statue of Liberty still qualifies as New York to London! Interestingly, the state line runs directly down the middle of the Hudson River, putting the statue firmly on the Jersey side, but the state of New York seems to have rather handily nicked Ellis Island and the Statue of Liberty by drawing a circle around them and planting their flag. Of course, being British, we would never dream of doing such a thing, not on such a small scale anyway.

I'd been monitoring progress with regard to the arrival of my boat and constantly waiting for good news that never came. Deadline after deadline was missed for loading and subsequent arrival, which was incredibly frustrating, particularly as the other guys' boats had arrived and they were busy doing their final fettling whilst I was left twiddling my thumbs and watching my funds fritter away. Initially, as each bit of bad news came, I got pretty angry with the guys in charge of shipping. Yet despite the fact that cock-ups had undoubtedly been made with regard to communication on their part, there was nothing that they could do to suddenly make a container appear or unblock the huge backlogs of shipping caused in part by the pandemic and in part by the incident in the Suez canal.

One of the knock-on effects of the pandemic was the huge loss of workforce which meant that there simply wasn't the personnel to move stuff around, whether that was crane drivers at the ports, lorry drivers for the containers or any one of a myriad of support services that keep the wheels of commerce in motion, which meant huge delays in everything. In the end, annoying though it was, no amount of shouting or brooding over the situation was going to help and I became used to the fact that the boat would arrive when it arrived so I may as well just enjoy the time whilst I could. After all, the adventure had been in my head for ten years so a couple of weeks wasn't going to make a huge amount of difference.

Whilst hanging around, I got to know my neighbourhood in Jersey City pretty well. There seemed to be a stark contrast to Manhattan in that it had much more of a village feel. Though it was just my impression, in Manhattan everybody seemed to be much more self-absorbed, all striving for an almost impossible goal with little time for anybody else; just across the river, by contrast, there was a much more relaxed vibe. This may have been helped by the legalisation of cannabis; though it had the same laws as New York, smoking in public seemed to be a whole lot more prevalent in Jersey City where it could be smelled everywhere I went. I'd read about the health benefits of some cannabis-based products, particularly with joint inflammation, and I was keen to get some in the event of injury.

Having smoked the sum total of two reefers in my entire life (on both occasions, to show a girl how 'cool' I was before coughing my guts up and making a tit of myself) I thought I'd go to a decent store where I could get some advice so looked up some reviews and found one in Manhattan. I decided I'd make a day of it, with some sightseeing on the way. It's a pretty easy city to navigate, everything being on a grid pattern, so I eventually found the shop which looked promising from the outside, pretty much like a posh pharmacy with everything neatly arranged and a number of assistants on hand to give advice.

Approaching a young woman, I explained that I'd like a topical cream to apply to the skin which could help in the event of joint inflammation. In reply, she stared back at me with bloodshot eyes, eventually managing to tell me that she didn't know but would get one of her colleagues. Unfortunately, her colleague, another young woman, was a good four metres away from where we were standing and, by the time the first assistant got halfway to her, she'd either forgotten why she was there or found something more interesting to do, ambling off to the other side of the store.

I assumed that she was waiting for somebody else, but no, she had in fact forgotten all about me. I then approached a chap behind the counter. He stood, somewhat glassy-eyed, staring off into the near distance, and when I asked for the same thing he replied, 'I don't know, it's all good, man.'

Fortunately, the word 'cream' did at least seem to register and he pointed me vaguely in the direction of a shelf where I bought what looked like a roll-on deodorant which promised to be an anti-inflammatory massage oil. Emboldened by the legalisation of CBD products and partial to a treat every now and then, I thought I'd buy a tub of CBD-infused jelly sweets for fun. Eighty dollars later, I left the store none the wiser as to the beneficial effects of cannabidiol but keen to see what all the fuss was about.

Though I was in no hurry to use the cream, I thought I'd give the jelly sweets a go when returning from dinner one evening. Having gobbled one down and waited for half an hour with no effect, I assumed that they weren't particularly strong and, quite enjoying the taste, had another couple as an after-dinner treat. Still feeling nothing after another half an hour had passed, I became a little bored so turned off the light and drifted off to sleep. About two hours later, I woke up with a raging thirst and my tongue stuck to the roof of my mouth, urgently needing a wee.

Unfortunately, whilst I was asleep, housekeeping must have crept into my room and raised the bed. It was now a very long way down to the floor, but carefully I lowered myself onto the carpet below and slowly made my way to the bathroom. Far from relaxing, it was one of the worst night's sleep I'd had since getting there, a never-ending cycle of chugging water and then lowering myself back to the floor, needing to pee. I was very glad when the morning finally came and the bed returned to its normal height.

Next on the list and hopefully a more successful culinary adventure was a search for my favourite expedition snack, *kabanos*, the Polish dried sausage that I'd enjoyed for many years. I found a Polish deli in an area of New Jersey called Hoboken, four or five miles from my hotel, and thought I'd take a walk over there to see what they had.

An hour or so later I arrived at a lovely little deli called Jola and met the daughter of the owner, a charming lady named Martha. Unfortunately, they didn't have any *kabanos* on display. However, they were able to order them in for me. When I asked how long they would keep if unrefrigerated but vacuum-packed, Martha told me they'd last a good four months which was perfect. After I told her that I would need 150, vacuum-packed in bags of ten, she looked at me quizzically before informing me that they usually came as a pair tied together. I was still building up my calorie count with my dehydrated rations accounting for about three thousand calories a day and I wanted to take in closer to five thousand so I thought that a double sausage, as thick as your little finger and about thirty centimetres long, would be an excellent source of some much-needed fats and protein as well as a delicious snack with a bit of texture. Having paid a deposit, I promised Martha one week's notice before I came to pick them up. Then, highly satisfied, I bid her farewell and headed back to the hotel.

I'd been in New Jersey for a few weeks by now, over a month since the original loading date of the boat, and it still wasn't even in a container in the UK. However, I'd been promised by the shipping agent that they were doing everything to get it to me as quickly as they could. Finally, on 19 May, I got the news that I'd been hoping for. The container had been loaded onto the vessel *Budapest Bridge* and was finally on its way.

I wasn't holding my breath, having faced all the delays and hurdles that I had, but it was hoped that the ship would take twelve days to get to New York and then another three or four days to clear customs so with any luck I'd be reunited with *Peggy* by the first week of June. Having come this far, it was a huge relief, as had it taken much longer, I was seriously considering postponing the venture for another year as there was a good chance that I would miss out on the feasible weather windows and put myself in serious danger of catching the first of the autumn storms.

From that point on, I became an avid 'dot watcher', taking every opportunity to check on Marine Traffic, a website for tracking vessels all over the world, to see how far my boat had got. Within twenty-four hours of departure, the *Budapest Bridge* had pulled into the Solent to anchor up and await the passage of a storm whereas every other boat, it seemed, was happy to carry on and battle into it. By now, I was so over the whole fiasco that any internal rage was quickly doused and the whole issue laughed about as there was little point in doing anything else. It seemed that I had picked the very wrong year to decide to even get to the start line, let alone row all the way back.

The other teams were now ready to roll out and had been given a potential small weather window on 25 May but a better opportunity on the 30th. I'd become quite close to some of them and, though insanely jealous with them having their boats ready for an imminent departure, it was great to be part of their pre-expedition buzz. The two solos and three of the four-man crew were all current or former servicemen and we'd had some great nights out together in New York.

On one occasion, we'd been invited to the Manhattan Yacht Club's floating bar, moored in the middle of the Hudson River. Bizarrely, on the way over, I got chatting to a chap on the boat with an English accent and it turned out that he'd gone to the same school as me and was a rower whom I knew from the year below me. Though I didn't recognise his face, a few years having passed since, his name was very familiar. Then again, you're unlikely to forget a name like James Bigglestone, or 'Biggles', as he was known back then.

Shopping continued in earnest and I decided to treat myself to a few creature comforts. I'd learnt from my time in the Arctic that the use of snack bags to keep you motivated throughout the day was a really good idea. I therefore went and bought kilos and kilos of trail mix and sweets which were portioned up into 150 separate bags. Next I found a South African biltong shop and got them to portion up five kilograms of biltong into 250-gram bags so that I could have one a week.

I'd been given a few decent tips by Mark Slats, a record-breaking ocean rower and Golden Globe sailing race competitor whom I'd met whilst in Antigua and fortunately I'd found the time to talk about something other than his rear end. He swore by crispy onions to help make some of the blander food options more interesting as well as giving a bit of crunch. He also gave me another genius idea that I'd thoroughly recommend to any ocean rower, namely taking a thermal food bowl which is an insulated food bowl with a lid. Normally, you heat boiling water and add it to the dehydrated contents in the bag. This tends to lose heat fairly quickly and invariably you end up with lumps of dry food stuck in the corners and a packet which is hard to rinse out. With a thermal bowl, you simply empty the dry contents into it, add the prescribed amount of water (I used a rubber measuring jug) and screw the lid on. You can go and do whatever you want for up to an hour and come back to a piping hot and fully rehydrated meal; the bowl is easy to clean out and you are guaranteed to get the entire contents of the pack rather than putting food remnants back into one of the holds where it will fester over weeks and months.

For me, there was also something a little more civilised in eating out of a proper bowl and the feeling of unscrewing the lid to get a big steamy waft of food was fabulous, particularly after a long stint at the oars, while I could easily add my own seasonings to pep things up a bit.

As the weeks passed, my hotel room started to fill up with more and more stuff. Quite what the housekeeping staff made of it, I'm not sure. Maybe they thought I was planning on hibernating or just had a serious snacking habit.

Whilst in New York, I discovered that there were two other boats looking to head out at the same time as us. One Czech guy called Milan who lived in New York was planning to get to the UK, and a team of three 'Irish lads' who were heading for Ireland. I put 'Irish lads' in inverted commas as I met them whilst we went down to the dock and they seemed about as Irish as Donald Trump, although one of them did have the last vestiges of an accent. They were struggling to get their boat ready, beset by a number of last-minute technical faults, but they were confident of getting everything sorted in the following weeks.

As for Milan, it was his second attempt after having fallen foul of bad weather the year before, ending up washed up on Long Island after spending days tied to a navigational mark during some horrible storms which failed to relent. This time around, he decided to take the earlier weather window, no doubt eager to get going, but unfortunately the weather gods once again did not smile kindly upon him and he had to abandon his attempt ten days after departure.

The later weather window of 30 May still looked good for the three other boats and they all made final preparations to leave. Getting the initial tide right was essential to see them safely out of New York Harbour and through the Verrazzano Straits into the open ocean. One of the solos had decided to take the early tide to give him the best chance of getting offshore before the weather turned and the other two followed twelve hours later. The word was out that the crews were made up of servicemen, both ex and serving, and the Americans did the guys proud with a lot of coverage. It was a great departure with news crews both on the ground and in the air, accompanied by boats from the NYPD and NYFD to see the boys safely out of harbour.

Dinger Bell, the first man out, was somewhat more covert with just me and a few others there to wave him off at three in the morning. This to me seemed a nicer way to go, just occupied with his own thoughts, rather than facing the pressure of having to do TV interviews and answer a hundred questions. To my mind, the focus should be on you and your boat, but being media savvy has never been my thing which is why, I guess, I had to pay for 75 per cent of the expedition out of my own pocket.

Watching them depart left a pretty big hole in the marina, but my boat had almost arrived so I was feeling upbeat. All the paperwork had been pre-authorised and onward transportation booked meaning that, the second the container landed, it would be put onto a low loader and brought to the marina. The arrival of the *Budapest Bridge* was imminent, the boat due to make two more stops to unload before finally mooring up in New York on 3 June. With any luck, *Peggy* would finally be in the water and ready for me to stow all the additional gear on it by the fourth.

Needless to say, the day finally arrived only to drag on with no sign of the boat. By late afternoon, it was apparent that it was not going to appear and, with the weekend fast approaching, arrival was postponed until early the following week. As luck would have it, since the three other crews had left and made it safely offshore, there had not been a single satisfactory weather window, strong onshore winds making departure impossible in a rowing boat. Long-term forecasts, however, were looking better with the middle of June a likely date.

Come Monday, I was fizzing with excitement to finally get my hands back on my boat and begin final preparations but, once again, delays at the dock meant that another day slipped by with no sign of her.

Finally, on 8 June, a huge truck pulled into the boatyard with what I hoped was my boat inside. It was such a relief when they cut the seals and opened the doors to reveal *Peggy* in one piece, just as I had left her back in the UK. An hour or so later, she was in the water and I was away from the dock (remembering to fit the rudder first on this occasion) through a tricky little turn and headed towards my berth. I had to rein myself in as, after such a long wait, I was busting to head out into the harbour and reacquaint myself with *Peggy* on the water. I knew, however, that there was still a lot of work to be done so I just enjoyed the moment cruising down the canal to my berth and watching the world go by in about as close proximity as I was likely to see it for some months to come.

The latest from the weather router was a possible two-day gap opening up on 14 June. With the eighth coming to a close, this gave me five days to complete all the little jobs that I'd wanted to do at home but had run out of time for. These were mainly to do with stowing and securing gear and had to be done in as ordered a fashion as possible so that I'd know where everything was and could easily locate it in an emergency.

I was pretty used to this given what I do for a living, but the difference was that I had to prepare for the real possibility that, at some stage, my world would turn upside-down which put a very different complexion on things. Though there were lots of waterproof hatches on board, there simply wasn't enough stowage to put everything in them for a five-month journey.

The four main holds on the outside deck were already fairly full with my dehydrated meals and energy bars. The two aft were packed out with the various drogues and para-anchors and the compartments forward were already three-quarters full with various spares and tools. It takes quite a lot of forethought and planning to put what you think you will need at the easy-to-grab end of these lockers as the last thing you want to be doing is desperately digging around for an essential piece of kit in the pitch black on a violent sea. The problem is, there are only so many accessible spaces so it was really a matter of performing a sort of triage to ascertain what I was likely to need on a daily basis, what I would need to be able to get to in a hurry and then pretty much everything in between. There was a fair amount of guesswork and, though I believed that I was doing roughly the right thing, I'd have really benefitted by spending a couple more days at sea on a longer passage to get everything sorted. However, there was always going to be a bit of adjustment once I got out on the open ocean anyway, so I wasn't too worried, as long as everything was secure.

I'd found some old sail battens in the shipyard which I cut to length for the aft cabin. They could be bent and wedged under a lip in there, pinning down all the 'wet' hardware such as ropes, lines and the anchor which I wanted to store away from my living quarters to keep things as dry as possible. It was essential that this was all very solidly stowed as the aft cabin also housed the steering gear and the threat of capsizing and the anchoring gear smashing into the rudder mechanism was very real.

I'd ordered a load of bungee netting off the Internet and set to drilling fixings into the cabin wherever I could so that all my ancillary gear including first aid kit, life raft, tool box, sleeping bag and other things that I wanted close to hand would be easily accessible. I fixed a couple of rows of pouches to the cabin walls so that all the small stuff like torches, cooking gear, cameras, sat phone etc. could be put in one place and grabbed at a moment's notice which finished off most of my preparations with regard to stowing kit.

I was still enjoying the luxury of the hotel so had the rest of the food stashed there whilst I sorted all the other gear out and I'd arranged to go back to Martha at the Polish deli on the afternoon of the tenth to pick up my *kabanos*. The weather was now pretty hot and working in the cramped cabin with bright sunshine and temperatures in the mid- to high-20s wasn't a whole lot of fun, but given what I'd signed up for, there was little point in whining about a little discomfort at this stage. What was nice was that my location just the other side of the fuel dock at the marina meant that I had a steady stream of visitors and well-wishers. I've never really craved company, but seeing the other rowers depart had left me feeling somewhat bereft and alone so it was a welcome distraction to show people around and tell them about my journey.

All was going well and I headed back up to Hoboken to collect my Polish sausages on the afternoon of the tenth as scheduled. Martha was just about to close up but had stayed open for me and I was greeted with a lovely smile. Everything that I'd asked for had been done and was being kept out the back of the store so I settled the bill and was given a big bag of Polish treats to wish me well. When she came struggling out of the back room with a huge bag of sausages I was a little taken aback – until her son emerged with a second bag, at the sight of which I almost fell over. I should have known better really, being in America; these were almost double the size of the sausages I was used to in the UK, being thicker than my thumb and half a metre in length. It turned out I had inadvertently bought around seventy kilograms of sausage and, though I really liked them, I was sure that we'd have a different relationship by the end of the row.

I'd planned on walking home but reckoned that I might have developed a hernia by the first corner, the load weighing not much less than a fully grown adult, so I gave in and got a cab back the hotel where I had to find a trolley to transport them up to my room.

One of the last things on my list and something that I'd been putting off for a while, given the fiasco the first time around, was setting up the BGAN satellite link. I didn't have high expectations of this and was prepared for the worst, but this time it was rather more urgent that I get it done.

The guy on the other end of the line must have had the patience of Job as, though not a technophobe, I'm far from being a whizz kid and became more and more wound up by the minute. Once again, it was a complete faff with hours spent on the phone and an intermittent mobile signal not making the procedure any easier, but eventually we managed to set up an email account and a few messages were sent via the terminal. I wasn't overly confident in the ability of it to work at sea, having struggled to keep it stable enough to maintain a signal whilst sitting on the dock, but by now I was happy to just get off the phone having wasted the better part of half a day mucking about.

As it turned out, the issue could have been resolved in about fifteen minutes. The problem was that I was using the wrong Internet browser which did not support the system that I had. All very frustrating, but as the system was always going to be a 'nice to have rather than a need to have', I was very happy to put that part of the preparation to bed.

It was now 12 June and the weather was still looking OK-ish for departure on the fourteenth. The nerves hadn't yet started to kick in and I felt satisfied that I'd done everything I could by the end of that afternoon. It had been a stiflingly hot and muggy day so I rewarded myself by going to the marina store, grabbing a six-pack of ice-cold beer and sitting out on the deck of *Peggy*. All the items on my checklist had been ticked and there was little else to do but enjoy the moment so I sat on my seat, leant back against the cabin door and cracked open a beer. There were still a thousand thoughts whirring through my head and I was very glad not to have anybody else there as I was able to concentrate on myself and the task in hand, slowly compartmentalising all the different hopes, fears and miscellanea about the adventure that filled my mind. The weather cooled and a rain storm came over, but I was perfectly content to just sit out there and enjoy the last vestiges of relative comfort, knowing that it might be a long time before I had an ice-cold drink again. After the last of the six-pack, everything seemed good with the world.

With two more nights in my hotel, I decided to make the most of it. I love eating good food and it was one of the things I would really miss whilst out on the ocean. I'd been a bit underwhelmed by the food in general since arriving in New York, most of it being pretty standard fare based more on quantity than quality and most places offering a fairly generic menu, but I'd discovered a lovely little neighbourhood restaurant between my hotel and the boat that did excellent food and had a great selection of red wine. I'd visited 'Bistro la Source' a few times and got to know some of the staff and clientele so I booked a table for that evening and spent a lovely night saying my goodbyes and being toasted by a few new-found friends. If I was honest with myself, despite my outward bravado, the nerves had started to build and I wasn't sleeping particularly well so thought that a slap-up meal and a bottle (or was that two?) of red wine might help to comatose me and stop me waking up every twenty minutes with a growing knot of anxiety in my stomach.

Though I've no doubt it did help, sleep was fitful as departure loomed. On the last night in town, I hankered for a taste of home for a final farewell so found a pub that served decent beer and a fantastic roast beef dinner. Even now, eighteen months on, I start to salivate at the thought of it! I was really happy to be alone as I sat there enjoying my last taste of civilisation and occupied with my own thoughts, rather than having to entertain anybody else, which is no detriment to my parents who had planned to come and see me off but had been unable to due to the travel restrictions.

Unsurprisingly, I didn't enjoy the best night's sleep and was pleased to see daylight creep around the edges of the curtain. All felt rather surreal, as if I were someone else watching myself going through the routine of departure. After all the training and preparation, today was the day that I kissed everything I knew goodbye and embraced the unknown. Thus as I waddled down to reception to check out, burdened with my sausage and trail mix, everything around me felt very weird.

Part of me wanted to shout out to everybody what I was about to do, but for the most part I felt an inner contentment knowing that nobody around me had any idea of my ambition, nor would they even be able to comprehend the magnitude of the undertaking.

I loaded my gear into a taxi which took me to the marina. It was a beautiful morning and all seemed well as I emptied the boot, putting everything on a couple of carts and making my way down to *Peggy*. There were a few people milling about, but none of them paid me any attention as I started stowing my kit. Departure was scheduled for 15:00 that afternoon due to the tides which would give me the best chance of clearing the Verrazzano Straits and getting into the open ocean. The weather forecast was looking OK: I would have twenty-four hours of light following winds followed by a further thirty-six hours of crosswinds before the predominant south-westerly wind would kick back in, pushing me back toward the shores of Long Island. It would therefore be a matter of making as much ground as I could to the southeast over the following days to build up a buffer to ensure that I didn't end up blown onto the shore.

The hours between my arrival at the dock and my scheduled departure couldn't go quick enough and I found myself willing away the minutes as they ticked by. My send-off was not quite on the scale of those of the other rowers, being modest to say the least. Bonnie Monteleone, a representative of an ocean plastics charity that I was representing, had kindly flown in for the occasion, and a bloke called Doug who had a boat in the marina and whom I'd spoken to a few times had promised to come and wave goodbye. I had said to him out of politeness not to go out of his way if he was too busy, which he took literally, so at half past two I simply let go my mooring lines, said goodbye to Bonnie and slipped out of the marina.

It may sound like a bit of an anti-climax after so much planning and effort, but it was exactly how I wanted it and, as I took the first strokes, the butterflies that I had been experiencing over the previous days instantly disappeared and I felt nothing other than excitement for what lay ahead.

13

NYLON: Crossing the Atlantic, the Beginning

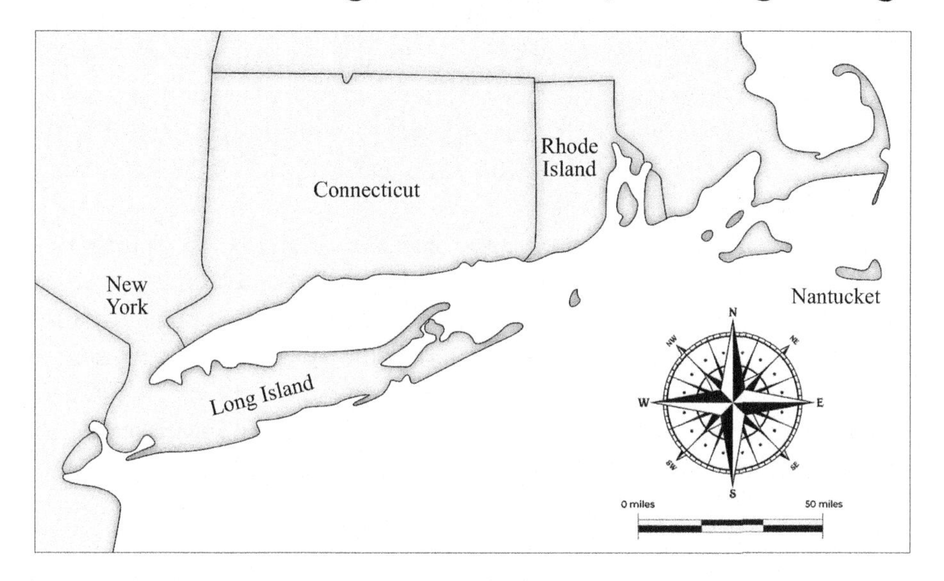

Rounding the corner of the marina and heading out into the Hudson, I suddenly felt an overwhelming sense of freedom and was on a huge high. It was only about a mile and a half to the Statue of Liberty and a further seven to the Verrazzano-Narrows Bridge, marking the end of New York Harbour and the start of the Atlantic Ocean, so I'd banked on taking around four hours to get there. I figured that this should give me just enough time to get clear of the narrow gap before the tide changed against me.

Navigation was tricky in these congested waters, but it was a good excuse to stop and take in the scenery every now and then. Most of the collision-avoidance had to be done by looking in my rearview mirror and judging as best I could, as to look ahead involved getting out of the rowing seat to peer over the top of the cabin. I had an electronic chart display mounted right in front of my rowing position so route-finding was easy enough, but there were a myriad of other small obstacles to avoid that weren't on the chart.

I was glad of my time in the Solent which was a similar waterway in terms of size and congestion and I made light work of dodging the various obstacles. Within half an hour, I was past Ellis Island and approaching the Statue of Liberty. It was now almost 8 p.m. in the UK and I knew that it was probably the last chance I had to see my kids on a video chat for many months so I excitedly called them whilst rowing past the Statue and showed them the sights. It was a strange feeling when I rang off, knowing that I wouldn't see their smiling faces again for some time.

Though I'd miss them terribly, I had already prepared myself for this. I had a load of photos on my phone and they had made me a 'good luck' card which was firmly glued to my cabin wall. Though a very poor substitute for actually being with them, it gave me an enormous amount of comfort. I would still call at 18:00 every day UK time to check in with Helene, but due to the cost of the calls, this tended to be very short and sweet just to let home know that everything was OK.

The scenery around me slowly changed, from the skyscrapers of Manhattan and Jersey City to the open parks just beyond them, then to the bustling commercial ports on the outskirts of the city where huge container ships loaded and unloaded goods from all around the world. I'd experienced similar shipping during my jaunt around the Isle of Wight, but nothing on this scale and it all felt rather overbearing, making me and *Peggy* seem very insignificant and vulnerable. As the hours ticked by and the Verrazzano-Narrows Bridge grew ever larger in my mirror, I looked forward to getting out of the industrial landscape and into clear water.

Eventually the huge bridge towered over me and the relief of exchanging the congested waters and busy shipping lanes for the widening expanses beyond was huge. I'd not made as much ground as I had wanted to on the first day, but I was satisfied at having come this far in the four hours since departure. By my calculations, the tide would start running against me in the next hour or so, so I was keen to get as far away from the funnel of the Harbour mouth as possible. Unfortunately, a headwind had been steadily building over the previous few hours so speed was starting to drop off and I was now down to one and a half knots which might well mean that I would not be clear enough of the Narrows to prevent myself going backwards.

Whilst contemplating the best course of action, fate intervened when the pulley wheel started offering no resistance and the boat was dead in the water. It was fairly apparent that the propeller had snapped, as I'd encountered exactly the same problem on one of the test runs whilst in the UK. Fortunately, I'd anticipated this and, not wanting to be stranded in close proximity to shipping and other obstacles, I'd only semi-stowed the oars. After unfastening a couple of bungee cords, I was up and running again.

There was a definite advantage with the prop system when going into light winds in that the back of the oars offered resistance when coming forward to take the next stroke, but the speed was about the same, the only difference being that I needed to use different muscles to pull myself forward. Though I hadn't felt a bump, I'd hoped that the prop snapping was due to a collision with a bit of debris rather than fatigue in the material. I was carrying three spare propellers, two with the variable pitch and one 'get out of jail' fixed pitch propeller, and I'd gone through replacement at sea with Jon so I was fairly confident I could effect a repair, but the place where I now found myself was too deep to anchor in. The choppy water would also make the operation very difficult and, with the wind and tide being as they were, I didn't want to stop there anyway, as I would have been swept back underneath the bridge in no time at all.

The chart showed a small island about a mile ahead. It looked as if I would be able to find a sheltered spot there to anchor in and swap the prop over so I carried on with the oars as the winds and tide started to build against me. An hour and a half later, with night having already fallen, I approached the island, going cautiously as the charts for this area weren't great.

The place was called Hoffman Island. It was a small manmade islet made upon a shoal in 1873 and named after the former New York City mayor and New York State governor John Thompson Hoffman. It was originally built as a quarantine station, housing immigrants who presented symptoms of infectious diseases upon reaching the immigration inspection station at Ellis Island, but now it was strictly off-limits and served as a bird sanctuary. This became fairly apparent as I approached due to the noise and the appearance of the rocks which, even in the dim light, looked as if they had been whitewashed, splattered as they were with bird poo.

I'd made it just in time by the look of it, as I could make out the tide now ripping past in the moonlight just fifty metres from my position as I sat in the lee of the Island. Rigging the anchor as quickly as I could, I threw it over the side and waited for the boat to settle to make sure that it was holding and that I wasn't going to get too close to the shore should the wind change. After a few minutes, all seemed well. I was tired and hungry, but my priority was to carry out the repair first and rest later.

We'd designed a removable hatch in the aft cabin that I could pull out to access the prop from inside the rear storage compartment. It might seem strange to those not familiar with boats that you can open a large hole in the bottom of the hull without sinking, but as long as the top of the hole is above the waterline, the water will not rise above the top edge of the aperture.

Still, I was a little nervous when removing the lid, having only performed the operation in broad daylight on Jon's driveway; but as the hatch popped out all was well, the only problem being the occasional swell passing through which caused the water level to temporarily rise and send a small amount into the aft compartment. Should I need to change the propeller in the open ocean, it was apparent that I would first have to transfer all the gear from the aft locker into the forward locker, not only to raise the back of the boat out of the water a little, but also to keep the gear as dry as possible to minimise weight as I carried on.

Once the hatch was out, I could clearly see that both blades had sheared off the prop. The procedure to remove the prop was simple enough; I simply extracted three grub screws that attached it to the shaft and then unscrewed it from the controllable pitch mechanism. Getting it back on was a bit trickier and again I'd have benefitted from a bit more time with the boat to carry out a prop change at sea (preferably in the pitch dark on a wobbly boat given the current circumstances), but after about an hour it seemed that I had everything lined up and I proceeded to mop out any residual water from the aft compartment.

It was now ten in the evening and I was very hungry. I hadn't planned on stopping that night, preferring to make the most of the marginal conditions to get as far offshore as possible. But my lack of progress in beating the incoming tide had forced my hand so I settled down for a few hours' rest and something to eat. I'd estimated that the tide should start to swing in my favour at about two in the morning. However, as I had no tidal atlas for the area, this was just based on my own observations and I hoped that the headwind I'd rowed into was just a temporary effect of the alternate heating and cooling of the land as night fell.

It had been a pretty full day and I was glad of the short if unscheduled break. The adrenalin from departure had long since worn off and I was nearing the point of no return; in short, I would soon leave behind any place where I could pull in and effect repairs. In the event of mischance, the only option from here until I reached UK shores, three and a half thousand miles away, would be to turn and head for shore which I was determined not to do.

Though I tried to settle for a few hours, I was acutely aware of my proximity to the rocks on Hoffman Island and I was up and down like a meerkat every time I thought I heard the cawing of the hundreds of birds roosting there get louder. Then, by one in the morning, there was little point in trying to rest any longer so I prepared to leave. This time, having learned from my lesson on the Solent, I'd attached a trip line to the anchor which came up easily and, having hurriedly gathered it onto the deck, I took to the oars to get away from land before stowing it properly. The wind had decreased a little, but the tide was still coming in and I struggled to make half a knot of speed. But half a knot forward was better than half a knot backwards, particularly knowing that I had limited time to get offshore before the weather turned against me, so I just kept rowing in the hope that the tide would change in my favour in the near future.

Hoffman Island is only four hundred metres long, yet it still took me a quarter of an hour to get to the other end. This was disappointing to say the least, but finally after an hour or so it had receded into the distance, only visible as a vague silhouette against the bright lights of New York. As the winds slowly died to nothing and then returned to the forecast direction, my speed started to pick up and once again I made decent progress. I was on a course perpendicular to Long Island, still trying to get as far offshore as possible in the short weather window that I had in order that I didn't suffer the same fate as Milan on both of his attempts.

The rowers in the three other boats who had left two weeks previously had all made the same decision and were now being whisked along by the coveted Gulf Stream, a fast-moving warm-water current which runs up from the southern tip of Florida and follows the US East Coast before petering out in the mid-Atlantic into a series of swirls and unpredictable back eddies. From what I could gather, the current was currently lying about a hundred miles offshore so it was there that I was hoping to get to for a bit of a free ride.

About an hour further on, I could hear the sound of waves crashing ahead and to my left, which was a bit disturbing as I checked the charts and could not see any shoals that might cause them. In the pitch black of night, I couldn't make out anything other than the occasional white crest in the near distance, but the sound alone was enough to give me a good idea of where I definitely didn't want to be. It did, however, give me a shot of adrenalin to get me through the small hours and I was mightily pleased when eventually the sound faded as I passed whatever tidal anomaly had caused it. Though it worried me a little, it only strengthened my resolve to get offshore as quickly as possible and into open ocean.

I could see the lights of Sandy Hook in the distance and to my left. This really would be the last port of refuge and the thought momentarily crossed my mind to put in and reassess the weather as this had always been an option. Some years before, another English rower, Olly Hicks, had restarted his campaign from this point having struggled to get clear of the New York Harbour area on his attempt to reach the UK. However, with the season already marching on and no sign of another weather window in sight, I decided to resist the temptation and take advantage of the conditions which were still in my favour. The thought of stopping here was, I realised, more of a case of me getting the jitters rather than being the result of any rational thinking.

Given the pressing timeline with regard to the weather, I'd decided to try and row two hours on, one hour off for the first forty-eight hours to give me the impetus that I needed. It was a pretty gruelling start to the voyage, most solo rowers having time to settle into a rhythm and gradually increase the hours on the oars as their bodies grew used to the toil, but it was born of necessity. The two hours on seemed to last longer and longer and the hour's break went in a flash, getting some calories down me and having a quick nap, but twenty-four hours in, I was making good progress.

As forecast, the winds started to swing slightly, still helping me but not as much as I'd hoped. Thankfully, they were very light but still less than ideal for the propeller, the bow wanting to constantly swing directly downwind and needing a lot of rudder to keep me going in the right direction. I was carrying two daggerboards, a long one and a short one, to help stabilise the bow and maintain the correct tracking, so I slotted the long one in. The autopilot was also struggling to keep up so I gave up on the propeller and opted for the oars as I could row using my right side predominantly which helped to keep me going the right way. The winds weren't strong and I was still making good progress. However, at this early stage it put a lot of strain on one side of my body and, by the end of the first day, I'd started to experience numbness along both arms and in one hand. Not great, but I guessed that I would just row through it and acclimatise as I went.

By the end of my second day at sea, the distant coastline had all but faded to nothing and I'd made eighty miles which I was very pleased about. The going was tough in the light crosswinds and I'd decided to straighten up a little with regard to them to give me a slight advantage, preferring to make good miles in the slightly wrong direction to ease the strain on my body rather than slogging it out in the right direction. It would mean a slightly longer route until I hit the Gulf Stream, but I was OK with that as I had reduced my leeway in turning the boat, that being the amount that the boat would skid sideways.

My hands were already heavily blistered from the effort and my back was aching, but I was taking painkillers whilst my body got used to the constant effort. I'd originally hoped not to have to do this, but with the length of voyage ahead of me and having learnt from previous experience that self-maintenance was very important, I succumbed just to make things a bit more comfortable. After all, there was little point in arriving in London in agony with a boatload of painkillers!

Just a quick lesson on leeway as it played an important part in the voyage and my ability to point in the right direction. As mentioned, leeway is how far you slip sideways when trying to go forward. The amount that each boat does this is very much due to its design and the speed at which it is traveling. A flat-bottomed boat with no fin will tend to easily skid sideways as there's nothing to stop it from doing so. A boat with a much deeper underwater profile, on the other hand, will tend to have a lot more 'grip' in the water and be able to resist a sideways push. Furthermore, a boat with a lot of exposed surface above the waterline will have a greater force acting upon it when the wind blows, which is handy when the wind is in the right direction but a huge impediment when it's not. Boat speed is an important factor too, as the slower you go, the more you have to angle the boat into the wind to work your way across it. Thus even in a 'beam wind' blowing directly across the boat, I had to effectively row into the face of it to maintain a straight course.

I knew that Rannoch boats were designed for fast crossings of the Atlantic from the Canaries to the Caribbean where the trade winds are fairly reliable and a light, flatter-bottomed boat with a larger above-water profile is a huge advantage. But here in the North Atlantic, it was a different story. The other three teams had opted for heavier, lower boats that would be able to track in a straight line far better than mine. When the conditions were good, however, I would be able to go quite a bit faster. I'd studied the weather patterns and discovered that, according to trends, I should get preferable conditions for around 60 to 70 per cent of the time with predominantly west-going winds to help me along. On the basis of this, I'd decided to sacrifice direction for speed.

Both Laval and the current world record holder had also used Rannoch boats so I guessed that it was a pretty good choice.

As the second day drew to a close, New York was just a distant glow on the horizon. The only thing still visible was the flashing light on top of the World Trade Center which I was determined to lose sight of over the course of the evening. Being a bit of a geography anorak, I loved the feeling of rowing over the curvature of the earth to make things disappear. As the night wore on, I saw less and less of it as I bobbed up and down on the waves before catching my last glance of it just before dawn.

Far from feeling afraid of losing the last vestiges of land, I felt liberated to finally be away and in the open ocean by myself.

On my third morning at sea, I came off a two-hour shift to find that the solar panels were not even providing enough electricity to power my chartplotter let alone anything else. It turned out that one had completely given up and the other was only producing about 30 per cent of what it should. Though I could have carried on, using the handheld water maker to produce enough fresh water to keep me alive, it would have left me with no communication or navigation equipment. I was hugely grateful, therefore, for the last-minute addition of the auxiliary socket on deck which allowed me to attach the spare solar panel.

Though I was now able make electricity, it was less than 50 per cent of what I had budgeted for. This meant I would have to ration usage to the absolute essentials: the main chartplotter in my cabin, the water maker and charging the satellite phone, nothing else, including the auto pilot which would help to keep me on track. As luck would have it, I'd tried listening to music on a couple of mornings, but I found it really irritating and much preferred to just listen to the waves and lose myself in my own thoughts. Not being able to use the stereo was therefore no loss at all.

I was carrying thirty litres of emergency water in the event that the water maker gave up which would leave me plenty of hydration for a few days. However, I found out later that day that it had been leaking, saturating my bedding in the process. Luckily, the weather was fairly calm and dry so I was able to hang everything out and get it dry-ish. Otherwise all was fine. The very light winds and very high temperatures made for hard paddling, but progress was good and in the right direction. My hope was that by the following morning I could stop rowing southeast and head more directly for home, with enough of a buffer between myself and the coast to prevent me being pushed ashore by the south-westerly gales which were forecast for the eighteenth and nineteenth.

Day four brought about a rude awakening and a real introduction to ocean rowing. The wind had freshened overnight and the swell began to build. Being inside an ocean rowing boat is surprisingly noisy, only ever peaceful on the stillest of days; otherwise the sound of the wind and waves slapping upon the hull is incessant. The change in conditions had me resting with one eye open, gauging how the boat was moving and reacting accordingly as the boat bobbed and pitched over each successive wave.

By now I'd broken my pattern of two hours on, one hour off, 24 hours a day, as I was happy to have got well clear of the land. I kept the same strategy during the day, but now I allowed myself six hours' rest during the hours of darkness. It being the height of summer, with the longest day just a few days away, I was able to stretch my target of twelve hours of rowing over seventeen hours of daylight which fitted in much better with my natural sleep patterns. Despite the constant noise and movement of the boat the previous night, I felt much fresher for the longer rest.

One odd phenomenon that I had noticed just before falling in to a fitful sleep was that I'd hear my parents voice in the various noises that the sea would make as they interacted with the hull of the boat. Not whole words or sentences, just something very familiar in tone that at first was a bit weird, making me wake up with a start but eventually, it became very comforting, almost as a reminder that they were there with me in spirit.

By now, the seas were up to around three metres and building. I had set the rudder over to try and make as much easterly progress as possible, but this left me rather vulnerable to the waves as I'd be hit fairly side-on by most of them however the night passed without serious incident and the boat stayed the right way up despite the frequent large rolls.

Come the breaking of dawn at around five in the morning, it was time for my sit on the bucket of contemplation. With waves regularly crashing over the deck, I thought it prudent to put on my harness and safety line and get ready to go outside. I waited for a wave to hit the hatch, counted a few more and then opened the hatch and clipped onto the safety line outside. What I was about to learn was that rarely did two waves crash over the deck one after the other. Thus waiting only increased the chance of being hit. As a large wave broke over the stern of the boat, I was unable to close the hatch as I'd attached my harness line to the stays outside. I tried to close it as best I could, but a huge amount of salt water gushed into the cabin as the wave hit the hatch, soaking my mattress. Fortunately, I'd got into the habit of stowing my sleeping bag every morning so that remained dry, but everything else in the cabin was suddenly damp.

With the forecast for rough weather for the next few days, there was no chance of drying it out as I had to keep all the vents tightly closed in the event of a capsize. Lying on a soggy mattress was fairly unpleasant, but it was a good lesson learned.

One essential bit of safety kit that I was carrying was an Emergency Position Indicating Radio Beacon (EPIRB), an electronic gizmo that would automatically go off and notify a rescue centre of my position in the case of activation. This could be done manually or automatically if the EPIRB found itself immersed in water. At work, we generally mount these on the exterior of the vessel, quite high up, in a protective housing with a special device which will spring the cover off should the boat sink. I'd simply installed mine in the bracket that was already on the rowing deck. However, with waves regularly crashing over the deck, I woke in the middle of the night to see the flashing strobe going off, indicating that it had been activated. I didn't know how long it had been going off for, but its activation puts a whole procedure into motion whereby a maritime rescue coordination centre will receive the alert. They will try to contact the registered owner of the unit or, if necessary, their emergency contacts to see if it is an actual emergency and, if they are unable to contact anybody, the big red button is pushed and a full-scale rescue is put into place.

I'd pre-programmed the telephone number for MRCC Falmouth into the sat phone in case of such an event. I now called them up to confirm that I was in a small rowing boat two hundred miles from New York in fairly violent seas, but was perfectly OK. At this, the woman on the other end of the phone asked if I wasn't a bit of a lunatic. I replied that I probably was.

The woman confirmed that they had received my alert, but unfortunately hadn't yet got the paperwork for the change in ownership or the emergency contacts. They had therefore tried to get the previous owners out of bed to ask if everything was OK. Not able to get through to the owners themselves, the coast guard called the first emergency contact listed, the owners' cousin in the US and, when that failed, their sister in the UK, at which point they found out that they were probably talking to the wrong person.

I stated again that all was OK onboard. However, I was asked to please read the sixteen-digit code on the back of the EPIRB to confirm that we were talking about the same unit. This was fine from the perspective of the very kind lady in Falmouth, but trying to read tiny letters while being tossed around in the middle of the night in a small boat wasn't the easiest thing to do. I'd purposely bought a cheap pair of reading glasses whilst in the States in case of such an event and stowed them in one of the emergency grab pouches lining the walls, but I was buggered if I could find them anywhere. Eventually, I managed by taking a picture on my phone and zooming in on the photo. All was resolved and the lovely lady wished me the very best of luck on my continued voyage. Hopefully, the cousin and sister of the previous owners were able to get back to sleep after being woken in the early hours to be told that their boat was sinking.

Other than that, everything was going pretty well. The propeller system had been working well in these difficult conditions with me able to get a steady pull whilst making my way across the wavefronts with relative ease. What was odd was that every now and then the mechanism would really stiffen up and it felt like I was dragging a big lump of seaweed on the propeller. I'd don my goggles on each occasion and poke my head over the side but couldn't see anything, but each time the increased pressure would diminish after a few minutes and the amount of effort I had to put in to propel the boat would return to normal. It would turn out later that when replacing the prop, I'd over-tightened it, snapping the controllable pitch mechanism.

Occasionally, a wave would slap the back of the boat causing the blades to deflect to full pitch, which was the equivalent of cycling uphill in your highest gear. A small weep had also developed where the driveshaft had gone through the hull, but compared to the amount of water that was entering the cockpit on a regular basis with the waves breaking over the deck, this was negligible.

With *Peggy* being designed to be rowed by two people, it had a larger open rowing deck than the solo boats and the well in the centre of the boat was able to hold about 350 litres of water. An automatic bilge pump would activate whenever there was more than a few centimetres of water in the bilge which would then cycle for thirty seconds after the well was dry. This would have been fine in normal circumstances, but with the solar panels playing up, the bilge pump was using too much battery power so I had to turn it on and off, all the time. The switch was inside the cabin so I'd have to wait until there was a decent amount of water in the bilge before opening the hatch behind me and arching back to operate the switch, then close the hatch behind me again whilst the bilge emptied in case another wave hit.

I'd already had a few knockdowns when the boat tipped on its side to 90 degrees when sideswiped by a wave, but thankfully it had bobbed back upright on each occasion. Had the cabin door been open, however, it could have spelled disaster, at best wrecking all my electronics and at worst sinking the boat. Once the bilge was empty, I'd have to do the same again, each time running the risk of a rogue wave hitting whilst I had the hatch open and further drenching the already damp and salty interior.

It was an irritating procedure, especially when I'd just finished only to be hit by another wave which would put a hundred litres or more seawater into the cockpit, but there was nothing that I could do about it. In hindsight, a waterproof switch on the outside of the cabin would have been great, but there was no way I was going to try and rig one up now, as to do so would mean drilling a hole through the cabin wall and I had no definite way of sealing it up afterwards.

Day six started well. The winds and seas were still high, but I made good progress and the sun came out properly for the first time in three days. This helped recharge the batteries, but after a few hours the propeller system developed a bit of a squeak. I applied some lubricant which seemed to have little effect and after an hour or so the little squeak developed into a bigger squeak which then turned, shortly thereafter, into a full-on death rattle.

After a call with Jon back in the UK, the cause was put down to failure of the main ceramic bearing on the driveshaft and, though I carried spares for most parts of the system, the only way this could be replaced was with a large hydraulic press. This sadly marked the end of the drive system which had been working so well up to that point. I was fairly gutted as it had been my 'genius' idea to design and build the system and a huge amount of time, effort and money had gone into developing it and bringing it to fruition. Still, there was nothing I could do about it so I set to work rerigging the boat to become a standard ocean rowing boat.

First thing was to remove the prop and the shaft to reduce drag so I jumped into the water with a hacksaw and started hacking away underneath the boat, coming up for gulps of air in between. It was hard work but lovely and refreshing, being my first dip in the ocean since I'd left New York. An impromptu inspection of the hull showed that she still had a lovely clean bum so I wasn't losing anything to friction caused by marine growth.

Next was getting to work topsides. Having got back on board, I found that the removal of the driveshaft had unsurprisingly left a hole through which the Atlantic was gently flowing, filling up the cockpit. I remedied this by inserting into the hole an AA battery, which was the perfect fit (a sharpie marker pen not quite having the girth). I stripped off anything inorganic from the pulley system and stowed that in the aft compartment and removed the heavy flywheel and committed that to the deep as it would only be deadweight from here on in. There was an arch in front of the rowing position which supported the chartplotter as well as the pulley that went to the flywheel. This was OK for short stints on the oars, but it was very easy to catch my hands on it in rougher conditions so I had to move it back about ten centimetres to prevent any future injury. It took a bit of time as I only had a hand drill, but eventually all was set to continue.

Though I was a bit pissed off with myself for trying to reinvent the wheel without ever having rowed a 'proper ocean' before, I got over it as soon as I picked up the oars and started paddling in complete silence. Of course, I'd been aware of the noise of the pulley system previously, and when I was resting the propeller would still turn causing a whir, but I'd got used to it along with the constant cacophony of the wind and waves; now, having got rid of the system and the noise that it created, life was blissful. Furthermore, getting back on the oars and feeling the blades pass through the ocean reconnected me to it and any regret that I'd had instantly disappeared, it now feeling like an altogether purer experience.

Conditions were still tough and I was constantly battered by the waves, but I found it totally exhilarating, one minute being in the trough of a wave faced with a three-metre, fast-moving wall of water, the next rising above it and surfing down the face as it broke all around me with a huge hiss and the whole boat vibrated with the speed, hitting over nine knots at times. My head spun with the thrill of it, but I had to keep my wits about me for fear of pushing too hard and getting sideswiped by the waves. On a few occasions, I had to let go of the oars and hang onto the rails as the boat tipped to precarious angles and I had little control over how I'd end up. Thankfully, we always came upright again.

I was having a great time, but being that close to the edge for days on end was exhausting and I was looking forward to an easing of the conditions.

By now, I was on the cusp of crossing the continental shelf and must have been very close to getting into the Gulf Stream. However, news from the weather forecasters was not good with a large tropical revolving storm developing a few hundred miles to the south and heading straight for me. Their advice was to cede some of the miles offshore that I'd fought so hard to gain over the previous week, which I really didn't want to do as I felt I was incredibly close to getting on the magic carpet ride that would sweep me towards home and give me a huge advantage but I had to go with the advice of the weather routers, so I adjusted my rudder and headed north of my intended track.

I had received a message before I left from the team of four saying that they had had some trouble in the area that I was heading for with a kind of counter-current that had taken them two days to get out of. They, of course, had the advantage of having two guys rowing constantly so were able to eventually punch through it, but they warned me to stay as far offshore as possible in the vicinity of the Nantucket Shoals. My current course kept me just over seventy miles offshore, which I hoped was enough to avoid the conditions that they had come across.

However, the approaching storm would first hit me with some strong southerly winds which would push me further towards land which was suboptimal to say the least. A knot of anticipation began to form in my stomach with the Nantucket Shoals being infamous for wrecking ships. They consist of constantly shifting sands, extending twenty-three miles to the east of Nantucket Island and forty miles to the southeast of it. As waves approach the shallow waters, they amplify into terrifying proportions. It would be a pretty awful place to find yourself in a storm so I was hoping to avoid them at all costs.

There was one positive in that after the change in course I saw my first sign of life when I came across the deep-sea trawler *Aces High*. The captain had obviously been a bit confused as to what he was looking at when he spotted me, hailing me over the VHF before coming in for a closer look. The signal wasn't great, but I managed to give him my email and asked him to take some shots and send them to Helene. After a five-minute flyby, with the crew all out on deck taking photos, I called him to say goodbye and thanks but heard no reply which I thought was strange until I remembered that I was butt-naked so maybe asking him to take some photos and send them home might have appeared a bit weird.

By the afternoon of 22 June, I was fifty miles southwest of the Nantucket Shoals; however I was making less than one knot in thick fog and the seas were rising ahead of the predicted storm. To make matters worse, I was in the confluence of three major shipping lanes which had my nerves jangling with visibility down to less than fifty metres. Though my AIS system was, to my knowledge, sending out a signal to other shipping notifying them of my presence, there was no proof of it doing so and I would be near impossible to spot as a radar target amongst the waves. Given my slowing progress and current position, I begrudgingly decided to deploy the para-anchor to stop me from drifting too close to shore.

The worst of the storm was due to pass in twenty-four hours, after which I thought I'd be able to resume my track. Though I knew the theory of launching and retrieving the para-anchor, I'd not done it in practice. Prior to leaving New York, I'd heard that one of the other solo rowers, Ian Rivers, had encountered problems with his anchor when the retrieval line (the rope attached to the head of the anchor to collapse the canopy and drag it back to the boat) had got wrapped around the parachute effectively strangling it and making it next to useless. With this in mind, and in deteriorating conditions, I decided to use a different method, tying a buoy to the retrieval line and attaching that to the head of the anchor so that when the conditions improved, I could row up to the buoy and retrieve the para-anchor. This would at least ensure that the para-anchor did not become entangled in the retrieval line.

Double-checking all my knots and with the anchor secured to the fixing point on the bow of the boat, I jettisoned it over the side along with the retrieval buoy and watched it drift away. The line soon tautened holding the bow of the boat into the wind and stopping me from drifting too far backwards towards the Shoals.

Having tidied up the deck and made sure everything was secure for the approaching storm, I retreated to my cabin for some rest. I'd made great progress up to now so was actually looking for an excuse for a bit of a break from the continuous battle against the conditions, although I would have preferred to have been well clear of the shipping lanes and away from the Nantucket Shoals. Monitoring my progress, I was hoping that my slip towards the Shoals would be about half a knot, but it was closer to one knot. I still had plenty of ocean between myself and the treacherous waters, but within an hour the rate had picked up, first to one and a half knots and then to two. At this rate, I would be on the Shoals in less than twenty-four hours which was a bit of a desperate situation.

I had no choice but to retrieve the anchor and make whatever way I could into the weather. I therefore went out on deck and made preparations to depart. During my time in the cabin, the fog had thickened making it impossible to spot the buoy that I needed to row to in order to retrieve the anchor. I tried rowing into the wind and waves in the hope of seeing it, but that proved impossible. I'd not planned for this eventuality – tied to the front of the boat, the anchor was way out of reach of the rowing deck. I spent the next half an hour trying to lasso the line from the safety of the deck, but sadly this proved fruitless.

The seas were now running at about three metres and increasing. The only option I had left was to get in the water, the prospect of which filled me with a certain amount of dread in the wild conditions but, with the Shoals drawing closer, I had no alternative. I grabbed my dry suit from the forward locker and put it on, only to find that having sat in my loft for the last few years, the rubber seals had perished so it was worse than useless.

With very little dry clothing to change into, I stripped off and prepared to jump in. There have been few points in my life where I've had to psych myself up to do something, normally being more than happy to commit to whatever was required, but this was one of them. Cursing myself for being such a f**king idiot for getting myself into this position and talking to Helene out loud, telling her that I was pleased she wasn't there to witness this as she'd have had my guts for garters, I jumped into the water with a line tied around me. The other end was tied onto a strong point on the boat, but this was of little comfort as I swam into the waves to find the line tied to the front of the boat.

What I hadn't accounted for was that the para-anchor does not float on the surface but sinks a long way down in order to secure itself well below the surface water so as not to be affected by the wind and waves. Consequently, the loop that I needed to fix the retrieval line to was a few metres underwater and under heavy tension.

Again, having no choice, I pulled myself down the rope, under the water, and managed to get my rope through an eyelet before returning to the surface.

Having to tread water and being constantly buffeted by waves made tying the simplest of knots very difficult, but after what seemed like an age, the line was secured. Unfortunately, I was no longer tethered to the boat but you can trust me when I say that the rope I was holding was never coming out of my hand!

I worked my way to the side of the boat and, with the adrenalin pumping, pulled myself out of the water with such force that I nearly disappeared straight over the other side! It was just one small step in the plan to get me out of shit creek, but it was one giant leap for Mark kind! I lay on the deck for a few minutes, catching my breath and chastising myself once more for having put myself in such a poor situation. All I could think of was Helene and the boys and how reckless I'd been, jeopardising my own safety not to mention putting the success of my voyage in peril. Yet now wasn't really the time for too much reflection, as I was still very much in the poo. My rate of drift towards the Shoals was up to two and a half knots and I was frittering away all the hard work I'd put in over the previous week.

My head spun as I tried to figure out how or why this would be happening. I could make neither head nor tail of it, but my choice was simple: pull up the anchor and row, regardless of how little progress I might make, or risk getting dragged onto the Shoals. The retrieval line wasn't tied to the head of the parachute so I had to drag the entire weight of the para-anchor filled with water from the depths and each pull, taking every ounce of strength and grip that I had, yielded only about twenty centimetres of line before I needed to repeat the process. The rope was eighty metres long and it took the better part of an hour to drag the anchor to the surface, but finally I saw the yellow canvas rising up through the water and grappled the last of it onboard.

I was exhausted, my hands were shredded from the effort and mentally I was completely depleted, but I had no choice other than to get on the oars and try and escape whatever was pulling me towards danger so I collapsed onto the rowing seat and started to row.

I tried to pull directly into the wind, away from Nantucket, but that was useless. Still going backwards, I set my mind to thinking how to best get out of this situation and came to the conclusion that there must have been an adverse circulatory current pulling me that I'd inadvertently hooked the para-anchor into. As with a rip current, there was no way of going against it so I decided to try and row across it instead. Progress was painfully slow, but eventually I started to make headway and I vowed to stay on the oars until I'd at least gained the miles that I had lost.

As the hours ticked by, my speed gradually increased and I breathed a sigh of relief. By ten o'clock that evening, I had nothing left in the tank and had to stow the oars and rest. The angle of drift was at least now taking me parallel to the coast and not straight towards it. If my observations were correct, this circular current would 'breath' in and out every six hours. Given that I seemed to be in an 'out' breath, I decided to rest for six hours, monitoring my track every hour. As soon as the current changed direction, I would get back on the oars and attempt to row across it until it changed once again.

My track showed a series of loops over the next few days as I fought to get free of this mid-ocean gyre, all the time shrouded in thick fog, but eventually I seemed to be making headway.

On my tenth morning at sea, I awoke to a state of mind that I have never felt before. The stress, anxiety and exhaustion I'd been exposed to over the previous ten days had taken their toll and I felt utterly broken and useless and unable to continue. For some reason I pictured myself as a defenceless chick in a nest and all I could do was pull the hood of my sleeping bag over my head and weep. In my mind, I conjured up a big red button that I could simply push to make the adventure end and whisk me back home to Helene and the boys. However, no such button existed other than to set off my EPIRB and call for rescue.

Slowly, after about ten minutes, I began to emerge from my torpor. There was no big red button, there was no safe harbour, I was still fit and healthy and I had a boat that worked. I reminded myself that I had put myself in this situation of my own volition and that there were literally hundreds of millions of people in the world who suffered every day with no end in sight and here I was, crying like a baby at my own self-imposed misfortune.

I hadn't entirely convinced myself, but I was on the road to recovery so I phoned Helene just to hear a reassuring voice. She was an absolute legend and literally talked me off the ledge. I was desperate for somebody to take the responsibility out of my hands and, if she had said at that point, 'Don't worry, you've done well but come home now', I'd have probably done so. As it was, she told me what I needed to hear: that I could do it and that everyone at home was rooting for me. It was the boost that I needed and after hanging up I felt a new strength and resolve to defeat this beast so I got back on the oars and pulled with an anger and fire in my belly born of having come so close to giving up.

Unbeknownst to me, Helene had got off the phone and broken down in tears at my situation. She'd never heard me sounding so low and longed for me to come back home safely, but she knew in her heart that I would never forgive myself if I gave up. There was an ulterior motive behind her support: she knew that if I didn't succeed, I'd only try and do it again and she was not going to put up with another year of my life dedicated to the row!

The whole experience of being in that mental state was quite shocking to me. A few people very close to me, all of whom I've seen as incredibly buoyant and positive people, have suffered bouts of depression and had talked of experiencing the exact same feeling of helplessness that I had felt in those ten minutes. Though it was only for a very short time, it gave me a whole new perspective on mental illness and the bravery of those who conquer it. Prior to that, I'd always been rather dismissive of people who claimed to be suffering from depression. I was more of the school of a hearty slap on the back and a "Come on, cheer up, worse things happen at sea y'know" being the remedy for people who are a bit down in the dumps. I now made a note to myself from that point on to make more of an effort to be empathetic towards people who might be suffering from anxiety which has subsequently served me well.

I was still far from out of trouble with the conditions not exactly great and the fog all-pervading. My batteries were running low due to the lack of sunlight and I was still travelling in circles on account of the current, but fortunately the circles were gradually decreasing. I remained on the continental shelf and, knowing that the Gulf Stream generally ran just beyond this, I decided to make a big push to get off it and hopefully catch a free ride at last. I hoped it was about forty miles east of my current position.

The forecast was good for now, but easterly winds were due to arrive by six o'clock the following evening so I had to get my skates on if I was to have any chance of finding the desired current. I rowed as hard as I could all day, putting in fifteen hours on the oars, and covered almost thirty miles, all of them in the right direction.

I was utterly exhausted but with another eighteen hours of favourable conditions forecast and an estimated ten miles to cover until I reached the Gulf Stream, I decided to take a six-hour break and resume early the following morning. The wind that had been blowing my way started to drop off at around four in the morning. This seemed odd as the wind dropping is normally a precursor to a change in direction so I got up and started rowing. By 06:00, the easterly wind had started to blow, twelve hours ahead of schedule. I only had six miles to go to where I'd been told by the forecaster that I would find a favourable current. I was desperate to reach it, but the wind quickly built to fifteen knots, gusting up to twenty, as a result of which my speed dropped to below one knot despite a huge effort on the oars, straining every sinew with each stroke.

As the wind came up, waves started breaking and it became impossible to get a decent stroke in the water; one in every ten waves broke across the boat, swamping me and filling the well with water, making *Peggy* ever heavier to drag along. The weather was too rough to contemplate opening the cabin to pump the bilge and the batteries were too low to use the pump anyway. The only positive from the arrival of the wind was that it did at least clear the fog and, for the first time in four days, the batteries started to charge.

After another hour of building winds, progress became impossible. My only choice was to redeploy the para-anchor and wait for better conditions which, according to the forecast, were a few days away. This time when deploying the anchor, I did at least tie a retrieval line to the fixing point at the front of the boat, but still fearful of tangling the para-anchor, I did not attach the retrieval line to the head of the parachute.

I was pretty miserable as I deployed the anchor, being so close to the currents that would assist me, and I was fuming at the forecasters who had got it so very wrong, but I was at least relieved to get in the cabin for a break and I resigned myself to sitting things out rather than torture myself trying to row in the impossible conditions. This was, after all, a marathon, not a sprint, and it was my hope that a few days in the wrong direction would soon be offset by an improvement in the weather.

Diving into the sanctity of my cabin in between breaking waves, I was at least safe and secure and able to rest whilst monitoring progress on the chartplotter. At least, so I thought until I looked at the screen. To my horror, I'd managed to hook onto the edge of the circulatory current which had plagued me for the past four days – I was being drawn straight back to where I had just come from. I monitored the regression for half an hour before deciding 'Bollocks to this!' Any direction was better than back towards the Nantucket Shoals and, knowing that the Gulf Stream was running from the southwest to the northeast, I figured that If I headed due south across the winds, then I may eventually bump in to it.

I entered a tug of war with the para-anchor, sometimes having to cede a bit of rope as the pressure in the line became too much for me to hold and taking up the slack when the movement of the boat allowed. After forty minutes of ball-busting effort, it was back on board and I was pointing the boat due south but making southwest over the ground, being blown 45 degrees off track – almost the exact opposite of where I wanted to go but it was still a better option than being swept back toward the coast. It was fairly counterintuitive to row directly away from home in order to get there, but it was better than the alternative.

After two hours of back-breaking work, constantly swamped by breaking waves, I started to see a change in my track over the ground as I started to swing around, almost imperceptibly at first, back towards the east. I was sceptical that I may have found the current that I needed, having seen maps of the Gulf Stream which showed it branching out and curling around on itself, but I decided to carry on. Two hours and just three nautical miles later, I was definitely into the right current. It was quite odd that I was pointing south in an easterly wind, but the boat was going northeast, 180 degrees away from the direction that I would have expected to be going in, but to be honest I couldn't have cared less how odd it was. The main thing was, I'd finally reached the Gulf Stream.

A huge wave broke over me and I couldn't have been happier. It was the temperature of tepid bathwater which helped to wash away the tears of joy running down my face. I was shouting and screaming for joy, saying thanks to Mum and Dad for giving me such determination and grit, and Helene and the boys for their unwavering support and belief in me.

Even the Rev Ev popped up again as I remembered a sermon about 'casting your nets into the sea once more', a tale of perseverance and faith.

There was not much left of the skin on my hands so I opted to attach the retrieval line to the para-anchor this time and I set it out once more. Upon deploying it, the bows swung through the wind and, stripping off my soaking-wet clothing outside to limit the amount of water that went into the cabin, I dived in and watched my track expectantly. Finally, I'd punched out of the gyre and was making half a knot northeast, against the prevailing wind, and was overjoyed to be doing so. I was still wary of being in a sidearm of the main current which could spin me off towards the coast, but for now I was happy to lay back and enjoy the ride, change into a dry pair of underpants and treat myself to a pack of biltong and my copy of *The Times* quick crosswords.

The following day felt like a completely new start to the row. The sea had calmed overnight and, though the wind was still against me, it was nothing more than a light breeze and the skies were the clearest blue. The relief at having made six miles overnight in the right direction was immense and I felt incredible. At one stage I'd awoken to check the tracker and found that I had stopped and gone in a small circle before continuing on my course. This coincided with a huge underwater canyon which must have interacted with the current to form a small eddy; at the time I was happy to just sit it out, too exhausted to contemplate doing anything about it. Getting up just before dawn, I was joined by a pod of three whales and could hear their clicks and whistles through the hull of the boat. It felt as if the ocean was rewarding me for having come through the trials and tribulations of the previous days and welcoming me to the warm embrace of the Gulf Stream so I decided to savour the moment with a leisurely breakfast, a 'Chuck Norris' shave (with cold salty water) and a swim in the balmy current.

The cabin was a mess as I'd had very little inclination for any housekeeping over the previous week and all the clothing that I had been wearing was covered in mildew. The mould had even started growing on the walls of the cabin so I took an hour to scrub, clean and dry out whatever I could. I removed one of the saturated cushions and put it on the cabin roof to dry out. Normally this would stop the solar panel from charging the batteries, but given that the panel was dead, it made no difference at all which I guess you could take as a positive.

By eight in the morning, the sun was already fairly high in the sky and it was apparent that it was going to be a scorcher of a day. I gathered in the para-anchor with ease this time, it being 'correctly' rigged and got to the oars again. Going was slow with the last remnants of the headwind remaining, but life suddenly felt a lot sweeter. I set myself a modest target for the day and decided to change my rowing routine from the regimented two hours on, one hour off and to see what felt right.

Truth was, I'd been struggling to keep up this regime, particularly towards the end of the day when the last two shifts seemed to drag on forever. Today, therefore, I thought I'd go with a fresh new start, rowing when I wanted to and resting when I felt I need it. I was still going to aim to row for twelve hours a day, but it would now be on my terms.

The hours slipped by with me immersed in my own thoughts, analysing how I'd felt over the previous days and looking forward to the adventure to come. I realised that I'd not discussed my fears and anxieties with anybody prior to departure, preferring to put a brave face on it and laugh off any misgivings I might have in a show of bravado, partially to convince myself that I was bigger and stronger than those around me. The truth of it was, of course, I was as fearful as anybody else would be, particularly in the last few days before departure. By contrast, Dinger Bell was more than happy to admit that he was shitting himself about the prospect of the row long before departure.

Coming from an ex-special forces soldier who had seen a lot more to be fearful of than I ever would, it seemed a bit strange to me, but I dare say he was probably a lot stronger for admitting his fear and coping with it, rather than hiding behind a mask of invulnerability.

The morning passed incredibly quickly and, before I knew it, I'd been rowing for three hours. The sun was now high in the sky and I regularly had to take my rash vest and wide-brimmed hat off and soak them in the ocean as a way of keeping cool. The blazing sun did at least mean that my batteries were charging which was just as well as I needed to make a lot of water to remain hydrated. At one o'clock, after five hours on the oars, I retreated to the cabin for an hour off to get some food and escape into the shade.

One of my cushion covers that was soaked made for an excellent sunshade on the hatch door so, leaving that ajar to get a gentle waft of breeze every now and then, I nodded off for a wonderful afternoon nap before the next session.

The day seemed to settle naturally into three distinct shifts, each one shorter than the one before, as I became more fatigued which suited me just fine so I decided to adopt that as my new regimen. The last shift was by far the best as the air cooled and the sun sank towards the horizon where it gloriously set. It was incredible what a difference twenty-four hours could make, but it was a dichotomy that I would become used to over the following months.

By 27 June, my wonderful magic carpet ride seemed to have come to a premature end when I woke up just before four in the morning to find that I was actually going backwards, but the good news was that the winds were due to finally change in my favour later that day. Getting back on the oars, the winds remained constant and though slow, I was still making tough progress into them. They grew a bit stronger that morning so after two hours on the oars I decided to take a twenty-minute break and a double ration of breakfast.

I'd arranged my holds so that two contained my main meals, one desserts and the other breakfasts. I'd purposely put them in completely randomly and would eat whatever I pulled out of the hatch that day. Deciding to have a double breakfast as I felt that I needed the extra calories to get through the morning, I managed to pull out a double helping of scrambled egg, cheese and caramelized onion which sounds delicious but was about as far from delicious as you could get. The dehydrated scrambled egg had the consistency and flavour of a car washing sponge and the cheese and onion formed a watery gravy upon which the lumps of egg would float around. But they were calories nevertheless, so I wolfed them down with all the enthusiasm I could muster. I managed to pull out a beef stroganoff with rice for dinner which was my second least-favourite but I at least had mixed berries and custard to look forward to later.

Getting back onto the oars after a quick break, the breeze was pushing up a slight chop and making progress slow as the boat hit every wave, sapping the momentum which I'd then have to strain on the oars to regain. But after a few hours, things died down and, by the afternoon, conditions were utterly blissful. The seas were now fairly calm and the ocean an incredibly peaceful place to be.

I know that the majority of ocean rowers like to have some form of entertainment to keep them occupied during their stints on the oars, but I found any sounds other than that of the ocean to be quite invasive and was quite happy to be locked into the moment and let my mind drift wherever it wanted to go. I was starting to enjoy the simplicity of life at sea, completely unencumbered by most of the things that we see as necessary in our daily lives and, with my day solely consisting of various cycles of row, sleep and eat, I felt incredibly liberated and privileged to be in this position.

I still loved my daily call home to Helene which I considered a luxury that pioneers of exploration in days of yore would not have had. Apart from that, I didn't crave any kind of company, preferring to just be in the moment. This was of course on the back of a few days of decent conditions and having only spent two weeks at sea, but I was happy to ride the wave of euphoria for as long as it lasted.

I rewarded myself at the end of the day with a bit of pampering involving a bucket bath, clipping my nails and my second change of pants since I started. I only had three pairs so with fresh water rationed to save on electricity, clean pants were a proper treat!

Historically, favourable conditions would be found on a fairly direct route from New York to the UK due to a phenomenon called the Azores High, a semi-permanent high-pressure system that sits just below the Azores and circulates the wind in a clockwise motion across the Atlantic. I was relying on this to give me the shove that I needed, but so far it had failed to fully materialise, only managing to hold for one or two days at most before being displaced by another pressure system which would bring adverse weather conditions, making the routing particularly tricky.

The weather guys back in the States were predicting long-term that the preferable conditions would be found quite a way south of the shortest route and they encouraged me to try not to stray too far north for now. The latest forecast was for strong south-westerly winds which would push me to where I really didn't want to be so it was going to be a bit of a battle once again. Already, I'd learnt a lot about how the boat reacted to winds from different sectors and how to keep it tracking as straight as possible using the different daggerboards and rudder settings so I was confident that I would be able to make the most of the forecast conditions.

Physically, I was holding up well having weaned myself off painkillers for my back pain. The only problem seemed to be a loss of feeling in my left hand with constant pins and needles, but that didn't hinder me except for a bit of discomfort at night which I tried to ease with regular massage and stretching. Mentally, I was in a good place, feeling that I had bounced back after my 'Black Dog' day earlier that week, but the forecast did have me concerned. As would be a common theme throughout the voyage, there was nothing I could do about it other than wait for it to arrive and tackle whatever problems it threw up as and when they occurred however the anxiety that would develop in the pit of my stomach was unavoidable.

June 28 had been a fantastic day in ever-increasing seas with some thrilling surfing, but by afternoon it was time to be a bit sensible and hunker down in the cabin. I was trying to maintain an easterly heading in south-westerly swells which left me a bit vulnerable to cross swells which could capsize me and, though I was wearing a harness and clipped in, I didn't much fancy being washed overboard and having to see where I popped up in relation to the boat.

The winds and seas had been steadily building all day and, after ten hours of rowing and the seas running at around four to five metres high, I thought it prudent to stow the rowing deck and lash everything down for the predicted storm.

This was my first encounter with a major weather system and the advice about coping with it varied from sitting on a para-anchor and letting it pass by to simply running with it and kissing my arse goodbye. The advantage of sitting on the para-anchor was that the boat would remain relatively still and the storm would pass over quite quickly, but obviously this would come at the cost of some very cheap and easy miles. Running with it (Laval's suggestion), on the other hand, would gain me some serious miles but I would have little control over where I ended up and would also be in it for a lot longer.

If the storm did intensify, there would be no safe way of going out on deck to rig a sea anchor so in the end I opted for a compromise, rigging a smaller drogue and a long line to the bow and lashing it all to the guard rail with a quick-release knot. If things got a bit too hairy, I could reach outside the cabin door and pull the release line and with a bit of luck the drogue would deploy and hold me steady into the wind and waves thereby minimising the risk of capsizing.

With everything rigged, I retreated to the cabin and checked that all vents were closed and all gear was securely stowed. I'd also taken the precaution of flooding the well in the deck (when I say I flooded it, the seas breaking over the deck did it for me; I just didn't pump it out) which gave me another 350 kilograms of ballast which would hopefully keep me steady in the water.

It was still light outside and the atmosphere in the cabin was stifling with all the vents shut, particularly as the sun set lower in the sky and was fully beaming onto the hatch, but with waves crashing over the cabin I had no other choice. I had adopted my earlier practice of waiting for a big wave to hit before cracking the door for just a second to get a waft of cooler air in every now and then, but this provided very little relief.

Just before dark, I heard the roar of a huge wave as it came barrelling towards me. Looking out of the hatch, all I could see was a wall of foaming water as the boat bucked and bounced before capsizing. I was tossed around in the cabin like a rag doll and gear that I'd thought was well-stowed suddenly seemed to be everywhere around me. As the boat self-righted, equally as violently as the capsize itself, the gear had another go at redistributing itself and a handheld radio flew through the air, hitting me above my right eye but causing no other damage that I was aware of.

My right knee was slightly twisted but the cabin was a complete mess. Apertures that I thought were waterproof were shown to definitely not be and I'd taken a few litres of water through various holes. Some had waterproof covers on the inside of the cabin which proved to be useless as all they did was dump more water into the cabin as soon as I took them off, despite my best efforts to catch the flood with my bowl. As an introduction to my first storm, I wasn't particularly enjoying myself and the same doubts and fears that I had experienced a week beforehand started to creep back up on me.

There was nothing I could do at the time other than try and clear up the mess that the capsize had caused and learn from the mistakes I had made. Apart from my stowing of gear which would have to improve, my biggest error was trying too hard to steer across the waves. I'd locked the rudder over so that my forward motion would keep the boat pointing in the right direction regardless of the conditions when what I needed to do was run directly with them. I duly straightened the rudder and removed the dagger board which would have helped to dig the bow in and flip the boat over and *Peggy* immediately steadied, not where I really wanted to go but in a much safer fashion and the miles to home were still decreasing which was the main thing.

Feeling a bit shaken and fearing the Black Dog knocking at the door once again, I called my rock, Helene, to tell her what had happened, mainly just to hear her reassuring voice. Once again, I wanted somebody else to make the decision for me to quit, but once again she told me exactly what I needed to hear. I asked her to ask the boys what they thought I should do in the hope that they'd ask me to come home, but my youngest, Harry, simply said, 'Never give up, Papa!' They were four simple yet powerful words that would resonate in my head and become my mantra for the rest of the voyage. From now on, I would do everything I could to show my boys that Papa never gave up, regardless of the adversity that he faced.

On a lighter note, I was making some serious miles, a bit ironic given the effort that I'd put into doing so already. But here I was, sitting in my cabin scratching my arse and going faster than I'd done on any previous day whilst listening to music and doing crosswords. Eating and weeing became a lot more exciting as I had to play roulette with the waves. Meanwhile, trying to boil water on a stove whilst the boat pitched and tossed was probably a little foolhardy, but the boat had definitely steadied after I changed my heading so I thought it worth the risk to get some decent food inside me. There was an ever-present fear of capsizing when I was trying to pee into a bottle which would not have been pleasant and the pre-planning of what to do in the event of capsize in order to minimise spillage was an exercise in itself. Apart from all this, everything was fine and the worst of the storm was set to pass by the following afternoon.

Though it wasn't the most restful night's sleep I'd had, I did manage to catch a bit of shuteye. The decision to run with the conditions until the situation improved meant that there was no point in constantly waking up to check my position and heading so I nestled into my bunk as best I could as *Peggy* rode out the weather like a champ. The following morning, I went for my daily sit on my bucket of contemplation but had to first bail out the 350 litres of water from the well and, by the time I'd finished, there was very little time for contemplation at all.

It was thrilling, however, sitting on my bucket, fully harnessed up and hurtling down the front of four- to five-metre waves, hitting speeds of up to ten knots. I'm guessing there's a world record for that somewhere and, if so, I was definitely in contention.

Afterwards, I grabbed my meals from the hatches for the day and retreated to my cabin for a bit of breakfast before getting on the oars. I'd been trying to keep the cabin as dry as possible which was a skill in itself whilst in big seas where even the act of having a poo offered no sanctuary from the waves. I'd found that the only way to do it was to lay a towel on the floor by the entrance to the cabin before leaving and then to be as naked as possible whenever entering the hatch, jumping in and closing it behind me as quickly as I could before the next wave hit.

It was this state of undress that I found myself in when, after boiling some water to make my porridge, I fumbled the stove whilst putting it away, singeing the tip of my penis and letting out an involuntary yelp. Certainly another valuable life lesson learnt but nothing that a bit of Sudocrem couldn't fix.

By ten o'clock, the seas were still high and the winds still strong, but I was getting restless and was keen to get the boat back on track and have some fun in the waves so I went back out and got ready to strap in. I fished my soggy sheepskin seat pads out of the dry bag I kept on deck (I was up to five now and felt like the princess and the pea, still able to feel every bum bone on the seat), slapping them onto the seat before unshipping the oars from their secure stowage position. It was only as I went to put my sodden shoes on that I discovered a grave error. I'd tied my shoes into the footplate but hadn't put my socks into the dry bag with the seat pads and was now one sock down.

They were made of bamboo so the environmental impact was minimal. However, I had been using the same pair of socks for the past three weeks so the biological hazard could have been far greater. The other sock did eventually come in handy when I decided to do a video blog whilst rowing naked.

It was lovely to be back out on the oars and making good headway in exciting conditions, but particularly good to be in fresh air rather than the stifling cabin.

Just after midday, I spotted a huge super tanker on the horizon, which was passing way ahead of my course, but as I carried on it got closer than I expected. I switched on my VHF radio (I had to keep it switched off most of the time to conserve power) to find that they had been hailing me for the past thirty minutes having assumed that I was in distress. An eagle-eyed watchkeeper had apparently spotted my tiny spec of a boat and thought it was a life raft of some sort and the captain had taken the time to divert this massive vessel to make sure that I was OK. It took a while to convince them that, yes, I was in a seven-metre rowing boat, four hundred miles from the nearest shore, and did not need any assistance, but eventually they believed me and turned around to get back on course.

It was a hugely reassuring feeling to know that there were seafarers out there who had the vigilance and professionalism to make sure that I was OK and I thank the captain and crew of *Iberian Sea* for going out of their way to check me out.

As they chugged off over the horizon, I was overwhelmed by how much smell the engines emitted. Being out at sea, there are no odours, other than my own (which maybe the super tanker picked up on long before they saw me) and the occasional fishy puff from a blowhole of a whale and, strange though it may seem, I found it rather comforting, having a whiff of something other than sea air and smelling of manmade stuff that was so familiar to me.

As the day passed, I noticed a shadow in the water tracking me and realised that it was a shark three to four metres long. Whereas the whales seemed to be more than happy to cruise alongside the boat and make their presence known, puffing out of their blowholes as they passed, there was something altogether more sinister about the movement of the shark, never more than a blurry shadow just beneath the surface. At first, I wondered if it was indeed a shark or just a trick of the light over the wave tops, but the occasional appearance of a dorsal fin gave the game away. The shark tracked me for a good two hours before slinking away, but I thought that I caught glimpses of it long after that. Not that I wanted to go for a swim, the boat making as much as four knots in the bigger waves with not a great deal of input from me, but I'd have definitely thought twice about doing so now!

Having spoken to other ocean rowers, I'd learned there was a consensus of opinion that it takes around three weeks to get used to life at sea. I was beginning to experience that now. As I neared the three-week mark, one of the things that struck me most was the incredible dynamism and ever-changing character of the ocean environment that you just don't appreciate when thundering along at fourteen knots staring out of the bridge windows of a superyacht.

This day was a prime example. The early shift in the morning went in a flash with long slow swells and a gentle following breeze allowing me to get into an easy rhythm and let my mind wander, fantasising about my first view of the UK coastline, anchoring up in a quiet bay and waking up to the sound of seabirds and the smell of land. The first two hours of the second shift went similarly, but fifteen minutes into the third hour a slight change in wind direction and speed threw me out of rhythm, so that I found it hard to string two decent strokes together, chopping at the water with my oars, trying to get a purchase on anything to pull myself along.

After a few weeks of fighting this I was coming to the gradual acceptance that this is the way of the ocean and that all I can be sure of is that if I could keep *Peggy* pointing roughly east, that each stroke was a stroke closer to home.

June had gone and I was into July, settling into the rhythm of life at sea. My only markers out here were arbitrary points sent to me by the weather routers that I would plug into the GPS to get some idea of my progress. There was a certain beauty in this, having no visual reference to gauge progress by and just pulling on the oars. It was in stark contrast to my row out of New York Harbour where landmarks seemed to take forever to pass or disappear and there was an undercurrent of pressure to perform with tangible markers to judge my progress against.

Once out on the open ocean, I made a point of not bothering to look at the chartplotter other than at the beginning and end of the day as it made very little difference; I just rowed in as good a direction as I could muster for as long as I could. Days were punctuated by essential tasks: topping up my water canister, preparing and eating food, resting and calling home once a day; the rest was simply spent at the oars. Small things that marked a break in the monotony started to make a big difference. Picking out a particularly good set of meals from the hatches, seeing something unusual in the water or finding a better way to get comfortable in the cabin all helped to differentiate one day from the other.

The one thing that was forever changing, however, was the weather. The Azores High had yet to establish itself and the much-hoped-for stable conditions that would enable me to make good progress hadn't yet materialised. Every four-day forecast always had a good amount of adverse weather in it, which kept me wary as to what the ocean would throw at me next.

One of my constant companions out on the water were the Portuguese man o' war jellyfish. Jellyfish are thought to make up as much as 40 per cent of the biomass in the ocean and I've had an interest in them since seeing a beautiful column of moon jellyfish at the London Aquarium that I found absolutely mesmerising. These almost sci-fi-looking creatures with their translucent bodies and, as far as we know, no cognitive function, seem to have some sense of purpose and to see this particular species making their way across the ocean, all apparently in the same direction (sometimes looking like they were making a better job of it than I was) was fascinating.

Strictly speaking, they are not actually a jellyfish but something called a siphonophore. The main float can be up to thirty centimetres long. They come in a range of colours – predominantly blue, purple-pink or mauve – and are filled with a mix of atmospheric gasses and carbon monoxide that they produce themselves. They are zooids and can deflate if attacked from the surface and temporarily submerge. They support a colony of creatures beneath them that are also zooids and genetically identical but fulfil specialised functions such as hunting, digestion and reproduction. Not bad for an organism with no cognitive function seeing that not that long ago in human history that was pretty much all that we were up to.

The man o' war hunts with its tentacles, stinging fish and other marine organisms and, though rare, they have been known to kill human beings too. Typically, the tentacles are around ten metres long but can grow up to thirty metres which made it a bit exciting when going for a dip!

On 4 July, as per the forecast, the next storm was about to hit me. A large low pressure system had formed to the northwest of my position and was barrelling its way towards me. The prediction was for forty-knot winds and sustained seas of greater than five metres over a thirty-six-hour period. It was the second major weather system to hit me in seven days. However, I felt a lot more able to cope with this one given what I had learnt from the previous storm and I was perversely looking forward to it as it would give me a chance to rest and to attend to a bit of self-maintenance.

By the early afternoon, I'd judged the seas to be big enough to justify knocking rowing on the head for the day and took time to stow everything properly, placing anything loose on deck in the various compartments and double-lashing everything that wouldn't fit below to the deck. Given that this system was going to hang around for a bit longer than the last and potentially be more powerful, I treated myself to an actual choice from the food hatches rather than having to sit there depressed at the thought of double couscous (the only meal that I had failed to finish due to it being so boring that not even my selection of seasonings could help it). I rigged the drogue once again for rapid deployment, but hoped that I wouldn't have to use it as my course had taken me into the 'sweet spot' of the ensuing storm which should push me in the right direction and be followed by a period of favourable conditions. With all that completed, there was little else to do but lock myself in and hope for the best.

I'd managed to set myself a program of stretching exercises which wasn't easy in the cramped confines of the cabin and anyone unfortunate enough to be looking in through the cabin door whilst I was performing them would have probably thought that they were looking at the wrong end of the last turkey in the shop on Christmas Eve, but it was great to stretch out some taut muscles at the end of a day on the oars. My bum was holding up really well and, apart from a few bruised bits, the stack of sheepskins were doing a great job at making the seat bearable. I hadn't managed to get rid of the numbness and tingling in my left hand, which was now also occurring in my right, but that was a very minor concern. Being in the cabin was also a good opportunity to catch up on some social media and, though I was unable to log into my various accounts, Helene would diligently sit and type out all the messages of support from people I knew, as well as those from total strangers. It was an incredible boost to my spirits to know that so many people were rooting for me and, along with my pictures of my family, these were my go-tos when times were tough and I was happy to read them over and over again.

The night was far from comfortable as the boat bucked and bounced over the waves and the wind howled through the aerials. Every now and then I'd hear the roar of a wave approach and feel the boat accelerate down the front of it and braced, waiting for the inevitable capsize which fortunately never came. It was a hell of a roller-coaster ride and one that I'd have gladly got off if I'd had the choice, particularly in the pitch black when I really had no idea of what was happening outside and could only imagine what it looked like from the motion of the boat. Thoughts of colliding with debris and damaging the boat were always on my mind, having heard of similar occurrences on other boats, but I reassured myself that it was a big ocean with not a lot in it so I'd have to be pretty bloody unlucky for that to happen and, anyway, there was bugger all I could do to prevent it so what was the point in worrying.

Come the following morning I'd already had enough of being in the cabin, but with the seas being as they were there was little point in being out on deck; I'd have just been exposing myself to danger and barely able to get an oar in the water amongst the wavefronts. But as midday approached, with the sun beating on the hatch, I had to get out for some fresh air.

The waves were still four to five metres high and travelling at speed, often breaking over the boat and setting us at all angles, so I harnessed up and hoped for the best. There had been an appreciable drop in wind speed which, though brisk, was no longer screaming and taking spume off the tops of the waves. It took about twenty minutes in the rough seas to simply un-stow the oars and other bits that I needed, taking care not to let anything go overboard or get broken in the process, but eventually I was able to start rowing again to try and make some progress as well as taking a bit of north out of my north-easterly track.

I'd been lulled into a false sense of security by the drop in wind and, within an hour, it was back and howling as violently before, whipping up the waves and making rowing impossible. I was grateful, however, for the short break out of the cabin and it gave me the opportunity to re-rig the solar panel to take advantage of the afternoon sun. Normally, I'd do this at least three times a day as the sun tracked across the sky, attaching it to different points around the boat to keep the panel as perpendicular as possible to the sun's rays to maximise the charge. But whilst locked in the cabin, it was less important as I needed to consume less water and therefore needed less electricity to power the water maker.

On blisteringly hot, still days, I'd need around twelve litres for cooking and drinking. But this figure dropped to as little as four litres on imposed rest days. Seeing the batteries charge to 90 per cent capacity rather than 80 did not justify the danger I'd have to expose myself to or the possibility of being hit by a wave as I opened the cabin hatch so I'd generally let the panel do its own thing in rough weather.

The wind abated during the night and the seas began to quell but, having only managed to snatch fragments of sleep over the past thirty-six hours and not being a huge fan of rowing at night, I decided to make the most of it and get some well-earned kip. The skies started to brighten at four the following morning and, after my morning ablutions, I was treated to a stunning sunrise on what promised to be a gorgeous day. After being in the confines of the cabin, it was blissful to be out on the oars once again with a light following breeze, lost in my own thoughts. Before I knew it, three and a half hours had passed without me even looking at my watch and wondering when the next break might be.

I was still very happy to let my mind wander but, although I found myself alright as a companion, guessed that I'd be very bored of my own company by the end of the trip. One thing that I did notice was how alien my own voice sounded, spending hours without saying a word and then suddenly breaking the silence with some utterance or another. Strangely, I'd also noticed that I spoke to myself in either a Yorkshire or South African accent if I needed to put my big-boy pants on and get on with something I really didn't want to do. Alternately, if I just wanted a chat or to amuse myself, I'd speak in French, well, my French at least. I think it might have confused any actual Francophones, but I knew what I was talking about.

Following the passing of the storm, conditions calmed and then the wind died altogether making it incredibly hard work on the oars. I felt like the boat had doubled in weight overnight, but it was a great chance to clean up and air the cabin as well as carry out a myriad of other maintenance tasks that were simply impossible to do in rough weather. Upon seeing a rain shower approach, I'd mop as much seawater out of the bilge as I could and use any rainwater caught to clean some clothes in a bid to keep the all-pervading mildew at bay. Changing into a freshly laundered pair of pants or T-shirt, or having a 'Chuck Norris' shave or a bucket bath, was a real treat following a passage of rough weather, making me feel totally revitalised. I even managed to dry out my mattress and bedding which made life on board a whole lot more bearable.

I'd made the mistake before leaving of repurposing my bedding left over from my previous boat, a lovely thick sponge mattress with a towelling cover. I knew that I would be sweating in the cabin so didn't much like the thought of spending my nights on a waterproof mattress and wanted something that would wick away the moisture. However, in thinking thus, I hadn't accounted for water frequently entering the sleeping quarters and so had effectively created a large humidifier which was impossible to keep dry despite my best efforts. I had at least got the choice of sleeping bag spot on; made by a company called Ocean Sleepwear, It was bulky but incredibly comfortable and included a Gore-Tex outer shell so remained dry and warm inside as long as I stowed it properly at the end of my rest periods. Over the past three weeks, it had started to gain a whole new layer of insulation, though with the warmer, calmer weather I decided that an inner lining of pubic hair and chest fluff probably wasn't needed so managed to get that out and give it a good beating and airing too.

14

NYLON: Crossing the Atlantic, the Middle

I was still making fantastic progress, far exceeding my own expectations despite the dodgy start, and in three weeks I'd surpassed the thousand-mile mark since leaving New York.

I'd made the mistake in the first week of looking at my position on the chartplotter and then zooming out to see where I was in relation to the journey as a whole. Suffice to say, it was less than inspiring and I vowed from that point on not to think of the bigger picture but to break it down into smaller, more manageable parts. Still, the thousand-mile mark meant that I was a third of the way across and officially 'in the middle bit' with my next big goal being the halfway mark which I hoped to pass by the end of the month. More significantly, I was nearing the end of the 'danger zone' that I'd identified from rowing statistics, the place where most attempts tended to fail, and I was building in confidence in my own ability to finish this.

There was still a heck of a lot of ocean to cover, but the thought of seeing land again was very much at the forefront of my mind. Though there was never any mention of a race between us, I had wondered if I would be able to catch the other boats which had set out two weeks before me. In this respect, I was heartened to hear the news from home that Dinger Bell was just a hundred miles ahead of me and on exactly the same track. Unusually for me, I felt no euphoria at having caught up with him, but I found the idea of being able to call him on the VHF to say hello utterly thrilling.

But a hundred miles on an ocean in two slow-moving boats with very different handling charachteristics was a very long way so I just kept my fingers crossed for now.

On the morning of 8 July, I awoke to a stunning sunrise, opening the hatch to the first light of day reflecting off the clouds in a whole host of pink and purple hues. The only thing marring this wonderful spectacle was the fact that the sunrise was at the wrong end of the boat and the last thing I wanted to see when travelling backwards to the east.

After a quick check on the chartplotter, I saw that no major damage had been done and I'd just described a big 'C' overnight losing four miles to the north and only a mile or so to the west. The conditions were forecast to be light initially from the northeast and then from the south so there would be no help from wind or current and I subsequently set myself a modest goal of thirty miles for the day.

The day did turn out to be incredibly still, the only puffs of wind no more than eight knots as forecast and bright sunshine. I'd hoped to get in a swim at lunchtime to cool off, but unfortunately the water maker malfunctioned so I had to spend my break seeing to that which also uncovered some damp bits in the cabin that needed to be addressed.

All was sorted within an hour or so, whereupon it was time to get back on the oars for the afternoon session. With slow conditions and thirteen miles to cover to get to my mileage goal, it was always going to be a bit of a push, but five hours of solid rowing later, with the sun having just set, *Peggy* and I achieved our goal with me having spent thirteen hours on the oars.

Since leaving New York, I'd made a point of calling Mum and Dad at least once a week. One day amongst other things (such as the latest football scores), they mentioned a friend of theirs called Denny who had decided to row with me all the way. She had pledged to get on the rowing machine every day at the gym whilst I was crossing the ocean and could apparently be heard talking to herself regularly, saying stuff like 'Come on, Mark, just another fifty strokes' and so on. This gained her a bit of a reputation, but fortunately she was quite well known, so the authorities were not notified to come and wheel her away.

It was always lovely to catch up with news of how my story was inspiring others but also tales of the normal. Many hours were spent at the oars simply thinking about all the things I was missing at home, such as doing the school run with the boys or stepping out into the garden and smelling the grass first thing in the morning. They were all pretty mundane things that we take for granted, but it required this kind of isolation for me to appreciate them for what they were. I was of course painting a rosy picture in my mind and a few days stuck in traffic would soon cure me of this utopian vision of my own domesticity, but it was a lovely thought to hang onto for now.

The morning of 9 July I was relieved not to wake up to another glorious sunrise, instead being greeted by a perfect rainbow over the entire stern of the boat. With squalls all around and winds gusting up to twenty knots, it was a bit of a soggy and difficult start, trying to maintain my heading to reach the next waypoint. After about two hours of rowing in cross swells with frequent 'cheeky slappers' (which by then had earned themselves several less-repeatable names) and making little progress, I decided to turn my bow a little more to the north to give myself a bit of a break in the hope that the news from the forecasters would send me in that direction.

After the first four hours, I took my break and checked the forecast to find that the plan had backfired as the waypoint had changed further south. Consequently, I once again pointed my bow across the waves for the next session on the oars.

Another slow four hours on, I was happy to take a break, but as the day unfolded things got considerably better. First I received a call from a Canadian coastguard plane, checking up on me, and had a nice chat with the crew who wished me luck and informed me that there was another solo ocean rower 183 miles to the northeast of me (whom I assumed must have been Ian Rivers). I then noticed a familiar target on the AIS system, the motor yacht *Gene Machine*, which I knew well as I had run one of her sister ships and had met the owners when they had come on my boat in Monaco with a view to buying it.

Anyhow, I called the captain on the VHF and he very kindly diverted his course, came over and pulled out all the stops to take photos and drone footage whilst circling *Peggy*. Having not seen another human for a few weeks, it was an absolute thrill to see them and I couldn’t thank Captain Brian and his crew enough for their efforts in coming over to cheer me on and provide some of the best footage of the entire trip. I am glad to say that I kept my promise to them when meeting up in Monaco a year later and took them all out for a few beers.

From then on, the conditions got better and better as the winds swung around to the west, so, still buzzing from my 'fly past', I stayed on the oars longer than anticipated and clocked up just under forty miles for the day with the winds now pushing me in the right direction.

The next day brought a bit of a mixed bag with decent conditions to start but the winds soon backing and strengthening until they were straight on the nose, bringing me effectively to a standstill. I flirted with the idea of ‘tacking’ across them, but it would have been of little benefit as the wind was coming from exactly where I wanted to go so doing so, when coupled with the leeway, would only result in some serious slogging just to go in a direction 90 degrees off course which would make me no closer to home.

I’d had a period of good progress so decided to award myself with a spell on the para-anchor to sit and wait for the conditions to change. I was happy to see, after setting it out, that I was making half a knot into the wind, having hooked into a favourable current. By now, the Gulf Stream had petered out into a jumble of swirls and eddies, as likely to be against me as with me, so it was very fortuitous to have found a helpful bit of current when I needed it.

I'd started to develop 'claw hands' from the continuous effort on the oars. This would cause me to wake up several times in the middle of the night with my hands locked into a rowing claw which I would then have to painfully straighten out. On traditional trade wind routes, this was less of a problem and would generally only develop much later in the voyage due to the reliability of the prevailing conditions which made the pull on the oars much lighter. However, here in the North Atlantic it was a very different story, particularly this year it would seem, when conditions were tougher than usual.

I had tried my cannabis-based massage oil, but think that any benefit might have had more to do with the massaging than the cannabis. At the time I quipped on my social media, 'Well, I've tried it for a few days now. Not sure if I'm doing anything wrong but I'm still waking up in the night with painful hands, the only difference being that I catch them wandering around the cabin at night looking for snacks and they don't want to get up until the early afternoon.'

Another physical change I experienced involved my appetite. Having had a month and a half in the US to put a bit of bulk on, I hadn't really felt too hungry for the first weeks, meal times being something that I scheduled to keep my calorie intake up rather than out of a gnawing hunger. Now, however, meal times were proving to be quite a big motivator and I often found myself fairly ravenous. I had burnt off a lot of my excess fat so everything I ate was pure rowing fuel. This had the benefit of making meals that I'd initially found to be mediocre at best incredibly tasty and I devoured them with relish. Given that I'd be on para-anchor for the rest of the day by the look of it, I treated myself to a double ration of everything and unsurprisingly slept well on a belly full of food.

Just after three in the morning the next day, I felt a freshening of the breeze and the swell picking up so, in the hope that it was the arrival of the predicted south-westerlies, I crawled out of my sleeping bag, put on my head torch and went onto the deck. Faced with the pitch black and a thick fog, I was dismayed and slightly confused that the conditions seemed to be coming from the northeast! Dazed after the deep sleep, the light bulb in my head finally flickered on and I remembered that I was in a rowing boat looking backwards so the compass and wind indicators actually read back to front so all was well.

The waypoint given to me by the weather router was only forty miles away. To reach it would need a solid day's rowing as it was across the wind and swell, keeping me south of the shortest route but in a favourable current. It was heavy going and as the GPS readout fidgeted around the two-knot mark, I was tempted every now and then to run with the wind and feel the effort ease on tired muscles and watch the speed pick up. It would have been simple to just go with the flow; however, my only viewpoint was in the here and now, as opposed to my weather routers who had powerful computers and complex modelling software as well as decades' worth of meteorological experience to assess my position and ultimately guide me to the best place to be for the coming days and weeks. So I trudged on in the direction they suggested.

Though their predictions were for the better part good, I was becoming disgruntled with them in regard to their lack of understanding of what *Peggy* and I were capable of. I had tried to explain to them on numerous occasions that I would only be rowing for around twelve hours per day, predominantly during daylight hours and, for the other twelve, *Peggy* would be drifting of her own free will. Yet when I received the forecasts, invariably they would be made for a boat moving at a constant velocity over a twenty-four-hour period. This was unrealistic and had to be continually readjusted.

I had been forewarned about the problem with this particular company by other ocean rowers. However, I wanted to employ a US-based weather router as I assumed that they would have the best knowledge of local anomalies along the East Coast of the American continent which was my major concern. These guys were also one of the market leaders in weather routing so seemed a safe bet. In hindsight, I would have been far better off employing the services of somebody who knew ocean rowing boats and their capabilities first and foremost rather than going for an all-singing, all-dancing weather forecaster.

With daily life on board now slipping into a very regular pattern, small things either good or bad could make a big difference. That afternoon I was unable to get hold of Helene and the boys with my satellite phone service giving me the message that the service was no longer available. After a few goes, I started to become quite anxious as I always called at the same time so that Helene would be available to answer and wondered what would go through her mind if she failed to hear from me. Within thirty minutes, I felt the Black Dog creeping up on me at the thought that I was very much alone out on the sea and would not be able contact Helene and the boys, Mum and Dad or the weather forecasters for the rest of the trip. I suddenly felt helpless, as the only way of reporting the problem required using the very thing that was broken and my mood quickly darkened.

Moments later, I remembered that I still had the BGAN satellite unit which, though I hadn't had a lot of luck in getting it to transmit, was at least a lifeline available to me. I wrote an email describing my predicament to Helene and asked her to get onto one of my sponsors who had not only supplied me with my handset but were also footing the bill for usage and then booted up the system, trying to find a stable place for the antenna to give me the three green lights needed to transmit the email.

The procedure for sending wasn't straightforward and the wait while the screen showed the 'transmitting' message seemed to last forever. Finally, however, I heard the familiar whoosh of the email being sent which sent a huge wave of relief through me.

I immediately brightened up and chastised myself for being so bloody stupid in letting the situation get me down without first properly assessing what tools I had to resolve it. It's not as if I hadn't done so many times in my life up until now, but I guess the circumstances in the past had been rather different in that fatigue and isolation had not been such big factors. Apparently, the fault with the satellite phone was purely down to a billing issue which was sorted within forty-eight hours.

The next few days brought ever-varying conditions, some row-able, some not so row-able, sending me zig-zagging north and south of my intended track but all with a good amount of easterly progress. By now, I'd become accustomed to making hay whilst I could and learning when I was better off battening down the hatches and letting the conditions do the work for me, although the stifling atmosphere in the cabin with all hatches and vents closed during these times was invariably miserable. Coming from different angles in close succession, the winds brought about confused swells which laid the boat flat on its side a good few times. It was therefore for the best that I just sat and rode out the worst of it.

This was to prove prudent as *Peggy* and I experienced our second capsize in a large squall with building seas. This time the customary bop on the head came from a flying water bottle that had come loose and clocked me just behind my ear. Unlike the handheld VHF radio which seemed to have come off worse from our previous encounter, the water bottle still worked afterwards. It also revealed that the first capsize had ruptured the waterproof membranes in the (not so) waterproof speakers, allowing a good few litres of seawater into the cabin but fortunately no sock was lost during this encounter and everything else was fine.

In the middle of the ocean, wildlife encounters were less commonplace, though I did have a petting zoo most mornings, waking up to either startled-looking fish gazing up at me through their dead eyes as if to say, 'What the f**k were the chances of that?' upon landing on deck or, better yet, collecting a somewhat more animated storm petrel out of the footwell.

Despite now being over a thousand miles from shore, every evening the latter would come around, seemingly fascinated by the white navigation light that I displayed, making a delightful chatter that sounded like a cartoon telephone call. Sadly, they liked to buzz by the light but couldn't see the thin wire aerials so every now and then I'd hear a clang and a flutter on deck. I'd rescued three so far and had enjoyed a lovely twenty minutes drying one out and warming it up one morning after it seemed that it had spent the night sloshing around in the bilge space. I had a lovely chat with it before it was ready to fly off, but decided to put some reflective tape on the aerials to hopefully stop the birds from crash landing. I was going to miss my encounters with them but it was for the best and, besides, there wasn't enough meat on them to liven up my couscous.

On 13 July, I had a very close encounter of the Dinger kind. Despite thousands upon thousands of square miles of ocean and innumerate permutations and combinations of weather conditions and currents, I received a ping on my AIS system to let me know that there was another vessel within a five-mile radius. It was obviously a small target as the signal was sporadic, which meant that the signal was only being received when the aerials could 'see' each other as they crested the waves at the same time, however, the system did manage to ascertain that the other vessel was moving at roughly the same speed as me and in the same direction.

I excitedly got on the VHF radio to try and hail whomever it was, but unfortunately didn't hear anything back. I also tried the sat phone, but no doubt they left that off as I did to conserve battery life (and to enjoy the fact that nobody could call up for a chat!). Though disappointed to have missed the opportunity to catch up with him and share my experience of this remarkable coincidence, it was nevertheless a great feeling to have come so close and meant that we were both going the right way (or were both hopelessly wrong).

Having struggled to stay far enough south in the strong south-westerly conditions, the weather routers were now urging me to try and maintain as much north as possible to put myself in the upper arm of a circulatory current which was running in a clockwise motion. I was only ten miles to the south of this arm, but the winds had swung around to the north-northeast and I was struggling to maintain due east, never mind gaining the necessary miles north. For nine hours I battled the seas, rowing with the rudder hard over and pulling on just one arm to try and maintain my course, but eventually I had to take a break and in one hour I lost all the ground that I had gained to the north over the previous nine hours which was incredibly frustrating.

Despite the entreaties of the weather routers, it became apparent that I would not be able to gain the required northerly latitude and so had to accept the hit to the south and row into the counter-current as and when I reached it. My frustration was compounded that evening when I received an email from my dad telling me that, if I could just get twenty miles to the north, I'd be in a much better position. I'm not an angry person, but just reading this made me absolutely furious. Though he only meant to give me some friendly advice, the message brought my frustrations to the fore. I'd spent a month at sea by now and battled some fairly adverse conditions, pushing myself to places physically and mentally that I'd never been before, and yet here was somebody sitting in the comfort of their own home looking at a weather chart advising 'if you could just…' with absolutely no concept of what that would involve.

The fire that this lit in my belly stayed with me for days. Dad's words kept going around in my head, keeping me up at night, and was a constant source of irritation as I slipped inexorably south over the following days, into worsening conditions, knowing that if I could have just stayed ten miles further to the north, I'd have been making far greater progress. I tried counselling myself with regard to this, but each time the email would pop back into my head, angering me once again. It actually took a full three days of going over and over this in my head before I finally let it go and was able to free myself of the mental morass that I'd got myself into.

It was quite an epiphany as I came to accept that there was no point in dwelling on the 'what ifs' of this journey. What was done was done and nothing could change the events of the past; the only thing that I could change was the future. It also taught me to accept the things that I could do nothing about and to concentrate on the things I could influence, so I suppose I should have actually thanked Dad for his glib comment, though I wasn't quite ready for that yet! Interestingly, after those three days, I was now forty miles ahead of Dinger and also sixty-five miles further south, such were the different characteristics of the two boats.

Those three days were pretty tough, with northerly winds gusting up to twenty-five knots and the side-on swells constantly soaking me as I rowed predominantly using one side of my body. Knockdowns were fairly frequent, displacing me off my seat, and the choppy waves would often clip the end of the oars, smashing the handles into my shins. I could have done my chosen charities a big favour if I'd had a swear box, though I would have been bankrupt by the time the weather next swung in my direction.

Despite this, it was not all doom and gloom. I'd seen some terrific wildlife with a huge pod of forty-plus dolphins having joined me as well as had a very close shark encounter. Normally they would hang back a good ten metres off the stern, but this one was barely beyond the end of the oars and at least half the length of my boat.

Furthermore, I'd passed the halfway mark in the my voyage, way ahead of my predicted schedule. Though there was still a long way to go, I decided to do a stocktake on my rations and found that it was fairly safe to push the couscous and the beef stroganoff towards the bottom of the holds and reward myself with frequent double rations of everything else. Funnily enough, this actually meant more to me than passing the halfway mark.

With the normal weather conditions failing to materialise, I came to dread opening the emails with the four-day weather forecast which tended to spell more adverse weather. Each time, I'd open them with the hope that things would improve and each time the report would give me a firm kick in the balls. Already 120 miles south of my intended track, the report on 16 July was no exception:

> *'The overwhelming wind regime with the developing lows and gales mentioned in your update earlier today will continue to be W-NW'ly near and north of the Azores. In addition, the N-NW'ly running in current in place will continue to be strong through at least later morning tomorrow, or just east of 39–30W. The best recommendation, as able of course, is to make as much E'ly progress as possible as to not get pushed further south. At this time, we're not anticipating a more favourable wind regime to make NE'ly progress to occur until at least the 24th as the low gale track shifts further north and ridging fills in closer toward the vessel's location. At that time, and really through the end of the month, we're expecting a more favourable pattern to develop with even SW'lys in place, allowing for more NE'ly progress. Do note that these developing lows this far south is definitely quite unusual for this time of year as climatologically it is more likely to have a much broader high-pressure ridge at this latitude. The lows and gales are typically farther north in July, which is what is expected to return by the end of the month as noted above'.*

Despite my epiphanies over the previous days and weeks, urging patience and acceptance, this was becoming a very bitter pill to swallow as the English coastline slipped ever further north and the angle of approach that I'd have to achieve steepened. At this rate, I'd be heading straight for the Azores and would be lucky to reach the coast of Portugal, never mind the UK. Only halfway through July and with good conditions not forecast for another week, my earlier optimism started to wane. The forecast letting me now that these conditions were very unusual and that I was shit out of luck did nothing to placate me and it took all my mental reserve to remind myself of everything that I had learnt about myself so far.

Once again, my go-to pep-up was remembering some of the stories that I had heard of the people that Global's Make Some Noise supported, people who through no fault of their own were battling chronic illness and would do so for the rest of their lives. There would be no stepping off their own journey to cheering crowds. A big burger, a few pints and a bit of stretching would not make everything better; all they could hope for was to make life a bit more bearable. Tales of their adversity had become my strength and remembering them made my struggles seem very trivial by comparison. I thus vowed to stop whining about my own misfortune as I was sure that they would give anything to change places with me and I would give anything not to ever have to go through their struggles.

That said, I doubt that I'd have been able to drag myself out of the hole that I was in if it had not been for Helene's support. She had come to dread a call from me any other time than the scheduled one as she'd know that I was low and needed to hear her reassurance and the last forecast had really knocked the stuffing out of me. She was, as always, amazing and helped me to put things into context as well as sending me all my wonderful messages of support which often brought me to tears. Probably my biggest bit of advice for any would-be ocean rowers is to make sure you've got a 'Helene' behind you!

Three days later, I was still battling against the constant northerly conditions which was hugely taxing on both mind and body, there was simply no respite. Although the forecast was for winds coming from somewhere between north and north-west, it always seemed to favour the more northerly of the possible wind directions meaning that I would invariably be heading in to wind. Just a shift of 10 degrees or so to see the wind indicator needle flicker a shade aft of the beam brought about huge relief as I tried to squeeze every degree of easterly progress out of my track with as little loss to the south as possible, but I finally cracked and on the last three-hour shift I decided that I'd just enjoy my time at the oars.

I'd settled into a pattern of three shifts of five, four and three hours respectively with an hour off in between which seemed to suit me very well, my time at the oars decreasing as I became more fatigued. The middle shift always seemed the longest, but I really enjoyed the last shift of the day and felt that, with nine hours of rowing already done, it was a bit of a treat to end that way. The days were already noticeably shorter than when I had set out and the fourteen hours required to finish my shifts were only just fitting into the hours of daylight, but being out there at sunset was always a wonderful feeling, especially knowing that I was rowing towards a well-deserved rest.

On this particular evening, I pointed the bows southeast and ran with the conditions just to give myself some respite from the relentless northerly wind and the relief was immense. No longer having to pull predominantly using one side of my body or fight the resistance of the rudder brought about an incredible feeling of wellbeing and, though I would lose about a mile further to the south than desired, I consoled myself with the fact that there was still a long way to go and it would make sod-all difference in the greater scheme of things and those three hours went by quicker than any others over the previous three days.

Neptune and his cohorts obviously took exception to my defiance the previous evening, sending me winds from the northeast and a south-going current. Waking in the morning to the sound of heavy rain on the cabin roof, I found that I had been pushed eight miles due south overnight and was still going southwest at over a knot! As I sat on my bucket of contemplation in the pouring rain, my only thought was that the winds had at least eased so I would be able to point the boat in the direction of the English Channel and make whatever way I could. Seeing that no warning of the adverse current had been given, I hoped that it was just a small cell that I would be able to punch through during the day so that I could start regaining some lost ground.

The rain was pretty relentless, but it was quite refreshing and allowed me to get enough fresh water in the bilge for a bit of washing, both of myself and my kit which was long overdue. Progress was slow, the first hours spent making no more than a knot, but I was at least going in the right direction, scrubbing the miles off the ever-dwindling tally. Eventually, the rain stopped and the wind slowly started creeping around to the west, allowing me to make better headway. The seas started to build which was a great sign as they are generally a precursor to the arrival of wind from the same direction and, by the end of the morning shift, it seemed that I was starting to get clear of the adverse current as my speed over the ground increased.

By the afternoon, the wind had settled to a gentle breeze and I was finally able to make some meaningful progress towards home. By the final shift, I was treated to near-perfect conditions. I was still headed by a slight current, but with winds and seas in my favour I enjoyed another blissful late session on the oars and was treated to a magnificent sunset.

The following day marked five weeks at sea. It was also the first day since the voyage began when the conditions allowed me to head directly for home and feeling each mile slipping off the total was mentally a huge boost. Having faced the conditions that I had, it meant a huge amount to be simply headed for my final goal, each stroke getting me a few metres closer to the UK. I knew that I probably had an absolute stinker of a forecast due as the conditions never seemed to hold for long and the forecasters had warned me of more turbulent times ahead, but my only hope was to make the miles that I could and hope that I didn't get pushed too far back when I couldn't.

Coming off the oars that evening, I was a little surprised to have only made thirty-five miles over the previous twenty-four hours, but having been able to do this in relative comfort made the actual amount fairly insignificant. Having passed the halfway mark, my mind was naturally drifting towards dreams of the safety of the UK coast and the welcome in London. I'd even allowed myself a zoom-out on the chart to see how far I had come and felt no disappointment when I did so. Yes, there was still a hell of a lot of ocean to cover, but I was closer to the finish than I was to the start.

On 14 July, I was told by the weather routers to try and stay above 42 degrees north to keep away from an adverse current which I was unable to do, slipping over 140 miles to the south and watching in despair as the numbers kept dropping. I'd set myself a threshold of 41 degrees that I must stay above, which was soon abandoned, as was the 40-degree marker, which was incredibly dispiriting. If I maintained that track, I would struggle to even stay north of the Azores, on a direct track for Gibraltar, a thousand miles south of the English Channel.

Yet by 19 July, five days later, I was ready to cross the Rubicon, back above the 42-degree marker that had been previously set and a heck of a lot further east. The numbers may seem arbitrary, but when in a huge expanse of ocean every milestone is a massive victory; the evening before, I had made it my mission to get back above that line of latitude.

The night had been fairly restless as I constantly adjusted my heading, a succession of squalls hitting me one after the other. The unstable conditions were indicative of a frontal system passing that would intensify over the coming twenty-four hours, leaving behind it finer weather but for now it was a matter of doing whatever I could to keep *Peggy* running in as straight a line as possible. Without an autopilot, my only way of doing this was to set parameters half a mile either side of my intended track on the chartplotter; if I went beyond these it would set off an alarm to warn me that I was off track and get me to set the rudder in the other direction if possible. The overall effect was to have my track looking like that of a drunkard in an alleyway, but it did at least mean that I didn't stray too far.

I was back on the oars at four in the morning under leaden skies and, at six, the heavens opened, thick grey torrents of rain lashing down on me. I decided to stay out on deck until the rain ceased as to open the hatch would have only added more moisture to an already dank cabin. By 11 o'clock, the storm was directly overhead and reaching its crescendo. The wind indicator seemed to be malfunctioning, maxing out at thirty knots but the sea state showed winds of at least fifty which howled around me, ripping the tops off the waves and atomising them into tiny droplets. The roar in my ears was tremendous and the rain hit me with such force that every part of exposed skin started to sting and I could no longer keep my eyes open. The impact of the gale on the oars as I lifted them out of the water rocketed me to the start of the next stroke and it almost took as much energy to restrain myself from being dragged forward as it did to make the stroke itself.

It was nature at its most raw and I was utterly exhilarated to be out in it, being whisked along at fantastic speeds, encouraged to row harder and faster to make the most of this incredible bonanza and I loved every second of it, fizzing with excitement as bigger gusts smashed into me and wave tops burst into clouds of spume drenching me further.

It was short-lived but what an experience. I felt like Odysseus tied to the mast as he passed the isle of the sirens, hearing their sweet song and left baying for more, but sadly the front passed taking with it my lovely south-westerly winds. I had at least crossed back to the north of my 42-degree line of latitude during my eight hours on the oars and the winds would, at least for now, let me stay that way. Again, the forecast wasn't great with more north- to north-westerly conditions which would send me back south, but neither was it as apocalyptic as I had at first feared and it looked like I would still be able to make some progress, roughly in the right direction.

I was still on a huge high for the last session of the day and, with the winds picking up again and having already had a buffeting, I decided (much like Odysseus's crew) to put in a pair of wax earplugs to drown out some of the noise. Putting this sense out of play had an incredible effect on numbing my experience of the deteriorating conditions. After half an hour of rowing, in building cross seas of four metres or more which broke over me regularly and took me to some very precarious angles, I suddenly had the strange feeling that being here in the middle of the ocean in a tiny boat, lashed by squalls, I felt utterly happy and comfortable. I spent the time thinking about how I should get around to restoring my vintage tractor and how to better clear up leaves off the lawn during the winter, not giving a second thought to the less-than-ideal conditions I was in. I simply felt at one with the seas and my situation and totally privileged to be out there with the absolute freedom to let my mind wander wherever it wanted, free of any distractions.

Funnily enough, Helene had asked me earlier that day if I was getting bored yet. The simple answer was no, I'd never been less bored in my life.

As had become customary during this rollercoaster of a row so far, the following day was bloody awful with the winds once again out of the north. Accordingly, in the first five hours of rowing I gained a measly seven miles and, worse still, had once again been pushed south.

The north- to north-westerly conditions persisted as forecast, once again making rowing very uncomfortable with waves constantly sideswiping *Peggy* and throwing me off-balance. The only thing I could do was to make as much ground to the east and limit my slide to the south as much as possible. I took a small amount of comfort when I heard news from home that Dinger was experiencing exactly the same conditions as me and was equally pissed off with them. The only thing of note during this period was that, for the first time in many years, I had the novel sensation of feeling the wind blow through my hair!

As progress slowed and with no let-up in sight, I came to the conclusion that my decision to double my rations on account of the great progress I'd made in the first half of the row may have been a little hasty. The thought of having a hold full of nothing but couscous and scrambled egg for the last leg of the journey filled me with dread. I therefore decided to get a bit creative with my meals – well, as creative as you can get with a dehydrated meal in a bag. Beef stroganoff was pretty low down the list, but I decided it would make a palatable soup when paired with couscous to pack it out a bit and, with a bit of seasoning, was actually alright. Scrambled egg remained a bit of a mystery and at one stage I even contemplated combining it with the much-coveted carbonara, but came to the conclusion that it would be an absolute travesty to taint my favourite dish with such an abomination of a meal. I had found, though, that by crushing the lumps of egg down to a fine powder they did at least absorb the moisture more readily and I wasn't left chewing on a piece of sponge in a watery, vaguely cheese-and-onion-flavoured slop and I was actually starting to enjoy it.

I always looked forward to meal times, being ravenous by the end of my stint on the oars despite constantly stuffing in as many snacks as I could during my brief stops during my shifts. I was very pleased with my decision to bring seventy kilograms of *kabanos*, though they had started to get a bit tangy and change to a slightly greyer hue, but no ill-effects were observed when eating them so I was still getting through a metre of sausage a day.

I'd also diagnosed that my ennui during the middle shift of the day was in part down to hunger which was when any negative thoughts would come to the fore. I blame my mother entirely by passing on the genetic disorder of 'hangriness' to me, as she also gets grumpy on an empty stomach, and decided to spread out my rations throughout the day which seemed to help.

On 22 July, the weather finally relented and the northerly winds started to drop, although I had once again been pushed south, back over my nemesis that was the 42-degree line of latitude. Much as I'd have loved to point the bows straight for home, I was being advised to remain south for now as the large circulatory current was still to the north of me and was running at about one and a half knots in the wrong direction. The idea was to wait until it weakened before trying to punch through.

As the morning wore on, the skies clouded over, the winds dropped to nothing and the sea became eerily calm, only the soft undulations of the residual swells disturbing the otherwise glassy surface. Since I'd started over a month beforehand, my progress had always been accompanied by the sound of the wind or the waves slapping against the hull but for now there was absolutely nothing. The silence became all-pervading and I had to stop and marvel at the utter peacefulness of it, at times standing on the rowing deck and shouting at the top of my lungs only to have the noise immediately absorbed by my surroundings. The rowing was tough without a helping hand from the wind, but the sense of complete isolation was an incredibly beautiful experience which lasted for the entire four-hour shift and into the evening when the faintest of breezes struck up.

The winds started to build in my favour overnight with my 'off track' alarm letting me know that *Peggy* was headed straight for home. The overriding temptation was to let her go, but I was mindful of the counter-current and spent much of the night fettling the rudder and centreboards to try and stay on track. I was desperate to head for home when I got on the oars and make the most of the conditions, having been swatted too far south with such regularity over the past weeks. After twenty minutes on the oars, I couldn't hold back so I emailed the forecasters to see if today might be the day that I could punch through the current that had been plaguing me for days. I knew that Dinger was in the sweet spot of the current, in the upper arm of it, and I had visions in my head of him wafting along ahead of me, happy as Larry on his para-anchor, having a cuppa and one of his beloved tinned pies.

Whilst their twenty-four-hour duty meteorologist sprang into action and put the necessary information into the highly sophisticated prediction software, I received the email below from Dad entitled 'Oi':

'Wake up you lazy sod, The wind's blowing the right way at last, take advantage of it.'

I thought I'd see out my shift before checking what had come back from the met office, but after another half an hour curiosity got the better of me and I gave them a call. They confirmed that, indeed, I could take advantage of the wind and proceed on course for the English Channel.

On the back of this, I thought of launching a budget forecasting service for mariners which would give succinct advice called 'Dadcast'. It would have to come with its own glossary for those who subscribed but didn't speak Cockney, a few pointers being: 'It's gonna get a bit taters'; 'expect a significant temperature drop' (taters = potatoes, potatoes in the mould = cold) and 'Nah, I wouldn't if I were you, it's looking pony'; 'inclement weather expected, advise caution for smaller craft' (Pony = pony and trap. I'll let you work that one out).

I hit the counter-current that afternoon. It slowed me down to around one knot, but with following conditions *Peggy* made good way over the water which helped to ease the stress on aching muscles. Every now and then I'd hit a lull in the current and get a taste of the speed I could be doing if it was not there which was very encouraging. I was also surprised to see how these eddies and counter-eddies would interact with one another and I could hear a change in current long before it was spotted as the fronts of two conflicting water masses met. Though relatively slow-moving, they were comprised of thousands upon thousands of tons of water which would cause the sea to 'boil' and could be heard from many miles away.

Rowing was always tricky in these waters as short choppy waves sprang up seemingly from nowhere and completely contrary to any existing swells, making work on the water difficult. There was also something a bit unnerving about being in these zones, which you passed in and out of, all too aware of the forces involved in their creation. The sight and sound of the crashing waves and whirlpools conjured up tales of yore about sea monsters swallowing boats and I was always relieved to be free of them

It was always pot luck as to which direction the next current would send me in, but for now we were making progress in exactly the right direction and the forecast was for much of the same over the next thirty-six hours.

Though still headed by the current, by 24 July I had clawed my way back over the 42-degree line in an ongoing tug of war with the conditions. Things were good for the time being, but the news was that the weather would soon change with the onset of more of the dreaded northerly winds, after which I would be hit with a south-flowing warm-water eddy. It was yet another slap in the face but one that I had become quietly accustomed to. Don't get me wrong, I still got pissed off at my misfortune, just with a greater air of acceptance.

The next day came bringing with it beam winds and waves. With the winds getting a bit lively and me still trying to maintain some of the northward progress I'd ground out over the past weeks, it got rather hairy as three- to four-metre waves hit me broadside. Mostly, *Peggy* would bob up and over the peaks and into the next trough, but every now and then a wave would break directly above us, so that we'd skid down the front of it, clocking up over four knots sideways which certainly livened things up a bit.

An unexpected consequence of being constantly buffeted by strong winds from my righthand side was that my eyebrows, which are bushy at the best of times, threatened to take over my entire forehead, flapping so much that they were constantly in my field of vision and really annoying me. At the first break in the day, I decided to prune them back using a pair of kitchen scissors and my mirror. Given the conditions (and the size of my eyebrows), it was a small miracle when I emerged from my cabin with my head still attached to my neck and my eyeballs un-impaled. That evening, I sent some statistics back home:

- 40 days gone.
- Miles from New York – 1,835
- Miles covered – 2,158
- Miles to English Channel – 1,235
- Daily average mileage so far – 53.95
- Average speed – 2.25 knots
- Highest recorded speed – 9.7 knots
- Biggest wave – 6 metres
- Dolphin encounters – 9
- Whale encounters – 3
- Shark encounters – 2
- Sausage eaten – 37 metres
- Socks lost – 1

Given that Laval had averaged 1.86 knots when he set a new world record over a shorter distance than I would be covering and the current world record holder had averaged two and a half knots in pretty optimal conditions, it was reassuring to see that I was doing pretty well. The numbers helped to dispel the blues whenever I began to worry about my progress overall.

By the evening of 25 July, I'd been battling the winds and current for two days. I relinquished the oars knowing I had to accept whatever the ocean might throw at me whilst I rested so I was mildly relieved upon waking on the twenty-sixth to find that we'd only lost four miles to the south overnight which was quickly regained the following morning as the winds dropped. It turned out to be a glorious sunny day, the first I'd seen in a while, and though it was a tough slog in very little wind and bright sunshine, it was still preferable to pinching my way across the waves. The current meant that I had to point the boat pretty much due north just to make a heading of east-northeast as the conditions knocked me sideways, but after nine hours we finally broke free of its grasp and, for the first time in quite a long time, my much-beloved evening shift matched up to its reputation when the relentless sun slipped behind the clouds and a light following breeze blew up to join me, allowing me to once again dream of reaching the UK. The next big target to aim for was a thousand miles to the English Channel.

In an ocean of ever-changing character it was remarkable to have a 'normal' day at sea, so much so that it came as a bit of a surprise when it happened. The winds stayed constant throughout, the sea state didn't alter, the weather was 'average', a mixture of clouds and sunshine, and the rudder remained pretty much central the entire time. Though refreshing, not having to worry about the Four Horsemen of the Apocalypse popping up over the horizon or any other unforeseen hazard, it just felt a bit 'meh'. I wrote at the time that if I could press a button and lock the conditions in for the rest of the trip I would, but then added, 'Who am I trying to kid? I'd be bored by tomorrow afternoon and gagging for some more exciting weather.' Fortunately, the weather forecast was due in the following morning so at least I had something to not look forward to. The decent conditions had allowed me to get further north than at any previous point in the voyage and I felt confident that I'd left the 42-degree Blues well behind me.

The weather omens weren't good when I went for my lucky dip into the food hatches and managed to pull out four meals, all of which were ranked in the bottom two of their respective classes: scrambled egg, porridge, spaghetti Bolognese and a rice pudding (to be fair to the rice pudding, it wasn't bad, just one of my least favourites) Coupled with the dark, overcast skies and a north-westerly wind, it filled me with a sense of trepidation as I opened the weather report. What I was hoping to see were lots of S's and W's and very few N's and E's but a quick scan told a familiar tale with way more N's than was salutary, accounting for at least two-thirds of the winds that were forecast.

This meant another five days of slogging across the weather and being knocked south, which would put another downhill on my already undulating track. The good news was that there in the five-day forecast were a couple of good bits amounting to about thirty-six hours of following conditions, most of which was due around my birthday at the end of the month, so at least there was something to look forward to. I'd set my goal of being within a thousand miles of the English Channel by that time and, though it was going to be tight, it was in theory possible.

The end of July approached and the weather brought a fairly mixed bag, as long as the bag in question was one-third filled with chocolate-covered peanuts and the other two-thirds were rabbit droppings, meaning that for the greater part it was crap with predominantly northerly or very light conditions making the going incredibly tough.

The pins and needles in my hands had spread into my forearms and I suspected nerve damage of some kind from the continuous strain, as I had no feeling in the skin on the back of my hands. Despite massage and stretching before and after every shift and a few times in the night, my hands were often locked into a rowing claw which sent pain across all my knuckles when I snapped my fingers straight. But apart from that, everything was holding together pretty well.

The days weren't without their highlights, which helped to keep my spirits up. One morning I saw a pod of whales, just twenty metres away. They nearly collided with a huge turtle that had actually passed under my oars not long before. It was fortunate that the turtle missed me as, given its size, had it hit, my rudder would have probably come off second-best. It would also have given me a fright big enough to put a dent in my dwindling supply of underpants.

On the days with little or no breeze and cloudless skies, I was at least able to clean and dry out the cabin, recharge the batteries fully and get some washing done. I had one 7-hour session directly into winds and seas which strained every sinew in my body, but I broke into the 20s with regard to my longitude (I'd started at 74 and London lies on the prime meridian of zero) and had managed to creep up to 44 degrees north which was 120 miles north of 42. In another session on the oars, I made incredible progress, averaging four knots in the right direction over a wonderful three-hour period before sunset.

On the evening of 30 July , after stowing away everything on the rowing deck, I sat down with my feet in the water in flat calm conditions, looking out over the ocean which mirrored the incredible skies as the sun set in blissful contemplation of the voyage behind me and the journey yet to come. The conditions stayed flat calm all night and I had the best sleep since the start of the adventure, a slow current only setting me back four miles southeast overnight.

15

NYLON: Crossing the Atlantic, the End

I turned forty-seven years of age on my forty-seventh day at sea, almost managing my forty-seventh metre of sausage to hit the treble, but fell one metre short of that particular target.

I don't know how but the forecasters had managed to sort out the best birthday present I could have wished for: overcast skies and following winds and seas all day. A fog descended on my sundowner shift, which was wonderful, muting everything and making the ocean feel almost cosy as my visual horizon closed in. More to the point, the fantastic conditions over the previous thirty-six hours had seen me smash the thousand-nautical miles-to-the-English-Channel barrier (a point that I'd put ten miles due south of Lands' End, the last bit of the UK before you fall into the sea). The weather wasn't looking great for the next few days, but I was into the final third of the row which I considered the home stretch.

Putting on my cold damp clothes the next morning, shrouded in a thick fog, bought back fond memories of just about every camping trip I'd had with my dad and the ATC in Wales where you'd tend to pitch the tent in the pissing rain and be grateful for the moment that you finally got under canvas and got a brew on, only to have to don your wet gear the next morning and do it all over again. Not everybody's cup of tea, I admit, but I always thrived on it.

Rowing in the thick fog, with the winds coming from directly where I wanted to go, brisk progress towards home was never really an option so I decided to strike the best balance I could between boat speed and direction and headed that way. I slogged my way across the waves, losing ground to the south, and every time that I stopped for more than a few seconds for a snack or a quick drink the bows would swing straight around and I would head off in exactly the opposite direction of home at one and a half knots which made break choices fairly simple.

I was a bit disgruntled as the forecast was for north-north-westerly winds, which these definitely weren't, so after five hours I relented and called the weather forecasters for reassurance that this wasn't part of a bigger system that had been overlooked. No sooner had I got off the telephone than the winds dropped, the sun burnt off the fog and the seas began to quell. The next thing I knew, I was dealing with a searingly hot day without the merest hint of a breeze.

In the space of an hour, the ocean turned to a treacle-like consistency which made me and *Peggy* work for every single metre. The gaps between the puddles that my oars made seemed to get closer and closer together as the four-hour middle shift dragged on, but I'd decided to treat myself to a lovely wash and swim at the end of it, just to keep myself motivated. Within seconds of finishing the shift, I'd stripped off what little I was wearing and jumped into the glorious cool of the ocean, which seemed to instantly wash away the sweat and strain of the day's toil, and I spent a good few minutes just marvelling at the feeling. Whilst there, I decided to take a look at the underside of the boat and was astounded at the amount and size of the organisms attached to the hull. I'd been looking after my own bottom very well, but should have paid more attention to *Peggy*'s. There were literally hundreds of gooseneck barnacles stuck to it, which must have been causing a good amount of drag. It was incredibly cathartic to attack the underside with a scraper and restore her to her former glory.

It only took twenty minutes and I told myself that I'd be making far more frequent inspections from here on in. With so much ocean still to row, even a 5 per cent increase in speed could mean gaining a few days. I even managed a bit of self-maintenance in my break as my ears had grown so hairy that they had started collecting the early morning fog much like a spider's web! A windproof lighter did the trick, but it would have been a better idea to have performed the procedure outside the cabin as the smell of burnt hair permeated the cabin long after the sunset shift that evening.

The dreaded weather report came through and even a quick glance at it had the butterflies in my stomach almost bursting forth. Three huge low-pressure systems were barrelling their way towards me, one after the other, with hardly a gap in between. They promised to be much bigger than anything I had encountered to date, passing closer and pushing up much larger seas. With the passage of each system, winds would be coming at me from all points of the compass and it wasn't going to be a matter of if they were going to hit me but more a matter of how hard and for how long.

It was now 3 August and the three successive storms were due to hit on the fourth, sixth and eighth. Though anxiety had started to build, I tried to keep it at bay remembering my experiences with *Peggy* thus far as she'd never let me down, regardless of what nature had thrown at her, and all I could do was to have faith in her to see me through this next trial. By now, I'd duct-taped up the exterior speakers, filled my solar-powered vent with sealant and plugged what I hoped was every other weep-hole that I'd found to minimise water ingress in the inevitable event of capsize so I was about as ready as I could be.

It was a strange feeling being at the oars the day before the storm, knowing what was coming and being helpless to prevent it. I felt like I was watching myself starring as the guy in the horror movie who goes on his own to check the fuse box after the lights go out, and though I tried to force any negative feelings down, I hadn't been this nervous since the day of departure from New York. There was a lot of rationalising going on in my head and the phrase 'It too shall pass' became my mantra. I just wished it would get on with it and pass bloody soon as the nerves were steadily building in my gut.

I wasn't helped by the sleep-deprivation from the night before as Peggy needed constant attention, bouncing off the sides of the right track as we were hit by successive squalls, but come the morning all settled down to what would be another flat calm day making progress slow and hard, but I knew that I'd be cabin-bound for quite a bit over the coming week so made the most of it.

It was another day of blazing sunshine and I took the opportunity to have another wonderful swim at the end of the middle shift. The rest of the time was taken up putting in a few extra fittings to lash everything down as best as I could. The swells had been gently building throughout the day and the winds started to arrive just before the end of the last shift so I finished up with some final preparation, filling my daily water container and bringing it inside the cabin, stripping the deck of everything that wasn't firmly screwed down and double-checking all the lashings before flooding the central footwell and retreating to my cabin to wait and see what the North Atlantic had in store for me. Having already ridden out two storms, I was confident that we could ride out another and decided to set the rudder straight and run with whatever came and start afresh from wherever I ended up.

The forecast proved spot-on with winds and seas rapidly building overnight and, by the following morning, conditions were too wild to contemplate going out on deck. With the winds already at thirty to forty knots and fast-moving waves piling on top of one another, reaching up to six metres in height and constantly breaking over the boat, all I could do was hang on as we were knocked down time and time again, always bobbing back upright. The maelstrom was forecast to reach its peak by around ten o'clock that evening, then lasting until the following morning, and I started to wish away the hours just to get whatever it was going to throw at us over and done with. It was a strange thing that the anticipation of what was to come was proving to be worse than the storm itself. Not that I was in a good situation at all; it was more to do with the fact that once I was in it, there was no more that I could do other than sit and wait it out, braced for the next big hit.

The wind continued to howl, peaking at over fifty knots, and the seas became fairly monstrous, with occasional waves towering over me as I looked through the cabin hatch at near-vertical faces and crests that broke over me time and time again. On occasion, the waves would lift us up onto their crests, upon which we'd accelerate, surfing down the face of them at such speeds that the whole boat would start humming and vibrating, hitting over fifteen knots on a couple of occasions. This was thrilling, but also a bit hairy, as I had no control over our direction in the general mayhem and only the vaguest notion of up and down (or backwards or forwards, for that matter).

I manned the steering lines that I had rigged to my cabin for such occasions. This gave me some steerage but it was of limited effect compared to the power of the waves and I'd resigned myself to the fact that it was only a matter of time before the 'big one' hit me. Prior to departure, Laval had told me that he had not once streamed a drogue and, despite suffering quite a few knockdowns, hadn't had to go through a single capsize, deciding the keep the rudder manned at all times and making the most of the conditions. I was attempting to emulate this, being also reluctant to stream the drogue that I had rigged, as to do so would mean that I would have to risk swinging the boat through 180 degrees and subsequently expose myself to being side-on to the huge waves which would almost certainly cause a violent capsize.

As it turned out, a violent capsize would be the least of my worries. Just before dark, I heard a thunderous roar and looked out the hatch to see a huge wall of black water, around eight metres in height and travelling very quickly, looming above me. I tried to keep control using the rudder, but the wave picked us up by the stern and we started speeding down the face of it as it broke.

What happened next happened so quickly and was so violent that it took me quite some time to process it. But it seemed that I rocketed into the trough just at the wrong moment, the bow of the boat digging into the water as the wave tipped the stern upwards, flipping me lengthways in a movement known as a 'pitchpole'. I somersaulted around the cabin, momentarily weightless, before the stern of the boat came crashing down, ahead of the bow and upside down, smashing me into the cabin roof and breaking a lot of the lashings holding down my equipment, which now lay all around me, acting as ballast and preventing *Peggy* from righting herself.

Looking out of the cabin hatch into the cold dark waters of the Atlantic did make me question my life choices at that moment. However, being upside down did mean that all was comparatively calm as less of the boat was exposed to the weather. Maybe a little oddly, I started to chuckle when my GPS alarm sounded to tell me that there was no signal. This was unsurprising given that there were very few satellites where the antenna was currently pointing, towards the bottom of the Atlantic some three miles down.

There seemed to be quite a lot of water in the cabin. I found this a little confusing given that I could only see a few weep-holes from previously unidentified sources, but now was not the time to worry about these. My life raft and immersion suit were to hand and I contemplated getting them ready. However to use them, I would first have to get out of the cabin which would mean opening the hatch and effectively sinking the boat by inundating it with thousands of litres of water the second I did so. My grab bag was ready for use if necessary (as was everything in the cabin which was literally all around me), but this would mean the end of the adventure and, with the forecast being as it was, I didn't much fancy sitting in a life raft for a few days waiting for somebody to get me. So definitely a last resort.

All this happened in the space of just a few minutes, though it was hard to tell as time seemed to slow down. After going through the options, I figured that my only choice was to try and right the boat from the inside; so as Peggy rocked back and forth in the incessant waves, I tried to judge the motion as best I could before throwing myself at the cabin wall to try and shift the centre of gravity in my favour. On the second go, it worked.

Suddenly what was previously down became up and vice versa, including my heavy toolbox that struck me on the shoulder and all the accumulated water which took the path of least resistance, into a conduit and through the locker containing all my communications equipment. I wasn't too concerned about this at the time as, had it gone the other way, it would have emptied into the main fuse box which would have been a whole lot worse.

I was battered and bruised and the cabin was a complete mess, with every bit of equipment having redistributed itself, but we were the right way up and it would be a good few hours before the storm abated so there was little else to do other than try and tidy up, stuffing everything I could into spaces as low down as possible to help self-right in the event of the same thing happening again. It was fairly inelegant, but the time for being fussy wasn't now and I was relieved when everything was once again fairly secure and I wedged myself in as best I could to await the next big hit.

The storm raged throughout the night but, come the early hours, the faintest easing of conditions was perceptible. It was an enormous relief to me though I was wary, having been through similar situations when storms like this had abated only to return with a vengeance. Resigned to the fact that there was nothing I could do, I drifted in and out of sleep, exhausted by the constant noise and motion of the boat, but as daylight broke it was apparent that the worst was over. There were still two more storms to come but they promised to be not as turbulent as the first so, having come through that one relatively unscathed, I was in remarkably good spirits.

The pitchpole had claimed a few casualties though. The water going into my comms cabinet had frazzled the router so I was no longer able to send or receive emails including my weather reports. All the deck navigation equipment was fried so, other than the compass, I had no indication of wind or boat speed and the chartplotter was refusing to switch on which would prove difficult for the coastal navigation ahead, but I'd tackle that hurdle when I came to it. The compass light had broken and my tracker which transmitted my position for people to follow my progress was also out of action. The source of the water wasn't from outside but from my daily twenty-litre drinking water container which had ruptured. This was really annoying as I needed to fill it daily from my water maker to provide enough for my consumption and it had shattered around the spout so no amount of duct tape was going to save it. Apart from that, all was OK.

I spent an hour that morning resorting all my gear from where it had been unceremoniously stuffed the previous evening and getting everything in some semblance of order. The cabin was still fairly soggy, but the main thing was that I was still afloat and still had oars, food, a way of making water and a compass, so remained undefeated. Had this happened in the first week, I'm not sure I would have been quite as defiant, but in the course of the row I'd become inured to the hardships of being alone in a small boat on the North Atlantic and subsequently felt fairly positive about my circumstances.

I'd taken a big hit to the southeast once again during the storm and, over the previous forty-eight hours, I'd managed to cover over 150 miles, yet I found myself only forty miles closer to home. Having been stuck in the cabin for twenty hours, I was very happy to get out and get back on the oars on the afternoon of 7 August and, though progress was hampered by residual swells out of the southwest accompanied by growing swells out of the northwest already being pushed up by the next weather system, I was at least able to make some progress eastwards in the small 'lifts' when winds helped to push me in roughly the right direction, though never by much which made the rowing rather frustrating.

The next lull came, signifying the next storm but, to my relief, the lull wasn't as big so I guessed neither would the storm be. Once again, I rowed until I was no longer able to do so, battened down the hatches and prepared to kiss my arse goodbye all over again, but any pre-storm anxiety was very much muted by the previous experience which left me feeling invulnerable rather than shaken as the conditions once again intensified.

I spent my time with small tasks which kept my mind occupied, devising ways to improve my own circumstances once I next had good enough conditions to do so. By the time the second storm hit, I was in a far more relaxed frame of mind and whilst the winds peaked at thirty-five knots and the waves built to six metres outside, constantly hammering the boat, I felt very much at ease tucked up in the cabin. Even capsize number four, happening as I rested in pitch-black dark at 2 a.m. the following morning, failed to phase me and I actually went back to sleep shortly thereafter, 'turning turtle' being a fairly well-trodden path by now with gear well and truly stowed and the minimal of checks required to make sure everything was OK. Admittedly, lots of stuff was already broken so there was a lot less to check or for that matter to worry about and I looked forward to the storm easing to allow me to put into action the little ideas I had to make the third one a lot more bearable.

First on the list was the water container which was a bit of a loss. Stupidly, before leaving New York (which seemed like a VERY long time ago) I'd wondered if the material it was made of was going to be tough enough for the journey. However, unable to find a suitable alternative of the required dimensions, I'd run with it. I'd been told a phrase by a stewardess I'd previously worked with many years before that I've carried with me ever since, often remembering it but for some reason not on this occasion, which I rued because it would have prevented a cock-up with the water container. 'If you've any doubt,' this woman told me, 'you've no doubt at all.'

I'd doubted that the water container would be OK and I should have made more of an effort to find something else as I'd found that my gut instinct had served me pretty well in the past, but had failed to do so and subsequently paid the price. Fortunately, it did give me an opportunity to 'MacGyver' a solution with what I had on hand.

Shortly after my birthday, I had to finally admit defeat with regard to my sausages. Opening a new vacuum pack would release a strange fishy odour and pulling out slimy grey sausages covered in rancid yellow fat was doing nothing to tickle my taste buds. I persevered for a few days, eating the first one out of the pack and binning the rest, but I didn't really want to risk food poisoning so decided to use the remainder as very good ballast.

It did however give me some excellent, flexible waterproof bags so, having emptied the putrid contents of one of the packs over the side of the boat, I disinfected and scrubbed it out to create a liner to the broken water container. I cut a small hole in one corner and dragged it through the spout hole, reversed it on itself and sealed it with self-amalgamating tape before reinserting the stopper/tap. I cut the top off of a tube of toothpaste and poked it through a hole that I'd drilled in the original lid of the water container and screwed the flip-top lid back onto the other side before jamming the lid of the container back over the neck, trapping the remainder of the liner and forming a perfect seal. The lid of the toothpaste was exactly the same size as the feeder hose from the water maker so created a perfect seal and ended up being better than the original.

Next I wanted to do something to stop me from getting knocked around in the cabin. I therefore put some fixings into the cabin to allow me to rig up the longer of the two daggerboards as a sort of bench that I could lie beneath, effectively pinning me to the floor whilst I slept. The only drawback to this was that I had to drill through fiberglass and, despite my best efforts to clean up the residue, sitting naked in the cabin produced some very itchy moments!

I was really chuffed with my little wins and felt more than ready for the next storm so, as conditions once again eased off and I was able to make some gains back to the northeast, part of me actually looked forward to giving two fingers up to the weather gods who seemed to have viewed me somewhat unfavourably so far.

As predicted, the third storm was not as strong as the first two and though seas were still pretty high, running at five to six metres with steep breaking waves and winds gusting up to thirty-five knots, I felt very much more in control of my situation. The seas were a bit more confused than during the first two storms which meant that I spent a lot of time getting blown across the fronts of the waves rather than going with them, but I hardly batted an eyelid as I spent another night in the washing machine, firmly pinned down as I was. I woke up next morning to fairly calm conditions which had not been forecast and I was a little confused.

The boat had tracked all over the place during the night, at times northwest, then southwest, and I was now drifting due south, but with winds now reasonably calm, I was able to get out on deck to enjoy some eerily quiet conditions. The track that I had followed made no sense whatsoever to me. The changing of the wind direction is generally fairly predictable with the passing of a low-pressure system, being an anticlockwise gyre, so will have a set pattern depending on where you are in relation to the centre. I wasn't going to complain, though, as having been battered for three out of the past five days, I was at least able to make some progress, albeit slowly in the light winds, which was also confusing me as the forecasters had predicted a period of decent following conditions after the passing of the third depression.

Just as puzzling was the sky. The light was somehow muted in all directions by a light haze, yet overhead the sky was a bright blue and the winds kept wafting in from all directions. A few hours later, the reason became fairly clear when I got thumped again, this time by northerly winds at the trailing edge of the depression I'd been through the night before, driving me directly southwards and strong enough that I could do nothing to prevent it. It transpired that I had managed to row and get blown right into the eye of the storm, a phenomenon I knew about but had never experienced to this extent.

I suppose that my exposure to the weather over the past weeks and months had heightened my senses to its whims, which is why the calm felt so very odd. Having suffered enough loss to the south and been battered already, I decided to sit this one out and relented by launching the para-anchor and waiting for the storm to pass. Being 'in the eye' was another great experience that you wouldn't feel the true meaning of in normal life when you can just go inside and close the door, but being this connected to nature and witnessing it first-hand in such a raw form was a humbling experience, reminding me that however big we think we are, nature is so much more powerful than we will ever be.

Eventually, the storms abated and, as forecast, the conditions swung in my favour. For now at least, I had a clear run home. Once again, it seemed that nature had decided to reward me for having passed its tests, but I was well aware of what a fickle mistress she could be and was determined to make the most of conditions before she changed her mind and gave me another kick in the teeth.

By 11 August, I'd surpassed the five-hundred-miles-to-go mark. I'd covered over three thousand miles from New York, 2,500 as the crow flies, and knew that, unless I had a major equipment failure, the crossing of the Atlantic was within my grasp. I'd heard that the team of four had made it to Tower Bridge that day; the same storms that had battered me had whisked them straight up the English Channel, the winds dying just as they turned the corner into the Thames Estuary to row back west into London. I was really chuffed for them and started to become excited about my own moment of victory.

The conditions were perfect for now with fifteen to twenty knots of breeze and long three-metre swells pushing me arrow-straight towards the

UK coast. For the first time in many weeks, my AIS alarm sounded to let me know that there was another vessel in the vicinity and it was heading straight towards me. I could just about make out a set of sails as I rose up on the peaks of the waves and I tried hailing the vessel over the VHF radio, but the signal was very weak. Fortunately for me, the other boat was just as curious as I was as to who would be out here in these less-than-favourable conditions for small craft, so far from land.

Understandably, being such a niche market, there is no category for 'rowing boat' on the AIS so I had to register myself as a sailing boat. The other vessel (as I learnt later) consequently thought it strange when, within a mile of *Peggy*, there was still no sign of a mast or sails. We had at least managed to make contact on the radio, however, and the skipper said that he'd come over to say hello. I was running directly downwind which is a horrible point of sail in a sailing boat in a big swell, as the boat will have a tendency to loll from side to side, making it very uncomfortable on board, and at one stage I had to stop rowing as he was making no ground on me, but eventually he pulled up close by.

It was interesting to hear that, despite being luminous yellow, in three-metre seas I was only visible to him when he was a quarter of a mile away; the rest of the time I was simply swallowed up by the waves. I found out that he was a solo yachtsman, George Arnison, on a beautiful old wooden sloop named *Good Report*.

He'd just completed the Jester Challenge, sailing from Plymouth to the Azores. This is a single-handed race for small boats that brings together sailors who aren't interested in all the stuff and snobbery that often comes with racing sailboats, being for like-minded people who want to pit their wits against the ocean. It is only open to boats from twenty to thirty feet in length and has no rules or requirements, no inspections or checks and no fees, but also no support and minimal organisation. Instead, the emphasis is on old-fashioned good seamanship and self-reliance which sounded great to me.

It was an amazing feeling to see another human being after all this time and George was kind enough to do a flyby and take some photos which he would send to Helene when he got back. Being British, of course we talked about the weather and I gave him my latest forecast which benefited him more than me in that the following conditions that I was so enjoying were about to come to a fairly abrupt end in the next twelve hours, allowing him to make a more direct course for Plymouth rather than taking a 250-mile tack (a sort of detour for sailing boats to make the boat go faster and smoother when the wind is in the wrong direction, which it invariably is!). Following our encounter, we wished each other luck and went our separate ways, me poking my head inside the cabin every now and then to see how he was doing and after about four hours I was slightly dismayed to notice his course abruptly alter and head where I wanted to go which must have meant that the wind had changed upon the passing of a frontal system.

Lo and behold, an hour or so later, following a violent rainstorm, the wind swung 45 degrees around and I was back to trying to pinch my way across the conditions. Fortunately for me, the wind change was so sudden that the swells hadn't had a chance to realign so I still got a bit of a shove, at least for the rest of the day.

The countdown to the UK was very much at the forefront of my thoughts and the nibbles that I'd been taking out of the overall mileages were turning into ever-bigger bites of the distance left to go. My next mental goal was to get over the continental shelf which is where the deep ocean rises up to the much shallower water that the European land mass sits upon. Traditionally, the interface between these two regions, where ocean currents are suddenly pushed up from over four thousand metres to 140 metres in the space of forty miles, can be treacherous. Much-larger-than-expected waves can be generated in this zone and the currents can be unpredictable as the differing water columns interact with each other. However, this upwelling of warmer currents also brings a great deal of nutrients out of the depths of the ocean and, in doing so, fosters a lot more sea life.

Though in not ideal conditions since the passing of the frontal system, I was still able to maintain a pretty good track and the winds remained strong enough to give me a helping hand roughly in the right direction. It was always such a delight to wake up to find that I'd made some free miles overnight and the weather forecast for the next four days promised more decent mileage. Of course, there would also be another storm system to contend with, promising high seas and variable winds, but what self-respecting four-day weather forecast would be without one!

Far from breaking me, the 'triple whammy' of storms had only strengthened my resolve; coming through them relatively unscathed only made me stronger. The forecast was predicting gales to hit me on the fourteenth and fifteenth and the epicentre, where the winds would be strongest, would pass only fifty miles to the north of my position. The conditions would almost certainly be uncomfortable, but trivial in comparison to what I'd already been through and I did not experience the same levels of anxiety or dread that I had previously had to deal with.

As had become customary, the winds dropped first, followed by the swell, before all hell let loose. Fast-moving waves once again thundered past me, four metres high and more, and once again we were thrashed around in the relentless washing machine. I even managed to top my previous speed record with one surf hitting 17.1 knots. It was pretty hairy out on the rowing deck, with regular knockdowns throwing me off my seat and onto the guard rails as I waited for the boat to right, but it was truly exhilarating as I sped towards the continental shelf. With the conditions already marginal and forecast to get worse, I battened down the hatches once again and settled down into my cabin for some food and a rest before whatever the night would bring.

Being so close to the centre of the storm, the wind direction changed far more rapidly meaning that there was a lag between the winds and the change in wave direction which put me side-on to the wavefronts. I was just about to boil up some water for that evening's dinner when a rogue wave came in out of nowhere and immediately flipped us over, but Peggy just flipped back up and shrugged off the water as if to say, 'Is that all you've got?' I'd done a full roly-poly up the comms cabinet, across the roof and back over the switchboard, following which I had to rearrange my cushions and a few other bits and bobs but otherwise all was fine.

These conditions were definitely smaller than previously experienced and I was hungry so decided to go ahead with my dinner plans anyway. This may have seemed a little foolhardy, but I kept one hand on the gas knob and prepared to throw the pot away from me should I get tumbled again. Fortunately, though a pretty bouncy ride, I managed to avoid this fate and afterwards tucked up in bed, pinned to the floor with my makeshift brace, a smile on my face and a belly full of grub.

I was to suffer two further capsizes that night, taking the grand total to seven, but after each one I did no more than have a quick scan around the cabin to make sure that everything was OK and went back to sleep. At around two in the morning, the AIS alarm went off which I suspected would happen as I approached a major shipping lane where goods from all around the world converged, destined for the ports of Northern Europe. Checking the chartplotter, I found out that I was headed for a hydrographic survey buoy, tethered to the seabed three miles below that recorded wind, waves and currents. I knew that there was one somewhere in the locality and was impressed that, thanks to modern technology, they'd been able to put a transponder on it to alert shipping of its presence. What was even more remarkable was that in 41 million square miles of ocean, I was on a collision course with it, my chartplotter telling me that I would pass within 0.05 nautical miles of it which equated to less than a hundred metres.

Though I always welcomed seeing something new at sea, I wasn't overkeen on coming so close to this particular obstacle in rough seas during the darkness of night so adjusted my rudder a little and woke up every twenty minutes to monitor my course until I was well clear. I was incredibly grateful that, while just about all my other electronics had failed, this bit of kit was still working. Had I collided with the buoy in the conditions I was in, the result would have been catastrophic, it being made of steel and three metres high. I'm not sure the UK meteorological office, whom it turned out to belong to, would have thanked me for my visit either.

As the centre of the storm passed to the north of me, the winds veered as predicted and I settled into the routine of edging my way across the wavefronts until the conditions allowed otherwise. I'd made some terrific progress to both the north and east over the previous days so wasn't too fazed about losing a few miles back to the south. From here on in, however, I would have to keep an eye on my approach which was something that had become a bit alien to me, having had the free roam of the ocean for so long, without having to worry about being a few hundred miles off course here and there. I was by now only 250 miles from UK territorial waters and that kind of deviation would have me bumping into France long before I saw the green, green grass of home.

I wasn't too bothered until I received the next forecast, a quick check of which revealed that the north-westerly winds were set to stay for three days which, if I was not careful, would bring me very close to the French coast. In fact, if I ran directly with the wind from my current position, I wouldn't even make the English Channel but would end up somewhere in the middle of the Bay of Biscay. A familiar feeling of frustration started to creep up on me as I considered the possibility of having come all this way and not being able to make the UK coast and the what ifs began creeping into my head. What if I'd stayed on the oars for a few hours more to gain a bit more north, what if I'd set the rudder a degree or two more over to gain a bit more ground, etc. But having been through what I had, I rationalised that every action that I'd made had bought me to this point and there was nothing I could do about it other than to keep on keeping on.

When I was 'in the zone' I'd play tunes in my head (Edwin Starr's 'Twenty-Five Miles' was a regular) or try to let my mind drift to anything other than the rowing. However, as I became more fatigued or frustrated, that proved impossible so my sole motivator was simply to count. A thousand more strokes until I stopped for a quick break, five hundred until I next looked at my watch, two thousand strokes until I checked on progress. It may sound incredibly tedious, but it worked. I've always enjoyed mathematics and I spent the time calculating fractions and percentages to break the shift down into smaller parcels and achievable goals. Not once did I stop at the projected target and there was always *If you can pull a thousand strokes, you can pull a hundred more, and if you can pull a hundred more, you can make it to five hundred more.* And so it went on.

Having made some impressive miles during the stronger weather and being so close to home, I found the slow progress across the mercifully light north-easterlies irritating. I was on the cusp of crossing the continental shelf. I tried, as best I could, to study the chart and guess where the remnants of the Gulf Stream were least likely to hamper progress as they curled to the south and headed toward the Canaries. But guessing was all I could do and there was little I was able to change anyway to influence the point that would see me emerge from the deep ocean.

On the morning of 16 August, at about 7 a.m., I was in a complete reverie, dreaming of a cheese and tomato sandwich, but not any cheese sandwich; this one was on homemade bread with mayonnaise and cracked pepper. The seas were calm and there was very little wind as my mouth salivated and my stomach rumbled at the prospect of real food. Then all of a sudden, out of nowhere, I heard a huge whoosh just to my right.

Quite how I didn't shit myself I have no idea. For as I looked over, I saw a huge humpback whale coming directly towards the boat, perpendicular to it and not fifteen metres away. The leviathan was twelve to fifteen metres in length, sleek and dark – it looked like a submarine cruising straight for my midships. Quickly gathering my thoughts, I double-checked the hatch behind me so that, if I was flipped, the boat would at least stay afloat. I held onto the rail, expecting the worst. However, at the last minute, the whale dived, passing under my boat with not more than a metre to spare.

To see this beautiful creature slide effortlessly beneath me within what felt like touching distance was an incredible experience. It felt even more magical when it surfaced twenty-five metres away with a calf.

Once the whale had passed and the adrenalin had worn off, I suddenly felt a terrible melancholy on account of the damage that man has done (and continues to do) to the environment. Though I had seen very few pollutants in the water on my way across, it is undeniable that we are poisoning the planet by our very presence and I suddenly felt not as one with the ocean, as I had done previously, but more part of a parasitic race which had no right to treat the planet as we do, thinking that everything will be OK when it most obviously is not. The deep sadness stayed with me for quite some time and

I shed a tear as I offered an apology to the whale. Again, I'm not a religious man, but the phrase 'Forgive them, Father, for they know not what they do' seemed particularly pertinent at this time as most human beings on the planet are just trying to live and hope for a better life, driven by materialism and blissfully unaware of what our overpopulation of the planet will eventually do to it.

The dark thoughts stayed with me and were only exacerbated when a pod of five stunning pilot whales joined me later that day, sticking around for three or four minutes, no more than five metres from the tips of my oars, before going on their way. I hugely enjoyed their company but felt that I was part of the problem, being in a plastic boat, surrounded by manmade things that were totally out of balance with nature, and I felt like a bit of a charlatan to have been graced with their presence.

The following day, I passed over the continental shelf. As if on cue, I was surrounded by a welcoming committee of hundreds of dolphins all around me throughout the day. Word was obviously out that it was fun to make this bloke out rowing on his own jump by sneaking up on him and two pilot whales surfaced not one metre from the end of my oars, blowing out as they did so and making me leap out of my skin once again.

According to the forecast, this was also going to be the final day of slogging it out against suboptimal conditions with the winds shifting to the west and southwest before some strong southerlies set in. Though the temptation was to head for the nearest point of land, I had to be careful in case I was too close to the rocky coast of Cornwall but nowhere near a sheltered anchorage when the southerlies hit which could wash me directly onto the shore. But for now at least, the track looked good.

On the morning of 19 August, I woke up to building swells and winds in the right direction having clocked up twelve miles overnight. I had just over a hundred miles to go to reach Falmouth. The forecast looked pretty bad and, having struggled with the unpredictable weather for the entire voyage, I realised that Mother Nature was going to have one more dig at me. In two and a half days, a strong high-pressure system would settle over Scotland. Travelling in a clockwise fashion, the winds would stream down between the East Coast of the UK and the European landmass before funnelling along the English Channel directly towards where I wanted to go. With gale-force speeds predicted, first from the northwest, then from the northeast, I would be blown away from shore and then back out into the Atlantic over the course of at least five days. Having come within touching distance of UK shores, I felt physically sick at the thought of this.

After closer analysis, however, and looking at the distance I had to go, I realised that I only had to average thirty-five miles per day to reach my goal before the high-pressure system hit. This was well within my capabilities so long as the conditions remained as forecast.

I took to the oars with a sense of urgency, every 0.1 of a knot counting, and though anxious, I knew that I could do it. Stopping briefly at 10 a.m. to fill up my water container (I preferred to do it early in order to give the batteries sufficient time to recover), I switched on the water maker only to find that it was not producing any water, which didn't entirely surprise me as it had taken a bit of a beating lately. I had the emergency ballast water should I need it, but with a long way to go to London, I set out to diagnose and fix the problem.

My first call, as usual, was to Helene. I asked her to try and get in touch with of Jim 'the water-maker whisperer' Macdonald. I'd worked with Jim on the 'Row to the Pole' project and had been to his workshop to strip down and rebuild a water maker ten years previously. If there was something he didn't know about water makers, it wasn't worth knowing and he'd become something of an authority on them, particularly within ocean-rowing circles.

Helene managed to just catch him as he was about to set off on a sailing boat in Martinique. This was fortuitous as, had she called a few hours later, he'd have disappeared over the horizon and out of telephone range. Jim's first bit of advice was to get under the boat and check the inlet. I wasn't too keen on doing this given that the conditions were starting to build with waves up to two metres and fifteen knots of following breeze. However, I had no other option so, armed with a screwdriver, I jumped in. At first, I had trouble holding on as the boat was moving at two to three knots, but apparently I made a pretty good sea anchor as it slowed down with me flailing about on the underside of it. The inlet for the water maker was well-clogged with more gooseneck barnacles which seemed to have sprung up in just a few weeks since the last scrub. I managed to quickly clear these with several dives under the boat.

Getting back on board with high expectations, I was a little disappointed to find that the water maker still wasn't working. However, another call to Jim had him taking me through a hard reset of the system which thankfully worked; I was hugely thankful for him being there for me when I needed him most. It had taken a few hours out of my schedule but, given the forecast and the progress I was making, I was still confident of reaching a safe harbour before the winds turned against me, though it would mean rowing late into the night and shortening my breaks to the absolute minimum, just enough to get a bit of fuel inside me.

The winds and conditions stayed with me as the day wore on and then turned into night. However, with a sense of urgency and the angst that came with it, I summoned the energy I needed to keep me going. Counting once again became my go-to strategy, although my biggest motivation was the thought of seeing Helene and the boys and Harry's words – 'Never give up, Papa' – were constantly sounding in my head. By 10 o'clock that evening, it was time for a refuel and a break for a few hours. I still had seventy miles to go to reach a safe haven and forty-eight hours to do it in before the weather turned against me. It remained within my capabilities, but it was going to be tight.

As a precaution, I thought I'd check with the weather forecasters that there had been no change and the predicted weather front hadn't sped up, mainly so that I could get some rest overnight before continuing. As it was out of hours, I didn't get to speak to my usual forecasters who, despite their lack of appreciation of what an ocean rowing boat was capable of (or, more to the point, not capable of), were fairly good. I'd been forewarned by other ocean rowers about the rather hit-and-miss forecasting from the out-of-hours team so stressed to the person I spoke to the absolute importance of getting this forecast right. Giving him my current position, I said that I would call back in one hour to give him time to collate the information that I needed. I then got back on the oars with the tension building inside me, picturing the weather front suddenly intensifying and sweeping me back out into the Atlantic, meaning that any rest was impossible.

After an hour I called back. The news that I was given was the sum of all my fears. The frontal system that would bring about the change in wind direction was going to arrive not in forty-eight hours but twenty-four, making it next to impossible to reach Falmouth Harbour before the deadline. I shook violently and tears streamed down my cheeks at the prospect of this and I asked him to double-check that this was the case and no mistakes had been made, stressing the desperation of my situation to try and impart the gravity of the news he had just given me. Despite this, he replied with a flippancy that made me want to reach down the phone line and beat the living crap out of him.

Knowing nothing of the coastline, he then gave me coordinates that I should try and head for. This was apparently the closest piece of land, a small and rocky cove that would have smashed *Peggy* to pieces had I tried to get her in there. Just before hanging up, he asked, 'Is there anything else I can do for you today?' A few suggestions sprung to mind involving various parts of his body and a food blender, but I said, 'No, you've done quite enough, thank you', before hanging up.

As I put the phone down I was a bit of a mess. I'd rowed three and a half thousand miles, been battered and bruised by an unprecedented eight storms, flipped seven times, lost the drive system that I'd spent a huge amount of time and effort building and developing as well as most of my electronic equipment. I had come through it all and yet here I was, so close to home, and about to be dealt the cruellest of hammer blows. For ten minutes or so, I simply couldn't rationalise or think of anything that might help, but slowly I shook myself out of my malaise and started looking at options.

My intended target had been St Mawes in Cornwall, a side branch of Falmouth Herbour. This would have offered excellent protection in the predicted gales, but it was now out of reach with the winds already swinging towards the south and slowing progress. Thinking it through, I realised that my best chance of reaching any kind of shelter was to make the most of the winds and head for the very tip of England. Though I could get there relatively soon, it was not ideal, offering little protection from the gales and the swells they would push up, while the coast in those parts was strewn with rocks. On the plus side, I would at least be able to get an anchor down and cling to the coast with my fingernails dug in until better conditions arrived.

With this new plan in my head, I decided to get a few hours' rest and some food as I'd need all the energy I could muster if it was going to work.

Getting back on the oars at two in the morning after having had a very fitful few hours of rest and probably twenty minutes of proper sleep, I attacked the task with everything I had. I used the anger from the phone call and the thought of seeing my boys as my fuel to power me through the night as rain poured down, a precursor to the arrival of the frontal system. I vaguely remember seeing quite a few fishing trawlers, but paid them no attention as the counting continued: *a thousand more strokes, two thousand more strokes, five thousand more strokes*. I'd been awake for the better part of twenty-four hours and, as the fatigue set in, I had to reduce my targets to hundreds of strokes to keep me motivated, but I carried on without stopping.

At one stage, I nearly collided with a trawler. I was aware of us being on a collision course but, given what I had been through, I simply thought, *F**k it, you can get out of my way!* Then, at a distance of no more than fifty metres and heading straight for me, he suddenly turned on all his deck lights, blinding me but giving me a fresh and much-needed dose of adrenalin. This wore off as the lights went off again and my mind started to play tricks on me so that I started to hallucinate.

First, it was my compass light which, in the dim glow of a fading head torch that I'd rigged up, turned into a big fat Russian *babushka* holding two enormous baubles, one under each arm. Then a washing line appeared to my right with a towel and a tatty jumper hanging from it that were flapping and getting on my nerves. My eyelids grew heavy as I rowed and the first light of dawn couldn't have come soon enough. Just before daybreak, I saw the beam from a distant lighthouse so I knew that the coast was tantalisingly close, but with the proximity to land came the possibility that I'd have to row into tidal currents which, with the southerly winds, could sweep me back around the 'toe' of England. Still, I continued, knowing that there was nothing I could do except keep on rowing and hope for the best.

The day dawned grey and overcast. In the murky light, it was hard to make out any land and I'd look over my shoulder every now and then hoping for a glimpse of the coastline, but to no avail. I could see from my chartplotter that I was only ten miles away, but there was still no sight of the tall cliffs of Lands' End and, slightly delirious from physical exhaustion and sleep deprivation, I started to doubt myself.

Eventually, however, unmistakable on the horizon, a grey smudge slowly started to emerge from the gloom.

Far from feeling relief, I still had a long way to go and was concerned as to where exactly I would be able to get to land. I was so tired and had been hallucinating for so long that I couldn't make any sense of where I was or what I should do or what the bit of land that I was looking at represented on the chart. It took all my mental reserves to snap out of my brain fog and figure things out.

I was aiming for the very tip of England. The only harbour that might offer some protection from the easterlies was Penzance. I didn't want to enter an actual harbour, however, as I feared that that would constitute the end of my voyage. I therefore preferred to be anchored out somewhere that could offer some protection.

The large tidal range meant that a lot of the sheltered spots would dry out which would break my rudder. I contemplated getting in on a high tide and trying to remove it, but once again I didn't know if landing on a shore, albeit a tidal sandbank, would constitute 'having made landfall' and therefore negate any claims of my row being non-stop to London. In the end, I decided to just keep going and reassess where I was when I got to the mouth of the bay near Penzance. I could make neither head nor tail of the weather which failed to relate to the forecast conditions; the strong southerly winds that had been predicted hadn't arrived, nor had the north-westerlies, but once again I put my confusion on this score down to my delirium.

By 11 o'clock, the rain had finally stopped, the clouds parted and I was treated to a beautiful day in calm seas. I was all in with nothing left in the tank, the tide had turned against me and I was no longer making forward progress so I decided to take a break. It was only then that it dawned on me: I had crossed the North frickin Atlantic!!!!

Well within sight of land, I first radioed the coast guard to announce my arrival before checking my telephone to find that I had a signal and immediately called Helene and Mum and Dad to let them know I had made it. I recall very little of the conversation as everything was a bit of a blur, though I do remember recounting my last thirty-six hours but thinking at the time, *Why am I telling them this? They were here all last night*, so messed up was my head.

Though I wanted to carry on, I decided to finally rest in the hope that a quick nap would help me to make the right decision for the next course of action. I had a slight fear of the tide sweeping me back around the tip of England, but I simply needed to rest and collapsed into my cabin with the hatch open and the sun shining on my face. I woke two hours later, soaking wet after what must have been a sizeable rain shower judging by the amount of water in my cabin and my soaked mattress, but I'd been totally oblivious to it. My nap did at least leave me feeling revived and having a phone signal meant that I was able to check the forecast. There was no sign of the early passing of the frontal system which the forecaster had got utterly wrong, despite my having urged him to take every care to make sure that it was accurate.

I'd phoned Helene prior to the start of this marathon to tell her about the forecast and how it could affect my progress. She'd duly posted this on social media and everybody apart from me knew that it was utter rubbish, but could not let me know, my telephone only being switched on when I needed it in order to conserve the battery. I had just pushed myself to row twenty-seven hours straight, had not slept for the better part of three days and had lost potentially sixty miles of eastward progress due to diverting to the closest point of land rather than continuing on course and getting to a port of refuge as planned. Yet as pissed off as I was at the ineptitude of the forecaster (or whoever it was who had picked up the phone that evening; it may as well have been the cleaner), I was incredibly relieved that I still had another twenty-four hours to make it to a safe anchorage. The tide was still running against me and the wind was now beam-on, but my westward slip on the tide hadn't been as bad as I had feared. I therefore took the time to have a bit of food and wait for the tide to slacken before pointing *Peggy*'s bows towards the furthest point of land on the eastern horizon: Lizard Point.

It was still ten miles away and then a further eighteen to where I wanted to be to consider myself as safe, but with a strong following tide it seemed perfectly feasible to get there in good time. The north-westerly winds were not due until later that afternoon, by which time I hoped to have turned the corner and got some shelter from the winds that I would otherwise have to row almost straight into.

There are numerous hazards along the coastline, which is littered with hundreds of wrecks sustained over the years, so I was cautious to stay far enough off the coastline to avoid getting swept onto the rocks but not so far away that I'd have to spend too long making up the ground to the north once I had passed the headland. The tide started to build and was whisking me and *Peggy* along with it and I knew from experience that there were some large overfalls off Lizard Point and that we were coming up to the spring tides when they would be running at their fastest. It was therefore no surprise when I heard waves crashing directly in front of me as the strong current passed over the shallow waters, much as it had done on my training run around the Isle of Wight.

With the fast-moving current, I was actually looking forward to it. However, I hadn't accounted for the ferocity or size of the waves being forced up and soon found myself in a fairly dicey situation. Far from being a flowing wavefront, the waves being generated were two metres in height, incredibly steep and constantly breaking. Once again I had to strain every muscle and sinew in my body to break free of standing waves which held me steadfastly on the spot rather than giving me the free and thrilling ride that I'd hoped for. It took me a full three hours of agonising progress, pummelled by the waves, before I was able to break free of their grasp and head onwards around the coast.

I felt that I'd done enough already to deserve a bit of a break. However, the delay in getting around the headland meant that the favourable tide was now waning and any hopes of reaching Falmouth Harbour that evening were disappearing fast. Again, I had no choice but to keep pushing if I was to make it before the change in weather scuppered any chance I had of getting to safety before the arrival of the winds.

One good thing was that the southerly winds had blown in as I came around the headland and I needed every bit of help from them if I was going to make any headway into the south-flowing current. I didn't have a tidal atlas for the area as it was never my intention to go into any of the large bays along the South Coast of the UK so I rowed on blindly in the hope that I would be able to make headway. I had no indication of speed over the ground on deck, all repeaters having fizzed and died some time beforehand. I therefore used visual markers to determine my progress as well as the feel of the boat through the water.

The alternative was to perform a rear-arching limbo move into my cabin with my feet strapped in to take a look at the only bit of electronics still working, the chartplotter inside of the cabin. With the wind still in my favour, the boat felt like it was moving through the water really well and, despite my exertions over the past months, I felt incredibly good. The visual markers, however, told a different story as the passage of the land started to slow meaning that the tide had turned.

After an hour or so of really good progress with *Peggy* gliding through the water seemingly effortlessly, I looked up and was a little confused as the coastline looked remarkably familiar. I had been so 'in the moment' and enjoying the feeling of easy rowing that I hadn't noticed that, for the three or four miles of water that had passed under the hull, I had progressed about a quarter of a mile. The wind was pushing me one way and the tide was ripping the other way, giving a net result of around zero progress. With the tide having turned, I knew that I was in for yet another battle as it would only intensify over the coming hours before relenting after six hours. To compound matters, the wind started to drop so I found myself travelling backwards.

The shore was too treacherous to try and drop an anchor so my only alternative was to row as hard as I could to stay in the same place. It was utterly devastating having come so far; all I wanted was to drop anchor in a quiet bay and rest, but that was no longer an option. By my calculations, the tide would not change until 2 o'clock the following morning so I would have to spend another night rowing flat out for six hours to stay still and then row four or five hours more to reach a safe haven. It was yet another massive blow but I knew I had to keep going.

As the hours rolled by, the current became stronger. At one point it took me fifteen minutes going flat out simply to gain one boat-length past a fishing buoy that was being dragged under the surface by the current. By 11 o'clock, I couldn't do any more and finally collapsed at the oars and decided to accept the inevitable. I slumped back into my cabin to see just how fast I would be drawn back into the English Channel.

As well as being totally exhausted, I needed to eat something if I was to gain any further miles. To my surprise, despite the tide hurtling past me, I was staying reasonably still. I went back outside, assuming that I had somehow snagged onto one of the fishing floats that I'd seen earlier, but there was no sign of an entanglement. It then occurred to me that the tide was so strong that it had set up a stopper wave that was holding us in place. There was just enough of a breeze to keep *Peggy* pointing the right way and the wave was high and steep enough to maintain her in a constant surf position. I might have had my fair share of bad luck throughout the voyage, but this was heaven-sent and I couldn't help rejoicing as I boiled up some water for a nice bit of supper and a rest.

I slipped backwards very slowly as the current overcame the wind, but for two more hours we more or less sat there. I had to set an alarm every five minutes as I kept nodding off and small variations in the current meant that we would surf either towards or away from the shore and small adjustments of the rudder were needed to counteract this. I also contacted the coast guard to let them know of my predicament and ask if they could give me any tidal information. They were unable to do this, instead asking, 'Do you need any assistance?' I was very close to crumbling.

By then, it would have been so easy to say, 'Yes, please.' I'd crossed an ocean, battled adversity and broken all my own expectations with regard to my speed. I could quite easily have thrown in the towel there and then, but I knew that if I had done that, I would never have forgiven myself. There would be other times during that night that I came so close to picking up the mic and asking for a tow, but for now I managed a weak 'No, thank you.'

With the tide starting to turn against me at about eight in the evening, I assumed that it would once again revert to being in my favour six hours later at around two in the morning after starting to slacken off considerably before that. However, just before 1 a.m., I noticed that I had started slipping backwards at an increasing rate. When that rate grew to one knot, mindful that I could snag the rudder on one of the many fishing pots I had encountered, I went back out on deck and started to row again.

The southerly winds that had been helping to hold me in position had all but died. This meant that the northerly winds would not be too far behind so I had to get moving. For the first hour, all I managed to gain was about quarter of a mile. But then, as the current slowly eased, I began making a little more progress. I'd only lost one and a half miles to the south, but travelling as slowly as I was it may as well have been a thousand, such was the effort required to get back to where I'd started six hours beforehand. Yet even this seemed like a huge victory. I still had eleven more miles to go, but as the tide slackened the wind started to build against me and before long I was once again straining at the oars to keep some momentum in *Peggy*.

I knew that I was being shielded by the cliffs to my right from the worst of the winds, but that would soon end as I crossed a large estuary and make the going a lot tougher. I could discern the lights of ships at anchor in the bay as well as some other navigation marks in the distance and made them my new targets. *Just keep counting*, I told myself, *a thousand more strokes, a thousand strokes an hour, ten miles, two knots, five thousand strokes, a hundred more, fifty more, halfway to the next hundred. Which hundred was I on?* I had to start again. So it went on.

The *babushka* was back with her baubles. So were the towel and the tatty jumper on the washing line. My mind and body felt completely disassociated from one another. I was running on auto. The winds built and swung around to be pretty much head-on, but I was beyond caring. I think that a group of small dolphins joined me, swirling the bioluminescence around as they played right next to the boat. It was like something out of the movie *Avatar*, but I cant be sure if they were real or not. The brightly lit ships at anchor in the distant outer harbour slowly came into sharper focus, but by then it didn't matter.

A hundred more strokes, seven miles, two knots, 3,500 strokes, thirty-five strokes... all I have to do is that ninety-nine more times. How long could it take to get past one 150-metre boat? Fifty strokes maybe, seventy-five allowing for the headwind, two metres between the puddles made by my oars... Is the boat getting closer? How many strokes was that? Just keep going to the next navigation light. How far is it? Why isn't it getting any closer? Just keep rowing. Three thousand more strokes and we'll be there.

As another dawn broke, the coastline came into focus and I could finally see the harbour entrance. The navigation light that I'd set as a point to get to before I took a break turned out to be the lighthouse at the mouth of the estuary. Finally, as I was in the last half a mile or so, I picked up some shelter from the land and the winds started to drop. Navigation was tricky as I had no read-out on deck so I had to keep stopping to look at the chartplotter in the cabin to check I was going the right way and then interpolate my heading to account for the fact I was going backwards – not easy in my frazzled state of mind – but eventually the small estuary that I had marked as my resting place came into view.

Still, there was work to be done against an outgoing tide and the counting continued as I neared collapse, but as I came into the final few hundred metres all was calm. It was early morning and not a soul stirred in the beautiful village of St Mawes. The water was flat and it was incredibly peaceful. I will never forget that image as I silently glided towards the harbour; even the sound of my oars entering the water seemed to be sacrilege, breaking the tranquility of the moment. I picked what I thought was a suitable spot, rigged the anchor and let it go over the side. Tying it off and waiting for it to settle, I was left with a sense of serenity and calm the extent of which I had never experienced before. I wanted to weep with joy, but I was too tired to do so.

For me, the Atlantic leg of the journey could not have ended better, in complete peace and solitude. After taking a full ten minutes to enjoy the moment, my moment, I made a quick call home to reassure everybody that I was OK and, though I really didn't want to, I thought it best for posterity's sake to make a video diary. Watching it back, I realised that it did no justice to the sense of relief I was feeling in that moment as words alone simply couldn't convey it. Up until the very last strokes, the North Atlantic had pushed me way beyond any limits I had previously experienced, but for now I was safe, well and in need of a rest.

16

NYLON: the Home Leg

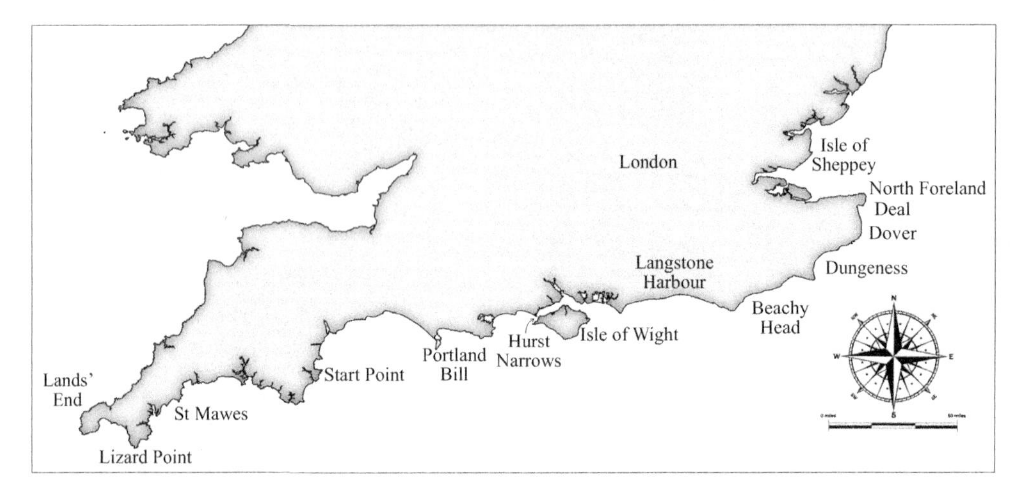

Despite only having slept for four hours in the past four days, I only managed a few hours' sleep as I was too excited to be back in civilisation.

I contacted the harbour master to let him know that I was there, where I'd come from and what my intentions were, and he very kindly shuffled some boats around to get me into a great spot where I'd be safe and secure in the days to come. I'm not a great one for social media but, now having the luxury of internet access, I logged on to my accounts and was overwhelmed by all the messages of support from all around the world which bought me to tears on a number of occasions. I was soon in need of cheering up all over again when I checked the weather forecast.

The news was not good with the strong easterly winds settled in for at least five days. This was very frustrating as I'd hoped to get to London before the end of the school holidays to spend time together with my family, but this delay would almost certainly put paid to that. I called Helene just to run it past her as she'd faced tremendous strain over the past months and I hadn't seen her or the boys for five months and I wanted to make sure that she was OK with me hanging around and waiting for conditions to improve. For the first time since I'd set out, this was the call where I really wanted her to tell me to carry on regardless and I'm glad to say she didn't disappoint, reminding me that it was always my goal to row from New York to London so I should stick to it, regardless of whether it took five or even ten days of waiting until I could leave.

We had discussed her coming down to see me with the boys, but agreed that it was probably best if they didn't as it might have broken my resolve if I was to see them and then have to say goodbye again. I therefore settled in to wait things out.

Peggy was an absolute mess, stinking to high heaven and very soggy, so the first job of the day was to get everything out and give her a good spruce-up. I was blessed with some beautiful late-summer weather so could leave everything out on deck to dry whilst I got to work, but after a few hours everything was done and the anchorage started to liven up. St Mawes is a very popular holiday destination and the combination of school holidays, great weather and international travel still being banned due to COVID meant it was going to get very busy.

Sure enough, it wasn't long before people began coming by, swimming out to see me or stopping on all manner of boats – kayaks, SUPs etc. – for a chat. It was so wonderful to be able to interact with human beings again and I relished the opportunity to tell a few tales about my journey. Offers of beer, pasties and ice cream were incredibly tempting, but I couldn't take them as it would nullify my claim of being 'unsupported'. I thus looked enviously to the shore where people were out and about, eating and drinking, as I sat on deck and boiled up another pot of water for another delicious dehydrated meal. I also had the opportunity to do a stocktake of my available food and, even with the five-day delay, I was able to give myself double rations. This was just as well as the waft of bacon coming from the shore in the morning and fish and chips in the evening made me constantly ravenous and, with the remaining *kabanos* now relegated to slimy packs of ballast sausage, I was in need of extra calories.

My first day in St Mawes was a bit of a blur with an endless stream of well-wishers, but as darkness fell everything quietened down and I was left alone in silence for the best night's sleep I'd had in a long time.

I was moored dead opposite a very posh hotel and close to the shore so I made sure that I got a very early start to 'contemplate' the day ahead. I was fairly sure that nobody really wanted to be greeted with the sight of a skinny, bedraggled man emptying his bucket as they enjoyed fresh-baked croissants and a glass of juice on their balcony! Knowing that I'd be there for some time and it becoming apparent that I was a bit of a tourist attraction, I decided to tidy myself up so I took to my head with a pair of rusty kitchen scissors and after a quick 'Chuck Norris' felt completely revitalised. The video that I had posted upon arrival, though attracting a huge amount of positive comments, also had more than a few pointing out that I'd turned into my dad over the previous five months with a mop of wiry grey hair and a well-weathered face. No offence to Dad, but I was pleased to take a few years off with a bit of a spruce-up.

As the day progressed, the crowds once again started to build. The local ferry operators, whom I'd got to know the previous day, started including me in their scenic tours. I'd get rounds of applause from boatloads of people every time they passed. It really was wonderful to have the support, but I was dying to get going again. The next safe anchorage offering protection from the easterly winds was fifty miles to the east so I needed a clear window of twenty-four hours before I could make my next move. Sad to say, this didn't look like happening any time soon.

Though I considered myself fairly unlucky to have been hit with these weather patterns so close to the finish, there were still three other boats out there. Dinger Bell was a good five hundred miles out and would be stuck on para-anchor for quite a while. The 'Irish lads' were making progress towards Ireland but having a lot of technical issues and it looked like Ian Rivers, the other solo rower who had set out from New York two weeks earlier than me, was going to scrape in by the skin of his teeth to the Scilly Isles. I'd also learned of another solo rower, Guirec Soudée, who had left Chatham, Massachusetts the day after me and was also somewhere out there; his GPS having failed him, he had to rely on passing ships to give him his position.

I can only imagine these men's frustration upon hearing the next weather forecast, which suggested that the easterly winds that were plaguing me would not abate until at least 2 September. It was bad enough being tortured by the aromas of life on shore, but at least I was safe, dry and comfortable. (Speaking to Dinger after he got back, he told me that he was happier to be out there and didn't envy me one little bit, being so close to temptation!)

I did have one very emotional visit from my dad and sister. Dad had been involved in a motorbike accident a week or so beforehand and was in a wheelchair, but he managed to hobble down the quayside and get one of the local RIB drivers to bring him over. Grappling him onboard as best we could, I thought that he'd got stuck as I held him but realised that he was sobbing and unable to move. I'd never known him to cry before and was pretty shocked and unable to think what to do. We are very close but showing our emotions is not something we do. Even hugs have always been frowned upon so to simply hold him whilst he let it out was incredible, reminding me that for all my trials and tribulations on the voyage, it had also been incredibly stressful for all my loved ones. Once Dad had recovered, I allowed him to put it down to his foot hurting.

As the days passed, I got to know quite a few of the locals who were all lovely. Every morning Sheila and her band of self-proclaimed 'geriatric mermaids' would stop by during their morning swim for a catch-up and to help me with my crosswords which I'd had to ration now I had lot of spare time on my hands. I received salutes from the crews of the gig rowing clubs for my efforts and was made to feel very welcome by everybody in the town, even receiving a visit from an 'actual' mermaid called Mischief who happened to be passing by.

It was absolutely no reflection on the townsfolk that I was gagging to leave, but I was starting to get a little stir crazy. The time there did have one huge positive in that I was able to talk to a lot of people about the charities I was supporting which really helped to put some more money in the pot.

I went for the occasional paddle, just to keep busy, but having so many other pleasure boats around made for pretty tricky navigation. Meanwhile, though I was desperate to break out of the harbour, the only lulls in the constant easterly winds lasted a maximum of twelve hours – not enough time to get to a decent anchorage once I'd left. There would also be a residual swell which I'd have to head into, which I knew from experience was tough going with the boat stalling every time the bow hit an oncoming wave. Though I didn't want to admit it, I was also a little scared by the idea of leaving the harbour in less than ideal conditions, all the arrows on the weather charts showing me exactly where I would end up if I didn't make it to a port of refuge. I was only just in UK territorial waters and a strong tide and winds would have me back out in the Atlantic within a day if I rushed the decision. The hope of a weather window on 2 September came and went with the high pressure firmly stuck over Scotland. Speaking to the local fishermen, some of whom had been working the waters for over forty years, I learned that they had never known such conditions during the summer. Then again, I shouldn't have been surprised, having learned that it had been the worst summer for storms in the Atlantic for forty years. Lucky me!!! I'd had to cut back on double rations and decided to have a four-day binge on my couscous-and-stroganoff hybrid meal so I didn't have a hold full of it for the last leg. I put a carbonara and chocolate chip biscuit pudding right at the bottom, reserved for my last night before getting to Tower Bridge, and I was ready to roll.

By now, I'd ditched the original forecasters and was relying on the advice of Simon Rowell, an expert meteorologist who had often guided other ocean rowers. He informed me that the next weather window was 8 September, an incredible eighteen days since I'd arrived, but it would only be three days before the dreaded north-easterlies returned for a short spell. It was therefore going to require a big push to get as far as I possibly could and I set my sights on the Isle of Wight which offered some decent spots to hide from the strong winds that were forecast. It was 175 miles away and, though the conditions weren't initially going to be much help, neither would they be against me.

Come the morning of the eighteenth, all was set and the tides dictated that an early departure was preferable. Having said my goodbyes to the wonderful people of St Mawes the day before and vowed to come back for a pint and a pasty at the earliest possible opportunity, I slipped out of the harbour and bid a fond farewell to the town that had been my sanctuary. It was a grey and murky morning with not a breath of wind as I exited the harbour mouth and headed out into the mist which muted the senses and increased my feeling of isolation which was glorious! I'd loved being around people during my enforced sojourn, but had forgotten how much I enjoyed the feeling of being out at sea, just me and *Peggy* when life became very simple.

The first step was a very short one, just five miles to the south, into the Helford Estuary, a stunning and unspoilt corner of the Cornish countryside. It was a bit counterintuitive as I'd actually have to row a few miles further away from London, but I needed to make some southward progress to counter the southerly winds that would push me back to the north during the first day of my progress east if I was to make it around the next headland at Start Point, sixty-five miles away. I'd passed the estuary in the pitch black of night almost three weeks previously. Then I'd cursed it for allowing the north-westerly winds to funnel down it, hampering my progress, but on this perfectly still morning it was an altogether different prospect.

We pulled into a stunning bay just inside the mouth of the estuary. After dropping anchor, I just sat and marvelled at the absolute tranquility. It was grey and had started to rain, but the only sound was of raindrops on the glass-smooth surface of the water and the birds overhead. The lush green shore was perfectly reflected on the surface of the sea and I couldn't have asked for a more beautiful setting to strike out from on the final leg of my journey.

Timings from here on in would be crucial as the tidal flow increased the further east I headed, squeezing the waters that flowed east then west approximately every six hours from the hundred-mile-wide mouth of the English Channel to the twenty-five-mile-wide bottleneck at Dover at rates that I simply wouldn't be able to make any headway against. The rate of flow was further exacerbated when passing headlands and promontories where there were tidal 'races' which could be up to seven knots, very handy if you happened to be going the same way as them but not so much if they were flowing against you.

The winds and tides were looking good for a departure at 7 o'clock the following morning so I tried to get some rest before my row, but I was too excited at the prospect of making progress to settle down and, by five in the morning, my fidgeting got the better of me. Though I knew I'd have to slog into conditions for a bit longer than anticipated, I would make a few miles in the right direction which would give me a bit more of a buffer zone to get around the next headland before the tide changed. I hadn't set myself any specific hours to row, it was just a matter of rowing as hard as I could for as long as I could and resting when I had to. As I set out that morning, the winds were from the south, but due to the leeway I had to head into wind a little just to keep on a straight heading to Start Point.

There was still a residual swell bang on the nose and occasionally *Peggy* would stop dead in the water as the bows slammed into a wave and I'd have to pull hard to get her moving again. However, slowly we started to make progress and the lights of the shore faded into the distance as we headed towards the middle of the bay. As the day wore on, the southerly winds remained but the tide gradually turned in my favour and we made tough but good progress. Before setting out, I was undecided as to whether I would row with the tide when it was with me and take the hit backwards when it turned or whether I would row against the counter-current to hold position against the tide and then rest when it turned to get a bit of a free ride. Ultimately, it wouldn't make the slightest bit of difference as the tides would even out and it was the amount of water that I could get to pass under the boat that would dictate just how far I got, but psychologically I didn't know what would be worse, rowing for six hours and making very little progress before jumping on the magic carpet and ending up further on while I rested, or making great distances only to have some of the big gains stolen away from me when I put down the oars.

As it happened, the southerly winds dictated that I didn't have to worry about such things. If I stopped rowing, *Peggy* would point her bows north and head into the bay, which I definitely didn't want to do, so I just kept rowing until the westerly winds arrived.

Late into that evening, I was joined by another group of dolphins splashing around in the pitch black, stirring up the bioluminescence once again which was completely transfixing and this time I was quite sure that they were real. I had noticed a complete difference in the behaviour of the dolphins I encountered in mid-ocean and those I saw in coastal waters; the oceanic dolphins always remained somewhat more aloof than their coastal counterparts who were obviously far more used to human interaction and seemed a lot more playful, coming much closer to *Peggy* and showing off.

I was getting fairly tired and by midnight, after nineteen hours on the oars, I needed a break. I was pleased with progress so far and confident on getting past Start Point the following day on the east-going tide and the southerly winds had started to shift to the west which was a very encouraging sign. I set my track alarm to let me know if I was going in the right direction, but thankfully *Peggy* looked after me with the minimum of fettling. I was up again at five for breakfast and back on the oars by six, by which time the conditions had picked up and become perfect for churning out some serious miles. The wind was now strong enough to counter and even make gains on the west-going tide so I decided to row eight hours on, four hours off to make the most of the favourable current. This was a serious morale boost, particularly as I shot past Start Point at five knots with a swift following current, and I rowed in to the first hour and last hour of countertide, when it is at its weakest.

The next major hurdle was Portland Bill which would be impossible to row past on a west-going tide, the current ripping past the headland at more than double that which I could sustain. My plan was to row a little into the huge bay before it to take advantage of a tidal eddy that flows in a circle and gives a little boost to the east as the current rages westward. I'd anchor up just in the lee of the Bill and wait for the tide to change at which point I'd pop out and get sucked through on the swift tide.

I made surprisingly good progress and as I neared the Bill I wondered if there was any possibility of me getting past it in time rather than waiting another six hours. Time was still of the essence due to the projected return of the easterly winds in the next few days, by which time I wanted to be safely tucked up somewhere, and though I initially discounted the thought, I couldn't help but wonder if it was possible.

Curiosity got the better of me and I decided to attack it with everything I had. I was ten miles out and had roughly three hours of tide running with me. If I could get far enough past the Bill in that time, I might just make it into the slightly slower-moving waters and at least be able to hold position until the tide once again swung in my direction. The boat speed was picking up all the time as we neared the tidal race. I was tired but exhilarated to see the lights on the land moving by so quickly, but I knew that it was far from over as I went past the lighthouse marking the tip of the promontory where the current moved the most swiftly. I'd decided to stay three miles offshore to keep out of the overfalls which had caused me such hassle when I had first arrived back in the UK and I didn't much fancy going through them at night anyway, especially as they would be even stronger than those I experienced at Lizard Point. It was now a matter of just how far I could get before the tide changed and just after I passed the lighthouse the boat speed started to drop.

We managed to get about three miles past the lighthouse before the tide turned and started racing against us. I still had a good following wind which helped, but I knew that I wouldn't be able to rest if I was to stop myself from going backwards. As the current built and the wind continued to blow, the waves steepened and grew due to wind-over-tide effect and I was soon surfing large steep waves. With the speed of the current, however, *Peggy* would slide backwards at two to three knots the moment I stopped rowing so I carried on into the night.

At the peak flow, I managed to make the sum total of 0.24 miles in four hours according to my GPS, but it was forward, not backwards, which was all that mattered. By two in the morning, I was pretty knackered, and knowing that the current had begun to abate, I decided to let *Peggy* take over whilst I grabbed some snacks and a very fitful rest whilst constantly monitoring the position. Soon, however, we started to eke our way eastwards and I was able to relax a little.

It was a very uneasy feeling being in coastal waters and just drifting on the tide in the hope that, if something was headed my way, they would change direction rather than bump into me. It flew in the face of everything I knew about being a seafarer, maintaining a proper lookout at all times being one of the cardinal rules. I'd become quite inured to it in the open ocean where the chances of bumping into something were pretty remote and they would probably have AIS. But in these waters, full of small pleasure craft, fishing buoys and a whole host of other obstacles and dangers, 'resting' only meant that I wasn't rowing and snatching micro-naps as and when I could.

One advantage of my delay in Cornwall was that the school holidays had ended so the amount of pleasure craft on the sea had hugely decreased and I hadn't actually come across many other people thus far.

With the current starting to build, it was going to be a sprint to get to the Isle of Wight and through the Hurst Narrows before the change of tide and, once again, it was going to be close as to whether I would make it in time. Having these deadlines constantly imposed upon me was taking some adjusting to and I found them rather irksome having had the freedom of the ocean where nothing like that really mattered. In my head, I'd always seen the

English Channel as being my 'victory lap' and had visions of simply rowing on the east-going tide and resting at anchor when it changed, preferably as hordes of delirious fans lined the shore and cheered me on. However, with the weather about to change against me once again, it wasn't to be.

In addition, I suddenly had pressure from home. Though I'd made terrific time up until now, far exceeding my expectations, I was being asked when I expected to arrive in London which put pressure on me that I could have really done without, as all I wanted to do was to enjoy the final furlong at my own pace. The charity I had been supporting even asked me if it was possible to arrive during Heart FM's breakfast show so that they could do a live outdoor broadcast. Fortunately, Helene was on hand to explain how tides work and that unfortunately, no, I wasn't sure that I could make it to Tower Bridge at 08:30 on a given day.

The Hurst Narrows mark the narrowest point (hence the name) between the Isle of Wight and mainland UK and all the water from the Solent gets squeezed through there twice daily. It was still about forty miles away and I'd have to take advantage of every scrap of wind and current that I could as well as rowing my socks off if I was to make it through in the nine hours that I had before the tide ran against me at such a rate that progress would be impossible. The alternative was to take a six-hour delay at anchor which might well mean that I'd be struggling to find a decent safe haven by the time the easterly winds arrived so I put on my big-boy pants once again and set out. After a few hours, the tide had changed in my favour and I made excellent progress, glancing into the cabin every now and then to see what speeds I was making and assessing whether it was going to be possible to make it.

Passing Bournemouth, there was a bit of a wind shift and I also had to adjust my course a little more to the north which didn't help as the winds were slightly more beam-on, but what I was trying to achieve still felt possible. I slogged away without rest and finally reached the Needles Channel, the approach to the Hurst Narrows, with forty-five minutes to spare, though I'd noticed that the surface of the sea had started to change and become choppy. I glanced back inside the cabin to see that my speed over the ground was starting to decrease fairly rapidly and it became obvious that the tide had turned against me earlier than anticipated. I was, however, still making progress, albeit slowing, and had passed the Needles lighthouse so only had about two miles to go and decided to press on.

Progress continued to slow as the passage narrowed and the current intensified against me. I could have bailed out and headed to the north shore of the Isle of Wight to anchor up and wait for the next tide, but I'd set it in my sights to get through the Hurst Narrows so pressed on. Passing a navigation marker about one mile out, I could see the tide rushing past it in the wrong direction but I was still making ground. My stroke rate increased as did my effort as I clawed my way towards Hurst Castle which marks the entrance to the Narrows and decided to head towards the north of the Solent, my goal being to ferry-glide across the current and get into the shallows at Keyhaven where the current would decrease and I would be able to drop the anchor.

By the time I reached the castle, the current was absolutely ripping through and I barely made any progress, literally just a few centimetres with every stroke whilst rowing flat out and blowing hard. I could physically see the tide line just a hundred metres ahead and to the right of me and was desperate to make it there to get into the slower-moving water, but it seemed to be on the very edge of possibility. Every once in a while, an oar would clip the top of a wave and just that tiny loss of momentum was enough to make me lose ground westward. I remember being so angry at the time at nature's cruelty in that, after three months at sea and thousands of miles already covered, I had to battle to make a hundred metres.

Of course, in hindsight, I realise that the agony was totally self-imposed. I could have easily anchored up two hours previously and simply made up the few miles on the next tide. It was only my own stubbornness at having set my sights on getting to the other side of the Narrows that had put me in this situation, but thoughts like that wouldn't have been very helpful at the time.

After about forty minutes of giving it everything I had, I slowly crept out of the main current and into slower flowing waters. However, I was now in the lee of the land and had very little help from the wind so, much to my chagrin, had to bust my guts to make it to water that was shallow enough to anchor in. Eventually, after one and a half hours of the hardest rowing of the entire journey and having made about five hundred metres in that time, I threw the anchor over the side and collapsed, panting, on the deck. It took a full ten minutes before I had sufficiently recovered from my exertions to pick myself up and get on with refuelling myself for the next leg.

I'd been in touch with Dad earlier that day to see if he could get the harbour masters at Lymington and Yarmouth to find a space for me to shelter from the easterlies. The answer was unfortunately no as they were full up. They had also pointed out to him that, unless I was through the Narrows by midday, I wouldn't stand a chance of getting to them anyway as the tide would have changed. It transpired that I had forgotten to take the hour's difference for British Summer Time into account when doing my calculations so had been rowing into the tide for the last three hours rather than the one I had accounted for (the first hour of tide being relatively weak and the extra hour having come from the fact that I had been travelling much slower than anticipated as the current built against me). So Dad was fairly surprised to hear from me when I told him that I'd made it inside the Solent and I was equally chuffed to have done so, having covered 155 miles in sixty hours. The really good news was that, having slogged my guts out for three hours against the tide, I'd only have to wait another three until it changed and I could get back on the oars and do it all again!

Though I didn't have any blisters, my hands were in a pretty bad state and I'd obviously done a lot of damage to all my joints throughout the journey, particularly having pushed myself over the past two and a half days when, every time I returned to the oars after a short break, it felt like my knuckles were going to dislocate with every stroke and pains shot across the tops of my hands and up my arms. Thankfully, the pain would normally subside after about twenty minutes. Either that or I'd just got used to it! Either way I could no longer close them beyond anything smaller that an oar which made simple tasks such as eating or brushing my teeth a bit of a challenge, but I consoled myself with the fact that actually rowing claws were just about all I needed just then so they would probably do.

After my efforts over the previous days, I set myself a very modest target of just fifteen miles that evening and was really excited at the prospect of being able to take it easy at the oars for the first time since the start of the row. Wind and tide would be with me and, once the pain in my knuckles had eased off, I was treated to a wonderful cruise along the Solent under a clear star-studded sky with a gentle following breeze. It was a wonderful time to reflect on the journey so far and consider what was yet to come – though far from over, it now felt well within my grasp. I even took the time to sit out and enjoy a dinner on deck as I was wafted along on the current, feeling very pleased with myself for all the decisions I'd made that had got me to this moment.

Later that evening, I passed Cowes where a party was in full swing at the Royal Yacht Club. There was music blaring and people were obviously having a great time, but I didn't envy them one little bit. None of them had experienced what I had gone through over the previous months and, despite all of the deprivations and hardships, I felt incredibly privileged to have the opportunity to be in the final throes of this terrific voyage.

I rowed gently into Osborne Bay, just beyond Cowes, that evening and once again all was flat and calm with not a sound to spoil the tranquility. I could have carried on for a few more miles but there seemed little point, the following day's row set to be a similar distance, and I'd already pushed myself enough to warrant an early knock-off. After dropping the anchor, my inner masochist was chastising itself for not carrying on just that little bit further as I had not pushed myself enough that evening, but he was soon told to bugger off so that I could get a lovely night's sleep.

It was now 12 September and the easterly winds were due to pick up that evening. Rather conveniently, the tide would change at 6 a.m. the following morning which allowed me a very civilised schedule to complete the fifteen miles to Langstone Harbour which I hoped would offer sufficient protection from the winds.

The journey there was fairly uneventful, though I did have to 'make like a meerkat', constantly popping up and down to check for the numerous ferries and other craft that ply these waters, but eventually I reached the harbour entrance unscathed. As I approached, a guy on a jet-ski pulled up and said, 'Are you Penny's brother?' By now, I'd hoped that I'd done enough to be known in my own right, but my sister had always had the bigger personality so I suppose it was only to be expected. I was kind of used to it anyway, being relatively unsociable and more commonly known as Harry or Louis's dad or Helene's husband.

I confirmed that I was indeed Penny's brother and it turned out that they were on holiday in Cornwall and had seen me when I first arrived at Lands' End so maybe there had been cheering crowds lining the entire coast after all. I'd just been too far away to hear them.

The easterly winds were due to last thirty-six hours, after which the weather seemed set to finally turn in my favour, not entirely of course, as there would be a few bits to struggle through, but that was hardly surprising given that I'd be rowing east to Eastbourne before following the coast north east to the Thames Estuary and then west all the way to London. Somewhat annoyingly, I was still being badgered for an arrival date. I put at between 19 and 21 September, but the preferred date, for everybody else at least, was Sunday the nineteenth as it would allow people who worked during the week to come and cheer me on. I'd seen the forecast and knew that averaging the forty-five miles a day necessary to make that date was possible but it would mean another massive effort coupled with a bit of luck.

The winds blew through as predicted (not by my original weather forecasters whom I had told in no uncertain terms what I thought about them and into which orifice they should insert their 'assistance') and, by the evening of the fourteenth, I was ready to roll, hopefully for the last time.

The route once again needed some careful planning, preferably with the hour for British Summer Time added to the tidal calculations, and navigation was going to be a bit tricky as I had no real reference on deck. I'd downloaded an app on my phone and rigged a waterproof battery pack to keep it charged, but try as I might I couldn't get the screen to stay on for more than ten minutes which meant I had to either keep tapping the screen to keep it alive or, more frustratingly, stop rowing and enter my passcode. This was fine for short-term navigation, though, so I decided to just use it when absolutely necessary.

The Solent and the Isle of Wight has an odd effect on the tides which worked to my advantage; despite the tide in the English Channel running to the west, I was able to sneak out of harbour and around the first headland whilst it was almost slack and once around Selsey Bill I'd have another nine hours before it started to run against me and I'd still have a few hours' grace at its turn as the current wasn't particularly strong inshore.

I set out in the early evening with a lovely north-westerly breeze giving me a shove as I rowed against the weak remnants of the current and made good time to Selsey Bill, twelve miles away. The Bill itself has large shoals and sandbanks so I had to make for a narrow marked channel which wasn't easy in the pitch-black dark and facing backwards, but I found the channel and turned a sharp left to head further up the coast. Unfortunately, this now meant that the lovely following winds were directly on the beam and, to make a good course, I had to actually head into them. I needed *Peggy* to be as nimble as possible if I was going to make the deadline as conditions were forecast to be a bit marginal at best so, saying a final farewell to them, I ditched most of my sausage ballast over the side, retching at the putrid fishy smell as I emptied the packets into the sea. I kept my emergency water supply, however, as I didn't much fancy drinking desalinated water from the Thames.

The winds freshened as I left the protection of the land and headed into open water and fairly soon, with them blowing forward of the bow, I was once again rowing through treacle. Clearly, I was in for a long night. I'd promised Helene to make every effort to get to Tower Bridge on Sunday 19 September, but having the constant spectre of daily mileages to make hanging over my head had me cursing having agreed to do so as it meant that I'd have to continue to punish myself to the bitter end. On the other hand, given the sacrifices that she had made and the amount of support she had given me, I couldn't help thinking it was a small price to pay. At least, that's what the angel on my shoulder kept telling me. The guy with the pitchfork on the other shoulder had some fairly choice words on the subject.

I would have loved to have headed further offshore to take advantage of the stronger currents and had a better angle on the wind. However, I was mindful that, by 11 o'clock the following morning, the tide would be in full flood against me so I'd need to be in shallow enough water to be able to drop anchor. As the night wore on, the *babushka* popped back up on deck. It was nice to see a familiar face, but apparently someone had taken the tatty jumper and towel down from the line as they were nowhere to be seen. Though I enjoyed having lights on the land to act as visual markers to see how I was progressing, it was also a curse in a way in that I was far enough offshore that they didn't seem to move at all and, to add salt to the wound, the winds had swung to the north and built up to twelve to fifteen knots so it took a huge amount of effort to make any headway.

I briefly considered trying to put into a sheltered spot somewhere as I was tired already and still had a long way to go. But I told myself that the boat would not do the work for me and the only way of getting to the finish was to keep straining on the oars and make the hard yards whilst I had to in order to put myself in a better position for when the winds finally swung properly in my favour.

I was constantly reworking the numbers in my head of the miles I had to cover, landmarks that I'd need to pass at certain states of tide and places where I might be able to stop in order to make the deadline. It was good as an exercise to help keep me awake, but a far cry from the freedom of the open ocean and definitely not the 'victory lap' I had in mind. I'd always known that this last 350 miles from the tip of Cornwall was going to be just as much of a test as the row across the Atlantic, but I guess I was unprepared mentally for just how tough it was proving to be. Every little wind shift had me cursing 'Oh, come on, just give me a f**king break', as it meant that I continually had to adjust my heading to stay on the necessary track. A quarter of a mile here or there in the open ocean was of no significance, but here it could put me on a direct course for a wind farm or a sandbank or take me into water where it was too deep to anchor. Stopping to rest was simply not an option as I'd immediately come off the line I needed to maintain.

It was a frustrating night, but as daylight broke the winds eased a little and I was able to make better progress. I spied what I thought were the lights of Brighton Pier which I headed for as I deemed that would be a good place to stop with regard to progress overall. However, the lights turned out to be the promenade in Worthing, ten miles short, which I was a bit gutted about. I was rapidly running out of steam but I knew that I could row *Peggy* at between two and two and a half knots so I just carried on until the speed dropped below a constant average of one and a half knots, meaning that the tide had swung and was now running against me (and I was getting too knackered to carry on). It was of great relief when, two miles past Worthing, at around five in the morning, the speed dipped below the threshold and stayed there.

By now, I'd been on the oars for a solid ten hours, most of that into wind, and everything on my body ached from the continuous effort. Even the anchor felt suddenly unmanageable as I slung it over the side in what I hoped was shallow enough water for it to bite and I was mightily relieved when the bows swung around and the chartplotter indicated that I was holding position.

Once again, I was dog-tired but at least I could get some food inside me and have a decent rest with fitful sleep whilst I checked that the anchor wasn't dragging in the increasing current. We'd made twenty-eight miles overnight, leaving only seventeen more to do before 7 o'clock that evening if I was to stick to my daily mileage total. However, my aim was to get as far as possible along the coast on the next tide.

The next 'pinch point' was Beachy Head, the tallest chalk sea cliff in the UK. Rising an impressive 162 metres straight out of the sea, its gleaming white face has been a landmark for sailors for hundreds of years. Interestingly, its name has nothing to do with a beach but is a corruption of the French name given to it, *Beauchef*, or 'beautiful headland'. It now unfortunately has a rather more macabre reputation as being the third most popular suicide spot in the world, after the Golden Gate Bridge in the US and the Aokigahara Woods in Japan.

Lying twenty-five miles east of my current position, Beachy Head is where the English Channel narrows to only sixty miles wide giving rise to stronger currents which meant that timing would once again be fairly crucial if I was to get past it. I would have until 8 o'clock that evening, after which any attempt would be impossible given the strength of the current and the lack of any discernible following wind to give me a shove. The tide had started to slacken by eleven in the morning so I pulled up the anchor (which proved to be tricky due to the state of my hands which struggled to grip the chain, but eventually I got it back on board) and made my way eastward, passing Brighton and Newhaven where it became apparent that I wouldn't be able to make it around the headland so I settled into a small bay just to the west of Beachy Head.

To be honest, I was pretty glad to have not made it as it gave me an enforced and decent break whilst I waited for the tide to turn and the spot I'd chosen was once again a beautiful, deserted and unspoilt anchorage that I had all to myself rather than the populated coastline that I had been tracking along over the past days. It was a short break to refresh mind and body and, after getting some hot food inside me, I managed to get a few hours' sleep. By this stage, I'd been at the oars for seventeen of the past twenty-four hours.

The tide was due to change by two in the morning so I got up at one to grab a quick bite to eat and prepare for departure. It was a magical spot and, though I'd have loved for the winds to have been blowing in my favour, at this moment on a perfectly calm night with the sound of the waves gently lapping on the shore and the white cliffs towering above me, framing a star-filled sky, I was happy to appreciate it for what it was. Hauling anchor with my gnarled hands and hooking onto the oars, it was a wonderful sight as I left the anchorage for the short journey parallel to the shore with the massive, glowing cliff dwarfing me and *Peggy* and making me feel very inconsequential.

I often become philosophical when in the presence of large geological features like this as they remind me of how insignificant our trivialities are in life. These huge rock formations were born a hundred million years ago and had existed through mass extinctions, ice ages, the birth and ascent of modern man and our wars, strife and troubles, yet remain relatively unchanged by any of it. Man will come and go in the batting of an eyelid of the life of these cliffs and, whatever we end up doing to this wonderful planet, they will bear witness to and weather it as they have always done.

Though life does get on top of us every now and then, I do try to remind myself of the adage 'It too shall pass' and, though our woes may at times seem endless, I am always of the belief that there will come a time when we can look back and reflect upon those periods, not with regret but with a sense of at least having endured and hopefully conquered the challenges we faced. I owe my optimism to my mum and dad who have overcome adversities the like of which I and my kids will never have to face, though I am sure that their generation will face a very different set of struggles with regard to the future of our planet.

Next on the list of 'joining the dots' along the South Coast was Dungeness, a pokey out elbow on the UK coastline opposite Boulogne in France where the Channel narrows further to just twenty-eight miles across. At first sight Dungeness doesn't look overly appealing, dominated as it is by two huge nuclear power stations (now decommissioned), but first impressions are quite deceiving in this case. The power stations themselves sit within a wildlife sanctuary designated as a site of 'special scientific interest', hopefully not from the discovery of seven-headed frogs and the like from the proximity to the power plant, but the warm water outfall from the cooling pipes has created a unique ecosystem that attracts sea birds from miles around. It is one of the single largest expanses of gravel in Europe and is internationally recognised as an important site for flora and fauna alike and, incredibly, one third of all of the plant species in Britain can be found here. It is still used as a military practice firing area, however, and during the inter-war years 'acoustic mirrors' were built here. These were experimental listening 'ears' that were designed to pick up and amplify sound waves as an early-warning station for approaching enemy aircraft and were sited here as it is apparently one of the quietest places in Britain. It turned out that they weren't very effective and were made obsolete by the invention of radar, but they can still be seen today.

Dungeness was thirty-six miles from my anchorage at Beachy Head so there was no chance of getting there on a single tide. However, with the news that westerly winds were due later that day, I set out with high hopes of rounding it on the following east-going tide. The winds were still of no assistance as I came around Beachy Head and past Eastbourne, making progress incredibly tough, but I was at least going with the current so got a bit of a shove. But as night turned into day, it was fairly apparent that getting around Dungeness was not going to happen so I set my sights on just reaching a patch of water shallow enough to drop anchor in to hold me against the tide which would be ripping though by 9 o'clock.

I was only just past Hastings when the tide began to slacken before turning and I was still a mile and a half short of any water shallow enough to drop anchor in so there was no time to stop and rest. If I didn't reach the shoal that I was hoping to get to, much of the ground that I'd gained that day would be lost to the tide, the prospect of which filled me with dread and spurred me on. There wasn't a cloud in the sky and the sun was starting to climb on a beautiful September day as I toiled towards the bank and gradually I grappled myself over the western end of it and just in time as the current was already running against me. Kneeling on deck and preparing the anchor for dropping as quickly as I could for fear of losing too much ground, I noticed the faintest puff of wind on my back and *Peggy* immediately responded, pointing her bows towards Dungeness.

Looking back towards the west, I could see small whitecaps forming on the water in a definite wind-line heading towards me. I honestly couldn't believe what I was witnessing and, if ever there was a time for believing in divine intervention, this was it. Watching the chartplotter, I saw that we weren't only holding ground but making way directly into the current, only just at first, but as the wind strengthened our speed increased. I looked to the skies, punched the air and thanked my go-to guardian angels, my cousin Jason and my Uncle Bert, for this gift. I was absolutely ecstatic at this turn in fortune and once again I was on the right side of the agony-ecstasy rollercoaster that had come to embody the entire adventure.

There were still thirteen miles to cover and I reckoned that, even if I could gain six or seven of those against the tide in the remaining five hours that it was running, I'd be in a great place to get around the headland on the next tide and still be on schedule for arrival on Sunday. As I continued to make progress, basking in the glorious late-summer sunshine and eating a spot of lunch, it seemed that there was a back eddy of current in the area that was further sweeping me towards the headland and my speed began to increase. To complicate matters, there was a clear line on the chart signifying the outer limits of the military firing area which I was approaching and before long the range master approached on his boat to check my intentions and notify me where I was heading. He asked that should I reach the boundary before firing ceased at 3 o'clock, could I kindly bugger off elsewhere. I double-checked the boundary with him and confirmed that I would stay clear until 3 o'clock at which he wished me luck, turned around and headed from whence he'd come.

This left me in a bit of a quandary. At my current rate, I'd be swept towards the boundary and be over it before the allotted hour. This meant that I would have to row to the south into the opposing current in the hope that it would be strong enough to sweep me back away from the firing range to the west, by which time I would be able to spin around in a loop and try again. It felt like a very odd situation to be in, having craved easy miles for so long and now having to relinquish them, but I should have known better as my guardian angels seemed to have it covered. Within half an hour, the counter-current that I was in started to ease and, though I was still making progress, it slowed enough that, by the time I reached the boundary of the firing range, it was almost exactly three in the afternoon and the tide had started to slacken.

I got back on the oars, grinning from ear to ear, thanking them and my outrageous good fortune in this happenstance profusely. I found it absolutely incredible that, after three months at sea and almost four thousand miles, one of the points of the trip I was expecting to be the most troubling, that being getting through the Dover Straits, would offer up such an incredible bounty.

As the tidal steam changed, I was whisked around Dungeness and, with the whole six hours of tide in my favour, was confident of making it through the narrowest part of the Channel, past the Channel ports of Folkestone and Dover and around the bottom corner of the UK to Deal where I'd anchor for the night. It was going to be another huge push, requiring me to cover thirty miles and heading evermore northwards, thus once again losing any advantage that I'd gained from the westerly wind. However, with the North Sea and the Atlantic taking turns to squeeze through this narrow gap, I had high hopes as, after all, I had the Atlantic on my side. We were fairly well-acquainted by now and I reckoned it owed me a favour or two.

It was to be a long night of rowing and I was a little nervous about crossing the harbour entrances at the busy Channel ports in the thick of night, with numerous cross-Channel ferries constantly crisscrossing my route. I therefore radioed the harbour masters of both, telling them of my whereabouts, and they were kind enough to alert all other shipping in the area. I must have been pretty tired by now as the *babushka* was back and I don't remember a great deal about the night apart from being blinded by the bright lights of Dover Port as I approached it. The winds weren't helping and I considered 'taking a short cut' through the port for a bit of shelter, but I didn't think the harbour master would have looked on me quite as kindly if I'd chosen to do so! I made pretty good progress past the Port, but fatigue was really starting to set in and, as the tide slackened, things ground to a crawl. There was nowhere to anchor safely and I wanted to be well clear of the Port anyway so the counting began again as I slogged on.

It was still eight miles to Deal and I was on the verge of collapse, but I got a faint puff of breeze from the stern urging me on. The counting once again got me through: *just three thousand more strokes and you can rest, break it down into smaller pieces and keep going, 250 more and you're halfway through the first thousand, six hundred more until halfway, last thousand strokes…* and so it went on until I reached Deal just after midnight and could do no more.

The euphoria of having reached my destination ebbed almost the second that I dropped the anchor and all I could do was collapse into my sleeping bag, shivering from exhaustion, to ready myself for the next leg. Thanks to my bit of good fortune earlier that day, I'd managed to knock sixty miles off the total in the twenty-four hours since leaving Beachy Head, of which I'd been on the oars for nineteen, and had subsequently put a bit time in the bank and whittled down the daily mileage to a hopefully achievable target. It was a huge relief to have done so as, though still tough, the chances of me making it to Tower Bridge on Sunday late morning had received a massive boost.

I was awake early the next morning having had a surprisingly restless sleep given my exertions over the previous days. But a combination of my body hurting and excitement over the prospect of finishing this adventure and getting back to everything that I loved had me tossing and turning for much of the night. The tide was due to turn at around nine in the morning so I took my time to chow down a few extra calories and try and enjoy the added rest. It was now 17 September and I still had eighty-seven miles to cover in the fifty hours before the welcome celebration was due to occur.

Getting there on time was going to be no picnic, but I figured that with five good spells of following tides, it was at least doable. I'd have to squander part of that advantage on this next leg as the north-going tide that I needed to get me to North Foreland, the last point on my eastward journey before turning a sharp left into the Thames Estuary and heading west for the first time in three months, did not coincide with a tide into the Estuary and with the winds forecast to now come from the southwest, albeit lightly, there was no way that I'd be able to battle into wind and tide to make progress westwards until the tide changed.

It was a fairly short ten-mile hop to the North Foreland light and I still had an hour or so to spare before the tide started to really run against me so I thought that I'd chance my arm and try and at least make some progress 'around the corner' and begin my journey west towards London. All was going well and I'd earmarked a shallow patch just off of the coast of Margate that I could drop anchor in but, arriving about twenty minutes too late, the tide had already changed by the time I reached the navigational buoy that marked the edge of the shallows. It was fairly apparent that the current was already running against me and was building by the minute and once again I was locked in a battle, going flat out just to make almost imperceptible gains. I knew that if I could just make a quarter of a mile towards the beach that the current would slacken, but for now I was stuck in the deep-water channel trying to race against a navigational mark which at times seemed to have the edge on me. It seemed utterly absurd that I'd come all of this way and yet was still battling to make every metre, but of course it was the same story as before in that my suffering was self-imposed; in short, I always wanted to make that little bit more progress rather than doing the sensible thing and simply anchoring up a mile beforehand and taking the tide as and when it changed. Though the journey had changed me in a lot of ways, it was obvious that some of the old habits were not breakable!

After forty-five minutes of intense struggle, leaving me panting at the oars after this 'sprint marathon', I finally made it to the shallower waters by the beach where thankfully the current slackened enough for me to make some progress. However, by now I was ready for a rest so only carried on for a mile or so before dropping the anchor and waiting out the tide. Due to my decision to row into it, I only had to wait a few hours for my opportunity to get back on the oars. Though I could have done with a bit more rest, I was keen to crack on and get as close to London as possible. Maybe, just maybe, I'd get my easy 'victory lap', albeit quite literally at the eleventh hour.

I had seven hours to make as much progress as possible and was hoping for a swift journey up the Estuary with light winds and a following tide. The route was tricky due to the numerous sandbanks and manmade obstructions, littered with fishing pots, mooring buoys and navigational markers, but regular checks over my shoulder and in the mirror seemed to have me missing them all for now at least, although things would get trickier as I rowed into the night. I'd not got far before the wind started to pick up from the southwest, nullifying any advantage from the tide and making it once again a hard slog. I'd decided to try and stick close to the coast to get some kind of shelter for as long as possible as I was told that the winds were due to die down later. This did put me outside the 'racing line' for the best current, but my muscles were now feeling very tired and I decided that an easier effort on the oars was the priority. Fifteen miles into the leg, I had to cross some open water to the Isle of Sheppey, leaving the shelter of the coast and exposing myself to stronger winds, but thankfully, as darkness started to fall, so did the wind strength so I was finally able to relax my grip a little on the oars and head onwards.

Fatigue was starting to catch up on me and I felt myself flagging, but I knew that if I dropped anchor now I'd be throwing away all the great progress made over the past days so I decided to carry on. The conditions were good, but I found this leg absolutely tortuous for some reason. Whether it was exhaustion from the previous days' efforts or the psychology of being 'so close but yet so far' I don't know, but I found these last few hours on the oars some of the toughest yet, constantly having to wake myself up to keep going and becoming a bit fuzzy in the process even though it was relatively early in the evening.

Navigation lights in the near distance seemed to take forever to reach and by the time I hit the channel for the River Medway I was becoming a bit delirious so I decided to stop at the next opportunity; I found a spot just out of the main channel to drop anchor and carry on the next day. I'd made forty-seven miles that day meaning that I only had forty more to go to Tower Bridge and three changes of tide to do it on. I wasn't taking anything for granted, but it finally felt like I was going to make it as planned.

Ever since I'd first conceived the row from New York to London, I'd always looked out the car window wistfully every time I crossed the Queen Elizabeth II Bridge at Dartford, seeing the Thames flowing underneath and wondering if one day I'd be passing beneath it on my way to claim a world record. For me, passing underneath the Bridge was always going to be the point at which I felt that I'd finally made it and I had high hopes of achieving that on the next tide, leaving me a relative stone's throw from the finish line the following day.

Hauling the anchor the following morning with clawed hands and tired limbs, it still felt as if there was room yet for defeat and getting on the oars feeling half-dead did nothing to quell this unease. As ever, however, it was just a matter of taking the next stroke and then the next until I could do no more so I put my head down and got stuck in. As I eased into a well-rehearsed rhythm and my body warmed up, things became a little easier, although the miles seemed to drag on forever as the flat landscape surrounding the Estuary slowly showed more signs of industrialisation. A seal had popped up to see me and became a travelling companion for a couple of miles as the Estuary narrowed and I could see why they called them 'sea dogs' with his cute face, whiskers and big eyes staring at me as I made slow progress.

The Estuary quickly narrowed to become a river – the Thames at last! – and the increased current hastened me along. Having been at sea for so long and despite the stay in St Mawes, the landscape suddenly seemed both alien and fascinating in equal measure. Even the large industrial buildings, wharves and piers began to take on their own beauty as I was whisked by them in the quickening current. To be in such close proximity to the shore and travelling at four or five knots was a great feeling. However, as I turned a sharp bend in the River just before Tilbury, I saw a navigation buoy named 'Lower Hope' which I thought sounded a bit downbeat so I took no heed of it.

A large cargo ship was on its way out of London accompanied by the pilot boat. The crew stopped for a quick chat and were blown away when I told them of my accomplishment. It was lovely of them to stop and take the time and they bid me a safe onward passage, telling me that there were no other major ship movements that day so I should have a clear route ahead which was good to know in the restricted waterway with limited visibility. So far, so good, but then just as I began to visualise passing under the QEII Bridge, now only eleven miles away, I was hit by an almighty gust of wind that seemed to come out of nowhere. It seemed that Jason and Uncle Bert had taken the weekend off and gone down the pub for a few beers to congratulate themselves on a job well done. From cruising south along the River without a care, enjoying the sights as I passed the outskirts of London, I was suddenly once again locked in battle with a fifteen- to twenty-knot headwind from the southwest which I found hard to control *Peggy* in, the slightest deviation off course meaning that the wind would catch the bow and try to spin me around. I only had three miles to get around the next bend, but I was zig-zagging all over the River and making very little headway, being buffeted by gusts from all points forward of the bow. Any rhythm that I may have had was destroyed as I had to haul with everything that I had on one oar to straighten *Peggy* up before rowing as hard as I could the regain some momentum before the next gust skewed me off course.

Though I thanked my lucky stars that this hadn't happened twenty minutes beforehand, as I would have pitched directly into the path of the oncoming freighter, it was small recompense for the effort I now had to put in to make any kind of headway. Anger started to boil up inside me at having to prove myself once again, having been tested throughout the journey, but with it came the resolve to defeat this new nemesis which seemed to have been put in my way as a final act of defiance by Mother Nature to thwart my ambitions. However, I was not in the mood to be thwarted!

The three miles took me two hours of ball-busting effort, but gradually I turned the corner and started heading westward once more; albeit having lost the advantage of the flood tide as the current started to slacken. It was a further six miles to the Bridge but that now looked like a lost cause so I searched for somewhere to anchor or tie up to sit out the tide. I was passing Tilbury Docks, a container-ship terminal which offered a 1.5-mile stretch of high concrete quay with no chance of stopping. The winds were still hampering me, but in the lee of the massive ships that acted as a buffer to the beam-on winds, I at least made some progress. Unfortunately, however, observing some other boats on swinging moorings on the opposite bank, I could see that the tide was on the turn; it was a fairly swift process when the flood tide turned to an ebb tide, all the water from the Thames River basin having been temporarily pushed back and then waiting to be released. Time was of the essence, but surrounded by the slab sides of these huge hulking ships, I had no choice but to row as fast as I could to find a place of refuge. I had no knowledge of this part of the Thames, but half a mile or so ahead I saw what looked like some small boat moorings so I aimed straight for them and rowed with everything I had left in me to get to them before I was swept back downstream.

I felt an incredible sense of relief when I found out that they were indeed small boat mooring buoys and I managed to loop a line around a free one as the tide started to race against me. I found myself tied up opposite Thurrock Yacht Club; the buoy had a name written on it, signifying the boat whose mooring it was and I had a fear that they might return and demand that I vacate the buoy. Only ten minutes after I had tied up, the current was already racing past at three knots and I wouldn't have stood a chance of repositioning myself so I looked up the club and gave them a call to ask if it was okay to stay.

I've dealt with a few yacht clubs over the years and they can be terribly snooty places with customs and practices seemingly designed to keep the hoi polloi away, but there guys couldn't have been friendlier or more welcoming; it seemed like a club for people who simply enjoyed life afloat, rather than wanting to swan around in pink shirts, cravats and blazers, swilling G&Ts

and trying to outdo each other in boat size or how much they earned (and obviously compensating for something else!) which was in my experience all too common. I spoke to the guy behind the bar and the weekend was obviously in full swing. I suddenly felt envious as I heard the glasses clinking, but knew that my moment was now less than twenty-four hours away.

Though I hadn't made the Bridge itself, I could at least see it from where I was and it was only a few miles further upstream. With five hours to kill until the tide turned, I sat out on deck and started prepping some lunch. I was constantly ravenous by now and looked forward to every meal time with eager anticipation. Throughout the row, time and tide had dictated when I could eat so to sit out at a civilised hour in warm sunshine and the protected confines of the River was a wonderful thing.

Just as I was finishing up, two guys from the Port of London Authority rocked up on the pilot boat. They had been looking for me and it transpired that Jason and Uncle Bert must have got back from the pub and sent these two as they were there to inform me that the Thames Flood Barrier would be closed at 06:30 the following morning as part of its monthly test. It was an incredible stroke of luck that they came by as it had been my intention that evening to stop a mile or so downstream of the Barrier, near Woolwich, which would have meant that, upon getting up in the morning to take my final bow, I'd have been faced with the steel gates designed to stop the city from flooding and I pictured myself rocking up and tapping on the 'door' to ask if anyone could let me in.

The day had been hard and the 'Lower Hope' buoy a sick joke, but the arrival of these two heaven-sent guys from the PLA made everything good again. The weather forecast was now for zero wind for the following day which was perfect as the Thames takes so many twists and turns that I would be rowing through all points of the compass so any wind would have been detrimental at some stage and the swift current that evening would be more than enough to ensure that I should finally be able to take my victory lap.

As the tide swung, I slipped the mooring and, by 8 o'clock that evening, I was finally on the home straight. Within forty-five minutes, I was under the QEII Bridge and I let out a huge shout of joy as I did so. The row had been so long in the making and had pushed me beyond anything I had done in the past, but now the time had come to enjoy the ride home. Navigation was tricky as I tried to remain clear of any river traffic that might be navigating out of London that evening, while the riverbanks are studded with all kinds of wharfs and jetties that deal with the dirtier end of business in the city. Huge scrapyards, waste-treatment plants and other heavy industry proliferate in this part of London, but I was still overjoyed to see it all as I passed by on the tide. As per the forecast, there was no wind and the lights from the various activities reflected off the surface of the water creating a confusing collage on an otherwise pitch-black night; though the darkness was limited to the River itself, the glow of the city illuminating the night sky. I was constantly on edge, wending my way down the River in the dark of night, but suddenly the industrial landscape gave way to a more urban scene and buildings that I recognised hove into view. Rounding a bend, the huge gate towers of the Flood Barrier appeared and I lined myself up to pass between them. It was quite nerve-racking as the current was so swift that there would be no backing out once I'd committed. However, I passed through without any fuss and headed onwards, looking for a place to stop.

I was heading upriver and thoroughly enjoying myself on the swift following current when I suddenly turned around and saw, to my horror, that I was heading directly towards three massive unlit barges moored side by side in the middle of the River, only a hundred metres or so away. The current was speeding me directly underneath their looming bows and I had to throw the rudder over and row as hard as I could to avoid them. With the speed of the current, there was no telling what might have happened had I not looked when I did and it could well have spelled disaster, but once again fortune had decided to smile upon me.

Up until that point, I'd been drifting along in a tired reverie. Now, however, I was suddenly completely wired on adrenalin and decided to stop at the next possible opportunity as I was keen to avoid a similar occurrence at all costs. With the city on both banks of the River illuminated by the lights of the O2 Arena, it was very difficult to discern any small mooring buoys. However, as I approached the next bend, I saw a line of boats on the far bank and decided to make a beeline for them.

I still had a few hours of tide left, but I'd envisaged the final leg of the journey up the Thames for so long I didn't want to pass it at night and miss all the historic sights and buildings for the sake of an easy morning at the oars. I would no doubt be up and about early anyway so there was no great rush to make any more progress that evening. I crossed the River and had to put in a bit more oomph to get back upstream to the mooring buoys, but finally I found a suitable spot to tie up, right by the O2 Arena and underneath the cable car over the River. All around me I could hear London in the full cry of a Saturday night with a concert booming in the O2 and regular party boats passing by. Part of me wanted to scream out 'What about me?' to get some recognition for what I had achieved, but for the better part I was just happy to be there by myself for one final night with *Peggy*.

Though it was late, having gone midnight, I was starving. I'd been looking forward to my last pack of carbonara for so long that it was all I could do not to open the packet and eat the dried contents straight out of the bag. On reflection, however, sitting there in my cabin with the hatch open, watching the world go by as I made our last meal together, seemed like the right thing to do. I was getting cold from having expended so much energy, but I snuggled up in my sleeping bag as the water boiled and heated the inside of the cabin and all felt very cosy, reminding me of so many times when *Peggy* had been my refuge.

Though excited to be going home, I had no doubt that there were elements of the adventure that I would miss terribly. This not being my first rodeo, I also knew that the human mind (or mine at least) has a wonderful way of remembering the good bits and forgetting the rest. Yes, I'd pushed myself to the limits of human endurance and, on many occasions, had cursed myself for putting myself in particularly tough predicaments. But when I asked myself if I'd change any of it, the answer was a clear 'Probably not.' The truth is that, without the suffering, I would have felt cheated and a darned sight less appreciative of the good bits. Whether I would consider doing it again, however, was a very different story!

Helene had organised a welcoming committee for the following day. I was to be at Tower Bridge at 11:00 sharp. A very kind chap, Ian Bayliss, whom I had met whilst I was quarantining in Antigua, had offered to provide a boat for her and the boys to see me up the Thames for the last mile. Just as kindly, the Thames Clippers company had offered a space on the Tower Bridge pontoon for me to moor up against. All I had to do was turn up on time.

Sure enough, I was awake before dawn, marvelling at the silence of the city. I decided to stay put for a bit and enjoy my last morning with *Peggy*. The weather was cool and misty and, apart from the occasional jogger, it felt as if I had the city to myself as I sat on my bucket for one last contemplation.

Afterwards, I went back to the cabin and snuggled into my sleeping bag, revelling in the silence as I took in the enormity of what I'd achieved. But then once the sun started to rise, the time for that was over as there was work to be done.

First things first, a final cup of tea and a bit of breakfast before a scrub-up for the pair of us. I'd hauled thirty litres of emergency water for the last four thousand nautical miles and decided to treat myself to a warmwater wash and shave, a clean T-shirt and my emergency pair of pants that I'd been saving especially for the finish. Next was *Peggy* and, after filling up my water bottles, I sluiced down her deck with the remainder of the water and cleaned her topsides.

I only had seven miles to cover, but there was to be no help from the flood tide as the barrier was closed. I am completely anal about punctuality so, though I intended to set out at 08:30, I decided to slip lines an hour earlier just to be on the safe side. Conditions were beautiful with the River mirror-flat as I made my way around the huge meanders, taking in the historic sights on the way, past the old warehouses converted into housing, on to the Greenwich Maritime Museum and the *Cutty Sark* sailing ship and further on upriver. I was joined by a load of rowers, out on a regular training session from the local clubs, and was happy to stop and tell them my story which was wonderful as more came to join us and I received more plaudits from them as I passed their respective clubs.

I was running a little early and caught my family unawares as they parked the car at Poplar Rowing Club (to which I would have to row *Peggy* back in order to haul her out following my arrival celebrations). Lots of excited waving and cheering ensued as they rushed down the slipway, but knowing that I would see them shortly I carried on. I stopped short of Tower Bridge and tied up to a huge mooring buoy to give everybody a chance to catch up as I was aware that a lot of people had taken the time to come and see me in, but I was happy to just sit and take in every moment of these last few miles. The kids waved excitedly was they sped past me on one of the Thames Clippers' boats, leapfrogging me en route to Tower Bridge to join the welcome, and I was filled with a sense of joy at the thought of being reunited with them and able to give them a huge hug.

The time came and at 10:15 I untied from the buoy and made my way towards Tower Bridge. I had butterflies in my stomach at the prospect of finishing as it had occupied my every thought for over two years and I'd been feeding off the image to keep me motivated for so long. I was just hoping that it would match up to my expectations. Though I knew how I felt right at that moment, I wasn't sure what my emotions would be as I passed underneath the Bridge and finally succeeded in my goal. Part of me was afraid that it would be an anti-climax; the old adage of it being about the journey and not the destination was at the back of my mind and, let's face it, it had been quite a journey.

As it turned out, I shouldn't have worried. Shortly after I began my final approach, Helene and the boys joined in behind me on the boat that Ian had borrowed. He was there too, accompanied by his wife whom I'd got to know well during my time in Antigua. When I was within half a mile of my destination, I heard cheers reverberating down the River and looked over my shoulder to see Tower Bridge lined with people who had come out to cheer me in and, as I got closer, the cacophony increased until it felt like I was being carried along on its clamour.

I picked up the stroke rate for a final flourish in the last couple of hundred metres, only to ease back when I realised that this was a moment not to be rushed. As I passed under Tower Bridge and looked up at all of those people cheering above me, I wanted to stop and thank every one of them, but stupid though it might sound, I felt that the journey wouldn't be over until I'd passed under the Bridge. Emerging on the other side, I tried to let out a cheer, but my throat tightened as I fought back the tears. I think I did manage to emit a small cry of triumph, but it came out rather strangulated!

The crowds had managed to cross the road and I was overwhelmed by the amount of people who had turned out to see me. Whichever way I had imagined the journey ending, it couldn't have done the actual occasion any justice. With no time for too much reflection, I spun the boat around and headed to the pier to set foot on dry land for the first time in ninety-seven days. It was an odd sensation, approaching the pier as suddenly people fussed around, helping with lines and all doing their bit, but it didn't bother me. Just to be in the company of others was great.

I was desperate to get to Helene and the boys and the second I stepped out of the boat and over the guard rail they were in my arms again. Mum and Dad were next and I think I nearly crushed Mum, lifting her off the ground as I did so. I don't really remember the sequence of events thereafter; however, I know that I had an interview with the BBC and another news channel, then had to row back out to rescue Ian and his family who'd had to tie up to a mooring buoy in the River, and finally ran up the gangway in a show of bravado, thanking everyone on the way.

Once the hubbub had died down, I was gagging for a drink and a burger so we all headed to the local pub, the Dickens Inn, for refreshments. However, I was mindful that I still had to row back to the Poplar Rowing Club to get *Peggy* out of the water, so had to settle for a single glass of Champagne. The best bit, though, was the tastiest, juiciest burger that I could have possibly imagined, dribbling down my forearms as I swallowed it in a few bites. It was a wonderful homecoming and to be able to sit outside a pub and thank everybody personally for their support was a huge bonus.

After an hour, though, I was desperate to get back home and relax with those closest to me so said my fond farewells and headed back down the slipway to *Peggy* for our final voyage together. As if on cue, the heavens opened, having done their duty and held back the rain for just long enough not to dampen the parade.

17

NYLON: the Conclusion

Arriving home that evening with Helene, the boys and Mum and Dad, all seemed a little surreal. Only hours before I had finished the biggest challenge of my life and yet, here I was, standing in my kitchen with a cold beer in hand, making a fuss of the dogs and just slotting back into family life. I'd fantasised about it for so long and had worried that the row may have changed me in some way, making it difficult to readjust, but I was shocked at how normal everything felt.

Come the second beer, it was time to have a long shower before getting dressed into some clean, dry clothes which was something that I'd also dreamed of. Then we all went to a local pub for a few more drinks and a meal. It was a very weird feeling being amongst everything so familiar, having been so remote from it for so long, but a couple of G&Ts and a bottle of wine seemed to take the edges off and I simply slipped back into being a dad, a son and a husband.

The following morning I got up, stupid o'clock as usual, put on some clothes and went outside. The sun was just coming up and I could see all the wonderful hues of the garden, smell its aromas and hear the birdsong which I appreciated more than ever as I picked some dog poo off the lawn and wheeled the bin out before returning to the house to empty the dishwasher. If there ever was a man happier to do so, I've yet to meet him.

It had been a journey of incredible highs, tremendous lows and everything in between. I'd learnt a lot about myself and consider myself incredibly fortunate to have been in a position to have so much uncluttered headspace to think about what mattered to me. I'd gained an insight into mental illness which gave me a far greater appreciation of those who suffer with it on a daily basis, found that I did actually enjoy being around people and learnt that it was OK to be nervous and show my emotions. But most of all, I'd learnt that the most important thing in my life was my family, without whom I would have never made it. Helene, in particular, had been incredible throughout, never wavering in her support of me.

Apparently, I've also become far more tolerant and patient with my kids, or 'soft' as my dad would put it, but I have no problem with that as I've realised the strength in it as well as feeling comfortable to tell them that I love them every day.

I'm yet to get a follow-up hug from Dad but maybe he'll break his toe again one of these days and need my consolation.

Dinger Bell finally reached the tip of Cornwall the following weekend and Guirec Soudée landed shortly after that in Brest, France 107 days after leaving Chatham on the East Coast of the USA.

Unfortunately, the 'Irish lads' had to abandon their attempt due to technical difficulties and were rescued by a super tanker and taken back to Boston

Ian Rivers landed in the Scilly Isles four days after I reached the UK coastline and, according to his team, was the first person to row the North Atlantic Ocean solo and unsupported.

Printed in Great Britain
by Amazon